THE MILLENNIUM TAPES

THE MILLENNIUM TAPES
(THE SEARCH FOR TRUTH)

Norman Alan Charman

The Book Guild Ltd
Sussex, England

First published in Great Britain in 2004 by
The Book Guild Ltd
25 High Street
Lewes, East Sussex
BN7 2LU

Typesetting in Times by
IML Typographers, Birkenhead, Merseyside

Printed in Great Britain by
CPI Bath

A catalogue record for this book is available from
The British Library

ISBN 1 85776 739 X

FOREWORD

How many of us must have pondered in a quiet moment: What is life all about? What am I doing here? What will happen to me when I die? Does God really sit on a throne in Heaven? – and what is Heaven like? Do you believe in ghosts or flying saucers? You should do, they are all relative, being part of the great domain of The Almighty. A ghost is merely a spirit that displays itself. Spirits are just like us, except they are in another dimension. Yet the very term 'ghost' conjures up enough horror to make many of us deny their existence. Why should an ordinary person, after passing over, be regarded as a mystical and frightening object? Small wonder that The Holy Spirit dislikes being called The Holy Ghost. In the same way our planetaire brothers from space despise being termed 'aliens'. The connotations of that word are equally obvious. What is so fantastic about spacecraft from other worlds visiting Earth? It really is happening. They have been monitoring us throughout three civilisations and with the world's population far bigger than it has ever been, it is hardly surprising that more people than ever before are beginning to notice them.

In 1969 a small group of people formed a Circle with the intention of throwing some light on these mysteries. As they sat around a specially constructed ouija board they were totally unaware that one of their number was a lady whose enormous potential as a trance medium – the rarest kind of medium – would eventually render that same ouija board obsolete. After several years of increasing pressure from ouija contacts to try trancing, she finally pushed aside her remaining fears and reservations and opened herself to trance contact. Her gift blossomed during the next two decades and the veil which separates the physical from the spiritual dimension was lifted. The obscurity of ouija contacts was replaced by informative conversation with real people, albeit temporarily, in their midst. The medium is not famous as she was non-professional, spurning the chance to make money from her incredible gift. Like the author, her sole object was to find out more about God, the afterlife and our place in the universe. She has succeeded beyond their wildest dreams. The Truth is more fascinating than

v

Science Fiction. It is said that curiosity killed the cat, but the Circle, in the great quest to know God, will be eternally grateful that The Holy Spirit chose them for indoctrination into the Power of Love. Tired of the platitudes of existing religions, which places a mystical God almost out of reach, they were given the chance to try to understand what it is really all about. From the moment searching questions attracted the attention of The Holy Spirit their destiny was irrevocably written. The quest for knowledge was to become a mission for the enlightenment of all. That they, with their naïve curiosity, should be chosen borders on the miraculous. The world needs to be prepared for the revelations of the New Redeemer, who has now reached the age of spiritual maturity. Not born on this planet, he was placed as a small child in the desert of the Middle East to be found by a childless couple who would adopt and raise him. 'This man will come to be recognised as the New Redeemer. He will teach, as did Jesus.' His task is to help us understand the immensity of The Immortal Power we call God and make our little blue planet more aware of the abundant life in the universe around us.

The information in the following pages has been given with love and patience by the Almighty Power of Love through The Holy Flocen (Holy Spirit), his deputy, The Blessed Efun, and Jeculin teachers from the most spiritually advanced physical races in the universe. A single visit by the Archangel Gabriel did much to strengthen the resolve of the Circle to continue its work in spite of often difficult circumstances. It was the absolute reassurance needed that it was the will of God that the greater knowledge being given should be known. Some long-standing biblical misconceptions were clarified with the help of Jesus Christ, his mother Mary, his Earth father Joseph and disciple Peter. Countless contacts from Space and the Earth spirit world have all helped to create some idea of why, what and where we are.

All of this was made possible by the unselfish mediumship of this great lady, Nita Hall, to whom this book is dedicated. Transcripts of contacts are, as near as possible, their verbatim response to questions and represent only a tiny percentage of the total number of contacts received. Many of the audiotapes from which they were typed are still in existence. The discovery that Theology and the Wonders of Space are inextricably intertwined has produced a result that is both exciting and revealing. Although this work flies in the face of many accepted scientific principles, it is presented as Science Fact as opposed to Science Fiction.

Norman Alan Charman

NITA HALL (Nitesi)

This book is dedicated to Nita Hall, a gifted composer, pianist and organist – and latterly a trance medium with no equal on this planet. Her many spiritual experiences throughout the whole of her life gave notice of a latent psychic ability that was being wasted until, in her more mature years, she pushed aside the fear of the unknown and allowed her ability to develop. Her only complaint during her years of service was that she was never able to experience the excitement of 'live' conversation with contacts that was being enjoyed by all the other Circle members during her trancing. She only heard it second hand via tape recorder. Without her selfless work over more than a quarter century the information in the following pages would not have been gathered and this book could not have been produced.

Only Spirits and Astrals could see the halo she wore as she offered her body to be used by contacts to allow them temporarily to become physical members of the Circle. It was this regular, cosy contact with the spiritual domain which triggered the universe-wide interest which followed. The audacious probe into unknown religious territory which she had instigated was, through their absolute belief in all they were told, eventually rewarded by being given esoteric knowledge of the wonders of God. This was allowed as part of an experiment sanctioned by The Holy Spirit who is the voice of The Almighty Power. The magical link with the spiritual dimension which she had provided for so long was finally severed on December 10, 1998 when her soul discarded a frail and tired body to allow her to enjoy the rewards she has so amply earned in the greater world beyond. Time alone will tell whether she will be recognised as a Saint in the new spiritual age the World is about to enter.

THE SEARCH BEGINS

The Circle's initial contacts with Earth spirits did not reveal very much as they simply didn't know, or if they did, were not allowed to say. The specially constructed ouija board was providing easy movement to any spirit wishing to make contact. A straight question such as 'Whatever happened to Hitler?' inevitably produced the counter 'Do not ask' – three little words which were to become a constant stumbling block when more direct questions were asked concerning the spiritual environment. Because of their incessant questions the Circle soon became known in the Spirit World as 'The Inquisitive Ones' and were gradually being accepted as serious researchers. They began receiving more influential spirits, even a Controller, who did answer more of their questions, but was unable to quench the thirst for, what was to him, forbidden knowledge.

The first Space contact was made by 'Friendly Alien' who turned out to be Eron, a non-humanoid, very reticent to elaborate on his life form. He was eventually coaxed to reveal that he had the body of a giant wasp, the size of a man. He was accepted for whom he said he was. It was because of the warm welcome given him that the Circle later received Hexlr from his planet which is called Quaslr. Hexlr is their equivalent to a Saint. He knew about God because Quaslr is one of the many planets which have benefited from a visitation of the Jeculins. When asked the most prized possession on Quaslr, Hexlr promptly spelled out 'Love' – and this was to be the recurrent theme of all contacts with our Space brothers, humanoid or otherwise. In retrospect the friendly wasps were an obvious test of belief, which must have been passed with flying colours for Space humanoids were soon to follow. Hexlr, a spirit of high standing, was known and respected on many worlds. It seemed reasonable that life forms with a greater intellect than our own would be able to learn and use our language if they had intended to visit Earth. The old British Empire has made English the most widely-spoken language and the monitored activities of American astronauts have helped make it an obvious choice for visitors to our world. Advanced civilisations have film libraries which

1

are visual encyclopaedias on almost every topic including languages. No planetaire (Space Traveller) would waste time visiting another planet if unable to speak the language. It is not uncommon for a planetaire to be able to converse in as many as 30 planetary languages.

As the months slipped by a strong bond of trust and mutual respect was being established with the contacts, some of whom were proving more co-operative than earlier ones had been. H.G. Wells, whose real name was Alfred, but thought 'H.G.' was a more imposing name for an author, claimed that he too had done serious research with ouija. He also remembered his group receiving Hexlr from the wasp planet Quaslr during his lifetime. Presor, learned leader of an ancient tribe long BC and Diogenes, now a spirit Controller, who did not wish to discuss philosophy on his visit, probably all contributed to Circle reputation as the 'Inquisitive Ones' being superseded by 'The Wise Ones'.

It is almost impossible to describe the exhilaration that was felt as meeting after meeting resulted in new contacts being made who were not only able but willing to try at least partially to demystify what has always been considered a taboo subject. From many of these were gleaned titbits about our spirit world, but their knowledge of God was just as limited as it had been in their physical lives. A visit from Solomon created a new 'high', but it also helped to explain why this surprising ignorance also existed in the spirit world. He provided the greatest test of the group's determination to try and discover exactly what God is. Solomon treated them as his children. It transpired that some had served him during his reign, which was his last physical life journey. His fatherly attitude changed when he found out the main purpose of the research. He told them they should not be doing this and if they continued they could suffer eternal damnation, but when asked 'How can it be wrong to seek to know more about God?' there was no reply forthcoming.

SOLOMON'S BARRIER

Despite the warning from the High Controller, a now somewhat anxious Circle continued with its research, but repercussions were soon to follow. There was a sudden dearth of Earth spirit contacts. After several disappointing sessions, Hyppolytes, another ancient Greek, made contact. A bit of a maverick, with scant regard for Controllers' wishes and almost certainly a free spirit, he turned out to be a good friend and ally to the Circle. He said there was now a barrier around them every time they sat which burned any spirit trying to make contact. He said he felt as though he had been scorched. It did not deter him from breaching the barrier several more times during this quiet spell.

Ironically it was Solomon's barrier that cleared the way for their Space friends to intensify their visits. The barrier caused them no problems. They were not even aware of it. Apparently more and more Space people were making long journeys to establish contact, then finding they were unable to get in because an Earth spirit was already in possession of the board. Now, with the exception of Hyppolytes, no Earth spirit would attempt to cross the barrier, leaving the way open for the fascinating friends from afar.

It was during this period, with the whole world agog watching the *Apollo 11* mission on TV, a Space contact told the Circle they had been watching our moonwalkers and had tried to make mental contact with them. They almost succeeded with 'the one called Armstrong' but had to desist when he became unduly alarmed. Following his moonwalk, Neil Armstrong became deeply religious.

April 1970 saw *Apollo 13* with all sorts of problems. There was even some doubt whether the crew would be able to get back to Earth. Our Space brothers had been watching over them too. They admired the bravery of our astronauts risking their lives with such crude equipment. A spacecraft had been shadowing the *Apollo* at a respectable distance until they saw the Earth vehicle go into its home orbit. They assured Circle members that had the astronauts been unable to get back they would have rescued them. Reports circulating afterwards said that the *Apollo 13* crew reported seeing a spacecraft, but this had been cut from the transmission and the crew sworn to secrecy. Even the more recent exploits of our round-the-world balloonists were noted from beyond the atmosphere.

END OF THE BARRIER

Word must have reached Solomon of the visit by the mysterious 'Flokkon' for the barrier was lifted soon afterwards. To the Circle he was just another welcome spirit from Space, for they could not see the magnificence of his presence, but for any Earth spirit monitoring their activities for High Controller Solomon the sight must have been awesome. 'Flokkon' was an intriguing contact. He came from an all-spirit planet where there are no physical lives. After his visitation the Circle were no longer 'The Wise Ones' to the Earth spirits. They had decided 'The Holy Ones' was now more appropriate. This visit, under a pseudonym, was the first of many by the greatest spirit in the universe and had not gone unnoticed. Subsequent contact with Solomon was more gentle than on the first occasion and there were no further warnings of 'eternal damnation'. His greatest concern now was for the state of members' mental well-being. 'You are seeking to know what is too advanced for your mentality and the reality is too great for your imagination. I watch over my children and I do not approve because it will boggle your minds.'

It was several years later, when receiving trance contacts, a Jeculin tutor announced dear friend Flokkon was really The Holy Flocen (pronounced Flossen), Holy Spirit of the Universe. He had deliberately kept his real identity secret because he had not wanted to frighten Circle members. He had succeeded. Until that revelation they had been calling him Flokkon and treating him like an old chum, although in their hearts they knew he must be someone of very special importance. In contrast, the spirit which really brought up goose pimples, when asked his name spelled out 'They called me King of the Jews.' 'Jesus?' 'Yes.' There was plenty of awe about on that occasion, although after the research had progressed to successful trancing, enabling him to speak directly through the medium, awe had been replaced by the feeling of brotherly love.

A cynical reader might wonder about the researchers' gullibility, but one of the first things they had learned was that spirits cannot lie. Truth is akin to love and comes from the soul. The name of Jesus has been, and still is, associated with love for 2,000 years whereas The Holy Spirit has remained an awesome mystery, even somewhat frightening and this has been further exacerbated by the unfortunate term 'Holy Ghost'. The minor inexactitude of The Holy Spirit introducing himself by spelling out 'Flokkon' was fully justified when considering the devastating impact Jesus had made with his more direct approach. There are more people like Jesus in the Universe, but there is only one operative Holy Flocen. Evil spirits, which fortunately are relatively few, will lie, but are easily detected by a person of reasonable spiritual advancement. This had never been a problem for the Circle as members had already been told they were to receive divine protection to facilitate their learning.

THE OUIJA BOARD

In spite of worldwide condemnation by the Church, the ouija board in itself is not evil. The evil is in the negative side of those who sit around the board and play it like a game. This can attract mischievous and sometimes evil spirits to the proceedings.

Too many participants think of ouija as a party game with unseen freaks from 'the other side' who are only there to provide them with entertainment. They do not seem to realise they are making contact with people who have feelings like themselves, people who deserve respect for their efforts in trying to aid attempts to make contact with their dimension. Decent spirits will shun any ouija group who only consider them as a butt for larking about. There are other spirits who are less particular – and less desirable – who would enjoy turning the tables on those who think them a joke and some of these are quite capable of turning laughter into tears. Ouija is not a game, nor is it to be played as such for the entertainment of its participants. Thousands of years ago scholars among the Ancient Greeks used it as a fairly reliable way to communicate with spirits. It remains so. The Circle had begun humbly enough with a ouija board.

Successful novice contact needs a minimum of four spiritually-minded people. Five to eight is an ideal group. A visiting spirit will select the person with the greatest medium potential to steer the planchette (or glass) without them even knowing they have become the vessel of the spirit's will. A spirit should never be summoned by name – they have their lives to lead as well as duties to perform. Before commencement a prayer for protection should be said and the blessing of The Almighty asked. Regular sessions can bring the exhilaration of contact with the so-called unknown, but the sort of spirits who may make contact depends on the purity of intention of the participants.

Ouija is not an ideal communication channel for spirits because the physical operatives rarely have the patience to allow the contact sufficient time to spell out everything he wants to say. Spelling a language is always more difficult than speaking it, even more so for a spirit trying to guide the arm movements of a potential medium.

Although the Circle had a strong medium to utilise, it was still sometimes difficult to resist the impulse to guess the end of the occasional long-winded sentence enabling the contact to go to 'Yes' or 'No' direct. To save bother they will sometimes do this even if the guess was not strictly what they had intended to say. So you get a 'Near enough' syndrome compared with the 100% accuracy of a spirit talking through a trance medium. For this very reason no information obtained from the ouija board has been used in this book unless it was later positively verified by a trance contact. The only exceptions are the ouija board visits of Tutankhamun and Soviet astronaut Yuri Gagarin, neither of whom made

5

any further contact despite having the chance to speak through the medium during two decades of trance mediumship that followed.

THE ADVENT OF TRANCING

Some three years after that first tentative step into the unknown with ouija, something happened at a meeting which was to spell the beginning of the end for it as the Circle's only means of communicating with spirits. It was the early 1970s and members had become more skilled and patient in dealing with ouija contacts, but there were a number of the unseen who had been pressing for Nita to try trancing. They thought such a powerful medium was being wasted on the ouija board. As the group sat around the table waiting for contact, one of them made a flippant remark that he could have been somewhere else at that time. A stinging rebuke from Nita – so out of character for her – took everyone by surprise. When the offending member asked what she had meant, she had no knowledge of what had been said and denied having spoken at all.

Without her going into trance, an impatient spirit had given his own demonstration of the benefit of direct contact. At a meeting soon after this incident Nita began trancing successfully and the ouija board was discarded.

A spirit 'gatekeeper' is a must for any psychic circle intending to do serious work with a trance medium. He is necessary to prevent the more rowdy element of would-be contacts coming in and wasting the medium's strength and valuable time. The Circle was to have the benefit of consecutive keepers over the next 18 years. They were all spirits of good standing who had volunteered to do the job after obtaining permission from higher up. Harry, Peter and Richard successively did sterling work for the Circle until its dissolution in 1985. Maurie was the new keeper on the reformation in 1990. His full name is Maurice Morris and he had been a financier in London. Harry was guardian of the cone during the steady increase in planetaire contacts which followed as trancing became the established routine. The contacts themselves were never routine, each one a delight to listen to and talk with. A religious leader or teacher was invariably among the contacts. The Jeculins and their associates from the light galaxies knew about the Circle and were answering many of their questions. They were told to throw out all preconceived ideas as they had been chosen by The Holy Flocen and were to be indoctrinated. Nita in particular would receive further indoctrination in her sleep. After some months of tuition from their Jeculin mentors, they had been given the affix 'asi' to their forenames. Nita became Nitasi, Norman became Normasi, Tom Tomasi and so forth. Further on, these had been replaced with the affix 'esi', which was a promotion to the senior title for true believers. Never having heard of a Jeculin with either title, it is possible the titles are reserved only for those fortunate people from spiritually backward races that have wholeheartedly embraced the knowledge and wisdom proffered by the Jeculins with the understanding it brings of the true nature of the great Almighty Power. Another peak was reached when the newly inaugurated Holy Flocen came and spoke through Nitesi for the first time in July 1976. The occasion was not as awesome as it might have been for the Circle as the beloved old Flocen had done his groundwork so well. 'Flokkon' as he had been for so long, had given out so much love in their ouija days members could feel less of the awe than such a great holy presence would normally command. Now he had gone to join Gabriel at the bosom of The Almighty and The Efun had become The Holy Flocen. The love was still there, its continuity uninterrupted. Nita's indoctrination included a visit from an angel with a special message for Circle members. To the message, which was in her own handwriting, she added the following footnote: 'All this took place when I was taking an afternoon nap. First the room became filled with a bright light and I seemed to be in another dimension. I saw no figure, yet I was aware one was near me. The voice was loud and distinct, yet distant. When I awoke after only a few minutes, I had these words before me in my lap.'

THE ANGEL'S WORDS

'Be not afraid and heed my words well. They are for your Circle people. We are on the verge of a great time of change. You of Earth face a time of challenge, but also of promise; of advancement, of prophesies coming true – a time of privilege, of daring and of love. Face up to your new horizons, new peaks and new liberations. Face up to life as The Holy Flocen asks you to do and do it bravely and unselfishly, for you are serving Almighty God, the only known God in existence. Yea, there be great and wondrous things ahead for Almighty God's true followers. Unbelievable things shall soon come to light and all chosen ones shall be the bearers of the Great Truth – all those who have the magnitude of knowledge and who live with and beneath the Holy Beam that joins the faithful cone, created by those selected people favoured by our protector, the great and holy Flocen, who is part of the Almighty Power we know to be God – the power of sacred spiritual love, the power that motivates us all. Wait, I say, wait patiently and all shall be revealed in good time. Seek not to question the truth of these words. Accept in humility and wait your time of enlightenment. Be joyous, knowing that great and gracious things lie ahead of you – the chosen ones – and never deviate from your path whereupon your feet now are firmly laid. All shall come to those who are humble and your eyes shall become adjusted to see and realise what is to be for you all who were chosen by the blessed Holy Flocen.

'If your eyes have been blinded by the light and sight of me, fear not, for your sight shall be returned to you as I depart and you shall sleep a short spell to revive you. Soskris and a blessing be upon you. I am an angel of God – an angel messenger. Soskris, holy woman called Nitesi and whose universal space name is Nitracypho, which means chosen child of God, Nitesi. Sleep, sleep. Peace shall rule within thy soul.'

Members had been asked to write original prayers to The Almighty. These prayers, which were read at the start of each meeting, were monitored to assess the degree of their spiritual advancement. Not only were they pleasing their mentors, but the accumulation of knowledge and the resultant wisdom being endowed was having a profound effect. Fear of death had already evaporated like a puddle in a heatwave. Normesi also found that he was becoming much more sensitive. He became aware that the fine hairs on his scalp were now acting as antennae which could detect the presence of a spirit if it was within close touching distance. They didn't bristle as hair does when a person is in fright or awe, they merely wriggled around in the same way as if a tiny spider were walking on them, but the reaction covered the whole scalp which would have taken an army of small spiders to produce such an effect. Stronger contacts produced the feeling of the hair being gently stroked – which it probably was. This 'antennae' reaction has happened hundreds of times since and is still reacting in the present day, often late at night when lying in bed awaiting sleep. However, all his attempts to make mental contact with the unseen visitors have proved fruitless. The way he viewed TV wildlife documentaries was changing too. What had been the thrill of seeing a magnificent lioness making her kill was now being replaced with a feeling of sorrow at the death of the equally beautiful animal which was to provide her meal. He could feel the predicament of the prey and it almost hurt.

On the human front, one began to realise that the hard 'macho' image, so respected on Earth, was really evidence of a neglected soul and weak spirit. He who tramples his fellow beings is an object for real pity. His

8

actions are strong, but his spirit is woefully weak. He has no love, spurning the life-force of the universe – Almighty God.

NO MATHEMATICS IN SPACE

Preconceived ideas of astronomy were totally shattered when tutor after tutor insisted that all the stars we can see in our galaxy are, in fact, planets. There is only one sun in each galaxy and the only sun in the Milky Way is our near neighbour. Quasars, those puzzling power sources which continue to baffle our astronomers, are probably real stars like the sun. They should look for one in every galaxy. If all the stars were suns, the whole galaxy would be bathed in light. Some of the starlight is reflection, although many of them have the intense light of their inner fires showing through, much like a bright electric light bulb would show through a thin china globe. Mathematics, so essential to the calculations of our astronomers, physicists and science in general, were invented by Earthlings and were peculiar to Earth. It was conceded that mathematics seemed to work for us, but they had no use for them, maintaining that Earthbound calculations were not necessarily viable when applied to the universe at large.

STEADY STATE

The galaxies are not rushing away from each other, although some Earth computations may give a different impression. Every galaxy is surrounded by neighbouring galaxies *ad infinitum*. It is impossible for a spacecraft to visit a distant galaxy by the shortest route – a straight course – without crossing all the intervening galaxies. The distance between galaxies is little greater than that which is between the planets within them. Each galaxy, whatever its shape, is encompassed by its own force field. The force fields are not created by superior intelligences, they are a natural phenomenon, as is the behaviour of the planets within each galaxy. Planets do not tidily orbit their own suns in a solar system similar to the one we are presumed to have. There aren't any other suns to orbit – not in this galaxy anyway. Neither the Earth nor any of its solar system neighbours orbit the sun. For simplicity's sake, imagine our whole galaxy as divided up into rough cubes of space with one planet in every cube. Each planet moves around its own cube in predictable manner, which is something that our mathematicians can predict correctly by Earth time about our near neighbours. They have even sighted stars apparently orbiting nothing – these are probably large planets repeating their pattern of movement within their own larger portion of space. But as you move out into deep space and encounter some of its veils and mysteries, Earth time begins to lose validity and even the so-called speed of light becomes just another enigma. What you see in space by telescope or naked eye could be happening now, not millions of years ago as astronomers believe. True light does not travel, it's either there or it isn't. It is a component from the beginning of creation, the exact opposite of blackness and one of the eternal mysteries of the universe that cannot be truly recreated by a searchlight or even a flaming sun. It is present in depleted form in our galaxy and in abundance in most other galaxies, enabling the eye to make astronomical observations as they happen. The speed of artificial light has been measured at 186,000 miles per second and the distance of stars from Earth are all based on the time it takes light or radio signals to reach them, but there are undiscovered conditions in the depths of space which can render these computations valueless. This calls into question the nearness of the stars, which could be a great deal nearer than the light-year distances suggested by Earth mathematics.

NO BLACK HOLES

There are no black holes or 'wormholes' in space. It is nice to have some of the anomalies in space explained away by equation, but there are planetaires who have had intergalactic space travelling capability for many millions of years and have never come across either of these anomalies. Because the particles of an atom revolve around a central nucleus it seems a natural progression that planets should revolve around something, yet there is no guarantee that even the moon orbits the Earth. A simple daily turn by the planet in a different direction from its slow spin which produces our day and night would produce the illusory effect of an orbiting moon. A spin within a spin. Apparently the moon is rather unique because of its closeness to Earth in relation to its near-planetary size. Although small compared to many planets, it is unusual for two of such size to be so close to each other. The moon's status cannot be compared with the moons of the giant Jupiter because of the colossal difference in size between Jupiter and its satellites. Held by the enormous gravitational pull of the giant, it is likely that they would orbit within that planet's space.

The Circle also learned that electricity, indispensable as it is to our planet, is finite. There is plenty of it, but it is finite. Once used it is no longer there for re-use. In contrast, the diffusion of either Cosmic or Vitrik after use does not prevent its availability to be gathered in again for re-use. If we do not find another power source before electricity is exhausted, imagine the chaos that would follow. Generators turning, but producing nothing. No more phones, lights, cars, planes, radio, TV or computers – society at a standstill. The day the Earth stood still – but not in the foreseeable future.

THE JECULINS

The Jeculins, their associate planets and those of Jeculin followers, all utilise an incredible, almost holy, power called Vitrik. It propels their circular craft at fantastic speeds on their missions of mercy around the universe. A space captain estimated he had crossed our galaxy in just two weeks of our time. When asked if he could match this, the Master of a Jeculin craft said he could cross the galaxy in five of our days. The maximum speed the Vitrik propulsion units can achieve has never been fully tested owing to the limits imposed by the ability of a craft's hull to withstand the stress of ultimate speed. The only time speed limitation orders were exceeded the craft and crew were all lost when it disintegrated in deep space.

All heavy work on their planets is done by emplinadors, which can range from an almost human robot to the vast factory-like complexes that produce their food and other necessities. Young Jeculins, after undertaking a period of compulsory duties, usually take up a vocational occupation. There is no need for money as everything is provided. High ranking officials are provided with a hopper. This is a small craft that can carry up to four people equally well on land, over water, or in the air. There is no day and night. Their skies are always bright. When Vitrik is used – and it is used for virtually everything – it dispels into the atmosphere, or in the case of spacecraft, back into space. This strange, limitless power undergoes a remarkable transformation due to continued usage. It gains in luminosity, producing the Vitrik effect – whole galaxies basking in eternal light. This continuous light has its effect on plant life. Spectacular flowers bloom in bright colours with an intense luminosity. The predominant foliage colour on Earth is green, whereas on many Vitrik planets foliage can be blue or red and green is just one of the many colours of flower blooms.

We are probably several millennia away from Vitrik – The Almighty would not allow us to have this holy power until we are worthy of it. All is not black however, as Cosmic Power is still waiting to be harnessed. Infinitely superior to electricity, but limited if compared to Vitrik, it will do everything electricity does and more. And it will provide the propulsion for real take-off and landing spacecraft to check out the nearest stars.

THE GREAT HAPPENING

As the autumn of 1978 turned to winter, some contacts began hinting at a 'great happening' which was to befall the Circle at the time of the Jeculin festival of Tarset (Christmas). The Efun himself referred to it and told them to prepare, but would not say what it would be. At the Tarset meeting on December 24 The Holy Flocen spoke through Nitesi to prepare them for the arrival of the beloved old Flocen who was coming to the meeting directly from the bosom of The Almighty to speak through Nitesi. This was something which had never happened before throughout all time. They were to hear the voice of their original Flocen for the first time. He who had spoken through Jesus 2,000 years ago, now briefly reunited with the group of tentative questioners He had so gently steered on the right path such a short time before. This wonderful meeting was to further elevate the Circle's status in the universe. Henceforth Circle members would be known as the 'Children of Light' and regarded as Jeculin Associates.

THE GALAXIAL BEAM

All genuine seances produce a certain aura glow. Members were told the aura glow of their Circle was so bright it could be seen from a great distance. The glow had become a beacon. Apparently, since receiving their new sacred title, a beam of spiritual light extending from far beyond the galaxy was shining down upon them. They could not see anything, but all of their spirit and astral contacts could. Jeculins making long astral journeys from their home planets were particularly appreciative of it, using it as a kind of spiritual 'wormhole' to reach the group more easily, but even they didn't know from where it originated, although members felt The Holy Flocen knew, even though he didn't say. They did not really dare to ask as the implications were so awesome. It did seem the quest for enlightenment had reached a peak that could not have been anticipated. It became clear they were now under holy orders to spread far and wide the knowledge that they had been given. They were to form from the Circle a new Church of God to be called 'The First Earth Jeculin Associate Church' and were told that in the new millennium it would become the greatest Church the world has ever seen.

It was arranged that Nitesi, Normesi and several other group members should go to a small spiritualist church where Nitesi would endeavour to go into trance. The Holy Flocen had promised his presence there. If necessary He would help her into trance so that He could speak through her. This He duly did. After declaring himself as The Holy Spirit, He spoke of the importance of love and of our brothers and sisters on other planets.

WHERE IS BELIEF?

It was a wonderful sermon and the captive audience of around 60 people, although probably hoping for messages from deceased relatives, was enrapt. It is now a matter for regret that nobody took a tape recorder to record those golden words. The rapture was somewhat dispelled by the lady principal of the church when she called for appreciation of Nita's efforts, adding, 'I'm sure that was a very good spirit we have been listening to.' Unbelief. She just could not bring herself to believe her little church had been graced by the presence of *The* Holy Spirit that afternoon. If her attitude was typical of the Spiritualist Church as a whole, their short-sighted aims have left them ignorant of many basic facts. No spirit would ever dare commit the extreme blasphemy of impersonating *The* Holy Spirit. The principal's male helper, who was also psychic, told Nita before she left the church that he had seen a beautiful white dove above her head as she entered the building. It is well known that The Holy Spirit often favours appearing as a white dove, less daunting for those with the seeing eye, although He can appear in any form to all mankind. Nitesi had announced that anybody from the church who would like to attend their meetings would be very welcome. To members' astonishment there was not a single inquiry about their meetings from an audience which one would expect to be brimming with potential future novice members to reinforce the Circle. Over the years there were occasional new recruits, but virtually all of these drifted away again. Although novice members were always told the prime objective was to expand the boundaries of religious knowledge, they were probably attracted by the lure of receiving regular contacts from space. But these same contacts were part of the indoctrination into the Power of Love and the erstwhile guests soon found that they had neither the stamina, nor inclination for this kind of psychic meeting. Regular Circle members considered them merely sensation seekers and therefore no real loss.

THE ASTRAL DOMAIN

The meetings progressed anyway and the variety of contacts still threw up the occasional surprise. Because of a general lack of spirituality Earth Astrals are very few, so it was a surprise when an elderly lady Earth contact already assumed to be a passed over spirit said, 'Oh no dear, I'm not dead', revealing she had been projecting her spirit astrally from her body for years. She was living quietly in London and had an almost blasé attitude to her rare ability. She had seen the bright light from the meeting while on one of her occasional evening excursions and came down to see what it was all about. She was the first of maybe half a dozen Astrals among hundreds of Earth contacts. Another, also English, said he had been at 'such a meeting as this' and was asked to relay a message which confirmed something that the Circle had already learned regarding their research into the history of the planet. Then there was a local clairvoyant who seemed to be bewildered at being able to speak through the medium. He was totally disorientated at finding himself at the meeting. The one who came the greatest distance was a monk who had been meditating in a Chinese temple. His limited knowledge of English brought this contact to a premature end.

Space contacts were invariably Astrals because it is a long and tiring journey for a spirit to make. They are unable to use the equipment that boosts their physical counterparts on their journeys. Astrals come directly from a booster chamber on their home planet, or take a much shorter trip by coming down from a spacecraft in the vicinity. Most larger craft carry a booster facility and this very fact illustrates just how well their spiritual reality is integrated with physical life. Astral travel is not the sole domain of humanoid peoples. Animals and many other life forms are able to do this. Waa-Waa was a dolphin. He and two compatriots had monitored our language before a brave attempt to make astral contact. He had great difficulty trying to use the voicebox of the medium. They came from a large school visiting the English Channel in the summer of 1978. Although only part of his replies could be fully understood, he gave his

14

love and told of his people's superior distance vision and their celebratory dance they perform by standing on their tails. This ultra high-pitched contact was all too brief, but still took its toll on the medium's throat. Over the following years there were several more brief dolphin contacts, the most recent being in late summer 1993. His name was Bikkel and he is a spirit. He knew Waa-Waa and said Waa-Waa was also a spirit now. Having some difficulty with the language, Bikkel's control of the medium's voicebox was admirable compared to Waa-Waa's shrieking efforts years earlier. (See transcripts.)

WILLING ABDUCTEES

There have been occasional instances where people of Earth, on meeting with planetaires, have been offered the chance to live on a more advanced planet – and many have accepted. One such person is Willlam Spence, formally of Oxford. He was a member of a psychic circle which had managed to make contact with planetaires. They were offered the chance to live on another planet, but with the exception of Spence most of the other group members thought it was a huge joke. He went alone to a prearranged rendezvous in the mid-1950s and was never seen again. No doubt police records of that time will have him listed as missing, believed drowned. In July 1981 he was allowed to visit the Circle astrally from the planet Curlieu to make himself known to them. His transcript makes interesting reading. The American mother of Eartha Arthur was another willing emigrant. She was taken to a planet in our galaxy where a romantic union produced Eartha Arthur. He owes his name to his origin. He thinks his mother, now passed over, later returned to the Earth spirit world. His description of their spacecraft, 'mushroom shaped with the works in the mushroom and living quarters in the short stalk' powered by a highly inflammable gas, suggests their technology is midway between our crude rocketry and the sleek discs of really advanced planets. They have settled for the much favoured circular shape, but like ourselves do not have Cosmic-Ray propulsion.

NITESI'S TRAUMA

In the mid-1970s it was not unusual for a meeting to last four hours. The Circle was strong and Nitesi was younger and fitter although suffering from ill health even then. The contacts stayed longer and had more time to talk. The really busy years were 1976–81 with a minimum of two meetings per week. The Circle was at its strongest with an average of five physical members present to back up the medium and hundreds of spirits and Astrals in attendance. Nitesi suffered further trauma in 1978 when her partner for more than 22 years left her for the arms of another woman. She had forgiven him, but stipulated he could not stay with her and continue to see the other woman. She was deeply wounded by his choice. He was not a Circle member, being frightened at the concept of talking with spirits and always contrived to be out and about on meeting nights. Many contacts sympathised with her tortured state of mind and the occasional reference to it may be found in some of the transcripts of that period that were selected for publication. One of just three remaining Circle stalwarts was lost in 1982 when Nitesi's brother Tom passed over. He was a practical man with an analytical brain and one of the last survivors of those who had seen the Angels of Mons in the First World War. Normesi had talked with him about this, suggesting they could have been large birds, but he was adamant he had clearly seen angels wheeling above the trenches. All those around him who witnessed this miracle knew they were angels. They had come for the souls of the thousands that were being slaughtered in one of the many senseless offensives which characterised World War I. He made contact a few weeks after his passing. He had been on a Jeculin course of instruction. Tom described passing over as a 'piece of cake' and nothing to worry about. His physical loss was the start of a downward spiral for the Circle which was further decimated by several 'part-time' members drifting away over the next three years.

THE LOST YEARS

The Circle became so weak that meetings were having to be cancelled at short notice. The meetings that did take place were badly attended and few and far between. Finally, towards the end of 1985, the unavailability of a suitable venue meant the indefinite suspension of further meetings. The Circle was reformed in January 1990 with the addition of several novice members and Nitesi in her 80th year. The spiritual strength was gradually built up again and until the end of 1995 a reasonably steady flow of contacts was achieved. They had been previously warned that Nitesi's ability to trance would gradually fade when she reached 80. With her persistent heart trouble and now virtually blind, this was becoming the

16

case. There were an increasing number of occasions when she was unable to trance. Meeting times became much shorter, rarely lasting over two hours. Contacts, when received, stayed little more than 15 minutes due to lack of power and in deference to her frailty.

The last great holy contact was on Friday, December 29, 1995. The meeting was graced by a visit from The Blessed Efun who had come on the express orders of the Lord Flocen to tell the true story of the birth of Jesus. (See *The Efun [1995] transcript*). 1996 began very badly. Nitesi, in her 85th year, very frail and almost blind, was struck down by a severe virus. She clung tenaciously to life during her ten-week ordeal. She won her battle and was able to trance successfully on ten occasions during the remainder of the year. Although weekly meetings continued into 1997, there were only three at which Nitesi felt strong enough to attempt to trance. It was at the third of these, on March 14, that she was successful in receiving what was to be the last contact as an operating research circle. His name was Noah and he was the spirit of an internal dweller who had not had to travel far from his home planet to reach them. His main sense of concern was for the health of the medium and to make himself known before her gift had completely waned. In one sentence he answered a long standing question without even being asked. 'I come from a planet which is not very far from you in this galaxy. You call it Mars.' (See *Noah [1997] transcript.*)

For the last 18 months of the medium's life the once powerful Circle was reduced to a weekly meeting between Nitesi and Normesi during which the contents of this proposed work were discussed. In one discussion in her final year (1998) she was adamant that the year was wrong in a 1993 Circle message about the New Redeemer 'in the year 2000 of your time'. Although unable to trance, her mind was still receiving night-time indoctrination and now that the year 2004 is upon us with no sign of a holy messenger, her acquired inner knowledge has been proved right. Fears for his safety must grow as violence escalates in the Middle East. Now read on and learn of the Earth's two previous civilisations and how the dinosaurs became extinct. Why the Earth is unique among civilised planets. Of birth and death and some of the secrets of the spirit world. Why you are here and how reincarnation gives you another chance, and another, and another . . .

THREE CIVILISATIONS

Here and now, you are a member of the relatively young third civilisation of this planet. Deep in Earth prehistory there was a thriving civilisation before the era of the large dinosaurs. Dinosaurs already existed during the First Civilisation, but the largest were no bigger than our present-day farm animals and certain smaller species were kept as pets. Some of the animals we have now were not originally endemic to Earth in those far-off days. The configuration of land was very different then with the land being more massed together, although there was always more sea than land. Our world was known then as Satallé. We were approaching their stage of advancement with our continued use of nuclear fission for energy and weaponry developing a situation which could have paralleled the one that destroyed them. Fortunately, with economic reasons causing a decline of interest in nuclear fission as an energy source the danger has somewhat receded, although the obscenity of the nuclear weapon remains a potent threat to all life. Our predecessors were proud of the comprehensive network of large atomic power stations covering the planet. They didn't even dream of making atomic bombs, as there was only one race of peace-loving people and one language. Atomic fission had been mastered and they thought they had made this energy source their servant. Satallé had its own small fleet of interplanetary spacecraft. They were slow by today's universal standards, necessitating the 'long sleep' which was ended by computerised resuscitation for crew members who were on the longer journeys. In those days regular visitations from space were warmly welcomed on our planet.

The visitors, however, were becoming more and more alarmed at the rapid growth of the nuclear network, with bigger and more powerful stations being added all the time. They warned that the constant enlargement of these facilities was creating a nuclear monster that would become uncontrollable and devour them.

Nuclear fission is evil in the eyes of The Almighty Power because the radioactive residues kill every form of life – the absolute antithesis of all

18

The Almighty is. Eventually the visitors became so worried they offered the citizens of Satallé sanctuary on their own planets. So many people wanted to take advantage of their offer of escape from the predicted disaster that the planetaires felt obliged to help in the construction of extra spacecraft with greater people-carrying capacity so that none who wished to leave would be left behind. The population was decimated by the evacuations, but many had stayed behind.

In the following years the planetaire visits became much less frequent and finally ceased altogether. The people of Satallé quietly got on with their lives. They missed the diversion of the planetaire visits, but were no doubt feeling their decision to stay had been fully justified. It was the quiet before the storm. The panic that ensued, as one after another of the great atomic complexes turned critical, was not to last long. The first explosion activated a chain reaction which culminated in the total destruction of all the inhabited land. What had been the First Civilisation was now a desolate wasteland.

DINOSAURS

The devastated planet, with its poisonous surface, lay neglected for millions of years as its poisons slowly eroded away. Even spacecraft gave the poisoned planet a wide berth. Then the gentle hand of The Almighty, in the guise of Nature, caressed the barren wilderness. Things began to grow and plant life began to partially clothe the lifeless desolation. Dinosaurs came out of the seas to set up their kingdom on land that now offered an alternative diet. They too had grown, their enormous size due to mutated genes over countless generations. Their great appetite had out-grazed their natural habitat and they spent increasingly longer periods on land making up the deficit, eventually becoming true land animals. For a long age the dinosaurs flourished, but the plant-eaters were not alone in their migration from the oceans of the world. Flesh-eating predators, attracted by such a bewildering array of food, were spending more time hunting on land than in the waters. Over the generations their genes responded, enabling them to adapt to the conditions equally as well as the herbivores who had multiplied to such an extent that the predation of the carnivores had little effect on their numbers. There is evidence that Earth was hit by meteors during the latter part of the dinosaurs' reign, but the resultant devastation was only a contributory factor to their final extinction. Compared to modern day Earth, the vegetation was sparse and gradually the enormous combined appetite of the herbivores was stripping the land bare. They had to travel much greater distances to satisfy their hunger and were dying in great numbers. The carnivores were satiated with meat during this period, but it was the beginning of the end for them too as their main source of food dwindled to extinction forcing them to turn upon each other to satisfy their appetites. Even the natural urge for reproduction took second place to the more urgent need for food. Soon there would only be the pterodactyls left to pick on the bones for their last meal as the scene closed on a remarkable period of Earth history.

THE SECOND CIVILISATION

Long after the demise of the dinosaurs, Satallé was repopulated by descendants of the First Civilisation brought by spacecraft from the planets which had co-operated in the evacuation of their forbears. This was the birth of the Second Civilisation approximately 17 million years ago. One race of people, but from a number of planets, most, if not all, in our own galaxy. For their new beginning they renamed our planet 'Wol'. Why they were denied bringing some of the technology they were used to is not known. Only the bare facts were available. It is quite likely they were segregated and trained to live off the land for their basic needs, much as archaeologists have done today for limited periods, to see how Stone Age people survived. But this was a planetary scale project and the newcomers had no 'mod cons' to return to. Certainly they had no specialists or trained technicians among them. Succeeding generations would accept the new lifestyle as normal and the beginning would become forgotten history. The settlements were largely based in the area which is now the Middle East. The inhospitable mountains and endless desert of today give no clue to what had been the lush vegetation and vast green plains of a veritable Garden of Eden. Gold was found in incredible quantities, never far below the surface, it was mined open-cast. Precious stones too, were found in abundance. Gold, in particular, had no commercial value. Streets of the cities were literally paved with gold and most buildings were at least partially constructed of gold brick, often patterned with gemstones. There was one precious metal, however, as iron ore was extremely rare in this geologically topsy-turvy wonderland. Trinkets and jewellery made of iron were highly prized and of great value. The cities of gold are still more or less intact many miles deep beneath the sands of what is now North Africa.

At its height, the Second Civilisation had reached the level of the Romans in their days of empire. Their city road surfaces were cobbled, while grit roads connected the cities. The capital city was called Tula, the home of the Sedlars, who were the kings and queens who ruled during the length of their civilisation, which was described as 'long' compared to the newness of our present civilisation.

There were drainage and irrigation systems that brought clear water from the mountains. Oil lamps were used for lighting. Their greatest king was Mené, whose fame was legendary, perhaps comparable to Solomon in a more recent age. Later they had a queen whose name was to penetrate through to the present civilisation. Her name is Athena and there is no doubt it is she whom the Ancient Greeks revered as a goddess. The nearest thing to war in her days was the traditional Colstan, a warlike game of tactics fought out like living chess. Players were selected by the Lords of the great houses from their own family and retainers to form a team which they themselves would lead into battle. It was an honour to be a Colstan player-warrior. With no need for a regular army, it was left to Colstan to provide the excitement and challenge the young bloods might seek. Every game drew large crowds of supporters, whose fervour was no less than present day soccer fanatics. Played in an arena sub-divided into small sections, players of opposing sides occupied opposite ends of the arena. Each player wore protective armour and carried some sort of weapon. They each stood on a square trolley with rear facing handles. Between the handles was an assistant who pushed the trolley wherever ordered. When the game commenced the opponents advanced toward each other to occupy as many sections as possible. To capture an occupied section, the attacker would be pushed alongside the occupant's trolley and they would fight until one of them was dislodged. No further details of the game are known, but suffice to say there were frequent serious injuries, and deaths were not uncommon. Athena had always hated the inevitable spilling of blood and finally banned Colstan soon after her ascent to the throne. The Second Civilisation was eventually destroyed by tremendous land upheavals and cataclysmic earthquakes. Information on this period is sketchy. There was no sudden end as happened with the First Civilisation, but it was the second time a peaceful civilisation had disappeared from this planet leaving no visible trace. The land ruptures had come slowly over a great many years with the intensity gradually increasing to an untenable level. The people were evacuated by spacecraft and this time there were no dissenters. Where and how cavemen evolved to become part of the age between the Second and the present civilisation is an enigma.

EXPERIMENT THAT FAILED

The present civilisation dawned tens of thousands of years ago when descendants from the second evacuation of the planet were put down to settle here. There was 'much jungle and blue water'. The 'wild' animals were friendly. There was no aggression and no fear. The new inhabitants relaxed into a new, almost idyllic lifestyle. Their tongue was not totally unlike the original Olde Englishe. Then came the great experiment that changed everything. A group of planets decided it would be a good idea to repopulate the Earth with 'volunteers' from their own peoples. They were probably largely miscreants and misfits whom they felt they could well do without.

By settling them on different parts of the world, they would be left to fully develop their own cultures and by the time the small pockets of population had expanded to any degree, the different races would have worked out how to share the planet in harmony. What a miscalculation! Then the plan developed an unforeseen complication. Over the next few centuries, as news of the experiment spread far and wide, more planets decided to join in. Soon our little world had a polyglot population occupying all the more desirable areas. This experiment made the Earth even more unique than it was already with its vast oceans of surface water. All populated planets have only one race of people, as it was on Earth during the first two civilisations and might have been today. They share their worlds, as we do, with other life forms, animals, birds, fish etc. It is this experiment which is probably the main reason why we continue to be monitored by spacecraft from other worlds. Meanwhile the new peoples of Earth found the trusting wild game easy to kill, but later generations had to hunt to stock their larders as the animals' trust in man was replaced by fear. The smaller game became furtive and more elusive to find, while the larger animals were becoming more aggressive. Inevitably, as national borders expanded there were frequent clashes between the different races. Our war-torn history had begun. The further unscheduled immigration undoubtedly tipped the scales towards the aggressive chaos of nations which still prevails today.

THE JECULIN PHILOSOPHY

The humanoid can be found throughout the universe, in every galaxy known to planetaires, although there are many planets solely occupied by other life forms. The human form is favoured by The Almighty Power because their innovative minds and sensitive fingers put them in a position, not only to help each other, but any other life form requiring help.

From a cluster of some 30 planets in a distant galaxy, Jeculins try to provide this help as they spread The Code of Love throughout the universe. The leading planet of this Jeculin cluster is called Cincea. They follow the Divine Will closely answering calls for help from distressed planets – often coming in response to prayers to The Almighty, to provide global help where needed. They know everything there is to know about our planet, but will not come to Earth in its present politically fragmented state. To achieve this, an Earth Council responsible for the whole planet must make the request. The United Nations is a step in the right direction. Unfortunately, with no real power to end despotic regimes which still exist in many countries and the inability to stamp out bloodshed wherever it occurs, they do not meet the necessary criteria. The original true Jeculins are few compared to the great variety of humanoid races throughout space, but they have many allies. Foremost are the Jeculin Associate planets which also live by The Code of Love. Then there are thousands of planets where The Code has been accepted and implemented as far as possible. They are Jeculin Followers. These great forces for good are like the physical arms of The Almighty, always ready to help in the event of some global disaster, ever seeking to draw us closer to understanding the Power of Love. The Jeculins themselves, like many Jeculin Associate races, are tall, averaging over 7 feet in height, with blond hair and very fair complexion. With the exception of The Holy Flocen's all-spirit world, they are the most spiritually advanced people in the universe. Their disc-shaped spacecraft are the ultimate in technology and they are true servants of The Almighty. The translation of what we call God is The Immortal Power, or sometimes The Almighty Power. The Code of Love stipulates that all life belongs to The Immortal Power and is therefore sacred. Consequently they do not kill anything. They will not even harvest corn or wheat until it has completed its life cycle or, in their words, become 'fallen grasses'. Animals are never slaughtered – they live until they die naturally. 'Wild' animals are fed and are no longer wild. Gazelle and antelope-type creatures walk fearlessly among the big cats and other erstwhile carnivores. Where does all the food come from? There are never any shortages of vital protein and there is a very good reason for this. The Jeculins regard the burial or cremation of corpses as a sinful waste of resources. They are not bound by Earth-type sentimentality to bury a departed loved one in a nice plot where, presumably, the rotting corpse can have a nice view of the surrounding countryside, or by man-made rules that stipulate that a corpse must be buried in so-called sanctified ground. In truth it would not matter if it was left in a desert to give the vultures a treat. On Earth it would matter to someone indoctrinated with the need for last rites, sanctified ground etc. because he does not change his beliefs immediately on passing over and the fact that he didn't have these rituals would worry him. The Jeculins do not have family units. They are all brothers and sisters, many of them genetically. Human eggs are taken only from the most perfect specimens recommended by computer. Semen is also selected in this fashion and both are stored until an increase in population is needed. Eggs are fertilised in batches and develop entirely from foetus to baby in a series of vitrik-powered computerised wombs, where their every need is monitored and provided for. As each baby reaches the stage of development where it would have been born as it is on Earth, it receives a complete change of blood. Apparently this blood change is an important part of their disease-free breeding programme. Sexual intercourse is regarded as an 'unspeakable act' and love-making between the sexes does not go further than kissing and concentrated petting in an established partnership. With the bearing of children discarded for so long, the female sexual organs have atrophied. This means a pregnant female would be unlikely to go full term for a natural birth.

They have extensive limb and organ banks containing all kinds of body spares which can provide a perfect match for any requirement. They are one very positive benefit from limiting the number of genetic breeding strains. Add to this their sophisticated medical equipment and it can be seen a perfect organ or limb match is a certainty every time. Even in an advanced society such as theirs, there is still the occasional accident. Many of their planets use a moving belt transport system connecting various points in their conurbations. There is nothing to stop the would-be traveller from jumping on or off these belts between stopping places and some people like to leap on or off just for the excitement when the belt is travelling at speed. These tall humans are extremely agile so mishaps are not as common as one might think, but it must be nice to know that if the worst possible happened there is a parts bank just waiting to rectify any body damage they might incur.

There is also horse racing, but not as we know it – they do not carry jockeys. Jockeys are not needed. The horses do not require steering or a few taps of the whip to do their best. These intelligent animals are trained to race each other to entertain the public and they perform according to

24

how they feel on the day. The horses enjoy their racing as much as the people who watch it. In a society which has no use for money, the only bets made are side wagers between individuals with personal trinkets at stake.

The Jeculins have much greater knowledge of the afterlife of their spiritual world. They have mediums too, immeasurably better than the standard on Earth, although they have complimented Nitesi as being comparable to one of theirs. The simple act of a soul leaving the physical and moving into its true home – the spiritual dimension – holds no terrors for these enlightened people. Contact with the spiritual dimension is even encouraged. There is no ritual sentimentality over an empty corpse. They know exactly where the person they knew and love has gone . . . and the corpse of that person will go, together with the carcasses of deceased animals and the 'fallen grasses' and no doubt many other things, to be cleansed and purified – and changed – to provide the proteins and nutrients to feed the planet. The exquisite fare that is offered and provided free in their great dining halls is truly out of this world in flavour and texture.

THE JECULIN FESTIVALS

There are four Jeculin religious festivals in a period corresponding to one of our years. For Circle benefit they were referred to as 01, 02 and 03. The fourth and most important is called Tarset and coincides with our Christmas time. As 01 also corresponds with Easter, it seems very likely that those momentous events on Earth 2,000 years ago were a part of the Divine Plan timed to relate with these great festivals which are observed throughout the universe by countless trillions of Jeculin followers. The first and major part of each festival is devoted to prayer to The Almighty and the festivities end with 'much celebration and drinking of nectar'.

ANIMAL INTELLIGENCE

Animal intelligence should never be underestimated. They know they can only live within the limitations of their bodies. Imagine having the ability to learn a language and no vocal organ to enable you to speak it. A good example of this is our own dolphins. They can shake off the constraints of the body by astrally projecting themselves to go out on learning missions.

25

They probably know more about us than we know about them. This was particularly well illustrated by Nik-Nik and Wula, two astral male dolphins who visited the Circle in June 1978. They each took it in turn to speak briefly through the medium. This is the gist of what was said. Nik-Nik: 'Love you. I go to the man and woman in boat like Wa-Wa *(another dolphin)*. We understand all they say to us. We love them.' Wula: 'I go to man and woman in boat as well. There are three of us that all go there one at a time. We all understand English and they think we are all the same dolphin. We saw the cameras when they were filming.' It is not difficult to regard dolphins as people in a different kind of body. There are plenty of animal intelligences to rival them throughout the universe.

SOULS OF THE ANIMALS

If we could make telepathic contact with our domestic pets, their degree of understanding would be a real eye-opener. In early 1986, Normesi felt it necessary to end the suffering of Cleo, his 12-year-old Alsatian/Labrador bitch. Her life had been prolonged with various cocktails of drugs, which were no longer taking effect. Her eyes were glazed with pain as he gently stroked her head, waiting for the vet's lethal syringe. The needle found its mark and her head sagged almost instantaneously. Then it happened. His melancholy was shattered by the words: 'Thank you. Thank you' running through his mind. Telepathy? Perhaps. Whatever it was, she got her message through. Everybody who has suffered the heartache of losing a much loved pet, be it a dog, cat, horse, bird, or even a humble hamster, should know that ALL ANIMAL LIFE HAS SOULS AND SPIRITS. When released from the body they return to their own kind in their spiritual homeland. There's even an afterlife for fish and insects. Animals are rarely seen on the human planes, although a place where the different spirits can intermingle is on a visit down to Earth – the physical plane. There are exceptions. Where the bond of love between man and animal has developed to an unusual degree, the animal could sometimes join the human on his allotted level. Ann Boleyn is often accompanied by her large grey Irish wolfhound and King Charles of spaniel fame is usually followed by half-a-dozen of the dogs that bear his name. The lifespan of animals, being generally so much shorter than that of humans, means their physical lives often come with a much greater frequency. Sometimes a human spirit can be born into an animal body. This has happened on rare occasions, but always when it has been the specific desire of the human. On any of the planets following the Jeculin Code of Love such a lifetime might provide an interesting diversion from the usual, but why anybody should request such a thing on our planet, considering the way many of our animals are treated, seems strange. Perhaps they can request a particular individual animal, such as the expected foal of a famous racehorse. That would guarantee a well-pampered life.

BIRTH AND THE RIGHT TO LIFE

In this modern day there is still much ignorance regarding birth and the right to life of an unborn child. Heartache is caused to expectant mothers of foetuses that have tested positively as having a genetic disorder, which inevitably leads to the birth of a spastic child. Mothers are tortured by the feeling that an abortion will destroy its right to life. Nothing can be further from the truth. A foetus, perfect paradigm as it is of pre-programmed cells automatically forming into a future being, is still only life in its most basic form, although occasional kickings caused by newly-created nerves flexing their control over newly-created muscles may give the impression of a thinking living being existing within the mother. Biological miracles of a near magnitude occur in our own bodies every day of life with complex operations going on which are not governed directly from the brain. The situation changes dramatically when the newly-born baby draws in its designated spirit and soul with its first independent breath. From that moment it is sacred, deformed or otherwise. THE SOUL DESTINED FOR AN ABORTED BABY WILL MERELY BE DIVERTED TO ANOTHER BIRTH AND HOPEFULLY A HAPPIER LIFE. The expectant mother should be asking herself, 'Is it fair to sentence a soul to such an existence?' Not everybody in the spirit world faces the prospect of another physical journey with a great deal of relish, although many with another failed physical life behind them, have no choice in the matter. While it is entirely justifiable to destroy a diseased foetus, abortion should not be used as a type of birth control as it is against Nature and Nature is a part of God.

The gradual elimination of hereditary conditions and diseases can be achieved by a combination of further gene identification and the voluntary sterilisation of rogue gene carriers. This would eventually put an end to having to make the choice between committing a formerly happy spirit to a lifetime in a frustratingly inadequate and often deformed physical body – or stopping the development of the empty human shell before it is able to claim its victim. This choice is only made difficult because of the lack of true spiritual guidance available to the expectant parents.

PASSING OVER – DEATH OF THE BODY

The time comes for everybody when a tired and worn-out body finally ceases to function. This is the only time that the soul leaves the body since it gained entry with the first gasp for air by the then newborn baby. The soul and spirit, as one, take their departure the way they came in – through the mouth. There is no problem for the true believer as they are merely returning to their home dimension after years of being largely restricted to only the physical senses of the body. On evacuating the body you find yourself floating and able to look down on what had been the physical you. There are many near-death experiences similarly described, but there is one vital difference – in their cases the soul has not left the body. The spirit however, which contains your awareness, had seized the chance to pop out for a look around while the restraining influences of the body were subdued. In fact, a mini astral projection. It is the soul that pulls the spirit back to the body if the spirit tries to make an untimely entry into the next dimension. There is a gossamer-like thread that connects the spirit to the soul. It will never break, no matter how great the distance of separation. Only the soul, that infinitesimal part of The Almighty, knows when it is the right time to evacuate the body. When that times comes, spirit and soul completely integrated, will leave the mortal remains. THE QUALITY OF YOUR EXISTENCE IN THE SPIRITUAL DIMENSION IS CHOSEN BY YOU ACCORDING TO YOUR ACTIONS IN THE PHYSICAL WORLD. This is what Jesus meant when he said you will receive your reward in Heaven. For the majority of people who have lived a reasonable life, without causing deliberate harm to others, the passing will be pleasant. If there was pain in the body, you have left it behind. The feeling of weightless freedom as you float above your now empty body will greatly mollify the pangs of regret at parting from your loved ones. It is the end of a life journey, and now you must move on. To Earth spirits willing to talk of the manner of their passing – and many won't – the tunnel sequence is fairly commonplace. After a few seconds you become aware of the entrance to a long dark tunnel. You know you have to go through it. Thank God for the bright light at the far end. How long that tunnel is depends on how far you have extended it by un-Christian actions during your physical lifetime. The tunnel leads into a large bright place where there are people waiting to help you and take you on to the next stage. You will eventually be taken to the spiritual level where you are to live until your next life journey is due. All levels of the spirit world cover the whole planet, which means people passing on to their appropriate level will find it reasonably near to the part of the world in which they lived.

A young male motorcyclist, killed outright in a gory road accident, was virtually catapulted from his body and remembered looking down on the mess and feeling relieved that he was out of it. He recalled going up among clouds and white-garmented people asking him about his religion and other questions. This was an unscheduled passing over. One lady who died of old age could only remember waking up on a grassy river bank. The white-robed figure of a man stood under a nearby tree. When he saw she was awake, he came over and asked if she was sufficiently rested. There are certainly more ways of passing over than the few that have been discovered, but one thing is sure – whatever you experience will be just what you have earned.

Babies and little children are always carried away by a winged angel. Very few spirits have wings. Those that have are angels. They are part of The Almighty's elite and always available for the most delicate of missions. An advanced spirit aspiring to become an angel, if selected, faces a course of intensive training. There can be no doubt by the time he gets his wings, he has really earned them. Every populated planet has its own winged angels. There is also a band of angels called The Singing People who are the special elite of The Almighty. They are not tied to any planet, never travelling singly, but always in numbers, singing the praises of the All-Highest throughout the universe.

There is no guarantee you will see deceased relatives. Unless their spiritual values are similar to your own, they may well be living on a higher or lower plane. Jesus said, 'My father has many mansions'. This was an understatement. There arc indeed many, many planes of existence. The highest are for those who have achieved the greatest spiritual development; the lowest for the unfortunate moronic types who will need many more physical lifetimes to grasp the basic fact that life and love should be synonymous. In short, if you've been a nasty person you will, after surviving the after-death experience you have earned, go to a low plane where everybody's disposition during life has been similar to your own. There will be the opportunity to receive instruction and improve yourself if you ask for it.

There are time zones which separate past from present, each zone spanning approximately 100 years. Even an advanced spirit needs special permission to cross a time zone. Each time zone has its own Controller who, along with his deputies, is responsible for all the planes within it. The Supreme Controller of our spirit world is Abraham, with Solomon as his deputy. Both of these great spirits have spoken through Nitesi and have since converted to the Code of Love as expounded by The Holy Flocen and the Jeculins.

HEAVEN AND HELL

People lift their eyes momentarily upwards toward the Heavens, where we are led to believe God lives, when making a quick appeal for forbearance, often over a trivial matter. The instinct that makes us do this is because the Earth's spirit world really does girdle the planet in the same way as the spirit world of every other inhabited planet girdles their own globe. But The Almighty is too big to live solely in the spirit world of one tiny planet. The Great Presence is everywhere there is life and the physical dimension is an equally important part of the Great Kingdom. The popular idea of Heaven, a mythical St Peter at the gate and God as a superhuman with Christ at his side, is pure fallacy. It shows the complete lack of understanding of just how great The Almighty Power is. Picture a universe with endless galaxies of forming stars and stardust. If the Power was already among the stardust it would explain His ubiquity. The only other alternative is that He came from somewhere else to organise the universe. But from where? THE ALMIGHTY IS LIFE IN EVERY FORM EVERYWHERE. Where the heart of The Almighty is situated is not for us to know, but it has been described to members as the bosom of The Almighty by The Holy Flocen, who is the Holy Spirit of the universe. The Bible quotes Jesus as saying God is in all mankind. Circle research verifies that we are made up of three parts: the mortal human husk; the immortal spirit, which contains our awareness; and the immortal soul which carries the knowledge of all our former lives, but appears to keep this knowledge to itself, except in cases where the spirit has reached a sublime level of empathy with The Almighty. The spirit belongs to The Almighty, but it must always be remembered that THE SOUL IS PART OF THE ALMIGHTY. The soul is very tiny and is not visible even to spirits. It is the job of the spirit to nurture this powerful link to the Great Father. On the physical plane this can be done by listening to conscience – the will of The Father transmitted to you personally by your very own soul. It seems far too many people are out of touch. Your terminal to The Almighty is like a telepathic phone link, yet so many have taken their phone off the hook.

RESTORING THE LINK

They do not communicate with The Almighty in prayer unless they suffer some catastrophe, then wonder why they feel so alone, yet His love is always there for them – but it must be a two-way exchange. These are the times people should meditate and think about their relationship with God, about their own lives and how other people might be affected by their actions. There must be much room for improvement or they wouldn't have closed off the link by stifling conscience. Listen to your heart and you are in touch with God via your soul. The more you listen the greater your sensitivity to divine guidance will become. Your heart tells you what is right and when you have done something good for somebody, where do you think that lovely warm glow comes from? It is a message of love from our Great Father to thank you for helping His other children. A genuine prayer for guidance will never be ignored. It must be spoken, or at least whispered. The prayer will be monitored and in quiet periods of reflection or sleep, thoughts will be put in your head which, when properly analysed, will provide the solution you have been asking for.

SPIRIT VOICES

Certain people claim to be able to hear spirit voices. Those that genuinely do hear these voices are blessed with a form of mediumship. Spiritualist churches use this type of medium extensively. There must be a lot of voice mediums who have turned away a mysterious voice from space at one time or another, believing it to be an evil spirit, or at least a mischievous Earth spirit. Once told to go away, a Space contact will never again return to where it was made unwelcome. By virtue of their greater understanding of the Power of Love, they are far more sensitive than we are and their feelings are instantly crushed by a brusque rejection. Unfortunately, like any other form of mediumship, this gift cannot be turned on and off like a tap when required. Voice mediums have to differentiate between their own thoughts and what has been interjected into their brain from an outside source. They are paid for each performance. If there are no spirits in the vicinity, or they are having difficulty in receiving during a performance, which happens often, they grasp at whatever comes to mind regardless of how it go there. They embellish upon this in order not to disappoint an eager audience hoping for messages from deceased relatives. Some of the congregation may be hoping for advice on a family problem, others just a message of reassurance. But this should be sought from the greatest relative of all, Father of us all, Almighty God. Once again their personal link to The Almighty has been forgotten. The relative they were hoping to hear from might be engaged on important duties; on the other hand, if on a lower plane, may not have the necessary permission to visit the physical plane.

VOICES OF EVIL

There are other, more sinister, voices that can be heard by a few people whose brains are attuned to that indefinable spirit wavelength. For them it is an unwanted and disturbing ability which at best can land them in psychiatric care, at worst can leave them charged with some unspeakable offence. These people are not Spiritualists, in fact they are right out of touch with our Great Father, making them prime targets for the ruthless outlaws of the spirit world – evil entities. They have been targeted because of their weak spiritual strength and, of course, their unwanted gift. They become confused because the voices are more impelling than their own conscience. This is why they have been selected for evildoing. Now they must pray – and pray hard – to The Almighty for protection until conscience once again dominates over suggestions of evil. This will happen when the spiritual link with The Almighty has been fully restored. If these gifted unfortunates could be reclaimed and properly trained they would be able to hear the emissaries of our Great Father instead of the evil miscreant spirits bent on causing them as much trouble as possible.

ALCOHOL TESTS YOUR SPIRIT

Everybody knows that an excessive intake of alcohol frees a person from inhibitions, such as shyness and worrying about what other people may think of you. A tipsy state of mild drunkenness peels away the fine veneer of superficial behavioural discipline and reveals the real you. If you wonder about the state of your spirit, which is the real you, analyse how you feel the next time you get tipsy. Does it make you warm to other people? Hail fellow, well met sort of thing. If it does, you haven't too much to worry about. Does it make you aggressive, ready to pick a fight? If you become violent at the drop of a hat, ready to smash anybody's face in to show how macho you are (wife-beaters take notice) then you are in real trouble. Bottom of the league. No love, no humility, no faith and no prospects. You are poised on the trapdoor that may eventually lead you to kill and The Blackness which awaits murderers. Even without killing anybody, the Bible's 'shadow of the valley of death' will seem a frighteningly large place to cross before getting to the lowest plane of existence in the next dimension. You have plenty to worry about because your spirit is out of touch with your soul which is God's personal communicator.

USE THAT LINK

There is no fiery hell and certainly no evil spirit powerful enough to be deemed as an Anti-God. There are evil entities, some with more than one name. The one that springs to mind first must be Satan. To compare Satan with God Almighty is like comparing a grain of sand with the sun. If The Almighty were a giant computer, it would have an end terminal in each one of us. Your soul is that terminal and the power it is hooked into is far superior to anything that drives computers. The strength of the messages we receive through this reflects the depth of our empathy with our Creator. It is these messages that give us the feelings described as conscience. Those unfortunates who stifle them – in effect killing their conscience – will inevitably end up in trouble. As they stray further, they create their own hell, here on Earth. The person who has chosen this path has isolated himself from the greatest power in the universe. The way back for the prodigal is to restore conscience and nurture it by following the path it indicates. The stronger the indication, the better the person you are becoming. The link has been reactivated.

THE BARD AND CCTV

Shakespeare believed that all the world was a stage and we are the players. Each of our lives a performance in a marathon play. The play is continuous while generations of players intermix for a brief spell before they disappear from the scene. How right he is! While some busybodies worry about the spread of CCTV surveillance cameras infringing our 'civil liberties' (whatever they are), the vast majority do not mind being filmed when it is for the general good. As the great bard said, we are all actors. For anyone with evil intent, being featured on CCTV should be the least of their worries. Every move they make is already being surveyed by the greatest surveillance system it is possible to imagine. We are all under scrutiny during the whole of our lives. Your performance on the world stage is noted by at least one of the millions of good spirits which are the eyes of God. Before you start to feel self-conscious about going to the toilet, taking a bath, or having a fruity session with your partner, it should be said that these same good spirits act only with the greatest propriety. They do not need to observe these actions and do not wish to anyway. Be sure that acts of murder, bestial rape, mutilation and any other repugnant behaviour by human upon human – or animals – is viewed by spirits. They would like to intervene, but their strength is spiritual and unlike those nasty poltergeists do not draw upon the untapped psychic power of children to derive their physical strength.

THE BLACKNESS

All life is sacred. For those who commit the ultimate sin – the deliberate taking of life for an evil purpose – there is something far more frightening in store than stoking one of the Biblical fiery furnaces. The Blackness patiently awaits to swallow the errant soul as it leaves the body whose spirit had led it into evil. The terror of a child shut in a darkened room as punishment is like a summer's day picnic compared to The Blackness. The Blackness is one place where God isn't. The evildoer has plenty of time to reflect on how much nicer were the places where God is. The cloying nature of this abomination is perhaps best understood by anybody whose face has made sudden and unwitting contact with a mesh of cobwebs. The cries of souls in torment can be heard, but they are always somewhere else and finding another poor soul to commiserate with would literally be like looking for a needle in a haystack. Time is not measured in the spiritual dimension, but we believe in extremely evil cases the unfortunate can spend the equivalent of several physical lifetimes and sometimes much longer, in this awful place. The very experience blemishes the soul, which can gradually heal however, after the miscreant has served several 'good' physical lifetimes. In the spirit world a person suffering the punishment of being suspended in The Blackness is referred to as being 'in static'. The average person will not see it. Soldiers in a kill-or-be-killed situation are not held responsible for their actions. Those who will have to pay are the initiators of needless wars. The Almighty helped the Western Powers to destroy the evil of the Nazi/Japanese Axis in World War II. With the demise of Godless communism, the new threat to world peace has already been demonstrated by Islamic terrorists. It is ironic that the system favoured by all Jeculin followers is a sort of holy communism, while the most fervent religion on Earth – five times a day 'Allah is great' – still harbours those who disgrace the name of Islam by persistently committing the most evil of crimes against Allah's children of other faiths.

MISGUIDANCE AND MISCONCEPTIONS

The warped interpretation of the will of God by Islamic fundamentalists has led them into far greater evil than any of the misconceptions immortalised by the Christian churches, which are more in the nature of embarrassments. For example, the term favoured by the Catholic Church, 'Holy Mary, Mother of God' is a blasphemous statement, but is no doubt excused and put down to ignorance. Mary is a holy person, but 'Mother of God' perpetuates the myth that our holy brother Jesus is God. The basic principles of Christendom, as laid down by Jesus, are good. The rot set in when a mass of petty rules, elaborate ceremony and mystique were created to try and place the church on a superior level to its communicants. The profession of law gains its ample pecuniary advantage in much the same way, bamboozling the general public with its mystique. 'Go forth and multiply' was good advice in biblical times for an underpopulated world. It meant a rule had to be set banning any form of contraception. The devout Roman Catholic is still suffering from it. And the world population expands nearer to bursting point. The foundations of the Western Church are crumbling under the continuous assault of sexploitation by an increasingly salacious society. The Church is slowly losing its battle against idolatry, but the idols being worshipped now are not cast in bronze, nor carved in stone. These false gods cannot be destroyed by a bulldozer, because they have made their home in the hearts of mankind, filling the vacuum created by an almost total ignorance of the wonderfully ubiquitous true nature of our Great Father. These deities are Sex and Money. How many lives have been wasted in pursuit of either one or both? The ignorance is caused by our outdated religions.

RELIGION AND SCIENCE

With the ever accelerating pace of technology, we are being left behind spiritually and there is now a big gap between the trailblazers of science and their religious counterparts, who have not advanced at all over the last 2,000 years. All the advanced peoples of the universe are as far ahead of us spiritually as they are with their technology. It is paradoxical that science will not believe in anything it cannot prove, or physically equate, whereas spiritualism, or religion if you like, demands absolute belief without proof. Yet that proof can come from within yourself. It matters not that this proof would not satisfy most scientists, for this is the kind of proof that satisfies the soul. It will not penetrate the blindfold of science. The paradox is that science, shackled by having to prove everything first, is racing ahead of spiritualism, which has boundaries without limit for the true believer. If the present lack of spiritual guidance obtains while science continues to break new frontiers, ethical problems will increase and compound. A case in point is total ignorance of the need to terminate Siamese twins as soon as possible after being detected. This unnatural abomination if allowed to fully develop will imprison two spirits at its birth.

CHRISTIAN AND MUSLIM

The Catholic Church that does so much good for those in underdeveloped countries, yet allows the continual indiscriminate slaughter of innocents by Catholic terrorists without even the threat of excommunication to the evildoers and those Islamic countries that fail to purge the evil terrorist perverts hiding among them only goes to emphasise the inadequacy present in both religions. Apart from the usual mandatory platitudes, neither religion ever contemplates taking stronger action against the killers. While the 'civilised' West blatantly flaunts sex, some Muslim women must cover themselves from head to foot. Mostly shut away in their masters' houses, they are banned from so many activities of their menfolk, they are essentially second-class citizens. Obviously the object of this compulsory 'bin-bag' *haute couture* is to prevent the carnal degeneration now evident in the West. In this it has succeeded – at the expense of having a fair and equal society. Yet the religion of Islam does not compel this excessive feminine cover-up, or the beating of women who inadvertently show an ankle. These same Fundamentalists, who also glory in the killing of innocent people of other races and religions, have twisted the teachings of the Koran to suit their own evil purposes. The destruction of New York's World Trade Centre towers on September 11, 2001 by hi-jacked airliners caused the death of thousands of innocent people and pain and sorrow to many thousands more. The initiators and perpetrators of all terrorism have much to answer for when their time comes. Whether their aims result from misguided religion or are merely political, The Almighty commands 'Thou shalt not kill' – and means it. It is a prime directive, not a statement of preference. These killers are not martyrs as they believe and have made themselves outcasts from our one God. The Blackness has engulfed the spirits of these kamikaze killers and awaits the last breath of those evil people who trained and sent them.

Islamic purists among Muslims believe the western term 'God' is inadequate to ascribe to the universal power they worship as 'Allah'. God becomes a common noun without the capital 'G' whereas in their language Allah is a unique noun which applies only to The Immortal Power. They think it encourages the belief that God is a far off super entity – a belief held by many Christians and shared by some Muslims. Common ground between Christian and Muslim is the acknowledgement that there is only one God overall. The Islamic religion recognises that the Great Power is within all of us (our souls) and all around us. In this respect they have achieved some understanding of the ubiquity of The Immortal Power as explained by Jeculin planetaires.

'ONE LIFE' SYNDROME

There are still people who say 'you only get one life'. Those who believe that often use it as an excuse to have a jolly good time and damn everything else – or anyone else – who gets in the way. Ironically this philosophy will ensure they will have many more of their 'one lives' whether they want them or not. Yes, you only get one life under a particular name, which on passing over you keep until your next life journey when you will be christened with a new name according to family. People who have had only one life are very few. Even High Controller Solomon almost certainly had previous lives before his final reign as an ancient king. Solomon killed men justly in battle, yet never had to face The Blackness – indeed he has never had to make another physical journey. The reason is the only battles he fought were for the protection of his people against opposing armies. There is a fine anecdote in the scriptures illustrating the wisdom of Solomon, where, when confronting the dilemma of two mothers disputing a baby's ownership, he told them the fairest solution was to divide the baby into two and give half to each mother. He knew the real mother would give the child away rather than see it die. A wise and benevolent ruler in his time, Solomon, when asked about this episode, said it never happened, but the logic appealed to him. In contrast Moses, of bulrushes fame, has had many physical lives since the days of BC. Perhaps he was not as holy as the Bible depicted. If he was such a saviour, he would not have had to make another life journey, unless he elected to do so. If this is the case, he has degenerated rather badly over succeeding lives. His most recent excursion was as 'Tops' Tilman, a chimney sweep around 150 years ago based, we believe, in Shaftesbury. He described his children as 'Little Bleeders' and exploited their small size by using them on his clients' chimneys.

THE BIBLE

The Holy Bible, the bulwark of Christian belief, was finally got together and committed to manuscript quite a long time after the events chronicled therein. This inevitably led to inaccuracies and, worse, some fairy stories being included which have given rise to misconceptions still believed to this day. Except for ardent 'Bible-thumpers', the rest of us are faced with a seemingly insoluble maze of intricately woven fact and fiction from which the truth does not always stand out as clearly as it should. The Bible is like a children's story book specially written for the simple people of earlier times. Surely the time has arrived for our comparatively sophisticated modern world to embrace the truths of our existence in the universe. The greatest truths in the Bible came through the mouth of Jesus, a holy spirit born into a body which was genetically half Earth and half Jeculin, but unfortunately many of his words were not recorded verbatim for posterity. He had difficulty getting the simple tribespeople of Israel to understand the vastness of the omnipotent Almighty Power which he represented. They chose to relate themselves to Jesus instead, elevating him to God-like status – something he is not and said many times he was not. It is this deviation from the message Jesus was trying to get across that has coloured subsequent Biblical writings enough to push any real knowledge of our Eternal Father into the background.

FAITH AND BELIEF

During the whole of the Circle's learning years Faith and Belief were always stressed as fundamental to their acceptance of the Jeculin Code of Love. To ask for proof would be sacrilege. It would be a symbol of disbelief. Yet to ask for absolute belief without subjective proof was no more than the present day Bible-based religions ask of their members, although the information contained in that good book is so sketchy that there isn't even a proper description of Jesus. There are whole chapters of irrelevant material which tell us nothing of the things that really matter. The stories of the Garden of Eden and God's creation of the Earth in six days make as little appeal to modern day society as the early astronomical theory of a flat Earth being centre of the universe. In fact we are situated in the only dark galaxy that transgalactic planetaires have come across. Compared to their own galaxies they have found it generally backward and undeveloped although containing a fair sprinkling of planets capable of space travel. There are even some less advanced than ourselves. And what did Jesus look like? His Earth father, Joseph Christ described him as having dark red hair that glinted. His eyes were very bright blue and light glowed through his skin. It was this luminosity that amazed the people he met. They called him 'The Glowman' because of it, but no mention of this is made in the Bible. His mother Mary briefly alluded to it when describing how the beam of light from the Star of Bethlehem penetrated the interior of the stable, saying, 'But then my child when he was born had the same light with him'. (See *Mary, Mother of Jesus [1982] transcript.*)

SECRET OF THE CRUCIFIXION

A holy person with a holy mission, Jesus was a medium. He often went in solitude to the garden to meditate and receive the Holy Spirit, a contact that revitalised him, strengthening his ability to carry out the difficult task that had been set for him. No doubt on some occasions when he preached The Holy Spirit spoke directly through him. There was no police force in the Israel of biblical times and the priesthood used early scriptures to keep the people in order, threatening them with the wrath of God if they strayed from the approved code of behaviour. Small wonder they found it easier to relate to Jesus, someone they could see, an apparent miracle worker, from whom so much love emanated. Certain happenings described in the Bible seem to have been invented merely to tidy up loose ends. The ascension of

Christ to Heaven falls into this category and appears to have been concocted to provide a suitable ending to our illustrious brother's holy mission. Jesus was not dead when his body was taken down from the cross, although all his life signs had dropped to an undetectable level before this was allowed. Nor was his body dead when it was entombed in the cave, sealed by a great boulder. Indeed, his life-force was at a very low ebb. It is not surprising that people were deceived by this when you consider that there have been many occasions, even today, when skilled mortuary staff have been startled by an apparent corpse coming back to life. Jesus told of how he went to live in the woods. He had a hiding place known only to his parents and Mary Magdalen. Knowing he was alive, a secret they knew they must keep even from his disciples, they brought food and drink for him and kept him updated with reports of his disciples and the progress of the holy word. Jesus must have made a good recovery from his crucifixion 'death' as he continued to live secretly in the woods until he eventually passed over at the age of 52 – 20 years after his ordeal on the cross.

MIRACLES

Perhaps the most controversial of the alleged miracles found in the scriptures was the Immaculate Conception. A 15-year-old girl, untouched by man, gives birth to Jesus. This is a particularly difficult one for some questioning Christians to accept, but Circle research reveals that this is a miracle that did happen. The conception was brought about when the Holy Spirit and Archangel Gabriel brought semen from a Jeculin laboratory and placed it sufficiently within her body to cause fertilisation. Considering the thousands of authenticated reports of poltergeists, mischievous spirits moving heavy objects, in extreme cases even throwing furniture about in full view of witnesses, who could possibly doubt the ability of the two most powerful individual spirits in the universe to transport one or two grams of semen across deep space? So we find Jesus was physically half Jeculin and half Earthman. This accounts for his irresistibly striking light-blue eyes, a standard feature of the Jeculins, but a virtual phenomenon to the Hebrew tribes that constituted the Jewish race. His spirit is holy and not originally of the Earth spirit world. Spirits will not visit the spirit worlds of other planets without prior invitation. Jesus, however, despite long-standing invitations to a number of advanced spirit worlds, still manages to spend the majority of his time in the environs of Earth where he is undoubtedly needed most. He is one of the few spirits who have the power to display himself and simultaneously speak audibly in the physical dimension. He did not use this power when visiting the Circle, preferring to speak through the medium. Perhaps it was another test of the blind faith of its physical members.

The miracles of Jesus healing the sick are also true. He was a healer of exceptional power, as well as being a medium. He was said to have turned water into wine. To anyone dominated by his powerful charisma the water must surely have tasted like wine. A hypnotist could achieve the same result. The miracle of the five loaves and fishes feeding the multitude is beautifully explained by disciple Peter in one of the transcripts. The greatest miracle of all must be the Star of Bethlehem which, until recently, Circle members were convinced was a Jeculin spaceship. This illusion was shattered just after Christmas 1995 when The Efun, acting on the instructions of The Holy Flocen, told a remarkably detailed seasonal story of the truth concerning the birth of Jesus. When asked if the Star of Bethlehem was a space craft the deputy Holy Spirit replied, 'No. It was a star ... It was an act of God.' (The Efun's Christmas story is among the transcripts.) The mind-boggling size of this miracle makes the parting of the Red Sea in earlier times entirely credible. Rather more recently, in the late 1970s, another miracle was in the making. The Jeculins were perfecting a method of creating an artificial planet from the stellar dust and litter which is plentiful in parts of the universe. In simple terms, a large body such as a giant rock with enough mass to attract small particles would be selected in an area where litter was in abundance. Rays focused on the target from different angles would attract matter over their entire length projecting it toward the target body slowly increasing its mass. After revealing this formerly classified information contacts gave no further updates on its progress.

LOOKING FOR LOVE

One of the features of our gradual spiritual decline is the upsurge of unorthodox religious cults which can look attractive to those who seek greater spiritual fulfilment than the established Church usually provides. Some of these cults entrap young seekers of knowledge, drawing them into a web of deception which can become very difficult to break away from, also alienating them from family and friends and often their cash as well. The pain and distress subsequently caused borders more on evil than

41

good. The 'false prophets' who administer these cults are not men of God or they would know that the way to God is love, not through entrapment. Love is all around us most of the time, often without being recognised, although it is easily noticeable when demonstrated to us by one's pet dog or cat. We humans seem to have a mental block when it comes to exchanging pure love for each other, yet simple things like the preparation of a meal by a wife for her family is an act of collective love for all of them. Anything that brings joy to someone else is an act of love. The joy that you give them is also being given to our Universal Father. A spiritually-minded person is aware of this and his brain is in greater harmony with spirit and soul, making him more aware of the ubiquitous presence of God.

At the other end of the scale, there are those whose brains are not in harmony with anything. People who deliberately provoke fights to provide an excuse to disfigure or maim a fellow human being. Presumably they want to impress others by how macho they are. There are hundreds of these incidents every year following the turn out of pubs, clubs and discotheques. Their spirits are pitifully weak and their vulnerability makes them commit mindless excesses that they will later regret. The Good Samaritan is a fool in their eyes. If they could but realise, while they continue to waste their empty selfish lives, that The Almighty is aware of everything they do. God does not want to lose any of the flock, not even temporarily, but these pathetic spirits, because of their weakness, are prey to any evil entity to guide their actions. They have shut out the love of our Great Father and it is they who must make the effort to restore that vital link which will revitalise their spirit. When you are young, the inescapable end of your life seems so far away that you push it out of your mind. This is natural, but don't push your relationship with God out of the window as well. If you kill anything that has a soul, you are killing something that belongs to The Almighty. This extends down to the smallest of animals. Microscopic life forms which destroy life, such as bacteria and viruses, are considered evil because of the suffering and destruction they cause.

THE BATTLEGROUND

As already disclosed, the humanoid is most favoured of all by The Almighty because of their ability to give help, not only to each other, but to less favoured life forms, which often have the brainpower, but not the hands and fingers to implement their ideas. This is why the battleground of

The Almighty is in the hearts of mankind. EVERY PERSON ON A LIFE JOURNEY BECOMES A PRIVATE BATTLEFIELD BETWEEN THE ALMIGHTY AND THE FORCES OF EVIL. It is up to each individual to win his own battle against evil. This is where evil must be conquered. Weaker spirits will face the greatest temptation and it is they who have to fight hardest to win their battles, but a victory for God in these more vulnerable battlefields brings more joy than the predictable defeat of evil by those who have the strongest spirits. Love, the irresistible power of The Almighty, is there to back you up – you only have to ask. Many things happen in this world that are not of Divine Will and therefore should not be blamed on God. Incidents happen and some people die before their time. Many such happenings can be traced to a lost battle in the continuous war between love and evil. For example, a person driving a car when knowing excess drink has impaired judgment, has lost a skirmish in his battle which could well have dire consequences not only for himself, but for other people's lives.

HEART AND SOUL

The heart is more than just the motor that pumps our lifeblood around the body. It is the heart that feels the warmth of love, not the brain. This fountain of life is the probable repository of the soul during its life journey. The spirit is occupied trying to influence the brain to do what is right and when it succeeds the heart is flushed with the warm love of The Almighty. The stronger your spirit, the greater its influence on your actions. Every-thing you do for the general good is an act of love to God and that love will be returned a thousandfold. THAT IS HOW A SPIRIT BECOMES STRONG. Heart surgeons should not be deterred by this knowledge from performing transplants as the soul and spirit would have already departed with the donor's last breath. Organ transplants and anything else that can save life has the full blessing of The Almighty providing it is not at the expense of taking another life.

OUR CHILDREN

We have much to learn on the guidance and development of children. Advanced civilisations indoctrinate their children from an early age, starting when they are babies. A gold wire is inserted into the virgin brain constantly feeding information for the brain to absorb. A great deal of this information is fed in while the child is sleeping. It is beyond our technology to do this, but it does illustrate the point that we start educating our children far too late. This is probably the reason why half your brain will remain dormant for the rest of your life, whereas our Space brothers use the whole of their brains to great advantage. They never have trouble with empty-minded teenage vandals, thugs or hooligans. Their teenagers' minds are fully preoccupied with what they would like to specialise in as they mature. They have a fascinating choice. The universe is their oyster. Our young children are left to play far too long. They eventually get bored and start making mischief to stimulate an under-used and unchallenged brain. This dangerous trend, left unchecked, is the root cause that produces those morons among our teenagers that have plagued society since before the time of Jesus. Education, of course, must also instil what is good and should be and what is bad and must not be.

DOES GOD ALLOW WARS?

Now that we have been allowed to know some of the wonders of our Eternal Father and how every individual has a personal spiritual link with the Great One, this conundrum almost answers itself. It is a realistic concept to think of God as the Universal Body with every life form in the entire universe as the individual cells. The Power of Love flows endlessly throughout, refreshing and sustaining, the bloodstream of life itself. Where love is given and received on a continuous basis the flow is strong, virtually a physical heaven, but where love is sparse and only found with any regularity in a selfish or sensual form the flow is weak and open to infection. The favoured humanoid life forms are the white cells, guardians against infections of evil. If they turn upon themselves, as they do all too frequently on this planet, they have failed to do the job for which they were intended and have created war – hell on Earth. As everybody's soul is an infinitesimal part of the Great Father, it can be argued that part of God is allowing wars. The part that caused war has turned away from and denied the Divine Will, disrupting the harmony of the Universal Body. It has become a cancerous tumour that must be eradicated by the surrounding cells. But what of the part of God that has allowed war? The surrounding cells are ourselves.

GOD AND NATURE

Physical existence is only the tip of a universe-wide metaphorical iceberg of spiritual life that also encompasses life forms which, although not accepted in modern times, were recognised by ancient mystics. The Spirit of Flame becomes physical only when fire is created, accidentally or otherwise. Many lonely people must have sat in front of a living fire in their own homes basking in the companionship of the dancing flames of a controlled burn. Conversely the Spirits of Wind and Water seem ubiquitously ever-present in the physical. The Spirit of Flowers is a Holy Spirit to all the individual spirits of growing things. Certain aggressive religions threaten the wrath of God, but there is no wrath of God. God is Love. Principal Western Churches acknowledge this fact even though they may not realise all that it entails. But the Immortal Power is in everything including the forces of Nature which sometimes hit the innocent, but often strike the guilty. Planetaires believe that Iran's severe earthquakes in the latter part of the last century was punishment for the Fundamentalists' murderous treatment of all other religious groups. Many of their innocent citizens also suffered. Even God could not sink the *Titanic* was the implication made by a magnate of its shipping line – Nature had other ideas and more innocents died. The senior cleric of York Minster made an outspoken statement which must have displeased The Almighty, for not long afterwards lightning struck a wing of the fine old building invoking the destructive power of the Spirit of Flame to complete the reprimand. Atheists will comfort themselves with the thought that it is all coincidence, but the unruly forces of Nature are merely mimicking the behaviour of God's naughtiest children who have turned from love to evil – some of them praising His name in the process. However, it is interesting that all peoples who follow the Code of Love, living in harmony with God, have achieved a working relationship with the Natural forces of their planets producing untold benefits for their civilisations.

POWER OF PRAYER

Prayer is a powerful weapon for good against evil. All prayers are heard. The more voices involved in any particular prayer, the stronger the probability of the request being granted. Miracles still happen and often go unnoticed. Sounds go well beyond earshot and carry on indefinitely through space, defying all laws of physics as we know them. Somewhere in space there is a gathering centre where words that were spoken thousands of years earlier can be heard. Only important conversations, statements, etc. are kept on record and special permission is required to be allowed to hear them. When an individual spirit like Jesus, or the Holy Mary, is overwhelmed by requests for help, the prayers are passed on to others for consideration. In a particularly deserving case they may intercede themselves. Unselfish prayers will attract much more support than selfish prayers from selfish people. Distraught parents wonder how our loving Father can allow their children to die from disease, or one of the many genetic conditions that beset us. It is not necessarily the Divine Will that they should die.

HELP FROM SPACE

Nearly every child in such danger could probably be saved by the specialist technology of our space brothers. The impracticability of this is obvious. Imagine hundreds of landings from space. Hospitals besieged by silver-suited 'aliens' arriving to take the ailing children back to their laboratories. A science-fiction writer's dream. The long-heralded invasion from space. It is easy to see why such an intervention is against the Jeculin Code. But the Star People do help us in rather more subtle ways. Their carefully planted anonymous experts are ever pushing our medical research in the right direction. They do not have the problem of bad genes back home. Any sub-standard genes that there might have been were eliminated thousands of generations ago by using only the most perfect eggs and semen in their reproductive programme.

THE GENE MILLSTONE

The recent breakthrough on Earth of being able to identify bad genes could eventually eliminate some hereditary conditions, but the millstone around our disease-ridden planet is the self imposed one of haphazard breeding. The so-called God-given right of every woman to bear children should be amended to 'bear healthy children'. If either male or female in a union carry hereditary defective genes they should not pass them on. Every child born to such a union sends out yet another ever-widening ripple of contamination into the lake of our breeding stock. So the heartache will continue for more families in the future. The greatest gift that all carriers of congenital diseases can give to our Creator is not to reproduce. How God can help us physically is partly down to ourselves, but what of the spiritual aspect? This is where the real strength of God can be felt.

HARMONY PROMOTES MIRACLES

The trouble is we are not spiritual enough. The perfectly attuned human body has the power to heal itself. This applies particularly in the fight against potentially fatal diseases caused by bacteria and viruses. The dreaded cancer is a condition brought about by internal strife within the body, making it turn upon itself the resources it has to destroy external infection. Body and spirit in harmony means the body is also in harmony with itself and, more importantly, in harmony with God. Should such a body ever need Divine help, it is ideally prepared to receive it. Of such stuff miracles are made. It all comes down to love. Universal love. Love of all things that breathe and grow.

COMMUNE WITH NATURE

Trees have great spirits. Try an experiment. Put your hands around the trunk of a tree and give it love. The aura of the tree will be aware of your presence. Lie down and gaze up into the canopy of its branches. Select a part of the canopy where you feel it would be nice to nestle. Empty your mind of everything else except this desire. Relax mind and body. Your only thoughts should be how nice it is among the branches. Feel that you are part of it. If you do this properly, you will achieve a state of oneness with the tree. Your reward will be a sense of well-being and a cosy feeling of security. The tree has returned your love. Everything responds to love – even disease. Love is the lifeblood of Almighty God and it flows throughout the universe. Plants, shrubs, flowers – they all have little spirits and are capable of returning the love you give them by flourishing in greater beauty and enhancing the tranquillity of your home and garden.

REINCARNATION

Reincarnation is a fact. Throughout each reincarnation the same groups of people are usually born around the same time as each other, not more than a generation apart. How many of us have looked at somebody whom we did not know, yet there was a familiarity about them which we could not explain. It is a momentary brush of spirits that knew each other in former lives. The new brain will not recognise them now, but for the spirit it has stirred half-memories of an indefinable past. Although your spirit may be unable to recall previous lives, it retains any gift or ability it previously possessed throughout your present life journey.

For example, a musician, composer, or artist will retain these abilities in all incarnations following their development of their particular gift. With a medium, the mediumistic potential will always be there in each life awaiting to be redeveloped. And the seeker of truth will search through aeons of time until his soul is satisfied. Many, many people have had dozens of earthly lives. The reason for living and living again is to provide yet another chance to expel evil from our souls and climb a little higher on the spiritual ladder, which, at its zenith, offers the sublime grace of complete empathy with The Almighty. Although we may never reach such heights, it gets better the higher you reach, as the higher spiritual planes are nicer than the lower ones.

PRINCESSES OF LOVE

The spontaneous outpouring of grief all around the world over the tragic death of Diana, Princess of Wales, in 1997 is a vivid illustration of the power of love. Diana appeared to emanate love and compassion to the people she met during her charitable and other work. Most of them would be aware of it. This is the true measurement of any spirit. How far short most of us would fall if we were to compare our own giving out of love in our everyday dealings with other people. After what must have been a glorious entry into the spiritual dimension, the greatest tribute ordinary people can pay her is to try and emulate her daily dispensation of love to all with whom they come in contact. The spirit world gained another diamond with the passing of Mother Theresa. Her love manifested itself in a lifetime of care for others. Compared to Diana, she kept a low profile with no media coverage of her daily work, but her welcome to the spiritual homeland would have been no less glorious.

STAR CHILDREN

Among the Earth's teeming billions there are hundreds of thousands, maybe millions, of Star Children. These are Star Spirits in an Earth body. They were probably drafted in to help the spirit world meet the growing demand for souls created by the population explosion of recent times. Their presence guarantees that every baby born will have a spirit and soul. A few Star Children have been with us since before Christ. Most of them do not know their spirits originally came from other planets. They are reincarnated as frequently as we are and they also return to the Earth spirit world to await their next call. This process will continue as long as needed, although any Star Child may be recalled to his own planet after serving a reasonable number of incarnations. In this event, emissaries would be sent to provide escort back. Star Children are unlikely to commit murder or any base evil act. It is highly probable that many of the people who make a stand against the evils and injustices of our world are Star Children without knowing it. The presence of Star Children, not only in our spirit world awaiting reincarnation, but many already living physical lives on our planet was only revealed to the Circle in 1995. At a meeting shortly after this revelation Nitesi and Normesi were gently informed that they also were Star Children; their first Earth lives dating back before the time of Solomon. They were to be recalled to the spirit world of Colinsia, their home planet, when their present lives ended. The Lord Flocen must have felt their consternation, for he subsequently sent a messenger giving them a choice of going to Cincea, Ocena or Colinsia. They knew nothing about Colinsia, except that its people had now become Jeculin Followers. Although honoured by the choice of going to Cincea, where they had so many friends, neither considered themselves as worthy or holy enough to go to the leading planet of the Jeculins. They chose Ocena who, like themselves, were Jeculin Associates and had provided over the years so many friendly astral contacts for the Circle. Ocena and its sister planets are at the forefront of spacecraft technology and their craft are among the swiftest in the known universe. Lodey, a teacher of religion from Ocena, reckoned every craft that is built there is faster than its predecessors. Speaking of Cincea he said, although there are no individual churches there, the whole planet is as one great church for The Almighty.

STAR PEOPLE

Star Children should not be confused with the Star People who live secretly among us. They have been set down here to assist our own advancement. These people are not aliens. Their presence here does not constitute even the remotest threat to our security. They are our brothers from Space, sent to stimulate and push our research in the right direction. Many spectacular breakthroughs have been made in the latter half of the 20th Century and no doubt, in medicine in particular. Some of these can be attributed to the anonymous work of our Space brothers whose sole objective is to help us in the constant war against disease and the many genetic malformations which are multiplied by indiscriminate breeding. When a breakthrough is achieved they step well back from the limelight and allow their Earth colleagues to take the credit. This reticence to fame is not entirely due to modesty. It is essential they do not draw attention to themselves, which would increase the possibility of exposure before their work is finished. When their mission is completed they rendezvous with a hopper (shuttle cralt) and are taken to the mother ship for the journey home.

UFOS

When will people start believing the evidence of their own eyes? A UFO is a flying object that behaves in a manner beyond the capability of terrestrial technology. If it can hover stationary, then zip off at tremendous speed, vertically or otherwise it is not an aircraft, bird, balloon or dustbin lid – and certainly not the planet Venus, in spite of ingenious official explanations. Likewise, a star-like light crossing the high heavens in an irregular manner cannot be one of the many pieces of our orbiting space garbage. A discarded piece of rocket casing, like any other object in orbit, must follow its trajectory – which is straight.

CROP CIRCLES

The proportion of crop circle hoaxes is probably much higher than those of reported UFO sightings, many of which are made in good faith. Most of the patterns made in farmers' crop fields can be done quite easily by hoaxers and there is little doubt the majority of them are, although information gained from Circle contacts revealed that virtually any spacecraft, if they so desired, could carve out an elaborate pattern from an orbital height by using a type of ray. None of their contacts would admit to such antics, but they were sure there were those who would. Their object was to try and shatter the arrogant belief that the Earth is the only planet with intelligent life in this part of the galaxy. The perpetrators are most likely from our own galaxy, because Circle space associates, although sympathetic to the reason, would consider such behaviour as rather infantile, as well as contravening The Code of Love which forbids the destruction of plant life before it has completed its natural life cycle.

CODE OF THE COSMOS

There are a number of reported instances of extraterrestrial beings landing and abducting humans for brief periods of scientific experimentation. An incident in the southern hemisphere during the 1970s involved 'crab-like' beings who abducted two males for genetic fertilisation purposes. These beings would also be from our galaxy. The description of their spacecraft suggested early crude space technology. They were breaking the universal space code which prohibits planetaires from landing on other planets without invitation, or gaining permission first. If this is denied, they must not enter the planet's airspace. The battleground of Earth however, is a very different proposition. With 200-odd nations, some at loggerheads with each other, there is no co-ordinated observation of our upper airspace. The strict rules observed by Jeculin Followers are often ignored by the more backward planets who view the Earth in much the same way as the empire builders of old when they explored the then dark continent of Africa. This does not mean our world is in danger from invasion from space. It's just that our divided planet is fair game for these minor transgressions that they would not dare inflict on another planet. All advanced peoples follow the code, which does not allow them to interfere with the life of an inhabited world. This does not preclude them from assisting the advancement of backward planets by infiltrating suitably disguised and documented scientists to stimulate their progress. Our world has been – and still is – perhaps one of the greatest beneficiaries from this philanthropic scheme.

In January 1979, there was a great deal of activity in our part of the galaxy. Because of the nature of the Circle's research they were now being more heavily monitored from outer space than the activities of American astronauts. It was thrilling, but no surprise to members when they received an astral contact with the captain of the leading ship of a large formation of craft from a federation of planets within the galaxy. During this period they received several of their spacemasters. They were on a reconnaissance mission and constituted no danger to Earth. Their presence had not gone unnoticed, the commander of an equally large formation of Jeculin associated craft told a subsequent Circle meeting. They had been monitoring the activities of the 'local' formation and were satisfied that they were not up to any mischief. Large formations like these are never from a single planet. They are usually composed of one craft from each planet taking part in the exercise. Both of these formations were in the shape of a giant 'V'.

The formation commander is the captain of the lead craft at the point of the 'V'. Intergalactic spacecraft do not fly in tight formation like our aircraft. Each craft is several hundred miles from its nearest neighbour.

OUR GALACTIC REPUTATION

There are many reasons why Earth is being continually monitored by other planets. We are notorious for being noisy, untidy, a danger to other worlds and perpetrating unspeakable evil every day on some part of the globe. Part of all television and radio signals penetrate the ionosphere and carry on for ever. Even the non-boosted spoken word has only just begun its journey when passing beyond human earshot. Advanced planets suppress their noise and very little escapes into space, while Earth is beaming out a rich cacophony of sound and pictures in all directions. Even the distant planet of Kari-Naris who, apart from their remarkable rejuvenation baths are far from the forefront of advanced technology, has equipment which can listen to Earth unwittingly broadcasting to the rest of the universe. The internal dwellers of Sudicarmus are just some of the many who can watch our television pictures from their home planet. (See *Rosha [1990] transcript*.) All television news, documentaries and other informative programmes are watched from space and analysed. There is no danger in this. It's all rather like our benevolent big brothers apprehensively watching their siblings toddling around a fireworks factory with a box of matches.

The real danger is down here. Poisonous particles thrown into space from atomic explosions fly through space indefinitely until they collide with something. The flashes of shells and bomb bursts, easily detected at great distance by the advanced optometry of spacecraft, supply ample evidence of the self-destructive tendencies of God's children in this spiritual backwater called Earth. Untidy is hardly adequate to describe the thousands of bits and pieces from former space projects that are orbiting the world. We are both unique and famous – or perhaps 'infamous' is a more apt choice of word. With such a diverse and crowded population and shimmering water covering four-fifths of the surface, Earth will always attract extraterrestrial viewers, many coming from other galaxies. They call us 'The Little Blue One'. They have never seen so much surface water before. On their planets the seas and lakes are surrounded by land.

OUR ORIGIN IS IN SPACE

We all came originally from space and FOR MOST RACES OF PEOPLE HERE THERE IS A PLANET SOLELY OCCUPIED BY THEIR KIND. The pyramids of Egypt each have a carefully aligned shaft which points to a star in the heavens. Where else but to the planet or origin of their people? Like most races on Earth they are from our own galaxy. There may well be more clues of origin hidden in the rock markings, cave drawings and hieroglyphs of other ancient cultures. Every life form on Earth can be found in the universe. Cebe was a tiny bundle of pure energy who came from a 'hot' planet. His only physical form was his energy, yet this transcendental being knew of the Power of Love. 'Cebe loves you' was his farewell. Cebe apart, there are so many humanoid and near-humanoids throughout space. There are little green men – and big ones too. Green is frequently the colour of internal dwellers. There are blue people and small people with large dark eyes. Reported encounters with the latter suggest they may be some of the very few planetaires that might be termed 'alien'. There is a large planet that is the home of people who average 12 feet in height. Then there are those with a closer resemblance to ourselves. The peoples of the Jeculin Associate sister planets of Ocena and Docena, with whom the Circle has had so much contact, are nearly a foot taller than us and have longer arms and legs. Their fingers and toes are also longer. And they, like the Jeculins, favour the lightning-fast circular craft that we love to call flying saucers.

53

INNER DWELLERS

The Earth, plagued with overpopulation on the surface, also has inner dwellers. There are many planets throughout the universe with inner dwellers. Usually an old planet with a hostile surface or an atmosphere no longer capable of sustaining life. The inhabitants have burrowed inwards to maintain their civilisation. Near neighbour Mars falls into this category and it was perhaps fitting that it was a Martian spirit who made the last contact through the Circle's great medium. Being the passed over spirit of an internal dweller establishes the presence of a spirit world there, but whether the physical civilisation is still in existence is open to question. It would seem prudent to assume that it may well be.

THE WATER PEOPLE

Our own inner dwellers are very much in existence with their civilisation pre-dating our present one by millions of years. They know nothing of our first two civilisations and regard we who have colonised the Earth's outer crust as interlopers. Their bodies are humanoid with scaled skin although faces and hands are smooth and hairless. Parts of inner Earth are far cooler than would seem possible, the inner fires having long receded from them as they sought easier paths to release the pressure by venting them through volcanoes much nearer the surface. There are places on the Earth's crust where the bed of our endless surface oceans lies back-to-back with warm inner seas, separated only by miles of solid rock. These seas are surrounded by land that is honeycombed with large caverns which contain the water people's paraphernalia of learning and records. The roof of their world is 'as high as the sky' and eternally lit from a source which they did not know, but believed to be holy. Vegetation and the myriads of small fish in the seas provide their diet. They too have whales and dolphins whom they consider to be their brothers. Hab-Blu was the second contact from the Water People and with his superior knowledge of English he stayed much longer and was far more informative than his predecessor 'Aquarius' whose vague details did little more than reveal the existence of his people. Hab-Blu had monitored and studied our language in order to make contact, but his people were grateful for the impenetrable barrier that separated them from physical contact with the world above. Their astral forays had kept them well versed with the goings-on above the surface. (See *Hab-Blu [1980] transcript.*)

54

JORPOA

The Cat People of the planet Jorpoa have small human-like faces with a cat-type body, perhaps a little smaller than our leopards, and a long prehensile tail. They had a problem with lions, the size of buffalo, who raided their communities and killed their people for sport if they could catch them in the open, but curiously would not eat them. The raids ceased after Jeculin emplinadors were put on Jorpoa to help the Cat People build earthworks around their communities. The earthworks were like dry moats with a steep slope on the outer side meeting a sheer cliff on the inner.

QUASLR

Quaslr is a planet occupied by two major non-humanoid life forms. Eron and Hexlr, first space contacts for the Circle, came from there. Their people are like giant wasps. They are intellectual and peace-loving. The other race, giant ants, larger than the man-sized wasp people, were extremely aggressive. They had no compunction about killing the wasps on their frequent raids, whereas the wasps knew it was wrong to kill. Quaslr had been visited in the distant past by Jeculins who had taught them about The Almighty and the Code of Love. It was an uneven contest with the ants continually annexing more territory and killing Hexlr's people in the process. The Circle did not know of this dire situation until Hexlr was able to speak of it through the medium several years on. Space contacts, Jeculins in particular, had become a regular feature as Nitesi's trancing blossomed under their help and guidance. A Circle request was inevitable. Would they be able to save the wasp people from impending annihilation by erecting some kind of Vitrik barrier? This was not as simple as it seems, because the Jeculin code does not allow them to use the Vitrik Hand of God to harm, let alone kill, life of any kind. They overcame the problem by erecting a barrier, the base of which extended far below the tunnelling capabilities of the ants. Touching the barrier would give the intruder an unpleasant shock, while a more determined effort would have a literally stunning effect. Ants ignoring these warnings and persisting in trying to break through the barrier would die in the attempt. This complied with the Jeculin code as any deaths would be brought about by the ants themselves. Thirty years on the barrier remains impenetrable. The gentle wasps of Quaslr, who would rather caress with their wings than sting anybody, have peace without fear. So another mission of mercy was successfully accomplished by the Jeculins and a whole race saved from eventual genocide.

KARI-NARIS

Kari-Naris, a planet in a distant galaxy from us, had a unique connection with Earth until a few years ago. The Kari-Narians, a race of humanoid people, can be black or white. Their whole lifestyle was an affront to The Almighty. With the aid of a regular rejuvenation process, involving immersion in special baths, a lifespan of 3,000–4,000 years was commonplace. In spite of the Kari-Narian 'year' probably being less than half of an Earth year, this enormous lifespan is still far greater than any other advanced humanoid civilization – including the Jeculins. The effect of the rejuvenation baths wore off more quickly the older a person became. Those who were so old that the rejuvenation had little effect were refused further baths. The ageing process manifested itself with unsightly sores and a general withering of the body. People like this were unpleasant to behold. They could not be allowed to spoil the hedonistic lives of the others. Banished from the surface, they were consigned to a network of deep underground caves. Food was dropped down to these unfortunates who faced a lingering death by degrees. But the caves had other inhabitants, who considered the aged themselves as an easy food source. The Circle's informant also told of evil scavenging creatures that lived deep in the caves. Nobody on the surface had ever seen any of them, but they could sometimes be heard by the people that brought food.

The Kari-Narians were rigidly ruled by a leader whom they called their 'great father'. All matings were decided by him and inbreeding was common at his behest. This megalomaniac even thought prayers to 'Our Father' were for his benefit. Occasionally someone would rebel against his whims. For example, a woman might object to mating with her grandfather. The punishment for disobeying their 'great father' was transportation to Earth for a period of maybe up to 60 of our years. To Kari-Narians, as with many other planets, Earth had the reputation of a barbaric planet and the sentence of such a term on our planet was a fearful prospect. The name they called their spacecraft translates rather quaintly as motion-machines. However, the amazing technology that had produced their incredible longevity did not extend to their motion-machines, which were slow by the standard of other advanced civilisations. This meant the long sleep of suspended animation for most of the occupants during their journey to Earth.

The deterrent of a long stay on our planet worked well until a certain woman who had served her term on Earth was returned to Kari-Naris. She began regaling her friends with the exciting things she had experienced while living here. She had fallen in love and married an Earthman in a place called England. The union produced a son, whom they called Paul. Mother and child were eventually picked up and returned to Kari-Naris. The Earthboy was different from other Kari-Narians, including his mother, in the most vital respect of all – he had a soul. The people of Kari-Naris, a strongly telepathic race, had no souls. They had spirits, but a spirit without a soul is likely to dissipate soon after the death of the body. Whether they ever had souls, is not known, but the dreadful ultimate sanction of The Almighty in the face of continued extreme evil is the birth of children without souls. This would result in a soulless planet like Kari-Naris, but the Circle's Jeculin tutors had no knowledge of this ever happening. Paul's mother was becoming a celebrity. Her tales of her adventures were destroying the fear of being sent to Earth. Rebels were beginning to look forward to the prospect of being sent here. Inevitably another planet was selected for the miscreants. A planet with no humanoids, populated by giant insects – a virtual death sentence for the deportees.

Over the years unrest increased. The Earthboy Paul was now a young man. He had always been sympathetic to the rebel cause and soon found himself elected leader of a secret organisation that had been formed to overthrow the 'great father's' administration. Rebels had been smuggling weapons from museums since the start of the unrest, as the only weapons allowed were in the hands of the ruler's guards and cronies. The numerical strength of the rebels was now becoming almost as great as the supporters of the old leadership. The more cautious were waiting to see if Paul's rebels would be strong enough to overthrow the regime many of them despised. They did not have long to wait. The rebels struck quickly by seizing control of the museums and armouries which were soon stripped of their weapons. Armed and confident, the rebels delivered their ultimatum to the 'great father'. 'Cede your power and save the peace.' He reacted predictably by ordering his guards to put down the insurrection. Thus followed a bloody civil war, costing many thousands of lives, which was finally resolved when the 'great father' was slain and his remaining supporters surrendered to Paul's men. The Earthman became leader of a planet in chaos. The Circle had several visits from Paul bringing them up to date with the situation on Kari-Naris. His predicament was to restore some semblance of order and to govern a severely disrupted planet which had never seen violence on this scale before. It was a job he felt ill-equipped to do. When told of the Jeculins, he asked if the Circle could get them to assist. This they duly did. The Jeculin code will not allow them to interfere with the internal politics of any planet, but on Kari-Naris this problem had now been resolved. The Jeculins responded swiftly to the request for help.

Advisers set up an administration headed by Paul. Old and sick people were rescued from the underground caves and put in comfortable establishments that had been specially built for them on the surface. The practice of putting people in the caves was ended. The resuscitation baths were closed until a decision was made on their future. All children fathered by former Earth-baby Paul would have souls. He had been put on a selective breeding programme and given drugs to boost his performance. It was believed his progeny would eventually bring the people of the planet into the great universal family of The Almighty. An exhausted Paul on one of his last visits told of how he was in the process of introducing soccer and other Earth sports to Kari-Naris. With his love of football this was no surprise. So probably by now Earth will have another link with that distant and equally unique planet.

SUICIDE? – ANOTHER WASTED JOURNEY

To anyone whose spirit is so low, they are contemplating putting a premature end to life, there is much to consider first. A young student, failing exams that have been built up as the be-all of everything, must feel it's the end of the world, but in the span of life it is really only a temporary setback. There are many famous and well-loved people who have earlier suffered similar setbacks. All living creatures are sacred and your own life form is no exception. They are sacred because they have been invested with a soul which is an infinitesimal part of The Immortal Power of the Universe who has ordained that you occupy the body that you have been given for its allotted span. There can be no greater reason for living than that. Your soul is also a communicator, but instead of being nurtured it has been sadly neglected. Neglect of the soul is by not listening to your heart trying to tell you what is the right thing to do. Continually ignoring these feelings and following selfish pursuits, sometimes to the detriment of others, has made you deaf to this wonderful guidance. You have turned your back on the love and Spiritual strength The Almighty can give you via your soul. The result is you have lost your way. Guidance can only be regained by asking in prayer. Keep on asking until your heart provides the answer. A fervent spoken prayer will always be heard. Thought prayers are not so easily monitored and should be left to those who are already in tune with the Divine Will. More mature people at such a low ebb must reflect on their past and what they must do to go forward. The greatest power in the universe is waiting to help them too. But they also must ask. No man is an island. We are all part of the magnificent wholeness which is life. Loneliness is self-imposed by denial of this basic fact. Dive head first into the pool of life and start reciprocating the love that is all around you. Failure in life can be turned into victory – measured not by wealth or influence, but by how much other people have come to love you. Those who do choose the coward's way out of life are unlikely to face The Blackness unless they have committed other evil acts. They will not receive many congratulations when they reach the other side after wasting another precious life. On the other hand it is not kind for a body to be kept alive artificially by machine. The soul is trapped in the body and will not leave until the body is dead. Likewise, the spirit is held in limbo because the body remains its home until the soul departs.

TIME TRAVEL

Time travel as depicted by science fiction writers is just a wishful illusion. Nothing can travel into the future because it has not happened. The only factor of time that matters is NOW. Now is endlessly inching into and absorbing the future which can go in many different directions and the direction it does take is entirely controlled by now, the point in time which nobody can pass. The past has happened and still exists in some hazy spiritual form. There is no physical way to the past, but it is possible for a spirit under guidance to return there for a limited period of time.

CRYOGENICS

Cryogenics is the impossible dream of those with no spiritual faith. They believe their bodies can be deep frozen until the advance of technology can revive them at some future date. They must turn away from this ridiculous dream and regain their faith. The faithless few who have paid to

59

have their bodies refrigerated in this way are being conned by literally cold science. The very fact that they doubt their continuance after the body dies suggests they can't believe in The Almighty Power either. This means they will pass on to a very low spiritual plane and will be having many more physical incarnations whether they want them or not. Supposing their old body was revived, it would be very likely they were already living physically as someone else. The placement of souls is by the Divine Will and there would be a danger of the revived body being nothing more than a soulless physical automaton. This Frankenstein-like tinkering is a pathetic attempt to explore new ground that does not belong to the physical. There are many frontiers of science, but this one should be left alone. These people need to rebuild their faith and confidence, while the money wasted on this misuse of technology could be put to much better purpose on other medical research.

TUTANKHAMUN (Ouija contact)

While the exhibition of Tutankhamun treasures were in London, during their world tour, the spirit of the young Egyptian king made ouija contact at a Circle meeting. He was greatly distressed by the removal of his treasures from his tomb. He said he would need them for when he was reborn. Nobody at the meeting could get him to understand that, if he was born again, he would then be someone else and consequently would not be able to reclaim his treasure. Contrary to the pictorial record of a dashing young king who enjoyed the excitement of battle and the kill when hunting, he loved all creatures and loathed hunting. He was just not hard enough to please the priesthood. He was wearing 17 necklaces – one for each year of his life – when he and his chief adviser were assassinated. The priest historians recorded their victim as they thought he should be seen by posterity.

YURI GAGARIN (Ouija contact)

Soviet astronaut Yuri Gagarin, forever famous as the first man to orbit the Earth, was another disgruntled spirit. He had sufficient English to spell out his tale of woe. He firmly believed that the Communist hierarchy had contrived the plane crash that ended his life. He had become an embarrassment to them. The fame that cemented his name in history had also caused his downfall. Idolised by the Russian people, he was becoming greater than the Soviet leadership. Almost a demi-god, he was considered to be a threat to the Communist Party. He would have to go, so an 'accident' was arranged. It must have seemed an equitable solution for a regime that even denied the existence of The Almighty.

THE EARTHBOUND QUEEN

Ann Boleyn was a very sad visitor to the Circle. She still felt deeply wronged by her liege, Henry VIII. On the day of her execution she told her lady-in-waiting to set out her red underclothing. She did not want the onlookers to see her blood staining her white petticoats. She was speaking rather quaintly in olde Englishe and was so melancholy Normesi felt impelled to try and cheer her up and brighten her attitude generally. She insisted she was totally innocent of the charges that brought about her execution. She admitted to frequenting the Tower of London over the intervening centuries, feeling unable to break free from the place where her young life was so abruptly ended. In this respect she had something in common with the teenage pharaoh Tutankhamun. They shared the same obsessive preoccupation with their last earthly lives to the exclusion of all else. This was preventing both of them from going forward to greater spiritual development. After Ann Boleyn had vacated the medium, another spirit came in and mentioned that she was carrying her head under her arm. Despite those headless sightings of her in the 'Bloody Tower', Normesi felt it was wrong for her to appear this way before those unseen Circle members who could see her. The next time she came to speak, he gently rebuked her about this, telling her it was most unseemly and certainly unladylike for a person of her quality. Later contacts said that whenever she visited the Circle afterwards to listen to proceedings, her regal head was always upon her shoulders and she looked very beautiful. After several years attendance of the meetings, it was noticeable that her speech was becoming much more colloquial. This change was put down to her conversing and listening to the more modern spirit members of the Circle. She preferred to be called Nan, the name she had favoured in her own time. It is extremely unlikely that gentle Nan will ever be seen again in The Bloody Tower. Her frequent attendance at Circle meetings just to listen and learn has made her more forward thinking. She has put her sad past behind her and has expressed a desire to learn more from the Jeculins. Even the sky may not be the limit for this good young queen who has made so much heart-warming progress that she should be an inspiration to each and every one of us to seek the boundless benefits of spiritual advancement toward the Power of Love.

GOOD QUEEN BESS

Elizabeth I honoured the Circle with her presence just once, but it was almost a confrontation. A total contrast to her gentle mother, her attitude of domineering aggression giving the impression of an extremely masculine woman. Having established her identity, she played the part to the full. 'You should be down on your knees before me – I am your Queen!' she thundered. She was respectfully reminded that we now have another Queen of England and allegiance was now to her namesake, Elizabeth II. When she had adjusted to the equanimity of the Circle, she revealed that she had had several physical lives since Elizabeth I, each time as a ruler, but none so powerful as Elizabeth. She would not elaborate beyond this. One of the few spirits with some recall of previous lives, she has retained the role of Good Queen Bess in the spirit world – a role she obviously relishes.

HENRY VIII

Ann Boleyn had been advised by another spirit that a few visits to Circle meetings might help to lessen her morbid obsession with the past. It was good advice. Elizabeth I probably came out of curiosity. Two impressive contacts from Tudor England. It gave rise to hopes that perhaps one day members might also hear the words of Henry VIII. This was never to happen, although he did visit the Circle on a non-meeting night in August 1990. To quote spirit gatekeeper Maurie's words, 'A few days past on a non-meeting night a man made himself known to me as Henry. He has been born seven times, called Henry each time and must remember always his life as Henry VIII because of the great evil he did then. He will try to attend a meeting.' If he ever did, it must have been just to listen, although one could well understand if the sight of Ann Boleyn among the spirit congregation precipitated his swift departure. It would seem he has not yet redeemed himself for his infamous reign of 'Off-with-her-head' marriages. Christened Henry seven more times is an almost unbelievable coincidence, but it is more likely a fine example of the enormous psychic power of the administrators of the Divine Will.

HAUNTINGS

The majority of people have an innate fear of the unknown. Tales of haunted houses and ghostly spectres bring the goose pimples out on most of us. We love to be thrilled by ghost stories, but would be transfixed with horror should we experience such an encounter ourselves. Most hauntings are either a spirit displaying itself in order to be seen, or moving objects while remaining unseen. The main reason for the persistent haunting of any place by the same particular spirit (e.g. Ann Boleyn in the Tower of London) is because the spirits involved in these sightings have made themselves earthbound by an overwhelming obsession with their most recent physical life. This has caused a spiritual vacuum which ignores their spiritual reality, preventing them from progressing properly into the spirit dimension and enjoying all of its advantages.

It is a near certainty that almost every building in the world has been visited by spirits at some time or other. Some buildings are more popular than others. A spirit visiting the physical plane will often pop into a house if something catches its interest. It may be just to watch a television programme, or see what the inhabitants of a particular building are up to. They cannot be seen as they are not displaying themselves. There is a strict code in the spirit world for spirits visiting the physical plane. They must not move objects in front of people or display themselves just to cause fright. This rule, of course, is blatantly ignored by outlaws such as poltergeists. These are not truly evil spirits. Poltergeists are merely immature mischief-makers who get their kicks trying to frighten the living daylights out of us.

FACING EVIL

Evil entities prey on the fear of the spiritually ignorant. The more fear they create, the stronger and bolder they become. This fearsome façade quickly crumbles when offered genuine loving pity, which is an embarrassment they cannot deal with.

FORTUNE-TELLING

There is a popular belief that spirits can foretell the future. Nobody can foretell the future. A spirit has a heightened intuition compared to our own and can take an unbiased, detached view of a particular situation. This can produce a prediction of what is most likely to happen. A good clairvoyant can only tell you what they think may happen, but nobody can tell you what WILL happen. Precognition is a different proposition. Premonitions, often of a disaster, provide a rare glimpse of a likely future happening. People who receive these futuristic flashes are usually fairly spiritual although some of them may not realise it. They have been picked to receive a warning of something which is likely, but not certain, to happen. Whether they can do anything about it is another matter.

PARAMETERS

Everybody can shape their future within certain parameters. A sensible decision taken at the right time can alter your future within these parameters. Anyone not satisfied with their lot in life should appraise their situation first, then ask for divine guidance. It will be given if asked for in prayer. Divine guidance will come from the heart, not from the head. Brain-based reasoning can be more selfish, possibly influenced by past bad experiences and poor environment. The best course of action always follows a balanced decision between heart and brain. This is a soul-based decision which will receive the help of God and bring you in closer attunement with the will of The Almighty, ensuring that your parameters will keep you on the path that has been preferred for your destiny.

THE HOLY FLOCEN

The most powerful individual spirit in the universe, The Holy Flocen, is the arms, voice and will of The Almighty. He has the ability when necessary – and it often is – to divide his power, in that he can be in several places at the same time, sometimes galaxies apart. He has trained for approximately 10,000 of our Earth years to be able to do this and will serve another 10,000 of our years as The Holy Flocen, before going to the bosom of The Almighty as his ultimate reward. He has a deputy, The Blessed Efun, a Holy Spirit in training. The Holy Spirit who visited Jesus's and the disciples' last supper was promoted to his glory in the late 1970s and it is The Efun of that day who is now The Holy Flocen. He accepts being called The Holy Spirit by Earthlings, but dislikes the term Holy 'Ghost' which is hardly surprising considering the frightening picture the word 'ghost' conjures up with its weird connotations. Likewise, our brothers in Space despise being termed 'Aliens'. The word suggests hostility, with the implication that they are a danger. Remember, aliens are interned in time of war. The few visits our planet has received from people who do not follow the Code of the Cosmos does not justify all Space visitors being referred to as Alien. However, they loved the name Normesi gave them so much that it has been incorporated in the universal space language, which is called Usietan. The word is 'Planetaire', meaning Space traveller.

GABRIEL

The Archangel Gabriel comes direct from the heart of The Almighty Power and if there is any personification of the Power of Love in one great being, it is He. Normally He leaves the bosom of God only for the birth – or passing – of a person of great religious significance. For this reason His only visit to the Circle created some anxiety regarding Nitesi, whose frail health frequently gave cause for concern. Fortunately He had come only to speak through her to the mixed congregation of Circle members and unseen spirits because it was thought special encouragement was needed. It was just as well He did not display, because His effect on the spirit viewers was awesome. They were literally flattened by the magnificence of the spectacle only they could see. In fact, in all the years of research no spirit has ever displayed to physical members. Much determination is needed and a great deal of a spirit's power is used to become physically visible even for a short time. Another consideration is that most of the responsible spirits who attended Circle meetings would not wish to alarm or frighten novice members who were introduced from time to time. It is easy to believe in what you can see – although even that is not enough for some people. Perhaps it was a continuing test that Circle blind faith remained just that. The visit of Archangel Gabriel and the following contact, planetaire Owen of Omega, whose astonished description of the scene physical members could not see, head the transcripts.

CIRCLE PROCEDURE

There was a set procedure which was followed at every meeting. Prayers that had been written by members during the time of indoctrination were read aloud. Each meeting was held under normal lighting, so after the prayers Nitesi, the medium, placed a pad over her eyes, held in place by her spectacles. Then an announcement would be made that the readings to follow may be interrupted at any time by a contact should Nitesi go into trance and vacate her body. Her own description of going into a successful trance was that as she listened to the readings the words grew fainter and fainter until her memory blacked out. These readings were usually of transcripts of earlier contacts, sometimes years old, but worth repeating. Whenever transcripts of The Holy Flocen or The Blessed Efun were used, waiting contacts, out of respect, would never interrupt until they were finished. Space Astrals who had made long journeys with the aid of a Vitrik boost only had a limited amount of power. The longer they had to wait to speak through the medium, the less power they had to maintain their contact for any length of time. To them the wait was an honour.

THE NEW REDEEMER MESSAGE

On the afternoon of Friday 20 August 1993, Nitesi, the medium, was sitting alone in her lounge, when a voice commanded her to switch on her tape recorder. She obeyed the instruction, knowing she would be helped into trance. When she came to herself again, she rewound the tape and found the following message recorded.

'Greetings to all who are here.' (This was a reference to the many spirits who stayed in the cone waiting for the next meeting.) *'My name is Uta and I am a special messenger from The Blessed Efun, who instructs me to inform you of this place that there is a new Redeemer born. Not born on this planet, but found as a small child in the desert in the Middle East. This child has been taken by a family of people who have no children of their own. They have adopted this small baby who now is a grown young man. In the year 2,000* of your time this man will come to be recognised as the New Redeemer. He will teach, as did Jesus. He will not be crucified. He will be a great leader of those religious people and he is with a Jewish family. The mother is called Miriam and the father is called Joseph. In*

---

*Five years later, in 1998, this information was corrected. Although unable to trance for more than a year, Nitesi was still open to night-time indoctrination. This resulted in her knowing things which had not been learned from contacts speaking through her. She was convinced 'the year 2,000 of your time' was wrong, but could not explain how or why.

66

their language it would be different, but as you do not speak any language but your own, I must try to conserve and use such words as you will understand. It is not known how long he will live, or what he will achieve. This is a matter for time to prove. But here he is and here he will be for as long as possible and he will have much to do and many to follow. His name is Senfa. He will be known as Senfa the Redeemer. A man of Jewish faith. No doubt many will decry him, but many, yes many, will follow. It will be a new time of believing. A new way of believing just as you have been taught now. You may not live to see the day when he becomes a great orator, but it will happen as I have told you. It is decreed that this shall come about. It has already started and you of this Circle have been taught much of what he will preach. It is hoped that you also would be able to preach the words given to you by The Holy Flocen, the knowledge you have, but if you cannot do so, none will blame you. You are good people. You are the holy children of The Holy Flocen. I am to tell you that although you are few now and cannot receive The Holy Flocen because of the sparseness of your gatherings, He is always and forever caring for you. Watching over you and guiding you if you will only listen to your hearts. Soskris to you all and farewell and thank you to the medium for this possession of her being. Soskris.'

Nitesi herself added the following footnote of her own thoughts: 'I must have put the tape on without knowing I had done so. Then came a deep sleep for about 1½ or 2 hours of the afternoon and when I awoke I vaguely remembered that something had happened. Consequently I listened to this tape and was quite amazed. It is quite a revelation that we have been given. I think we are very honoured to have been given this information.'

IN RETROSPECT

God, The Almighty Power of Love, is far more immense and diverse than Earthbound religions realise. Omnipresent throughout all life in the universe, nothing escapes the attention of the Universal Body. The Archangel Gabriel is the embodiment of all that the Power of Love is. He lives at the bosom of The Almighty with all the Holy Flocens of previous ages and never had a planet of origin as they had. The Personification of God only leaves to visit Earth and other planets where his name is known and revered when the occasion is great enough to warrant the presence of God in a more personal and comprehensible form.

The Holy Spirit (known to the rest of the universe as The Holy Flocen) comes from a holy planet where there are no physical lives. He has the unique ability to divide his power, which enables him to be in more than one place at the same time when it becomes necessary. He is the voice of The Almighty Power and God's First Officer in the respect of performing the Divine Will throughout the universe.

There are other holy spirits which perform The Almighty's will. The greatest of these is The Holy Flocen's deputy who also comes from the same holy all-spirit planet. His universal title is The Blessed Efun who will serve as the Efun for approximately 10,000 years in Earth time before becoming the new Flocen upon the elevation of the present one to the bosom of The Almighty.

Jesus Christ, like all of us a child of God, is one of many holy people throughout the universe who carry out missions for The Almighty. Athough he did not actually die on the cross, his many hours of suffering with body wounds while nailed to it is of more significance than if he had passed over during his ordeal. All those who have suffered since and may be suffering now should remember that he suffered voluntarily for the love of God. He will always be special to us because of his mission to try and enlighten our savage world.

Now The Almighty has seen the necessity to send us a new Redeemer to destroy the misconceptions that are rife in all our present religions.

Though equally holy, he is not Jesus reborn and all faiths must listen to his message. When The Holy Flocen speaks through him the words you hear will be coming directly from Almighty God. His fame should be worldwide soon after the turn of the century.

Reincarnation fuels the physical life/death cycle. We have all had dozens of previous lives. Older spirits may have had hundreds of past lives. The probable reason for your present life is that you were not good enough in the last one. Your spirit still has to learn that you cannot return God's love fully without loving all life, because The Almighty is in all life. When everybody does this there will be no more murders, no more wars. We have a long way to go.

The reward for a good life of service is very alluring. Life on an idyllic higher spiritual plane – and being given the CHOICE of whether you have another physical life or not. The punishment for an evil life is a term in The Blackness, something much more horrifying than the fairy-tale furnaces of a mythical devil. When the soul is purged, further incarnations are mandatory in circumstances which may or may not be ideal.

The greatest sin is the taking of life without necessary cause. We are temporarily excused the humane killing of animals for food because we are backward and at present know no better and there are still many other planets in our dark galaxy where animals are bred and killed for their meat. Cleanliness IS next to Godliness. Wanton sex and unnatural sex acts remain an affront to the Power of Love.

A poor spirit can manifest itself physically in the form of bodily weaknesses and various maladies. Psychiatrists are admitting to this by conceding that some medical conditions can be psychosomatic. A condition of the mind. But where else can the physical link with the spirit be, other than the human brain?

There is no likelihood of Earth being invaded by so-called 'aliens'. The overwhelming message from space is love. The only war-like aliens in our galaxy are non-humanoid, usually reptilious or like giant insects, but although they are the principal life forms on their planets none are even remotely capable of space travel. The occasional large formation of spacecraft operated by planetaires which might be seen in the vicinity of Earth may well look big enough to be an invasion force, but all of the craft obey The Code and are not about to invade any planet. Their missions are just fact gathering and general reconnaissance. If they have been sighted by official space observers their secret reports to their superiors could easily frighten any government into denying even the existence of extraterrestrial craft.

If the First Civilisation had acted on planetaire advice, they would not have destroyed themselves and part at least could have survived the cataclysmic geological upheavals that ended the smaller and more concentrated Second Civilisation. The world would not have been settled by immigrant races and our planet would now have been one of the most advanced in the galaxy.

Earth type names are found throughout the universe. This is not coincidence. It is because the immigrant forbears of our present civilisation were put down from a variety of planets onto a deserted world that had lost its two previous civilisations.

USIETAN GREETINGS

'Soskris'	–	a loving greeting which is also a blessing
'Krisselt et alcien'	–	a welcome in love
'Krisselt et salis'	–	a farewell in love

RECORDING THE TRANSCRIPTS

Approximately the first four years of Circle research were conducted on a ouija board with the proceedings being covered by jottings and notes. Only what was considered important messages were noted verbatim. With the advent of trancing they started taping contacts on a reel-to-reel tape recorder. Unfortunately almost all of these old tapes have been lost or stolen during the last quarter century. In the late seventies the switch was made to cassette recordings, which were handier to use and easier to store, although some of these have since been lost. All the cassette tapes since 1980 are still intact however, except for a handful destroyed by recorder malfunction. Many of the early tape transcripts which generally contain longer contacts have had Circle members' questions eliminated as far as practicable, but after resumption of the Circle in 1990 it was decided to leave many of the questions in the transcripts to more accurately portray the intimacy of the two-way conversations that took place. With over 60 tapes still available, it was difficult to select those which have made the greatest impact on the research. Obviously The Holy Flocen's words are paramount, but there is something to be learnt from virtually every single contact.

THOSE QUESTIONS ANSWERED

Did I exist before I was born? – Yes, living happily on one of the myriad spiritual planes surrounding the World.

Why can't I remember this? – Because when your body was born and you took up residence with its first intake of air you were immediately restricted to its physical senses with an empty brain which has nothing to remember.

Where will I go when I die? – That depends on you. Your good and bad actions in the physical world are balanced to determine the height of spiritual plane you are qualified to live on.

Why can't I remember previous lives? – Because these memories are locked in your soul and not accessible to your spirit.

What is the difference between my spirit and soul? – Your spirit is you and your total awareness, in fact all your senses. Your soul is an infinitesimal part of The Almighty. Now you don't need to ask how can God possibly know what everybody is doing most of the time.

I am frightened of dying. Should I be? – Only if you are a murderer or downright evil.

How can a killer redeem himself? – By doing as much good as possible for the rest of his life.

What happens after death to an unredeemed killer? – The awareness of being lost in an endless black void for an indeterminate period until the poisoned soul has been purified and all the evil expunged from the spirit.

Is it wrong to abort an abnormal foetus? – No, it's commonsense. The spirit destined to occupy it will be mightily relieved. It is very important that the foetus due for termination does not draw breath on exposure.

I have just lost a baby that was stillborn why? – The reason why the spirit and soul due to occupy it have had to divert at the last minute is obscure, but it is far, far better that this has happened rather than the baby lived for a few minutes before dying. Your personal tragedy after months of expectancy of a life that might have been remains, but if it is any consolation, just remember that the baby has not died – it never lived.

Is euthanasia a sin? – Not if it is caused by the overuse of powerful drugs to relieve pain in the late stages of a terminal illness.

Is suicide a sin? – Yes, it is self-murder. The waste of a precious life which could have much to contribute to the general good.

How can I best serve God? – By being kind and giving help when it is needed to all God's children and creatures.

NITA'S DESCRIPTION OF THE CONE

One evening in July, 1978, Nita went into her customary trance, but with no contact taking her over she used the opportunity to describe the meeting to members from an astral viewpoint. The following narrative is taken from a notebook of that period as the relevant tape is among those that have been lost.

Because you are wondering what I do when I leave my body, I am going to tell you just this once. I am attached to my body by a silken thread, which is silver in colour, so I do not go very far. I do speak with people who are near me. From them I learn varying things. Inside this room there are many spirits, at least two are astral and they add their auras to the cone. The cone is like a sweet paper we used to make, but very large and like foam rubber. It is very luminous. Outside I can see Peter. It is as if there is no roof. I can see the walls, but no ceiling. Your aura is OK, Colin. There is nothing to worry about, but you must stick to one path, for if you follow many paths you will split yourself asunder. Norman, you have many problems. You do not wish to split this Circle, yet you do not wish your home life to be affected. You owe a duty to your home, but also owe an allegiance to the Circle. Rest on my love, there is enough for all ... I can see through the walls if I wanted. The cone goes through the ceiling. Surely they must realise the cone is full of love. All I can see is the cone and the spirits, the dolphins, waterman and a lady. If I wanted to I could speak to them, but I must not break the silken thread. What I can feel and think and see out is different from what I can feel and see when I am in my body. I cannot tell you how I actually go into trance, but I must be helped by other beings. In a trance my body does not respond to me. That cone is so illuminated. It goes so far up. It's so gorgeous. You can pass through it although it looks like foam rubber. I am going to go now. I did see the Singing People *(angels)* and heard the Singing People, but I did not talk to them. I am a bit more ethereal. Everything is a bit wispy out there. I will go back now. So much love for you. Draw upon it, rest upon it. Bye- bye.

(Note: In those early days Nita had still to learn that the silken thread which connects spirit to soul was unbreakable.)

PETER (Circle guardian) – That was my idea – thought it would be nice for you as there was no one around who wanted to come to you to talk.

SUMMARY OF THE TAPES

Many of the earlier transcripts have had Circle questions eliminated to allow continuity of information whereas later ones, which retain two-way conversation to impart the informality of the meeting have occasionally been slightly abridged when nothing of further importance was forthcoming.

Tuesday 15 July 1980   **ARCHANGEL GABRIEL** [The ultimate in encouragement from The All Highest

                             OWEN [Male Astral from planet Omega describes the scene he encountered on his arrival after the Great One's departure]

29 December 1995   **THE EFUN** [Tells the story of the birth of Jesus with previously unknown detail]

12 July 1976   **THE HOLY FLOCEN** [First trance contact by the newly inaugurated Holy Spirit]

28 February 1977   **THE HOLY FLOCEN** [His comments on the failure of a spirit to display herself for the Circle and their difficulties in trying to follow The Code of Love]

24 October 1978   **THE EFUN** [Speaks of medium's domestic heartbreak]

21 November 1978   **THE HOLY FLOCEN** [Prepare for a great happening for Circle at Christmas meeting]

12 December 1978   **THE HOLY FLOCEN** [Preparations for Special Tarset and tribute to Nitesi's stand against evil. Tells of experimental Circles on other planets]

75

24 December 1978	**THE HOLY FLOCEN** [The promised happening]
	THE BLESSED OLD FLOCEN [The Holy Spirit who spoke through the mouth of Jesus]
	THE HOLY FLOCEN ['Now are you in amazement?']
	NAOMI [Member of Circle spirit congregation]
	UNIDENTIFIED EARTH SPIRIT
	NADIA [Spirit congregation]
	HARRY [The Circle's first gatekeeper]
20 February 1979	**THE HOLY FLOCEN** [Speaks of the immensity of The Almighty and the help Earth secretly receives from Space people]
22 May 1979	**THE HOLY FLOCEN** [One day all religions of Earth will amalgamate]
27 May 1979	**THE EFUN** [The request for help for Kari-Naris has been received]
16 March 1980	**THE HOLY FLOCEN** [Explains the holy trinity]
30 March 1982	**THE HOLY FLOCEN** [Message of encouragement]
26 March 1985	**THE HOLY FLOCEN** [More encouragement for a depleted Circle]
29 September 1995	**THE HOLY FLOCEN** [The final visit]

BIBLICAL FIGURES

3 December 1978	**JESUS CHRIST** [Explains how carrying bitterness and animosity sears the soul]
11 May 1980	**JESUS CHRIST** [His life and death on Earth]
8 June 1982	**MARY, MOTHER OF JESUS** [Secret of the crucifixion]

14 July 1995	**JOSEPH CHRIST, HUSBAND OF MARY** [Talks of Jesus and Mary]
21 January 1979	**DANIEL** [Tells of Nitesi's halo and her mental torment]
11 February 1979	**PETER, THE APOSTLE** [The miracle of the fish and loaves]
8 April 1979	**ELIJAH** [Speaks of the Bible and alterations from the original text]
13 November 1990	**SOLOMON** [An enjoyable and philosophical reconciliation]

SECOND CIVILISATION

21 November 1978	**CILLATONE** [The chief attendant to Queen Athena speaks of her time]
27 May 1979	**MINOA** [The king refers to visits by strangers in silver suits]
17 February 1980	**MENÉ** [Advancement of the great king through Jeculin teaching]

THE AFTER DEATH EXPERIENCE

5 October 1982	**HAROLD WATKINS** [A sceptic at one of the weakest meetings of the Circle]
2 October 1990	**WILHELMINA** [Met by a winged person]
9 October 1990	**HELEN** [Delightful informative lady]
30 October 1990	**MARY** [Great information from this lady]
14 December 1993	**WALTER** [Detailed account of his experience]
21 December 1993	**FRANK** [Thoughts of a former aethiest]
5 April 1994	**HAROLD** [Dramatically prevented from giving further information]

| 13 November 1990 | **GEORGE** [Came to the Circle after exposing a fake medium at a séance] |

*   *   *

| 12 December 1978 | **NURSE EDITH CAVELL** [Describes the presence of an evil entity at the previous meeting which was one of the few meetings which Normesi was unable to attend. It was also the only time such a monstrosity had dared to enter the Circle] |

SPACE CONTACTS

| 10 October 1978 | **FEELAM** [Male Astral, Cincea. Answers questions on time travel] |

| 22 October 1978 | **LE-BOS** [Male Astral, Wool-Bi. The Almighty is in everything] |

| 31 October 1978 | **HILLY-HOCK** [Message from a world of bison] |

| 12 November 1978 | **BELLON** [Planetary Leader. Very informative] |

| 7 January 1979 | **SPACE MASTER** [Astral, our galaxy, from one of the many craft that provoked an epidemic of UFO sightings at that time] |

| 9 January 1979 | **SMITHY** [Male Astral, Space Master. Some details of their ships] |

| 14 January 1979 | **HOGAR** [Space Master. A real Vulcan who thought the creators of the Star Trek TV series must have had some space contact. His planet is called Vulcanie not Valkarie] |

| 16 January 1979 | **TINKLE** [Male Astral, Space Master from planet Mobil. Formation leader from Jeculin fleet monitoring the fleet of Circle's previous visitors. Startling revelations on the help given to our moon astronauts by Space people on more than one occasion] |

| 15 April 1979 | **LEDAN** (Male Astral, Historian from Ocena. An old friend] |

78

22 April 1979	**ICLA** [A short visit from the head of Jeculin tutorage]
	JENNY [Little Earth girl spirit describes the beauty of Icla]
24 April 1979	**NESTIA** [Fincia, Spirit of female Jeculin astronaut lost from spacecraft talks of her spirit world and how space travel affected her personality]
	TINSIE [Female Astral from Opea. Could they be ancient ancestors of the Japanese?]
24 June 1979	**OODGIE** [Male Astral, Space Master from Issiko. Has viewing beam which penetrates walls]
3 July 1979	**OODGIE** [Back in the vicinity]
11 May 1980	**ATINAR** [Female Astral, Spacecraft Group Leader from Suklar. Confirms the close proximity of galaxies to each other. No 'black holes' either]
June, 1980	**RIKKA** [Male Astral from Cincea. Imparts the religious knowledge he is imbued with]
October 1980	**GRANAD** [Male Spirit from Fu-Lieu. Talks of the after life with special message for Ann Boleyn]
October 1980	**BO** [Male Astral from Wesoly on far edge of our galaxy. Speaks of his world and its introduction to The Code of Love]
October 21, 1980	**LUKI** [Female Astral from floating city Karrigotta. Absorbing.]

* * *

11 November 1980	**CHERRIK** [Astral, Planet Turpi. Told the meeting that Ann Boleyn, who was present, had said she couldn't bear to miss a meeting because she was learning from all she hears]
2 December 1980	**HAB-BLU** [Male Astral. Earth inner dweller. Fascinating details of Earth's inner civilisation]

* * *

79

| July, 1981 | **HEMMERY** [Male Astral. Jeculin Formation Leader. Another large formation passing Earth] |

July, 1981   **ODELL** [Female Astral. Ocena. Life on her planet and other chit-chat]

28 July 1981   **WILLIAM JOHN SPENCE** [Male Astral. Formerly of Oxford. Willing abductee now living on another planet]

March, 1982   **FEDA** [Female Astral, Ocena. Talented lady talks of her planet]

8 June 1982   **PELO** [Male Astral. Space Master from Docena. Warns of nuclear danger and finiteness of electricity]

*   *   *

22 May 1979   **KERSHAW** [Male Astral. A call for help from Kari-Naris which prompted the Circle to ask for Jeculin assistance]

25 March 1980   **PAUL** [Kari-Narian Planetary Leader talking of developments on the planet]

15 June 1982   **PAUL** [Some Earth games now played on Kari-Naris and Docena will be supplying them with modern spacecraft]

*   *   *

22 April 1982   **FILIA** [Male Astral, Grocenia. A doctor gladly suffering frustration due to lack of illness on his planet]

21 December 1982   **TARAN** [Male Astral. Space Master from Ocena 2. Reveals the capture in America of an Ocena 2 shuttle craft and its five occupants]

12 March 1985   **SON-RA** [Female Astral, Welis. Observer checking mineral content of various planets.

26 March 1985   **FREEDY** [Male Astral, teacher from Ocena]

AFTER CIRCLE REFORMATION IN 1990

13 February 1990   **ROSHA** [Male Astral from Sudicarmus. This inner dweller tells of the monitoring from his own planet of Earth TV pictures]

21 September 1993   **BIKKEL** [Male dolphin spirit. Message of love]

5 October 1993   **HEK** [Astral Jeculin surgeon from Lacinea on mission to another planet]

19 April 1994   **TONDELAYO** [Spirit, son of Crazy Horse, the great chief of the Apache nation. Is to be Nitesi's escort when she astrally vacates her body while trancing]

10 May 1994   **MOL** [Female Astral from Cincea. Brief contact with important confirmations]

24 October 1994   **FEELAM** [Astral, Space Master. Cincea. Speaks of Mol's knowledge of Earth history]

5 December 1994   **HILSA** [Female Astral. Religious teacher from Osirus-Osirus. Communication between worlds]

1 May 1995   **PHILBERT** [Space Master, Bincia. Fairly jocular conversation which again confirmed our TV programmes are closely monitored]

4 August 1995   **FRONTA** [Colinsia. Nitesi and Normesi are Star Children]

11 August 1995   **UNIDENTIFIED EARTH SPIRIT** [More personal information]

18 August 1995   **MESSENGER** [Nitesi and Normesi are given a choice of spirit worlds]

     MAURIE [Comment from their loyal 'gatekeeper']

     WILTON [Space Master of planet 'Twenty-One'. The repopulation of Earth with people and animals]

25 August 1995   **HALLODE (LODEY)** [Male Astral. Teacher of Religion from Ocena welcomes the choice of his planet]

27 October 1995	**ALICIA** [Female Spirit, Cincea. Has to stay four days in the Circle cone to build up power for her return journey]
8 March 1996	**SEWAY** [Male Astral, planet Longsin. A buoyant message of hope as the Circle declines]
19 July 1996	**HELGA** [Female Astral, planet Wumpi. Some of their spacecraft are triangular]
23 August 1996	**CY-BY** [Astral, planet Wisbye. Speaks of some of Nitesi's music having been recorded and broadcast between planets]
1 November 1996	**FREDERIQUE** [Male Spirit, our galaxy. Planets in our galaxy which speak language almost identical to English]
8 November 1996	**NONI** [Female Spirit, planet Merry. Followed by 'gatekeeper' Maurie]
15 November 1996	**LOLAH** [Female, from Wesoly, far side of galaxy. Followed by Maurie]
14 March 1997	**NOAH** [Male Spirit from Mars. Internal dweller. So many questions and no time to ask them. The last contact]

THE TRANSCRIPTS

ARCHANGEL GABRIEL

Tuesday 15 July 1980

Children of Light. You who are the chosen ones. Chosen by The Holy Flocen. I do not come very frequently to any Earth people, nor to people of other planets. Perhaps only once or twice. Of course your meeting times – I find it necessary to stand ... *(Nitesi raised herself from her customary armchair and stood for the first and only time during a trance contact)* ... Well my wings are too large to be encompassed in a tight chair. Gaze upon me. Try to see through this medium the spirit that inhabits her. You may never ever have this opportunity again, but I have come to you in great love, in deep faith. I am Gabriel. I am known as the Great Light of the Lord. I am indeed here because you need some encouragement to help you to continue in the great work that you have been given to do. This work is not of your choosing, but was chosen for you and you are children of The Holy Flocen, who is part of The Almighty, and The Blessed Efun who also will follow, The Holy Flocen's successor. I am quite different. I am ever with He whom you call your Almighty God and whom we call The Immortal Power. I come to you of this Earth and I go to people on other planets, where I am known by the same name. And on every planet you will find small sons named after me. Even on your own planet there are a few, but not many there to take this name. It is a powerful name, for I carry the light of Almighty God and this light I am bringing to you to bless you all and all of you who are here astrally and spiritually and to bless first your medium without whom you could not ever function. I am old as time. I will never die. I dislike the word die, but there is no passing for me. I have been ever a spirit and will remain ever the spirit Gabriel through all eternity. I am the one and only Gabriel.

Are you therefore from The Holy Flocen's planet?

I have no planet, my son. I am God's – The Almighty God's great power and I could not complain. Join me in love, join me in prayer. Ask ever that The Almighty smile upon you and that the power remains forever within you. This I ask for you and this you must ask for yourselves. Be not backward, be not afraid to try and bring those to you whom you must bring to you, for you are the leaders of this new Earth Jeculin Brotherhood's Associates and you must do your work accordingly. Be of good faith. Be of good cheer and be ever thankful for the small part of The Almighty that dwells within each one of you. Each one of you. If you wish to take my hand ... (*Each member received a blessing*) ... I cannot stay with you for my time is very limited, but my power, that is ever strong. I might never come again to you, but if I do you will know that I am gosh.

Bless this good medium who works so hard for you and for us and bless all those who love her. Soskris ... You will seat the medium, for I am leaving now. Be sure you seat her, or she may fall. I leave you now. Soskris.

Later the same evening after a respectful interval the next contact gave the following graphic account of the scene he encountered on reaching the meeting.

OWEN (Male Astral – Planet OMEGA)

To you, Holy Children of Light, The Flocen's own chosen ones, I come here this night and I find many spirits prostrate upon the ground immersed in deep prayer. Astrals also in some state of shock. I enquire the reason to find you have been visited by a great and holy power, greater, or as great as The Holy Flocen. I wish I could have been here to have seen this great and wondrous entity. I am disappointed that I did not arrive a little earlier. Still you have people here who are impressed and as you have a medium waiting to receive and I have only a short time boost, I must come to you and speak. You do not know me as yet, but you will. I am called Owen and I come from a planet which I do not think you have had any people from yet, for this planet. It is called by a word that you use upon your Earth, the meaning of which is the best possible. The word is Omega and that is the name of our planet. I am Owen. I am not a teacher. I am not an astronaut. I am not a leader. I am Astral.

Male Astral?

Yes. I come because of hearing of your great and beauteous beam. The light that comes down to meet your beam being as Jacob's Ladder, as has been heard of throughout all times in the universe.

Is there such a thing as Jacob's Ladder?

It is an – oh – I cannot think of the word – anomaly. But that light which you see is the light I've described as being Jacob's Ladder. This I have learned from your own ancient Bible. We do not have a Holy Bible as yours. We do have a great book. Yes. I think all planets have a great book, and I suppose your Holy Bible is your great book. But our great books are really more historical than religious. Our religion comes from inner knowledge and from teachers who are fore'er there to make sure that there is nothing that we do not know. Our inner knowledge is there, of religion, which you do not have. Until you have been taught it you know nothing. Our children have religion instilled into them from the moment of their birth. I think you have been told this from peoples of other planets. About the early teachings of children, so that by the age of four or five they have learned all it is possible to learn by night indoctrination.

Yes, a sort of pillow talk

Yes, pillow talk, yes. I say night – we do not have night. I say night for your benefit. It is sleep time indoctrination and there is also a gold wire by which you can have instruction – gold wire treatment. This is for the more advanced people. It is not everyone who needs gold wire treatment, only the great technologists, the great scientists. The high-up ones, who are the leaders of planets and not necessarily the only leader, but the high ones of the planet. And the councils of the planet, they all need gold wire treatment.

We had a very excellent demonstration of the effect of gold wire treatment from a recent contact

Yes, can you tell me?

Cu-Ell from Omnicenia. He received three gold wire treatments to learn our language. He spoke haltingly and hesitantly and a little bit laboriously. Before he came to us again he had two more gold wire treatments and he spoke the most proficient English of any of our contacts.

Yes, this is possible. And for some of us this is a means of learning your language that we may come and be able when we get here to converse with you fluently instead of haltingly and childishly. I have been learning your language over a very long period. I did not need to take gold wire treatment. I have learned it from the libraries and also from listening in this Circle. It is a very good way to learn, to listen.

You are very proficient yourself

Thank you. Yes, I am happy to be here. I am astounded at the state of your – shall we say – congregation. Your visitors here. There are many. I am Astral. I see a lot of Astral people are here and I am told that those who are spiritual are still prostrate upon the floor and still praying. For you have had a great visitation, perhaps the nearest you may have to Almighty God. There are those who have perhaps more right to be in speaking than I, but I have not been in to speak before and all seemed reluctant to come in after your great visitor, but I am brasher than most. But I felt I could not waste this medium, nor this journey that I had made here tonight hoping to find an opportunity to speak with you. It is a very great honour to be allowed to utilise the same body that has been used by such a great and holy spirit.

He said he was known as Gabriel on all planets.

This is so.

Do you know whether he can split himself into a number of places as The Holy Flocen does, or does he always go as one great entity?

88

I think he goes as one great entity.

No wonder everybody is flattened in awe.

I think as a rule he is – I do not wish or care to say this. No, perhaps I best say it, but I do not think on this occasion that his purpose was for this. He usually is – I cannot find the right words to describe. He usually goes to places where very important holy people are expected to pass. I do not like to say this. I do not hope that there is some holy person here who is expected to pass.

He did say he would only come once or twice to our meetings and this is the first time.

And he did say why he came to your meeting?

He said to give us encouragement.

Then he did not come for the other purpose, for which I am very pleased.

So are we.

Yes indeed, but he can also come at the moment of birth. This has been known. Not for everyone of course.

Like as for Jesus.

As for very special people. Very special holy people. And he has a function. He is indeed directly from our Immortal Father.

He did tell us this. He has no planet.

Exactly. He belongs and lives in the power of what you call Almighty God.

And you call The Immortal Power.

That's right. Yes.

So you see you have had a tremendous visitation and no wonder all these people here are either in shock, or in deep prayer in great submission to Almighty God. I do not see the spiritual ones for they are not displaying themselves, but I do see and have been told by the Astrals that there are some who can see the spiritual ones, for I have been shown the spiritual ones.

Of course we were masked by our own physical limitations.

What a pity. If you could have seen what I have never seen, but what I realise must be the most wondrous sight in the universe. For the light must be greater even than that of The Holy Flocen. I feel as though I am so brash to be here using this body after such a person has used it, but a – no, not a person. An entity. A presence. Ah, but Almighty God. And much that I meant to say to you has gone from my mind, which is only natural. However, I have made your acquaintance at last and I will hope to come again and you will no doubt remember Owen and Omega and you will perhaps have others from Omega.

89

Is it in a distant galaxy?

No, it is upon the perimeter of your own galaxy. We are close enough to have become Jeculins.

But you are in the Earth galaxy?

We are on the verge of the Earth galaxy, then there is a force field.

So you are within the Earth galaxy force field?

Yes, but very close to the force field. You understand?

Yes. We understand.

And very close to the force fields of the other five are Jeculin peoples and planets.

So you have Jeculin ships coming into our galaxy asking your permission to come through?

Oh yes, quite frequently. If they pass close to us, we are the ones they ask to come through. We are quite a well-known planet. So well known that you even have a word on your planet which is the name of our planet, which you use for varying purposes.

It is the name of a letter of the ancient Greek alphabet.

Really. I did not know for what use you have the word, but I do know you have the word upon your Earth. We call it Om**e**ga but some call it Omeg**a**.

You're Jeculin, you said?

Oh yes. We have learned to become Jeculins.

Not Associates, but absolute Jeculins?

Well, I suppose one must say Associates, as we were not originally Jeculins. We were not Jeculins. We have become Jeculin Associates. Yes, Associates is correct.

Are you far from Wesoly?

It is a long way from us. Almost the complete opposite side of the galaxy.

That also is a peripheral planet, I believe.

It is now Jeculin Associates, I know that, but I think this was due to your teaching.

Yes. They came to us and we put them in touch with our Jeculin brothers, with whom we are in frequent contact.

Yes – there is a slight disturbance and your medium –

It is the telephone.

I feel the medium is eager to return.

It is being attended to.

Yes. These sort of things are apt to make the medium wish to rehabitate. I have lost all I had to say to you. It is gone.

No doubt you will report back on the scene that met your eyes.

Oh yes indeed and I will try to come in again. I have been here in the meeting many times. I am what you would call one of your regulars. I am as you to look at. Well . . . as near as can be. Slightly less clothed.

Do you see Vitrik warmth from the adjoining galaxies, or does the force field cut it out?

No. The force field cuts it.

But your space is fairly light, is it?

Yes, quite light. We get it from the next galaxy.

Which is Vitrik, no doubt.

Yes, I dare say. I am not absolutely certain.

Do you use Cosmic Power?

Well, it's not called Cosmic Power. It is not Vitrik, but it is not what you use.

Is it found in space?

Yes.

And has to be stored?

Yes.

On the ships, not gathered in like Vitrik ships gather it in?

No. Nothing like that. We do not call it Cosmic Power.

No. It's an Earth term.

Cronin, it is called.

Do you use gas tanks to store it?

Cronin tanks. It is a kind of gas.

Is the actual Cronin itself a type of gas, or is it just it's a good agent to hold it?

I am not technically minded, so I cannot answer. I do not suppose you can answer concerning your electricity any more than I can concerning Cronin. Yes, yes, all right, all right – she says she wants to come back. So I will leave you now and try to return to you again. In the meantime I think you must think very deeply on your visitation of earlier this night. For I am sure that it has great depth of meaning for you. Soskris to you all.

Thank you for talking to us.

Much love. I come in love and I wish to give great thanks to the medium.

Go with our love, Owen.

I go in love and I leave my love with you. Soskris to you all.

Soskris.

THE CHRISMAS STORY
(Told by THE BLESSED EFUN)

Friday 29 December 1995

You know me well. I am The Efun. Thank you for remembering who I am. I have been instructed to tell you that the love of The Almighty is ever with you. These are the words of The Holy Flocen. He sends a blessing for you all and he thanks you for being so constant and true. You and Nitesi – Normesi and Nitesi have never ever let him down. Now I have a story to tell and I want you to listen for it is the story you know, but you do not know all the details. I am trying to tell you the story of Mary and Joseph and Jesus. Mary and Joseph came to the inn and they were refused and told there was no room for them. If they had been wealthy there would have been room for them, but because they were poor people with no money, there was no room at the inn. But the landlord, who saw she was heavy with child, said 'Away with you to the stables. You can stay there free of charge.' So they went to the stables. Mary, on her shaggy old donkey, its hair all matted and rough and spiky, its eyes almost closed with tiredness, for they had come a long, long journey. But they went to the stables and in the stables it was unclean. Very, very unclean. And Joseph said, 'You cannot have the child here, Mary. Better far that you go under the trees where it is clean and just the ground.' 'No, no' she said 'I feel the child is about to come. I must stay here under this roof.' And then came the sound of approaching tramping feet. Three camels appeared and on the three camels were three kings. These kings were not friends, but they came together for they had come together on the line that they had followed the Star of Bethlehem. And so they came to the stable and Mary had not yet given birth to the child. They got down from their camels and with Joseph they started to scour and clean the stables, so the child could be born into cleanliness. They did not know who the child was, or what the child was. They only knew that it was the right thing to do and since they had

92

followed the Star of Bethlehem, they had to stay and watch the birth. So they cleaned and they cleaned and even the camels came and licked with their great tongues and cleaned the manger and cleaned the straw and licked the walls clean. There was no water, but they found an ancient vessel, a bowl-shaped vessel, which perhaps had been used for milking in earlier days. And they cleaned it, but because there was no water, they cleaned it with urine. And then, when the babe was born, it came forth covered in blood and it needed to be bathed and the kings and Joseph urinated again into the bowl, so there was warm liquid to cleanse the child and this was done accordingly. And when she dressed the child in swaddling clothes, for she had prepared them before the birth, the little hands, the little feet and the little face were uncovered, but the rest was covered and it was then that the three kings threw themselves upon the ground for they saw that the child wore a halo and had a glow on his skin and they knew he was the new king. Even the camels went down on their knees and bowed their heads and the old donkey neighed once, gave a great shiver and then he also went down on his knees and put his head to the ground. And when Joseph looked at the donkey, he saw that where he had been old and ugly and shaggy, he now looked beautiful, clean and shining, for it was his mouth that had cleaned the manger where the baby now lay. So there was cleanliness there and there was love and there was adoration. And the kings knew why they had come this long journey, but they put their presents that they had brought with them under the tree that they found in the corner of the little stable and they put their baubles and their jewellery under the branches of the tree and that is how the Christmas Tree came into being. This is also how a great voice came and spoke to them. They knew not from whence it came, but it spoke and said, 'Every seventh day shall be a mass day and every time that the year has passed and this time of the year shall come again, shall be called Christ Mass Day' and that is the word Christmas Day. That is where it came from. And the kings bowed down before the little king and listened to the voice which was really the voice of The Holy Flocen. And they stayed for several days within that stable, providing Mary and Joseph with food that they had brought with them and wine that they had brought with them. They could not bathe the child in wine for the wine was cold and the child must be bathed in liquid that is warm. But the child was well cared for and well loved and well fed by the mother. And the mother drank the wine and the wine went to the baby and the baby also enjoyed the wine in that way. And so the three kings remained there with them until the time that Mary was fit to get on the donkey and travel forth again. I'm telling you this story because I have been told to do so by The Holy Flocen. For it is the true story of Christmas. I will leave you now.

May I ask you –

No. I have no time to remain.

Just confirmation of one thing. The Star of Bethlehem. That it was a spacecraft?

No. It was a star. And it came down so close to the stables that it illuminated everything within it. It was the most beauteous thing. It was an act of God. And I have to leave you now my children, but I have done what I have been told to do. I have given you the true story of Christmas. The story of Christmas is well known, but only in patches. No one gives it fully. No one describes how the babe was bathed in urine. No one describes how the Christmas Tree came into being. The baubles and the jewellery that were left there were given to Mary and Joseph and to the baby. And that is the way Christmas came into being. And now you have Christmas every year, but you have every Sunday. You have – or you should have – a Christ Mass every Sunday. There should be every seventh day. I have to leave you now for I have many other calls to make. I leave you with love and I thank you for receiving me and I thank her for allowing me to use her body and her voice and her brain of course and I will come again when I can, but you must not expect it too often. I have much to do, but I love you all. The Holy Flocen's chosen children.

We love you Efun.

I bless you. May The Almighty be ever with you. Soskris to you all, blessed Children of Light . . .

FIRST TRANCE CONTACT BY THE NEW HOLY FLOCEN

12 July 1976

Blessed are they who believe in The Almighty. You who are the chosen ones, listen while I speak for the very first time through a person. I have not before utilised this method. Do you recognise me? I am The Flocen. I thank you for receiving me. I have never used a voice before, but then I have not been The Flocen for very long. There are no others who could receive me – I am here for you because you believe.

There are many things as yet undone, many tasks to be performed. You will succeed in all you attempt because I shall be the guiding power behind you, and you need never fear, for I will not allow that anything shall ever harm any single one of you. Give your hearts. Give them freely, give them to the best of your ability and make your efforts to do the work as it comes to you. You will realise all that you have to do, and you will do it because I say so. I will ever be behind you, even although you do not feel or see me, you will know in your hearts I support you and give you strength.

It is my very sad thought that our first Flocen, who was so close to you, could not have used this means of communication, for He would have done better than I, but I will use it again. You will however understand I cannot come as often as He, for I have new duties and much work. To take up where He left off is a great thing to do, but it takes much time, and I am as yet inexperienced.

You believe in me, I know. I believe in you. You are those that we chose, to do the work that we chose for you to do. You have done great work, because you have done things that have been brought for you to do, and you have achieved much without my assistance, although much with my assistance. But most you achieved before I came to office. I am sorry if I sometimes seem to neglect you. You must understand it is because the universe is immense, and there are many places where I am needed. I know I am needed on Earth, perhaps more than anywhere else, but I cannot give too much time as yet. Later I will be able to give much more time.

You may touch Nitesi for my blessing, but be careful and do not wake her before I am ready to go. I suggest you wait until I have said my farewells. I have to welcome a new member – Lorraine. I welcome you to this circle. In addition I have to say I am happy that Christo and Jinder are now ASIs. She will wake. I will leave you with love and the blessings of The Great Almighty. Farewell. Soskris.

THE HOLY FLOCEN

28 February 1977

Soskris, my dear children. I greet you in love, and the love of The Almighty is ever with you. Soskris, Soskris. I do not wish that you should be perturbed by the fact that you have tried to see the vision of a spirit visitor. You must not be perturbed, for the spirit is strong in intention, but weak in production. I do not think it to be your fault that you have not been able to see, nor her fault that she has not been able to display herself as she wished to do. I am aware that you wish to see, but it is not necessary for you to see as long as you believe. They say that seeing is believing, but this is not true. Believe, and you will see with your mind's eye; there is no need for you to see visually. Just as there is no need to see me for you to believe in me, you believe in what is true, and truth is all you need to know. I give you love, dear children, and a blessing. I give you all a blessing. Soskris. Soskris. And for her, Soskris, Soskris. And as she says, for those who are absent, Soskris. Let that carry out and go far away to those who are not here with you on this occasion. My love is always with you, dear children, and I am close to you in my thoughts, if not in person. I realise that at times there are things that cannot please me entirely. There are things that you cannot forego as yet, nor can you succumb to my wishes. It is not that you do not wish to do so, but that your habits of a long while are hard to break. I realise now that I ask much of you in many ways, but you will come to serve me and Almighty God truly and then you will know the perfect peace that will come into your souls, knowing that you are pleasing The Almighty. I think you realise that it can be done in time and you must make the efforts of your own accord. In whatever you do, you will have my blessing, even if you go against our will, even if you go against my instructions, still will my love be with you and ever the love of The Almighty, for He has chosen you. I say 'He' because there is no other way to express in your language, except to say The Almighty, which sometimes sounds inadequate to cover all we mean to say. I would say you are doing your best to abide by the Code of Love. You are all unable to feed yourselves without breaking the code; of this we are aware and fully conscious and we do not blame you for what you cannot help. It would take many centuries of your time to correct the eating habits of a people so mixed and varied as yours of this planet. Perhaps one day, it will come to pass, but in the meantime you can be true to yourselves and to your faith and live as cleanly as it is possible for you to achieve under your present circumstances. I love you all, and because I love you all I know that in your love for me and for the great Almighty you will do your best, each and every one of you, to uphold the code as far as it be humanly possible. I have used the word 'humanly' advisedly, for there are no others quite like you. You are so mixed and so mixed up; try to live with true love. The love of the spirit is greater than the love of the body. The love of the spirit is Holy love, sweeter love, fonder love, truer love, and it goes to help The Great Almighty. Remember that. Remember also how deep is my love for you and how true I feel you will become. Soskris, dear children. Soskris.

THE EFUN

(Holy Spirit, Assistant to The Holy Flocen)

24 October 1978

I say to you all Soskris, hoping that you do still realise the depth of meaning that lies within that one, simple word. I have been troubled that you have lost some of your records, for he who came to speak with you last meeting, after Le-Bos, brought a message of great importance. It is fortunate that you managed to write down at least some of his words, if you could not write them all, which is quite understandable, for we are aware that you cannot write as quickly as a person may speak.

You know, of course, who I am. I am The Efun and you must have realised that from my greeting. Soskris again to you, dear children. How sad to see so few, yet do not feel despair, for others will come to you in due course, but it is up to you to try to seek them out, that they may have the opportunity of enjoying the knowledge and truth that is taught to you. I hope you will all remember this. I give blessings to this poor, good medium, this one who tries so hard to serve you, despite any effects of illness or heartbreak, which she appears to experience at this time. It is not the easiest thing for a medium to make herself available when health is poor, or mind is greatly disturbed, as is hers. One little thing I will tell you – I have helped her into her trance, and I will bring her back when I have finished, which may mean that you will not receive any more contacts, for she is not at all well. But she is brave, and she is trying to face up to what in your life is a very, very difficult and hard-to-bear situation. One thing I must tell you that she, in her consciousness will not tell you, is that each living person on this Earth is imbued with an enormous ego. It is the same on other planets, but perhaps not so prominent, but when ego is injured, it causes great distress to the person. Also you suffer from another thing which we do not have in the same way, which is called pride. Hurt a person's pride and you have wounded them almost mortally! It is hard for a person of your Earth to recover from a wound of pride. All of you possess that. Once we had it, but we have it no more, for we have found the better way of life, and all our peoples who are Jeculins are able to eradicate and keep themselves free from such happenings. They do not live together as man and wife. They live together as families, certainly, but because we have cleansed them of the need for physical love, they cannot hurt each other. This is what injures and hurts you people of this Earth, and until you can cleanse yourselves of this desire which you think to be natural, it will continue to be so. It was only created that you might re-create yourselves, and at a later date you will not need to do this. It will be a long time from now, and you of this room will never see that day.

I bring you love from all those that you know, and all those that you respect, and wait to listen to. I bring you also a repeat of the news you were given, when you were told that something is going to happen for you – some unexpected blessing that will be placed upon you. You may look towards it with joy, and you may be as you were once before. Remember you were in some little awe of what was about to happen to you, when you were made our First Earth Jeculin Associates. I cannot tell you what your surprise is to be, for it is a gift, and until you get it you are not to know what you get, but you may expect it and look forward to it with joy. Be joyful, my children. Be strong in faith, be true of heart, give love how and where you can. I mean of course spirit love and not physical love. Give out, and you shall receive in. Give out to all those that you know of on other planets, and from them you shall receive double what you can offer. You are the most fortunate of Earth people, that you have been selected to form this circle, and become the ones that we shall teach to break your world into a new way of living. There will come the time when you must proceed to make public what you have learned, and we have suggested that it shall start with a writing taken from the many papers and tapes that you have, from which you shall select the parts that are necessary to teach others the true path to Almighty God, and the true path to a happy future in your life to come.

When you pass from this life, it is not the ending of a life, but the beginning of a new life. That new life for you who are following the true path will be beautiful and full of ecstasy. I bless you all. I love you all. I am able to say to you that The Flocen also sends you his true and heartfelt blessings. I am not able to stay, for I have much to do elsewhere, but I have come to you because you are sitting here, in need of contact, and may not be able to get it unless someone strong enough is able to help your medium, our dear Nitesi, to get into her trance. In her present state of perturbation it is not easy for her to achieve the trance, which she needs for

100

us to utilise her. Likewise, it is not easy for her to get back unless she is helped. Therefore, I must go now and help her. I leave you with great love, which I wrap around you all, and especially around her. Soskris dear children. The love of the Almighty and the Holy Flocen be ever with you. Soskris.

THE HOLY FLOCEN

21 November 1978

Soskris to you all – those who are seen, and those who are not seen. Soskris to you all. If you wish to touch my hand, you may do so. Soskris, Soskris. Come forward you others. Soskris, Soskris, Soskris, Soskris, Soskris. Dear children, Soskris to you all. I am The Flocen. I bring you the love, the true and holy love of The Great Almighty. It is upon you now, my children, and it is yours to keep, not for a day as you call it, nor for a night; not until my next visit, but for all time, for you are the receivers of the Holy Love of The Blessed Almighty, whose emissary I am for I speak the words that cannot be spoken by The Almighty, and the touch which cannot be given, except through me, and with the voice that cannot be heard, except by those who have been chosen to listen. So, holy friends and dearest children, remember always, no matter where you are that the love of The Almighty and of myself, whom you call The Holy Flocen, is ever with you, beside you in all things and at all times. Because of the terrible and hurtful things that have happened to our dear medium, Nita, without whom we could not operate until one of you are brave enough to take up the same job, for her I say a special Soskris, for she needs us and she needs the blessing that I bring. I want to say, the love that she bears – I do not mean the physical love, I mean the love of her spirit and soul which she gives first to The Almighty and consequently to me, but she has this special love, for there are two kinds of love of the spirit. There is love for The Almighty, and love for one selected person. There may be many loves in the life of any person on this planet; there can be many loves, but not true loves – mostly it is sensual or physical attraction. When it is spiritually given, with no thought outside of the spiritual, true love, which these two people have shared together. Both have loved spiritually. Now he has gone from his true path which lies beside her, to seek a sensual love, which is truly not love at all. It could also be that he is seeking a possessional love, where he will receive more than he could from Nitesi,

102

who has already, to my own knowledge, given much of the physical things that people of your Earth desire, and in many cases, require. Yet still, he cannot help but spiritually love her. If she can realise this, perhaps she will feel less abandoned, less hurt, for to hurt a spirit is to hurt also the soul. It has damaged the soul, the spirit, the heart, the aura, the brain and all the essential things connected to our dear Nitesi, without whom none of us could ever speak to you, until one of you can take over her duties. Pray for her, as we do. Pray that she may get ease of mind, and that she may realise that there is no severing of the spirit love once it is given, no matter how great the desire may be to run after the other kind of love, which we are not in favour of, and which disgusts us, for it is surely only meant for the begetting of children, you having no other means available. Now I will talk to you of other things. First, let me remind you that she needs your love and support. She needs, more than you can imagine, to be shown that she is cared for, no matter how little the effort, or how big the effort – she will appreciate all that you do in that direction, for she will help anyone else in that same situation to her utmost ability, of this you may be sure.

Now we will speak of the great thing that is to happen. I am not going to inform you of its true nature, because we wish it to be a great surprise, as well as a miraculous gift. You will never, in your minds, be able to imagine what is coming for you, but let me assure you that you will be more than happy. It can only be for those who are present on the day of Tarset that you make your meeting time, and be sure you do! It is only those who are present who will be able to share this wondrous and most unusual gift. It is to make you happier – to show you more truly that we are pleased with your efforts, few though you be, as you are staunch and true to your beliefs, and that you are following the Code to the utmost ability that you can. We know your difficulties, and you cannot escape them until your whole world has been converted, which will take a long time. You *can* and *do*, I know, live as truly as you can, and refrain from doing those things you know would cause pain to me, or to The Great Almighty, or even to The Blessed Efun. So continue in your ways, my children. Believe and be happy, believe and be loved truly by all those who visit you, particularly my love. I bring you the love of The Almighty. Do not let anything deter you from your path. Do not let any person, no matter what they say, lead you astray, as has happened in the case of poor Colin, who tries so many paths that he can find no steady place on any path, being too eager to find some more sensational manner of believing. This person he speaks of as being The New Messiah . . . No, No! If there were a new Messiah, it would be told to you who are our chosen people, and that person would be brought to you, for you *are* our chosen people and the first to be made as Jeculin Followers on this Earth. You are the beginnings of the beginnings of the great expansion, the great conversion. It may not come in your lifetimes, but you are the ones who are beginning it – to learn the truth, and to spread the word where and how you can, remembering always that you must not force any opinion upon any person who is not ready to believe. Try hard to help them to believe, and give your physical feelings nowhere but to those that you consider worthy to remain your steady mate for all time. Spiritual love and physical love – join these together, since this has to be on your Earth, and this will be your perfect match. Without that you would be lost people. You must understand that we know what goes on. We know also much that goes on in your minds ... not to wish to be inquisitive, but to guide you onwards towards your true path, to help you always over the stiles as they come, that you may land safely in our care upon the other side, and leave your troubles behind you. This is also for Nitesi. We wish to help her, and when her time does come, we shall call her and she will answer, but you must be sure that she does not try to attempt to come before we call her. I know it has been within her mind and I know also that she says she finds life pointless – just another day to live with no meaning – that is because she is so badly injured, within. There *is* a point in each day, and she must try to find it, and try to live more happily, as she will do eventually. In the meantime be loving, be patient and give great care to her, for she has been, and is always very good to you all, and to us, who have trained her. She is good to us, for without her there would be no voice to speak to you. Even if you went back to your old method of communication, which you call the ouija board, you cannot get true messages from it, unless you allow each spirit to spell out their whole message entirely. If you try to guess the messages, quite often they become different to that which was intended, and the spirit will be too tired or weary or conflicted to put you right, or perhaps not even understanding what you are writing or saying. So we prefer that you shall continue in this way, and we prefer that she shall be able to go on conducting this circle for quite a little while as yet. First she must get better, and then great things will happen for you, but without her getting better, a specially great thing will happen for you all. That includes those who sit within this room unseen, and those who rest in the cone unseen, or those who just float around on the borders of the cone, for the cone is not truly strong enough to support many at this time. They also will receive this great and beautiful happening, which is coming to you all. So you who sit in this circle that I can see, but these of the circle and this dear medium cannot see you – tell others that you know, tell the important ones who have been here before, tell the father of Nitesi, and the sister who came to help her when she assumed that her passing time had arrived – tell them all that can get here to come here, that they might also be present at the great and wonderful happening. Soskris. Soskris, blessed children of The Almighty, the chosen ones, the ones we love, the ones who have taken the true, straight path, which shines so bright. You will all, one day, ascend upon that bright, lighted path, until you come up to meet me personally. I cannot say in the flesh, but in the spirit, and I will one day appear to you, if you will only open your eyes and look, to be able to see, but I will give you fair warning that you may prepare yourselves. Soskris, blessed children of The Almighty. The love of The Almighty is ever with you, therefore so is the love of Me, whom you call The Holy Ghost, The Flocen, Soskris. Bless you child, Nitesi. Get well. Get healed within the spirit, the heart, the brain. Bless you, child.

THE HOLY FLOCEN

12 December 1978

Soskris, beloved children of The Great Almighty. Soskris. Come, touch that I may bless thee. Soskris, Soskris. For your greeting, I thank thee. I come to bring you great tidings. You shall know now when 'tis to be the great day. Soskris, dear children, Soskris. Soskris to this dear child (*Nitesi*) who has stood up to her test, and passed with high, flying colours. It was a test. She is indeed worthy of any honour we can pay her, for always she is true to her word, and her promise to The Almighty, that she will do all in her power to serve The Almighty, and all His emissaries, which includes myself. A blessing be upon you all, for the love of The Almighty *is* with you – this I can assure you of. Be sure that you realise this is true, for only through my voice can this be passed to you, and its strength will give you strength, and help you bear your troubles, and her to bear her troubles more easily, and with less discontent. We are aware that she has suffered, and suffers still in a lesser way, but the suffering is within the heart and mind, and therefore within the soul. The spirit she gives freely, but the soul she cannot give away for it belongs in the body as long as it must live but the spirit she is ready to give and vacate her own true housing of the spirit so that we, and others, whoever they be, except those who are evil, shall enter her, and utilise this body, this voice, these hands, this brain – all given joyfully and with no thought of self. Therefore we bless her and call her our Holy child. You are all our holy children, but she is very special to us.

Now we will talk of Tarset! You shall tell me, and I shall try to adjust it to the time, when cometh your Christ Mass day. On a Saturday, a day before your meeting day, is Day One of Tarset – that is the day of prayer for us, and you will join in that day of prayer, when and as much as you can, remembering this is a very special Tarset, for you in particular, and for some other planets that have been carefully selected for the same reason that you are selected, for we have other experimental circles in places where they are not yet truly Jeculin Followers. It does include the planet on which the

106

Ornamental people are, for theirs is a circle much as your own, started at much the same time and in much the same way. So, for you the first day of Tarset is two days before your Christ Mass day, day two is your meeting day anyway, which I think you call your Christ Mass Eve. Day three will be your Christ Mass day, when I do not think you can come for a Circle meeting because of family ties. Day four will be your other celebration day when I do not think you would want to come either. I am trying to point out that the best day for your meeting at Tarset would be your normal meeting time. This is the day we have selected as being the most convenient for you to have the great happening that is going to be more than a Christ Mass present, more than a Circle's Special Tarset – a really, truly special Tarset, that has never to my knowledge ever happened before. This is to be a once, and probably once only happening. I mean for you. It will happen for other planets, upon the same day, but yours is to be first, but they will go on through what you would call night, for they have no night. So it matters not to them what time the happening will come. If only it could affect the rest of your planet! It is a great, and beautiful miracle that is going to happen and you shall be the recipients upon this planet, and on other planets where there are other Circles learning to become Jeculin Associates, perhaps not even so advanced as you, it shall happen for them that have been selected. There will come many Spirits from planets that are already Jeculin, that they may take part in what is to happen; to be present will be considered an honour beyond description. I can tell you little else except what you have already been told and that is to be sure that she is crowned and gowned, to be sure that you wear white garments on the upper parts of your bodies and to bring as many people as you can. You Spirits and Astrals that are here, and you people up in the cone – bring as many as you can, that all may know, see and hear. I have nothing more to say, dear children, except that you are the truly chosen ones, and it is for you that this special, tremendous happening is to be permitted for from it you will learn how great is love. I can tell you no more for I would be breaking the great mystery, and mystery is what it truly is but you will know, when the day arrives. Candles, if you please. If you have any, light them – you do not need to be in the dark, oh no, but make yourselves as close as is possible to the time when you were made The First Earth Jeculin Associates, The First Jeculin Earth Church. Blessings, blessings, dear children. Soskris. Soskris to each one of you. God is with you; The Almighty loves you well. Soskris, my children. Soskris, dear medium. Forget your troubles if you can. Try to bear that hurt which lies within you with the grace and graciousness we have taught you. Soskris, dear child, Soskris, dear medium – all of you.

SPECIAL TARSET

(Tarset – holy celebration time for all Jeculin people)

---

24 December 1978

THE HOLY FLOCEN

No, she is not in trance. Her spirit stands here and touches me and permits me to speak with her voice and utilise her body. I am here to give you all a great blessing and prepare you for the blessing that is to follow. I am The Flocen. Soskris to you all. On this occasion is to happen the great happening that we have promised you, which has never been before, and may never be again. When it happens, I ask you to go upon your knees and bow your heads, as you would if you were in any church, remembering that this is your church. All of you are to have the same blessing. Even he who is not one of you shall be blessed in the same manner that you shall be blessed, and you shall remember the joy of the blessing throughout all of your lives, into eternity. I will tell you now, it is a miracle that is happening. It is not for you alone – it is for all those that are present that you cannot see. It is for those that rest within your brilliant cone, for this night it is indeed brilliant. It is also for those that cannot get within the cone, but rest around the outer edges, listening with ardent ears, for what is about to pass concerns them as much as it concerns you. First I will ask you to remove the crown, for it is not necessary. It is heavy upon the head, and I am not comfortable that it fits not properly. I thank you.

I am here to prepare you for what will come, that you may feel the awe and the beauty of what is to happen. I wish you to realise that it is the greatest honour and the most joyful thing that can happen to you all. When I cease to speak, there will come a voice from long ago, that you have never heard speak through this body, through you, dear child Nitesi. I will not stay long, for I must not delay the great happening. When you hear the voice, although you have never heard it before, you will know to whom you are listening. You will know by the very words that come to you. So, I am leaving you now and later I will return.

THE BLESSED OLD FLOCEN

A blessing upon you all, my own beloved children! This is a great concession that has been given, that I may be permitted to depart from the bosom of the Great Almighty to come to you in person, not in thought, but in person. Once, and only once is this to be permitted. I wish you all to come and touch. Touch, dear children, beloved children of years ago. I am your old Flocen. Soskris, blessed children. Soskris to you all. Soskris I say to you, for I bring you a blessing of God Almighty, whom I am a part of. If you wish to touch and touch again, touch as much as you will, for you are touching God. I love you all.

I have come from my resting place, that I might be with you once more, to be able to see you in person, to be able to speak with you in person, as we have done over so long a period in the past. We were amateurs then, you and I also at making contact through the older media, the ouija board, which now lives away down the coastline and is sadly misused, but of that we will not speak.

We will speak of this blessing that is being brought to you. It has never been known before, that a Flocen may come back to this Earth, or any other planet, but it is the will of the Great Almighty that to encourage you in your ways of following the Jeculin path, I should speak with you just once in your lifetimes. Just once you shall listen to my words. Just once you shall be as my brothers and sisters. I have made this journey away from the bosom of The Almighty, and into the body of my good and sweet friend, who has served me well for so many years, and now serves the new Flocen in the same way. Hopefully she will serve The Efun one day, when he becomes Flocen, but not in this lifetime. Yet it may be that she will not continue that duty, for I feel she will be able to become a free spirit, which can eventually rest with me upon the bosom of The Great Almighty.

Love me always, as I love you. Do your best to carry on and go forward in the path you have chosen. Remember the crossroads where you had to make your choice – to go forward into this new life of belief into this true path of light and glory, or stay with your old Earth spirits, under the control of those who knew not of us. Boldly did you choose, and I was proud of you, for you followed the word of The Great Almighty, you

109

followed the will of The Great Almighty, and none will ever turn you from that path. I believe in you now, as I always have. I will believe in you throughout time. I will love you throughout time, even as I rest upon the bosom of The Great Almighty. Love is eternal, and can never, ever end. All is beauty when you have love. All problems can be solved when you have love. All of life is within your hands when you have love. Love one another, love The Almighty, love the new Holy Flocen and go forward to do your work, as I know you will. You will indeed. God is with you, holy children, the chosen ones of The Almighty. God *is* with you.

Now must I leave, but the Holy Flocen, who is now your link with The Almighty will be with you still. He will return to you. This has been your promised happening, and there is no greater happening that could have been found for you, unless it were to see, but your eyes are not yet open. In time they will be, but you will not see me. You will see the Holy Flocen that you now call 'My Lord'.

I will leave you, for my strength is not great, not for travelling any more, and I need the rest after this journey to you. God be with you all, for His love *is* with you, and in having God's love you have everything that life and this world can offer. I have yet to perform this same duty for other circles such as you, who are waiting for me, so I must not exhaust my strength. To each one of you individually, even he that I know not, I give great love, and in giving that great love I am giving each single person a tiny part of The Great and Blessed Almighty God. Soskris, my children. Soskris my own blessed children, Soskris.

THE HOLY FLOCEN

Now are you in amazement? Never did you think that such a thing could happen! It is indeed a miracle, which perhaps I will never have the honour of performing. I am as honoured as you that this has happened, and that I also have been able to take part in this wonderful thing that has happened for us all. I am the Holy Flocen, but to have listened to the words of He who went before me to the bosom of The Almighty, to have listened to Him, to have taken part in your ceremony – I am as astounded and overawed as all of you must feel! I feel that I also have been blessed, and I feel love within this circle. Where there was love before, now there is magnificent love, and those that are without your circle that you cannot see are also to have received that beautiful blessing, straight from God. All of you in this circle, all of you around in this room, all of you above in the

110

cone and you who cling to the outsides of the cone – you are all blessed by what has just happened.

Take now your nectar and thank The Almighty that He has permitted you this great, great privilege, unheard of, unthought of. Blessed God, we thank thee! We thank thee, Blessed God! Soskris. Let her come back and know what has happened. If she does not already know, she must know now, for she deserves it as much, if not more than all of you. Soskris, beloved children.

NAOMI

You are so fortunate to have heard and know that you have spoken with not only the Holy Flocen who is our leader of these times, but also the truly Holy Flocen who has become part of The Great Almighty. If you did but realise, you have indeed spoken with, and listened to, and been blessed by God Almighty. I am fortunate that I have been allowed to listen and witness this great and tremendous event! I am not one of your Jeculin people, yet I am here usually in your room, in this place you call your temple of love to The Almighty. I am of Earth, and I have spoken with you before. I am called Naomi, and as I say, I have spoken with you before, but never have I been in such great awe as I have been on this night of Tarset. I *am* converted to your way of thinking. I am, for I have listened so many times to the words that come through her blessed mouth, words of the great ones that utilise her body, even as I have utilised her body. How good can a person be, that they permit their spirit to fly from their body and allow others to use it, and speak through it. You should all realise that you are indeed blessed to have such a person to call your own medium. She has passed into a small trance. She goes I know not where, nor does she remember when she returns, as you know. It gives me (and others like me) the opportunity to tell you how grateful we are, to be allowed to remain in this place that you call your temple, to listen to such great ones as we have heard here this night. It is truly a miracle that you have been given a small part of Almighty God, and I also have received my portion. I am humble. I am tremulous with joy. I am in awe, as no doubt you have felt, for I know that all those spirits that are here to visit you and sit within this room are, or have been filled with awe. With me, it has lasted still. Even as I speak through her now, I feel that I am glorified to be able to use the same voice and body that has been utilised, not only by the Holy Flocen, but by He that passed before and became a part of The Great Almighty, the Holy

Power of Love, without whom none of us would ever be alive. Be happy my children, my friends, that you have been selected to learn all that you have learned. Be joyous that you may carry this memory throughout your lives into eternity, where perhaps you may again one day meet the Blessed and Holy Flocen, who is now a part of The Almighty.

To be touched, to be blessed as you have been, and we have been, has made us feel that true humility is a living, breathing thing, and we are a part of it, as are all of you. I will not stay long. The Old Flocen looked so beautiful, so very, very beautiful, with such a glow, such a magnificence that it is impossible to explain, but so very, very old, so old it is impossible to describe. Yet was His face full of light and beauty and His whole being a glow of light and love. I have never seen such beauty in all my life, when I was living or since I have passed, and I do not expect ever to see it again. Never will I forget. *Never* will I forget. I bid you farewell.

UNIDENTIFIED EARTH SPIRIT

The child Teresa is ill and should return to her bed and a doctor should be fetched. I am an Earth person, and I speak truth. The child is ill. I am an Earth Spirit and I know what is right. I love you all. I love you dearly and I thank you for allowing me to be a part of your blessed, blessed circle, and to be allowed to use this body after it has been used by so great and blessed a person, not only The Holy Flocen that we all know and love, but the Great Holy Flocen who has passed to The Almighty's breast, who has come forth to speak with you through her. Do you realise how great this truly is? Do you know how much she is reverenced by all who utilise her? She is holy indeed and will never do harm to anyone. I leave you in love and I thank you for permitting that I should be here at this wonderful, beautiful happening. Soskris. Nadia is here. She also wants to thank you.

NADIA

Yes, yes! I am here – hello, hello! Why are you not in bed Teresa? Now it is over, you have to go. We think only of your well-being, dear child. We love you, we want to see you well. You have been here for Tarset, but we want you to enjoy your Christmas, just as we shall. I bless all of you, as far as it is within my power to do so, and I give you all my love and my grateful thanks for allowing me to be one of your circle, that I might hear and see such a holy procedure, such a wonderful happening, and such beautiful, beautiful people. I can hardly believe that I have been allowed to take part in this happening with you. We are told it might never happen again, but once was enough. We will remember throughout our whole lives as spirits, throughout even new lives, if we go to be reborn – it will be there in our brains, and something will bring it back to us, for it is something that could not be forgotten! It is a miracle! I love you all. I would like to kiss you all, but I do not feel that you would perhaps want that. So instead, I say I love you, and I will wrap my love around you, to keep you safe, to keep you warm, to make you better, dear child. I hope to help to make you better. I say now, farewell and Soskris. I go.

HARRY

Hello, everybody! Hello! You knew I would come! This is Harry. Pop has been here, but he could not remain, for he has so many duties, but I was able to remain, thanks to him. We are all here. There are so many, you would be surprised. There are so many in this room, in the cone and without the cone, floating around free some of them, or clinging to the edges of your cone. Your cone is glorious tonight! Peter is out there, taking care of all of them. Peter is a good man, and is much in awe of what has happened, for although he had an inkling of what was about to happen, he did not know for sure how great it would be. We are, all of us, mightily awed by this great happening, and all are humble to have listened, to have been permitted to hear the words of He that comes from within the very centre of Almighty God.

Almighty God has touched us all this night! How more blessed can we be? Who can ask for more, or wish for more? I will return to you when I can. It may not be for some while, but do not despair – I shall be back with you, and I'm only sorry that I cannot remain with you now. I feel that your medium has become most tired. She has done much this night – much for you, much for us and much for them, the Holy Ones. She is indeed a Holy One herself. I will help her back. She may need help, for she is not well, but she is getting better from her traumatic experience.

I will go and fetch her back. I will say to you all – much love dear friends, dear brothers and sisters. Look upon me with love, as I look upon you, and always remember how greatly you have been favoured, to be able to have heard the voice of One who is part of God Himself. We are all so fortunate, and so humble at having been able to listen. I go now. I am tired, and I must find her first. Perhaps she is with Peter, but I will bring her back. Fear not – she will be all right. Farewell, Soskris.

THE HOLY FLOCEN

20 February 1979

Soskris to you all. The love of The Almighty is ever with you. You may touch my hand, if you so desire – it is a blessing. Soskris, holy children. You are holy ones, all of you, for you have been chosen to carry forth this work. You did not seek to do this work – it was put upon you, and you have done well. But you will do better and ever greater things will come in your path. I know of the sad, demoralising time that our beloved medium has been going through and that she is suffering still, although she says little now. I realise that you have all helped and prayed for her, but it is not easy for her to shut away such a large part of a lifetime and forget it as if it had meant nothing, for it meant much to her. I bless her, I bless her. I pray that the thoughts that hurt and the memories will depart and leave her quiet in the head, brain softly resting, thoughts become more tranquil, heart beat less wildly. From within here, dear holy child, dear Nitesi, you must give out all hurt, throw it away and keep only love in there. I know love and longing are sufficient to make illness upon your body, but you will conquer this in time with the help of all your friends. So I say unto you Nitesi, and you will hear my words when you awake, you *will* get better. You *will* get well again! We need you here! You are our medium – we have no other to take your place as yet. Sadly do we need that one should come forward and say, 'I will be ready to take over at such times as she may feel unable to do it.' Yes, this we need, and this you, my good holy children must search for – a good, strong medium who can do trance work as Nitesi does, but failing that take any medium, providing you have one. I ask you not to revert to the ouija board unless you are forced to do so. I am speaking now of the time when you will no longer have Nitesi with you, which must happen one day as you all well know.

I speak now to welcome you the young one, dear holy girl, Bridget. A blessing upon you. Dear, Holy Almighty God will leave his love with you and you will come with your feet upon the broad, white path and step with

115

these others ever towards the great eternity of love and beauty that is our Almighty God. Understand that God is the power of love, and that within each being is a part of God, for the spirit and soul that lives within each being is a part of God. It does not return to God when it leaves the empty husk that is no longer needed, when the soul and spirit depart, but goes forth to do work for Almighty God, and only returns to another body if there be much to atone for in your earlier life. That is fully understood.

I have been here, listening to you speaking before your meeting. You are anxious to contact masters of space ships, to find out if they will make contact with you and give you some visible proof of their being. Now you know that we do not believe in asking for proof of anything. We believe that as religion has always been and must always be, there must be blind faith, starting in The Almighty, but with people this is different. These people are not The Almighty, although each contains an infinitesimal part of The Almighty; the soul and the spirit of each being is that part, as it is with all the animals, trees, blades of grass and the fern and corn. Anything you can mention contains a part of The Almighty, for everything has its own spirit, and that being so, is a tiny part of The Almighty, the immense, wondrous, beauteous and unbelievably magnificent Almighty, who is the Great and Holy Power of Love.

Now, we speak again of these people you wish to contact. I approve that you have sent out a message asking for these masters of ships to contact you. You say in preference, those from your own galaxy; perhaps you would be wiser to ask for masters of Jeculin ships, whom you are sure would do no harm to any of you, for they are not able nor permitted to destroy or kill anyone or anything. You already know that there are some Jeculin people upon your planet. They have been put down here, but no craft is landed to put them here. They have been put down by our own secret means, and being already sufficiently educated in your language and more highly technical than your people have the ability to be, they have been placed in positions that are appropriate, where their brains can teach other brains to open up some of the dead cells, which are never in use in your heads. It is necessary for you to get these in use before you can realise the greatness of the advancement of other planets, even in your own galaxy. You have allowed more than half of your brains to become atrophied. This is sad, but they can be revived with help, and eventually *will* be revived with help, but only those who are to do some justifiable work with what they are being taught, to advance your planet. It is done in a way that the person concerned is not fully aware that it is being done. They are asked to take certain tests for certain things and they are

116

electrically wired to certain instruments. This happens frequently amongst the higher people in science and without their knowledge, they have another portion of their brains opened, and into that portion has been planted a memory given to them from a Jeculin to help them to bring forward their work. They will get credit for it and the Jeculin will stand back and claim nothing, and be as one who sweeps the floor, or tidies the instruments, or negotiates small knobs.

Tomesi, I know that you have a person who is anxious to get hold of certain objects – this is all very well in conjecture, but you have yet to find the person who will agree to do this thing, and none will be able to do it without consulting higher authority of their own planet. These people must be fully assured that if they come close enough to your planet to do such a thing as lower some object to your Earth, they will not be attacked, otherwise they could obliterate half of your Earth in one second. The only reasons that your people have not fired on spaceships is firstly because they are not usually in range and secondly because they would be afraid that if they fired at such an object, they would in turn be fired upon, and the firing from above would be far greater than they could send up. This they must surely understand. They must have very poor, small brains if they cannot understand such a simple thing, that if some object is shot through space towards a flying object, it has not got much chance of hitting it, for you know as well as we do that a space craft can move at a speed of a thousand miles a minute, and the poor little missile would go futilely into the air and merely explode and bring damage back to Earth, but if they were to fire upon you, their range is far greater than yours and the area they covered would be so immense that it would be an impossible situation for you.

I have something I would like to say concerning a member, a person who has sat at your meetings on quite a number of occasions – not a great number of occasions, but who is frequently interested to know what has taken place at your meetings. That person is the promised planetaire. I am not able to give you the name, because I am not wishing to disturb your minds in any way, so you must use your intuition to find out which of the persons who have been present at some time or another within your circle and are not present at this moment, might possibly be the one to whom I refer.

Does this person know that they are of another planet?

That I am not allowed to answer, but I am not even sure I could answer you truthfully, for they may not know who they are. Some do know and some do not. When they are dropped already a man-being or a woman-

117

being, then they will know that they are, but when it is a spirit brought from a Jeculin world and given into one of your children, then they might not know, although they might suspect at a later date that this could be so.

I regret that I cannot remain with you longer, for your good medium is growing very tired, and I cannot exhaust the poor woman any more. She is already sick and exhausted and full of drugs which we do not care for, but we know she is under sedation and must take them if her medical man says she must do so. You will excuse me please, beloved children. Remember that my love is ever with you and surrounds you to keep you from harm. Soskris to you all. I love you all well. Soskris to each of you. Beloved children, I touch you, I bless you, especially dear Nitesi, for you need help more than any. Soskris.

THE HOLY FLOCEN

22 May 1979

I come to you on this occasion for the purpose of helping you to lighten your souls. For this I feel you need encouragement. Your numbers grow few and I feel you need to be encouraged to carry on the good work that we have set you to do. I am The Flocen. Soskris to you all, blessed Children of Light. This title has been given to you for you have earned it, and few though you be your intentions are still good, and therefore do you deserve the name of the Children of Light. Always have I called you my blessed children, but now I must call you the Blessed Children of Light, for that is the desire and wish of the great and wondrous Almighty God, whose words I speak to you.

Keep to your good work, for it is needed that you should continue, and nothing must permit you to allow any of it to slip away – you have not been taught over these long years for nothing. You have a mission ahead of you which you must adhere to. You shall learn in time to come what your mission is. In the meantime you must go on as you are – the devoted children who give their time, their prayers and their love to The Almighty and also to me and to the Holy Efun.

If you look deep within my words you will see that I am giving you love from The Almighty. You can have no greater gift upon this Earth, or upon any other planet. You shall be known throughout time, for you have achieved what no others have achieved before you, not even yourselves in previous lifetimes – you have never reached the stage you are now in. This is why you have been made a church, because you are devoted, because you are the founders of the First Earth Jeculin Brotherhood Associates. When you do eventually have a church, you will have that upon your fascia and you will also have The Children of Light. All who enter your portals will be as children of light, providing they believe and follow the code as near as it is possible for a human being to follow the code.

119

There is nothing held against you for visiting this Christian Spiritualist Church. You do not need it, but it is good that you are inquisitive enough to want to go, and it is good that what you experienced there you found to be true and to be helpful to you. That which has not happened yet cannot truly be foretold. These are Earth spirits, and maybe they imagine they can look into the future, but I assure you that all spirits (other than Earth spirits) know nothing of what has not happened, but everything of what has already happened. There are some people who have foresight, a heightened intuition, and these people are not to be denied or trifled with, for they may truly believe in all they are telling you. If you believe them it is not detrimental, but do not be disappointed if these things do not come to pass. There is no reason at all why you should not go to the church or to the development circle where you have started to attend, where even our medium has been and had good experience. Truth cannot be denied, but none must claim to know the truth when they have not been taught it. They can only be taught it through the means which you now possess. One day, all the religions of your planet will try to amalgamate, and that will be a great day. All people must believe. All those that believe in Almighty God, no matter in what form they see God – they are believers who have only to change their ways to the true path, the path of light, and to realise that Almighty God is the Power of Love. Once they have been taught this, they cannot help but to follow your path.

With our medium attending a church, she may one day be asked to speak. If this is so, she will be greatly guided, either by myself or most certainly the Holy Efun. She will speak (even if not in a trance) the words we will give her to speak. We will indoctrinate her beforehand, so that if she is called upon to speak she will do so with confidence, and know that what she says is right. She will lead them gently, not brutally or gauchely. She will lead them gently one more step towards the truth, so that it may be folded out before those who listen, that they will know there is more for them to learn than they already know. Those that go to that church go chiefly to hear from their loved ones, but also they might be interested to know that Almighty God is interested in them. She will be given instruction so that when the time comes, she will know what to say when she is asked to speak. No matter where she be, she will know what words to speak without offending any or frightening them away. We shall help. Ask your medium sometime to stand up and say to you what she would say to a congregation full of strange people. It could be helped and rehearsed, but it needn't be, for she *will* be helped and will know what to say. If you are good followers and you know she is to speak, you will be there when she speaks to give her substance behind her words, to give her the strength of your love and uphold her as we will.

You know that 02 approaches and that I will endeavour to come to you on that night when you meet, which will be the second day, the day of celebration and the wedding of your dear friend Labona which we will also be celebrating. Have as many present as you can gather, for it is a celebration time. Labona's wedding is a new innovation, one that we hope will lead to many more of the same kind. It is a trial and error situation, but it is a start, and it is chiefly through you people that it has come to pass. So you see, small though you be, you can still influence people galaxies away and upon the High Council. Remember that, and act accordingly.

I bring you love; love of The Almighty, love of the Blessed Efun and I bring you my love. I wish I could speak to you in my own language, for then I could say it all so much more beautifully, but you would not understand. If you so desire, I will speak to you just a few sentences. We use a few words to mean many things.

So lindie fin solibom ... So fissen, fissen so to lumpa, to lumpa to Almighty God.

I have just told you of my love for you, my love for The Almighty and that you shall always, always be Children of Light, children of Almighty God. Soskris, blessed Children of Light. Soskris.

THE EFUN

27 May 1979

Soskris to you all, holy Children of Light. In love I come. I am The Efun. I have come with glad tidings. We have received the call from Kari-Naris and the invitation to assist them to re-establish themselves and this we are going to do. These are indeed glad tidings, for we cannot go without being invited. We realise that we go to a world that is practically heathen – never mind; we shall help them all we can and teach them as we have taught you and maybe in time to come, they may regain their souls, but first they must learn. First they must learn not only of The Almighty and all His great powers but to learn how to adapt themselves to a new way of life. This is the most important call we have had in a very long time for it is to us a great work of mercy to help these people. We pray they will learn quickly, that they may be granted souls, that no more need they live those vast lives and never more to be put beneath the ground to die and wither away. For those that have souls there is no death; death does not exist for it is only the husk that is shed and the soul and spirit together pass from the husk which has served its useful purpose for a lifetime. There is no such thing as death for the soul, therefore must we do all we can to help these people who have none. I cannot tell you that those who are already below will be given souls for I do not think they will be in a position to learn. Those that have already been sent below are withering to a horrible diseased death. There must be no more people sent below; people must not be kept alive so long. It is an impossible age that they live to. Also we could establish the system where their seeds are taken and the best are matched. This would be by far the best method of helping them – to stop copulation altogether, to make it unlawful. Those who have fought for a cause realise there must be violent changes. To fight for a cause you must have the knowledge that violent changes *will* be your lot for a while, for they are trying to break the habits of a world that have been established for centuries upon centuries. I can tell you nothing of the early times of Kari-Naris – none knows why they have no souls; it is something that must have happened before time records were kept and unless they have some means themselves of telling us what happened to them we will never know. We have not yet decided in what way they shall progress, but they shall have advisors and people who will not only make laws for them but see that they are laws that will be kept. They have asked for our help and they will be given our help. In this way they must accept the help as we wish to give it. They are not able to change their ways themselves; they have not been able to think out ways in which they can change. That is why they came to you and asked for assistance. You, of course, are not as advanced as we and would not know how to truly advise them although such advice as you did give was good and honest advice. It will not be an easy task for us to enforce a different style of living on a planet that has lived so freely and in a wrong manner. They will have to obey us if they wish our help, otherwise we must leave them on their own. The advisors will go very soon; already a selection has been made of scientists and administrators that will be suitable for the planning of the new world, a new kind of civilisation which as yet has no souls. If they learn as we wish them to I feel sure they will eventually gain their souls, but they must change their ways. There must be no more revolution. Those that are the winners must be humble and kind and not treat those left of the losers as enemies; they are, after all, brothers and sisters, so closely united that it is impossible to segregate them. There will have to be a complete segregation and rehousing. The time when Kari-Narians gain their souls will be a time of great celebration and perhaps a cause of a special Tarset. It *is* such things as these that do cause an extra time called Tarset. We do not often have great things like this happen and we have not solved all the problems yet by a long way, but we have many things in mind to help them if they are prepared to pass up their old ways and subjugate themselves to those that we will send to help and advise them to a new and better, cleaner, fresher way of life. If any come to you, you will instruct them as well as we do for you have the knowledge.

There is also jubilation in another centre. That is that it has come to our attention that dear Nitesi is to at last go forth and spread the word. For this she has been trained over this long period. Now comes the time of fruition when she shall go forth and speak the words. She will have help; she will need it. In her brain is all the knowledge that she requires and if she does not bring it out of her own accord we shall be there to prompt her telepathically, or even to come through and speak through her. If she manages on her own it will be a great triumph and it is something that has

123

greatly pleased all who know about it. It is the beginning of your expansion. She must invite those who wish to know more to come. Of course, they cannot all come at once; they must come by appointment and be assured that there will be no charge. All they will need to give will be their time and she will do the teaching. I should think you could hold 14 or 15 at a time in this room. We are happy with the events as they are taking place; we are also very happy in the parts you have played in the lives of Le-Bona and La-Bona. You must not disregard the fact that you have in some ways been largely responsible for the re-establishment of marriage. Marriage has always been considered a holy thing, though not the way you conduct it upon your planet, for you are apt to discard it as easily as you take it up, whereas in the old days none were discarded. It is for this reason that we ceased to have marriages because of the discarding. Now if we restart this old custom, if it is successful for La-Bona it is possible that others will ask the High Council for permission. This could happen on many planets and it all comes back to you and Le-Bona and Vinnette's people asking for help which you got for them. It is highly probable that the other group of Kari-Narians living on Theopolis will be given souls for they are living with good people who have beautiful souls.

We do not approve of the killing that has happened upon Kari-Naris and yet we realise that something of this nature had to happen to cleanse that world. We are only now learning the ways of that planet for it has been ostracised throughout the centuries, much the same as the Earth was after the destruction of your First Civilisation. We did not come back to you until we realised that atomic power is again being misused.

I will if I can be present on the occasion of La-Bona's wedding but I do not promise. There will be much jubilation and I wish that you also should celebrate as you always do at our holiday times. I leave you in love now. I leave my love wrapped around you to keep you warm and comfortable so that you know how deeply we love you. I bless you all, my dear ones, children of The Almighty, the chosen ones who have worked so hard. Your reward is coming. Soskris.

THE HOLY FLOCEN

16 March 1980

I speak with you on this occasion because I feel you need buoyancy. You need to be buoyed up because you have so sadly become diminished in numbers. Although you have many who sit with you here, so you need never fear however small the meeting appears to be, like it is only one or two who listen, for there are many who are your unseen congregation. Remember that always. Therefore you are not alone and others wait upon you to hear who shall speak through your medium. I love you all, blessed children. You are indeed my children. I am as a father to you for I have chosen you from all those who believe and band together. I chose you for you were the first to listen to a voice from another planet and not doubt. Because you did not doubt I did realise that you were those who should be made the chosen ones as you had been before in previous lives. It did not mean because you were before in previous lives believers that you would necessarily in this life be still believers. But I found that you were and therefore I taught you gently, gradually, leading you to things that you knew not and casting from your minds the things that were not right and proper to be there. It is of course good to be a churchgoer, to believe in Almighty God, but there are things that are preached in churches that are not utterly true and there are false gods worshipped where there should only be the Great Almighty of whom I am a part. We know that your blessed Jesus was a holy man and a son of God, but your people claim him as God and this should never have been permitted to happen for he does not desire it and nor do we. Yes, they call us a holy trinity. I will explain to you there is a holy trinity. It is indeed Almighty God, myself and all of you who truly believe. So that you who are many become as one, which makes a trinity. But Jesus is one of you and was one of you during his short lifetime. Remember that. Reverence him as you will for he was indeed a prophet and a holy man speaking the words of God that I put into his mouth. He was a holy man. He is still a holy man.

(Unfortunately no further words from this great teaching tape are available. The tape was not turned over as the words were also being recorded on another machine. Now it seems that tape is no longer in existence.)

THE HOLY FLOCEN

30 March 1982

Soskris my beloved children. My blessed dear children it is long since I have been with you. I greet you in love. I enclose you in the warmth of my love and wrap around you the wings of my love that you may rest in peace upon my bosom, for I am truly your father and you are truly my children. I regret that it has been so long, my dear ones, since I have been here to visit and speak with you, but I do not forget you and I would have you remember at all times that you are all dear to me and it is through my giving of your recognition, Tom, that you have now an 'Esi'. Therefore do you understand that you are within my love as are you also, you who are called John and also within my love. And you Norman, Normesi and dear Nitesi are forever in my blessed love. And you are to me blessed people for I have made you so and before me the old sweet Flocen made you his special venture. His children truly, now my children. It is wonderful to be able to see you again, but I never forget you, nor do I ever forget to inquire how things are going with you and all that happens to you. All that you do and say comes to me through various sources at various times so that you are never away from me. It is for you that this love is here for you to lean upon, to draw strength from. You must never feel as though you are alone even though I may stay from you a long while, but you understand that my duties are many and I cannot spend too much time with you. I cannot indeed stay with you now. My visit is very fleeting, but I thought as I was passing near that I would come in and speak with you for this short time. I have been on another occasion, but you do not now meet on the other night when you used to meet and on that occasion I was disappointed for you were not holding a circle. Now I will tell you I must leave you with love, but I say to you again have faith in yourselves and faith in what you know you have to do and help each other as much as you can for this is your duty. This is what has been designed for you to undertake and these are the things you all must do. To love each other and to give to each other. To be giving as well as taking. What you give will be given back to you tenfold in time. I have told you this before. The love of The Almighty is ever with you blessed children. Soskris. Soskris my dear ones. Blessed children, Soskris.

THE HOLY FLOCEN

---

26 March 1985

It is long since I have spoken with you, but you do not forget me and I do not forget you. You are my dear ones. You are my great experiment. You are the ones that I planned so long ago to bring gently and gradually to learn all that you must learn. Blessed children you have for many long years studied hard and now you are almost at a stalemate, but you must not give up. You are still my great experiment and I shall love you always. When I say I shall love you, you know I speak for the Great Almighty. Blessed children, blessed children. I love you as you know. Remember always that you are mine. Dear sweet children, try hard, try to regain some of that which it would appear you have lost, but not from your minds or your hearts. It is only that there are few of you now, yet let me tell you that far away from you those others, who were once so close to you, still, as you, think and feel the same and try to establish, or keep in touch as you do. There are those strayed away from each other, separated from each other and separated from you, but they are still my children, still my people and I still love them as I know they love me. It is hard that they have partners that do not believe as they believe, yet their hearts are still mine. Nothing can take that away. Remember always pray to the Great Almighty. He is your father and I am also your father. Blessings be upon you. I tell you the love of The Almighty is ever with you.

129

THE HOLY FLOCEN

29 September 1995

I greet you in love and I tell you the love of The Almighty is ever with you despite my long absence. I thank you for recognising me. I come because I hear you need to be told. You need to be told and therefore I have found the time to come in. I know you were reading my words from long ago and it is long since I have visited you, but I never have you out of my heart. You are always there and I am always praying for you that the good that you have achieved will continue to support you in your low status that you now have unfortunately arrived at. But it will improve. You will improve. I cannot come to you as I used to, nor can The Efun, but I will come when I can and if I feel you deeply need me and I feel you do now. Because it is so long, so very, very long since I came to bless you all and I do bless you all. I am sorry that you are such a small group now, but you are a true group and as long as you stay close together you, who believe, will be blessed by me and by The Efun and by Almighty God. I cannot say more than that. It is the greatest thing I can tell you. For you there is always love. For you have done good work over a very long period. You have carried out almost impossible tasks in the past. You have recruited and you have lost, but never mind my dear beloved children, never mind. You are still the greatest. You are still revered throughout the planets because of the work you have done. You are called 'The Children of Light' and that is a name which is only yours. You who belong to this particular circle, under this particular medium, the best one that we have. We honour and love very deeply this medium. Thank you, all of you for being here. Thank you for listening to me and please accept my love. If you wish I will reach out my hand and you shall touch if you so desire. Bless you my child (Chris). Bless you my child (Val). Bless you. Bless you (Normesi). I cannot remain with you for I have much to do. Blessing for her (Nitesi) and better health for her for she suffers greatly with this pain and she suffers with this loss of the eyes. I cannot do anything about that but *you* can. *(**The Holy Flocen** *pointed at Circle member).* For you have been given the power to the best of your ability. I bless you my son for you are also very holy.

My Lord I would like to say that you are always in our hearts and we always know that you are there for us, wherever you are.

I am glad for you. I am loving you always. And so I leave you now with my love wrapped around each one of you and when it is my love that is wrapped around you it is the love of The Almighty that is ever with you. That blessing is for her. Soskris. Soskris my blessed children. My great experiment.

JESUS CHRIST

---

3 December 1978

Blessed children of God, thy Father, my Father – I greet thee in love and say unto you Soskris. I come again in love, to speak with thee and bring thee comfort, and hope that all of thy needs shall be eventually granted, for love is with you, wherever you go. Mine is with you, and the love of our blessed Father, the great Almighty is ever with you, for you have been chosen, just as I was once chosen.

Jesus I am. Say with me – Soskris, Soskris in the name of the Father. I feel a little less tension in our dear medium – more calm, more settled, perhaps not freed of pain or hurt, and not freed of anguish. Yet I feel that there is no bitterness. Maybe my words when I came before have helped her to guard against bitterness and dissension. I do realise that it is hard, for I have lived this life that you live. I have lived it to my sorrow and yet what I did was for our Almighty Father. I think that our Almighty Father has taken the bitterness from within her soul, for when bitterness sets its seed into the soul the soul will remain eternally damaged. I see now that it glows with the brightness of forgiveness and I am happy, for I feel that I may have been able to help her when I came on the last occasion. I would like you all to remember, not only her but you others, and you of the silent visitors of which there are always many, including myself at times, when you know not that I am here. I wish you all to remember that bitterness is something that can destroy the beauty of the soul. Therefore, no matter what occurs to you, try hard not to allow it to make you bitter, for if thy heart and mind become bitter, then will your soul be seared, and the sear will not heal. It will not heal while you live. We consider animosity to be near to bitterness. It must be avoided by all, because when this sets in, then the tongue speaks wrong and unkindly words. All of you here, you living ones, you passed-on ones, you astral projections – all of you have been taught that you are on a mission and your mission is based upon love. Love can never be put aside for animosity or bitterness – this must never be

132

allowed. She has said (and I have heard) that love and hate are close together. Yes, they are, but love must be the strongest power, for love is within your soul, and your soul belongs to The Almighty, who *is* love! Hate is near to love, but love must come out on top. Do you understand the depth of meaning of what I am saying to you? It is imperative that you understand! Everyone has the ability to love, and everyone has the ability to hate – it is good and evil. Do not ever allow that the evil should overcome the good. The good must come out to overcome the evil, and cast it aside. That is why I said to her on the last occasion when I was here not so very long ago – THOU SHALT NOT BE BITTER. Bitterness, hate and animosity all club together to try to destroy that single beam of love, and there you have three fighting one, but the one must grow, and grow, and grow, and grow until it can overcome them! They will be cast away. That is why I say to her – forgive him. Just as I cried out to my Father and your Father – Forgive them, for they know not what they do! Forgiveness is holy. Gentleness is holy, and she has become in our eyes a holy person, and you of this circle, you in particular who are present, you two living people (Normesi and Teresi) we consider to be holy people. She is your leader and priestess, and she is the one that has been filled with indoctrination, yet she is still human, and must experience human feelings, just as I have experienced human feelings when I was alive. They have suggested that I was ... homosexual you call it now. They have also suggested that I went with loose women. I am going to tell you – my life was *not* perfect! Not until the time came when the words were given to me, and only to me, to go out upon the hillsides and preach the words of the Lord. I am not the Lord – I speak the words of the Lord. They call me Lord because I speak the words, but the Lord is our Father, and our Father (through the Holy Ghost whom you know as The Flocen) has given me the words to speak, and I must speak them! Just as she must speak what I say!

She is in a trance and I have helped her. I developed my mediumistic powers at the age of 30 and she developed hers at about the same age, but was afraid to utilise them. She has always had mediumistic tendencies, right from a very early age. She had spirit friends to play with when she had no children around. She called them fairy-tale people, but they were spirit friends, and she believed in them, and they helped her through a very lonely childhood, with no other children to play with and brothers who were older than her.

I cannot remain. I am sorry, but she now wishes to return. It is because of the sound of the ringing bell (telephone). It has called her back. I love you all. I look upon you as the blessed ones of The Almighty. I look upon you as the chosen people. You are doing your best, just as I did my best. Thank you for listening to me, and will you please thank her for receiving me, and tell her I love her dearly, as I love you all. I love you who are here and still living, and all you passed-over spirits. You Astrals from other planets that are present, I love you. Come to me, I gather you to my heart. Soskris, dear children, Soskris. Soskris, dear medium, dear sister. Get well, get well. Keep love in your heart and forget all bitterness. Take hurt from your mind and remember only the joys. If you must love him, it is no sin, for love is given into your heart by The Almighty. Bear with him, be kind to him, and help yourself to get well. Soskris. Soskris.

JESUS CHRIST

---

11 May 1980

You who are called the Children of Light, who are my brothers and sisters and also my children. I bless you all with the power that was given to me so long ago when I lived upon your Earth. I am Jesus.

Soskris.

Soskris my blessed brother and my good friend. I am the white light that she saw. I have helped her into trance, for having seen my light she could no longer go to trance therefore did I have to help her. I am come in love as ever and to tell you that the love of Almighty God is ever with thee. I am come to speak to you on things that you often forget. That love is the most important of all emotions. More important than self love or personal love or wife love or family love. More important than work and discussions of work. More important than earning money which I know you need to live by as once I needed it also. And I did work as a poor carpenter to earn money for the bread that I ate and to give to the poor. That which was over and above my needs. This I did from the time I was a grown man, which in those days was at the age of 14 years. One became a man much earlier in my young days than you do now. I wish you all to think, not just you Normesi and I think you are Johnasi and all you others, Astrals and Spirituals. To think deeply upon the meaning of love and what is expected of you in love as was expected of me. To forgo your selfishness, to overcome your meanness and give that which you do not need for yourself to those that you know need it more. Whether it be in money for people of this Earth, or whether it be love for all you others as well as for you of this Earth. You must give of yourselves to keep the place that you have gained in the eyes of The Holy Flocen, that the churches call The Holy Spirit or The Holy Ghost, but you know that The Holy Spirit is called The Holy Flocen. It is a much more beautiful word than Ghost which is an unkind and hard word and conjures up unpleasant thoughts whereas The Flocen conjures up beautiful thoughts. If you have anything you wish to say to

135

me, I am glad to answer you if I can. I certainly would like to converse with you rather than to lecture you. So speak my friends, say your piece and let me answer if it need be answered. I will tell you of love. Love is the very inner part of a person's being. Love is within the soul and the spirit. Love is not for self and must not be for self. Love is meant to give to others, but foremost to Almighty God, our Heavenly Father. Let us say heavenly although we know there is no such place as heaven. Yet is our Father Almighty and Heavenly. It has a beautiful sound to it and we are happy to use this expression. For anything that is beauty is love and anything that is love is beauty, but all love is Almighty God. However you try to think about it, always remember within each one of us, and I mean all of you as well as myself, is the holy spark of love which is part of Almighty God, making each one of us a tiny fragment of the great and wondrous Power that can never be fully understood, but must be reverenced throughout all time and throughout all the universe, all the galaxies, all the planets. All must reverence the great Almighty and remember that only through The Almighty are any of us ever allowed to live and if we do wrong then shall our lives cease to be. You will say now why did your life cease to be and I will answer. I endeavoured to do that which was put upon me to do. That which I was born to do. Yet I did not do it sufficiently well, therefore did I have to pay the price like any felon upon the cross. Think not only I was to be crucified. Millions were crucified. I was but one, but I was the only one who wore a crown of thorns and who had the nails driven through hands and feet. Others were roped to the crosses, but others had their stomachs slit and their entrails would hang out. At least I did not suffer that humiliation although they made a cross cut upon the place above my heart which bled freely. I did not die of my wounds, or my hanging upon the cross. As I have told you before, I passed into unconsciousness both from lack of food and from loss of blood. But they assumed me dead and permitted my followers to cut me down, where I was carried to the tomb and laid within and the great stone was placed across the aperture that none could move. Yet was it moved because they were faithful, they were my followers and a holy force was given to them that they could move a stone – mere men – to move a stone as heavy and enormous as those that you now call Stonehenge. A special force was placed into their bodies that they should be able to remove it, that they could rescue me before suffocation took place and I was carried forth in the deep of night. And in the morning came they who were not my followers to find the stone moved right away and the cavern empty. They say I rose again. 'In three days he rose again from the dead.' In three days I was revived from dying. Revived from my coma that I could stand amongst the people and put fear into them. This was meant to be, that they should at last recognise that something greater than their understanding could happen. It was not truly meant to subterfuge. It was meant to try and educate the uneducated. To bring belief into the hearts of those who did not believe. Yes, eventually I did die.

How long afterwards?

Quite a long while.

What happened in the meanwhile?

I had to keep myself from public view and hide my face behind a cowl when I went forth.

So after you showed yourself –

I went into hiding. But I did my good deeds whenever possible and I taught my followers and my disciples how to continue my work. Then did I know it was my time to go and did go quite peacefully in the arms of my mother. Still a young man, but not as I was taken from the cross. A whole man, not a mutilated body. So people remembered me and called me king and made me God which I did not want to be. And I told my disciples 'tell them that I am not God. Tell them I am a son of God. Tell them I was a son of God.' That yet they would not put me upon a pedestal and make me into a god. Yet did they do so, for they needed something tangible. A God they knew, had seen. This was wrong. God you cannot see, but God is all around us all, not only now, but at all time.

You must have been very psychic, in fact a medium.

I was a medium. I was indeed a medium and I have been one of the very few mediums who had real true mediumship where there are so many people who pretend to be mediums and are not truly so. Those that are truly mediums are very few and far between. Perhaps one or two in each country of this world, but many upon other planets, but not many in this world. So if you have one, yes indeed, you are fortunate. You are truly more than fortunate to have a medium who is a true medium and not a person who pretends to hear voices that do not exist. One who will speak only the words that other spirits speak through her, whether they be astral or whether they be spirits it matters not. Yet sometimes you will hear her speak, for her subconscious will come to the surface and she will tell you, 'This is me. I have things hidden deep within me that I must talk to you about and she will talk to you and you must believe when she talks to you for it is important. She is then baring her soul to you and for this you should reverence her and treat her as she deserves to be treated as a holy priestess.

Circle member: Can you tell me who puts thoughts into one's mind?

You put thoughts yourself into your mind unless you are being given transmissions from other spirits who will then put thoughts into your mind which you could not have thought of your own accord. This is a great gift and if you have it, nurture it and try and bring it to fruition that you may be able to speak the words that are put into your mind which you know you were not capable of thinking yourself. Do you understand John?

Circle member: We've been told that Jesus chased the moneylenders out of the Temple –

Of course, of course. I was just as wild as any other young man of my age. I could get just as angry. It wasn't a lack of love, it was because it angered me that moneylenders should try to make money out of such a source. To lend money to poor people to go into a temple? It was wrong that they should ever have to pay to go into a temple. No one should pay to be able to speak to Almighty God.

They had to pay to go into a temple?

Yes and for that did the moneylenders sit there. To lend the poor people that were asking a boon. You know the meaning of that term? Isn't a boon a gift from God? And paying for it to the priests of those days. It angered me. Yes, I scattered them. Yes, I beat them about. Yes, I would do it again. I was no meek and mild man in my normal self, only meek and mild when I was speaking the words put into my mouth by The Holy Flocen, my Holy Spirit, my blessed Father. For the Holy Spirit was indeed my Father to me and still is. As He is Father to all of you.

Jesus, you are not originally of Earth. Did you perhaps come from The Flocen's planet?

I came – I am not permitted to tell where I came from. I am only permitted to tell you that I was not an Earth spirit, but was born into that tiny child of Bethlehem. I know this now. I knew it when I was ten years of age. Yet was I told then that I must wait until I became 30 years of age before I could utilise my power. Then would I be helped with the work for I was still only a peasant man. A poor peasant man. A worker, working for his living in a very poor area and living in a very poor manner with hardly clothes to my back or shoes – or sandals as we used – for my feet. But I was content.

You were a great spirit really with a poor peasant brain at its disposal.

Much greater than that was the knowledge that was given to me later that I might speak and let it flow from my mouth without ever thinking a word of it. No need to think for the words were put into my mouth. There are few people that have this ability and you have one in your medium. I do not wish to say that she has the same strength that I had. That I have had. But I will tell you that hers is a very special knowledge and a very special duty which she performs in a very special way without ever, ever saying I will not do this. I can remember the times when I have said I won't, or I can't, or don't make me. Yet she never says this. I reverence your medium, just as I know she reverences me. We are brother and sister even although she is not of my time, nor was she ever born in my time. She was born before, she was born after and has been born again and again, but she was born long, long before me. She is an older spirit than mine. I think you know this. And you also Normesi are an older spirit. You know this also.

I know I had very early times.

Yes, earlier than mine. There you have a slight edge on me, for you have lived many times before I ever came from my home planet to be one of you.

And we've learnt so little in so long a time.

Because you have learned earlier and forgotten. What you have learnt you have forgotten over and over and over again. Now for the rest of this time of your existence upon this planet you must remember what you are told. You must remember and carry forth your work.

Was the reason that we couldn't carry this knowledge with us and into a further life because we turned away from it before we died?

Yes. Yes. Yes. Long before I ever existed. You had knowledge that I had and that she now has, but you turned away and would not go when you should have been taken to a far planet. You stayed with your world preparing perhaps to die for your world than to abandon it. Perhaps you were right. It is not for me to say you were wrong. I have now reached the end of my time. I wish to bless you all. A blessing upon you dear children, Children of Light, the chosen ones of The Holy Flocen, therefore of my wondrous Father and of Almighty God. Soskris.

MARY, MOTHER OF JESUS

---

8 June 1982

I have only been born once. I am called, no – I am known as the mother of Jesus. Jesus was my child. My dear blessed son and it is true that I did beget him without any physical contact with any living man. But I did have a visitation from a glorious angel that I thought to be the angel Gabriel but I do not know for certain that it was, for now I believe it might have been he who you call The Holy Flocen. And he did come to me spiritwise and did impregnate me spiritwise. But it was a glorious, beautiful experience. A wonderful – but love – a love that cannot be put into words. A feeling that cannot be described in words and from this beautiful joining I became pregnant with my dear son. My beloved child. My child was a holy child because he came from the person of great light that I thought was the angel Gabriel. I was not a very holy woman, yet I was a good clean woman, A girl really. Not of many summers. About 15 summers when I became the bearer of this precious child. And people thought I had been bad. That I had behaved wrongly with a man. And lo my belly swelled with the child growing within. Then they would point their fingers at me and call Joseph, the Jew who accepted me as his wife even though he knew I was carrying what he thought to be some other man's child. But it was not. It was indeed the child of God or the child of the holy angel Gabriel as I thought at that time. But now I think not the holy angel Gabriel, but the beautiful silver light of him that you call The Holy Flocen. Can you imagine the wonder, the beauty of having such a person enter your body and leave there a seed that would grow into a man. And eventually that man became the greatest man of all men. For a very short while he was indeed the King of the Jews. The only real king at that time.

Mary, may I ask you a question?

Yes, you may my son. I am happy to be here with you for I know you have been seen by my son.

We have, yes.

And he loves you well.

As we love him.

But you must not think he is God. He is the child of God. You are children of God for you have been chosen to do holy work. Ask your questions my son. I will try to answer them.

Jesus, we understand, did not die for quite some considerable time after he made his appearance after you with friends rolled the boulder away.

This is a great, great secret. You must not, you must not spread this rumour.

But it is a secret that I would think should be known. At the time I can understand the secrecy. At the time.

Let me explain something to you. This is a terrible way to take a life and most of those who were upon the crosses were dead when they were taken down and they thought he was dead and allowed us to take him down.

Did you think he was dead?

Yes, but he was not dead. He was in a coma and we did not know this until he came to us afterwards and told us that he had been in a coma. So we did place him in the tomb and rolled the great stone, which took many, many to put it in position.

What made you go to remove his body, was it to bury somewhere else?

Something told us we must go back there to see him and what made us, we will never know unless it was the will of The Almighty. To remove the stone once it had been placed in position was a wrong thing to do, yet we were forced to do this and do it we did. There were many of us who moved the stone. Just as many men put it in position.

Did they all experience the need to go to –

Yes.

Not just you?

No, not just me and not just me with Mary Magdalen, who was as my daughter, for she loved him dearly. And he forgave her for her wantonness and made her clean again. Made her as new, for he loved her new. But we went back and rolled away the stone and he was not there and we will never know how he moved the stone to let him out. Did the angels come and move the stone to let him out? So they say he arose again from the dead. But he was not truly dead, so he told us when we met him again. For we met him outside. He showed himself to us and to all the people. All saw him and he said, 'I am risen from the dead. I am come to you again. I am still your Jesus.' But when the people went away and he went with us into the forest and he said, 'I shall live here, in the forest. I shall live as the birds and the bees and any of you who wish to remain with me may do so. But I will not demand that any should.' But some of us wanted to stay with him.

Did any of the disciples stay with him?

No. They went off to do their work not realising he was still living. They thought him dead. They thought that it was an apparition that appeared to them when he came and said, 'I am risen from the dead.' They felt it was a ghostly spirit that they viewed.

When you first saw him, was your first feeling of awe, or sheer joy?

Joy. Does the questioner know that I had another son? Do you know this?

Err. No.

And this son I had by Joseph, not by the Holy Spirit.

What was his name?

He had many names. He was called Jesus' Brother, but he had many names and I called him My Son. I do not know what they have called him, or whether he is shown in the Bible that you have. But he was a living boy and man after Jesus and Jesus knew him and loved him as a brother.

Did he follow the teachings of Jesus?

Not as strongly as he would have liked to do. He was not so strong in his belief. He could not follow in his footsteps, although he did follow him, but not with the same depth of feeling, but then he was not the holy person that my son Jesus was. My son was a great and holy spirit.

Did you know that Jesus, we have been taught, was not a spirit of Earth at all but from a very holy planet?

This I do not know, my son, but it is possible. That he did come from my body, was the child of my body, was born as they say in a manger when there was no room for me at the inn. This is true this story. This is the true story of his birth and did come the three kings, who brought their many gifts and the shepherds were there.

The star in the sky which led the kings. Did it appear to be very low in the heavens?

Yes, very low indeed. Almost you could touch it. You couldn't touch it but you would think you could reach up and almost touch it.

I wonder if it was a space craft from another world.

It might have been, but I cannot say it was or was not. We were very ignorant in those times and I'm not very much better educated now.

You saw this star yourself?

Yes.

Was it one colour or did it have many colours?

142

Oh it had all colours – it was beautiful. It was like a rainbow compressed into one star.

Did it flash at all brighter and dimmer?

No it was just bright at all times. It was so bright it nearly blinded me and it came down to beam upon me as the child of God. It even penetrated into the poor stable where I was housed and even the little donkey that was there with us, my donkey, was bathed in the light of the star, but then my child when he was born had the same light with him.

A silly question, but do you recall the name you called your donkey?

No, I do not. It is so long ago, my son, and I suppose it does not seem important to remember some of these things. Most of them are forgotten by most people, but I know that these stories are told and I wish to speak with you to verify and tell you that part of it which is true so that you will know that what I am speaking of is the true part of what you have heard. Some of it is what you would call made up, pretence. But no pretence in what I am telling you and no pretence in the birth of my sweet, beloved baby.

How many summers did Jesus live beyond the time of the cross?

Oh. If he was 30 and he was two years teaching before they crucified him and then he was 32 and it was when he was 52 years of age so he lived for 20 years after the crucifixion.

In the woods?

In the woods.

And you saw him frequently during this time?

No. I did not see him all the time, before, I saw him when he first went to the woods, but not later because you see I had to go back to my husband who would not understand if I went to live in the woods, for he would not live in the woods with me.

He told us that he died in your arms, however?

I went back when I heard the time was approaching. I was told. I was given inner information. This of course is not the language that I normally would be speaking. For we are Hebrew people.

Yes, you are speaking very good modern English.

I am proud of this, but then I have had many years of listening to try to learn.

Where have you listened?

Everywhere that I can go.

And English is widely spoken?

Oh, yes. And people are talking of Jesus and there I must listen to see what they say.

Do they recognise you when you go?

No.

They don't realise that you're the mother?

No. They do not know I am there. I can appear if I wish. I can appear or disappear. I cannot appear and speak I can only speak. I couldn't appear now.

Yes, we understand.

But if Jesus were here, he could for he is so much stronger in spirit. He could speak and be there for you to see, if he wished it. If he wished it. I have seen him do this for people. Only for a few minutes – a few moments.

For living people?

Yes. There are many who believe and would like to see.

It is said that if anybody wants Jesus to come to them enough, he will come to them.

Yes, this is true. If anybody wants the Holy Spirit to come to them he will come, if they want it hard enough. They might not see him, but he will go to them just the same.

There is of course a tremendous difference between The Holy Spirit and Jesus. The Holy Spirit can be in many places at the same time.

This I know. This I do know. But now my power is low. I am unable to sustain it so I must not remain with you for much more time.

It was wonderful of you to come and talk to us.

I have been longing to do this, but I will not put myself forward. I will only come when there is a clear way in.

Are there many spirits here to hear your words?

Yes, but I was admitted first and given thanks to come.

That's hardly surprising.

I do not have any holy light like my beloved son. I am only an ordinary spirit.

But you are a special person.

Because . . . is the mother of God, but this is not true.

This is blasphemy according to our religion.

This is not true, I cannot be the mother of God, but I was the mother of a very holy spirit that was not, was not – I cannot find the right word – was no man involved in the making – is the seeds difference.

Will of divine, of course.

Thank you, that was beautifully put. And now I will say I must leave you with great love and sweet gentle love to remain with you after I have left you.

There are many Roman Catholics who pray to you, but you cannot handle all these prayers – are they passed on?

I do realise that many people pray to me, they do call 'Hail Mary'. This is true and I am from many different languages called upon and, as you say, I cannot hear them all. I am ever constantly aware that people are calling upon me to intercede for them in certain matters of their lives which is not always possible for me to do, though I would like to try wherever I can. Certainly could I ... from the Holy Spirit that help be given to them if they need it. But you must not detain me longer.

Our love is with you.

I thank you and my love is for you. I leave my love with you. May the blessings of The Almighty be with you.

JOSEPH CHRIST, Husband of Mary, Mother of Jesus

14 July 1995

You are writing about my child. You are writing. You are writing about her who is the mother.

Are you the mother?

No. I am not the mother.

She was your child?

No, she was my wife. My name is Joseph Christ. I have not got a lot of time and I will not be able to continue if you interrupt too frequently. I am not very intelligent, but I know you are writing about the events of my lifetime and I want to help you. I know that you are troubled by some things. I am called Joseph Christ. Christ is a surname. I am not able to go into many details away from my story because I have not got the ability to speak in your present time language. It is difficult for me. I am, of course, a Jew. You know. Jesus was the child of Mary and because I did take her as wife to save her from being in dire trouble from becoming pregnant when she was not a married person. I protected her by marrying her and accepted the unborn child as my own. Therefore did the child become Christ, for that is my name. And he was called Jesus at a later date. As a small child he was called The Unnamed One.

Did you have one word for that meaning?

Yes, in Jewish.

What was it?

No, do not ask me these things. You do not realise I am not educated. I need all my powers to speak your present time speech. I come for your helping, no, to do helping.

To help us.

Yes. Because I have heard that you are making this great effort to put into a book all that . . .

146

The Truth. We seek the Truth.

It is not what you read in the Bible. The Bible was made to frighten the ignorant of which I was one. So, in fact, was Jesus, for he also was an ordinary man. A commoner.

But he was a medium, like the person you use.

Yes, but that came when he was grown man, not before. He was a simple boy with dark brown red hair. Red and brown, or dark brown with red colour and very bright blue eyes. No Jew ever had such colouring.

Did that cause some wonderment?

Yes and always from this, my boy, came bright light as though he glowed through his skin. His eyes were blazing blue and his hair was dark bright red. Glinting red.

Was his skin lighter than the average Jew?

Yes and it was as though light shone through it and amazed people who met him. But he was a very quiet, shy unobtrusive boy. He was always happy to help anyone and to do whatever he thought was good and right. He was not a wild hooligan like the others of his age. Gentle. Kindly. Always trying to heal or mend and good to his mother and good to his brother, who was called brother of Jesus. He had no given name.

He was younger, of course.

Of course, yes. He was after by three years.

Was it common in your time for people to be given these picturesque names with a number of words meaning something?

Yes.

Like the Red Indians of North America.

Yes. You see you are interrupt and I forget. I do not want to forget, but I cannot help forget. I come now to say he grew to man and he said 'My father,' that was me, 'I must go to the people and call them to follow me. Will you help me? I need 12 good men.' These he called his disciples and gradually we found his 12 men and they huddled together. Sometimes in the houses, sometimes on the hillside. Sometimes in barns and they conferred and talked. Always they listened to him. The Glowman. They called him The Glowman. And then he started to heal people and he became a great and wonderful healer. And he said, 'I must talk to the whole congregation. Not in the temples, but on the hillsides. You must gather them for me my disciples.' And so the disciples gathered the people and brought them together. And he stood and spoke, but when he spoke it was not like him speaking. It was like others were speaking through him, for he used words and languages that he had never known. For he was but a simple man with no great education and worked as a carpenter.

147

Woodwork. Trees were cut and he made beautiful things from, but he didn't like the trees to be cut because he said they were living things and must not be treated with disrespect. However, that is the work we did and he did. But after he went to the people he did no more work and he lived off his disciples and was begging, which seems wrong, for we had enough for him. But he wanted not our money. And then he make the great sacrifice. He was condemned as being one who misled the people. There were of course crucifixions every day. Many, in various places. Rows of them. There were people who stole a loaf of bread could be crucified. To steal is wicked. And women were stoned to death, but once when the Mary Magdalen was to be stoned for being a prostitute Jesus stood before her and held up his hand so (*the medium raised her hand in 'stop' fashion*) and they threw the stones and not one stone hit her or him. They all went wide, above, below, beside, but never on either of them and he said, 'Now you see the power of God. You shall not stone this woman. She shall not do wrong again and I take her under my protection.' And that is how he saved her life and from that moment she became absolutely his property and he went no more with young men, but did stay with Mary, the Magdalen. His mother did not approve, because she (*the Magdalen*) had been a prostitute. But I understood his goodness and knew that he had made her a better person. And I forgave him as did his disciples. I will have to return to you another time because my strength is now going very fast.

You have only been born once then?

Only once.

As your wife.

As she has only been born once. She was a good woman, who was a virgin woman. When I married her, although she was pregnant, she was a virgin woman and she has always been a good woman, but she has never been born again. She can come to you if she wishes.

She has been to us, did you know?

No, I did not know.

13 years ago.

Well you are fortunate. I hope she will come again for your benefit. To help you, because you need help with what you are doing. But you must take care of your medium. You will not have her very much longer and I do not know what will happen when you've no longer got this medium to help you. I cannot stay any longer because I am now almost without any strength.

I shall ask our congregation to give you love.

I will love you always and I do bring you love from these with whom I still associate. I am not able to stay. I say the blessings of God are yours and to that I will say Amen.

Go with our love, Joseph.

DANIEL

21 January 1979

I feel greatly honoured to be able to listen to the words of The Holy Flocen. How humble, how gentle and tender his words, such humility to admit his inability to cope in that early time of his reign. You will remember me when I tell you that I am called Daniel. Soskris, I will say, for I have learned to say Soskris through the Great Ones who have learned before me. I am here in this room to be with you, that it is known you have been chosen by The Holy Flocen and The Great Almighty to be the holy ones who shall be the foundations of a great and virtuous church wherein shall be much reverence always no matter who speaks through the medium. Reverence shall be here for she has become blessed and wears a fine halo as well as a great aura. She has had the halo only since you have had your great Tarset. I will say to you all I could wish that I were of your time, that I could be a living person to sit within this Circle and join with you in prayer and join with you in learning for you are indeed following a great path, a great, wide, shining path which leads you eventually to the very heart of The Great and Holy Almighty God. I was considered good in my time but compared to you I was not in the same way. You are good for you have been chosen. You may not yet be perfect but time will perfect. To have been chosen, you must have been good to start with; to have been selected to be the leaders of a new and holy church, the only true church of Almighty God. This must surely be the greatest honour that can be paid to any people of any planet. You are those people, few as you are, yet there are many here – Spirituals, Astrals and those who wait within your cone that is so bright and goes so far into the sky and those that cling to the outsides of your cone hoping to be able to pass through and come in through the centre to speak through this blessed medium. I am sad for I realise that this medium, blessed though she be, suffers from natural despair and torment which is caused by love of a being – not for love of The Almighty, not the spiritual love, but the physical and mental love that we of this Earth have always been accustomed to give to one and one only person. We may have minor loves throughout our lives as we all have done and all must do but there is always one great love and if that is lost to the person that has had it, then is that person destroyed in a manner as if part of the body has been torn apart, torn away, and tortuous pain remains in its place. The brain is severed with tortuous thoughts. Half the thoughts on one side are gentle, forgiving, remembering, loving and the other half tormented and remembering the bad things and in a way blaming not only the person concerned but themselves as well for what has happened. If only we could wipe these two sides into one place and smooth it together, the good must overcome the bad, yet none can do that. The spiritual love cannot hope to be withdrawn nor can she hope to withdraw it but at the moment she suffers and I can feel it. He does not suffer the same – he suffers mentally, she suffers physically. He is physically satisfied and has a woman to hold within his arms. She frets for those arms to come back around her. He cannot withdraw his spiritual love. However much he tries to bury it beneath other thoughts, he cannot do it. Spiritual love cannot satisfy physical longing. She has the need of comforting, of nursing back to being herself so that again her eyes will shine brightly as each day breaks and she will look forward with happiness to each day, instead of which she looks to it with dread that there is yet another day to pass through with this torment and the hurt that distresses almost beyond her abilities to contain. I can feel all this and I offer my love in consolation but that is not what she needs. What she needs are warm, forgiving arms to hold and to stretch out her arms forgivingly to hold the one she loves. I doubt this will come to her, therefore I fret for her. Let us pray to God:

> Dear Father Almighty, help this your good medium who has served you well throughout these many years and will continue to do so as long as the breath lies within this body. Help her and give her some consolation, any consolation will be appreciated. We pray this, Almighty God because we love her. Amen.

I have not felt such pain before. I have experienced it in my own life but not to the extent that she does. But then perhaps I was not such a person as she, perhaps not capable of giving so much love as she is capable of giving. There are those that can and they are not many. There are those that live upon the surface and they *are* many. For him it might not have been his true soul-mate; for her it may have been, yet he has accepted her love throughout these many long years, and she has given it unstintingly,

151

unselfishly and for ever forgivingly for the wrongs that he has done in the past and even now she forgives. This I feel, all within her; it pains me as it must pain any who visit through her, for all must feel what she feels and experience what she is going through. Each one takes a little unhappiness away with him or her because of this. We all say the same: God help her. Amen. I will not remain with you long for I have a long journey to make and we have no boosting chambers as they have upon other planets. I have learned about the other planets through those great ones who have taken to being followers of the Jeculins – David, Solomon, great Lord Abraham, Moses. I know I am not fit to class my name with theirs yet I am spoken of in the Bible but that was for the strength that Almighty God gave me to overcome evil. I was protected by Almighty God in the lions' den. I offered my soul to Almighty God and asked for preservation and I got it.

I am sorry that I cannot stay for I find that although she is in some despair and it distorts her thoughts a great deal, yet I am happy here with you, speaking with you. As a man I speak with you whereas before I scribbled letters upon a board, not very effectively, for I was not then very conversant with your language as you speak it now. Love each other, love all things living, all beings living or passed over, all Astrals that visit you, all animals, creatures, birds of the air, animals that are free, animals that are caged, domestic animals, the things that grow upon the ground, the flowers that bloom and quickly die, the trees that stand tall and grow ever towards God, reaching higher and higher in their efforts to reach The Almighty – love them all, but most of all love Almighty God and The Holy Flocen, before anything else. Before man love, before woman love, love Almighty God and The Holy Flocen and The Great Efun. Love them and you will never go wrong and you will be cared for and protected by The Great and Holy Flocen and The Holy Efun who is good to you and visits you frequently. Soskris. A blessing be upon you all, good creatures, good people who are in this room. A blessing be upon you all. May Almighty God ever watch over you all. Bless this child. Bless this poor, aching heart. Ease this poor, tormented brain.

152

PETER, THE APOSTLE

11 February 1979

In these hands I bear love; love true and holy, not physical love but blessed, glorious, spiritual love, and I bring it all for you all who are present. I bring it also for her, without whom we could have no contact. Love is the sweetest, most glorious thing. Many use the word, few understand. Imagine in my hands a bowl filled with love, and from this bowl may all take as much as you need. Be not greedy, for there are many who need love.

I am an ancient person from ancient times and I have been spoken of and written of in your Bible which, I have come to understand, you no longer believe so fully in and for this I blame thee not. Take a little love my friends, all who are here. I will receive love from thee as I give love to thee. You may call me by a name that is famous – I am called Peter. I was a disciple of the great and holy Christ. I understand now that we worshipped Jesus Christ as God, for we felt the need to have a visible God. Many times did he say, 'Call me not God, for God is my Father, and I am but a son of God, just as ye all are.'

You must remember that the Bible has been transcribed over and over again, until if you could possibly find the original written work, you would not recognise them as being the words now in your Bible. I am trying to adapt myself to your modern-day language, which was not my language, for we all spoke Hebrew or Egyptian and some of us spoke Arabic, but chiefly it was Hebrew and we all had big, hooked noses, which do not exist so much now among the Jews as they did in the earlier times. Ours was a troubled time. Indeed, all times are troubled, but to each one it seems the most troubled times were when they existed as a living person. Of course, I am passed over, but I have not done any more journeys and do not think I will have to do so.

I have heard of your learnings from many of the people of my time, including my dear, saintly brother, Jesus. We were as lovers, so deep was

153

our love. Not physical lovers, but spiritual lovers, for we loved each other deeply and dearly, as did many others of the disciples. It is said there were ten or twelve, but there were more than twelve and all spiritually bound to Jesus, as he was spiritually bound to us. There were women amongst his followers who loved him well, as we did, and also who occasionally gave way to lust and loved him in lust. But man's needs must be served, however holy he be, and a woman who has grace enough to receive the lustful love of such a one as he has been greatly and highly honoured. The people, had they known, would have stoned her. He does not claim to have been a celibate man. He does not claim that he was not what you now term homosexual. In those days, many of us were homosexuals, but the word was called homo, which was derived from the Latin. It was no disgrace. It was, and has always been considered a disgrace when females permit such lustfulness to take place between themselves – that is frowned upon, and always has been. Yet, there were some of those, but they were cast out – not necessarily stoned, but cast out away from those who were good, and not allowed in the homes or lives of those who disapproved of such matters.

In this good woman who is your medium, your great rock to which you must look and lean to receive the contacts; to this dear, kind woman I give heartfelt thanks that she has permitted me to utilise the body and voice. She is able to accommodate not only me, but many of the highest of all those who can come to you, of whom we have learned through such people as Solomon, who was earlier than us but nevertheless, he has taught us of later times. We have heard also of what you learned from Jesus Christ and it is a new world that we live in. This is what he tried to teach so long ago, but we did not understand then that he was trying to tell us that God is Love. We did not understand this. We thought that God was an old, old man, seated on a great, ornate throne behind pearly gates, through which you must be admitted by another Peter, not myself. There have been many Peters, but the one we believed would admit us is called Saint Peter and that is not I. Those gates were there, as far as we knew, long before I existed. We have now learned there are no gates. Consequently, there is no Saint Peter doing that job, and there is no very ancient, venerable elderly man. We know now that God is not a man – God is Love.

God is the love, and into each soul that enters body upon the moment of birth is one small part of Almighty God. It is a stupendous thing to realise after so long. It has been many hundreds of years, perhaps thousands, that we have believed in an old man and searched for the gates of heaven and

154

for the throne surrounded by angels, with this great old man who is called God, but that is a fairy story. There are many heavens, some you make for yourself and there are many hells, all of which you make for yourselves, or through others harming you. This good one that I am using here, she has tasted hell – is tasting it still, but it grows less. We will offer our prayers that it will disappear altogether. Thy prayers and my prayers and the prayers of all those who love her. There are millions who love her, for through her, millions have been converted into followers of the Jeculin peoples and their code and the code of the Great Almighty.

I have never seen the Holy Spirit. I would like to see the Holy Ghost, the Holy Flocen as you call him, and as we are learning to call him. We are far more contented and advanced now, for we are learning the truth which is different to what we believed was the truth in our own days. I have to tell you that there is only one path, a great, wide, white, glowing path, and once you have found that, you must not stray, for that is the path to Almighty God, that is the strength within you. The part of God that lives within you is seeking ever to get your feet upon that path, so that when the time comes for your body to be of no more use to your soul and spirit, then will the soul and spirit be able to continue upon the path, but if you have not found it, then no doubt the soul and spirit will have to be reborn. I have dreaded that I might have to be reborn, but it seems that I have slept nearly 2,000 years until Solomon awoke me and said, 'Come, my son. We have much to teach you of other worlds, of other lives and a greater truth of living!' Since then, I have been learning and have taken with me all my brothers and sisters that I could gather, that they might also know the way to the great, white holy path.

We have had glimpses of queer vessels shooting across the sky, but in our ignorance, we believed them to be a dying star. I cannot claim that I have recognised any such craft as you describe, though I would dearly love to do so. I can claim to have met many people from other planets, which in my day we did not believe in. We did not have electricity and no means of illumination at that time, except by flamboys or candles. Flamboys were large sticks with a heavy knob on the top which was dipped in some oil which we used to keep the floating lights burning in oil lamps.

I have a long beard which is worrying me at the moment, for I should have had it dressed before I came to see you, and I have long hair parted in the middle, which I keep pulling off my face to stop it from hiding my features. I wear a long, white robe which is trimmed with gold embroidery, with large, bell-shaped sleeves which trail to the ground, which makes it a little dirty at times, and sandal shoes. Upon my hands I have two rings which are different to these on her hands. One resembles a scarab and the other is very large and set in heavy silver. It is a stone that you call moonstone. They are both very heavy and weigh the hands down.

It was only because we were the first believers in Jesus that we were called the apostles. We went out into the countryside, not always with him, sometimes alone, and we would call people to us to listen, while we repeated the words that he had taught us, and we shouted them upon the hillsides, so that they could be heard far and wide. The story of the feeding of the multitude in the Bible is grossly exaggerated. There were many fishermen and the fish came. There were only a few to start with, but as it became obvious that more were needed, the fishermen rushed away and got more and more fish. The people who were able to do so and who had sufficient gave their loaves. We did not consider it a miracle, except that so many were able so easily to catch so many fish, and that so many were able to willingly forgo their own provisions to provide so many loaves. That was the miracle, for people in those days were so mean and would no doubt be called stingy. They would not part with their belongings, but for Jesus they did. I have not seen water turned into wine, nor have I seen the seas parted, but then perhaps I was not present at that time. I will not say that it did not part, nor will I say that water was not turned to wine, only that I did not see it.

We all saw Jesus after he was supposed to be dead. Women, in particular Mary Magdalen (Maudlin, we called her. In fact, she was called Miriam, as was the mother of Jesus) they were wiping his lips with the juice from berries which gave him, as he licked it in, a sleeping draught, which helped him to endure the great pain of being nailed upon the cross, and they did place a crown of thorns upon his brow which did puncture his head, and the blood ran down his face and into his eyes and even into his own mouth. They did slit his breast where they attempted to expose his heart. Many others were treated in exactly the same way, the difference being that since he was called the King of the Jews and it was the Jews who denounced him, he was nailed upon the cross, whereas the others were thonged to the cross, and therefore he died a slower and more painful death. But he did not die on the cross. Unconscious, yes – presumed dead, because they knew no better, but we knew better. Of his manner of passing, none of us truly know. We know he was within the tomb and that we had placed therein bread, wine and water for him, should he need it, which he did, for he revived, though tattered and torn and bleeding profusely from head, hands and feet and upon the breast. We rolled away the stone (the Marys – the mother, the Maudlin – and some of us disciples who had denied him, and tried to make up for our wicked denials of being part of his hierarchy). We rolled away the stone, and he came forth, bleeding but alive. He sent us on our different ways, and told us that we must continue to teach all that he had taught us, to speak all the words we had heard him speak upon the hillsides, to gather the people and preach to them, and if we were forced to die for doing so, then we must die bravely. After that, we saw him no more – he just disappeared. Whether the Miriams knew or not we could not tell. If they did, they would not speak. It was as if their tongues were cut from their mouths, for they spoke no word. Joseph also disappeared (Joseph was the Earth father). He too was seen no more. If you wish to know more of what happened at that time, you will have to ask my Lord, Jesus, if he should come to you again, but I do not think he will wish you to ask him that. I feel you should let him keep just one of his secrets.

You know of course, they say he will come again. If he comes again, you will know him, for his eyes are so strange. They could not disguise themselves from you. They are blue and they are not the eyes of an ordinary man. You may be right that he was from another planet, but I cannot confirm it. One thing is certain – he has a great soul and, looking into his eyes, you will have to follow him.

I must leave. I have enjoyed this visit, and I am grateful that you have received me and listened. I am also most grateful to this dear woman of your world who devotes herself so unselfishly to this work that she does, and she does it for the Great Almighty and the Holy Flocen. Unto her I wish to say my deepest gratitude for allowing the use of this body and voice, for allowing me to converse with you, my brothers and sisters. God be with you always. Bless them all, dear God. Farewell my friends. May God be with you in all you say and do.

157

ELIJAH

---

8 April 1979 (1st day of 01)

Soskris dear sons and daughters, brothers and sisters. Soskris to you all. I have not been with you for many years. I am called Elijah. I was and still am a man of the people, but a holy man. A man who believes as you believe and wanted to teach as you now teach, who was a chosen child as you are chosen children, for you now are called the holy Children of Light, which is a great honour and one that I never attained. I was alone in my beliefs for none would believe me. I tried to teach them but they would not listen to me. You are having the same difficulties but you do not go out as I did amongst the people and shout from the hillsides, 'Come to me and listen to the words of God!' Times have changed, but I know of a place where you can do this. It is in the Hyde Park in London and you are allowed to go amongst the people and speak your words and if they shout you down or even stone you, stand steadfast and say your piece, each of you upholding the speaker. Where there will be one to speak, there will be many to stand behind the speaker and protect the speaker. Each of you are capable of doing this thing. Whether you will or will not, time alone can tell. I am anxious for you to have more converts for I failed miserably but you have already done a great work of conversion, spiritwise. I have followed the Jeculins so I am quite entitled to say Soskris.

I do not doubt that my words are in the Bible, but who reads the Bible and believes in it now? Very few. Many read it, but the words do not sink into their brains – they skim over the words and take not the meaning, find not the truth that lies within them and the Bible has been greatly altered since my day. It is indeed a masterpiece of covering up the truth with so many words. We had not so many words – we could not have stored the scrolls if we had.

I wish to speak to you of the people that you say have no spirit of love (Kari-Naris). You show much pity for them, but I feel that you must be wrong for they must have a spirit of love if they are loving people at all,

158

even if they have no souls. They have a spirit while they exist, but I think they must have a much longer lifetime than we have. Four thousand years is a long life and how do they manage to keep themselves young? If they did not have these rejuvenating baths that you speak of they would be like wrinkled walnuts after the first thousand years had passed. Did she not once, very long ago, write music about the secret of the marble baths? How did she gain that knowledge? She must have had some telepathic communication to be able to write that story. Even if this is not so, the story has a good, logical way of thinking. If you do as you are supposed to do and then do what you are not supposed to do, is it not philosophically right that you should be changed to a statue? I do not agree that it is harsh, if you break the rules.

I am interested in these people because I think they should have souls. I think a concerted effort should be made that we should ask that spirits be given to these people. You shock me greatly when you speak of their incestuous way of life. I was the leader of our people in my time but I would permit no incest to be allowed. Always, since time immemorial, no incest has been permitted between father and daughter, brother and sister or mother and son – it is the most wicked of acts that can be committed. Can we do nothing to help them? If they are forming a rebellion, then they are on their way to salvation. I think I must call for a great meeting and call for many, many people to support me in this, that we shall attempt to save these people from themselves or from their leader. I am a controller. I can call on many, many people, all sorts of people from this planet, but not on people from other planets, but this I understand you can do and this is why you are called the Children of Light. You have been chosen to do this work, and if your progress is slow, you must not blame yourselves for progress is bound to be slow under such circumstances where you have no pulpits to preach from, no open air places where you may go to preach, except the one that I have mentioned. There you would find many to follow you, but you would have to build your temple near to the place where they can go, for they would not be able to travel the number of miles even though you now have very modern equipment to travel with. I have learned a lot about you and I see that at times our ways were much better – not so evil. We had a little fighting at times but not a great deal; they were religious wars mostly. In the name of Our Father, war is wrong. Crusades were wrong for they fought in the name of God. The real problem is that there are too many controllers of too many little countries. They should all amalgamate as one.

As I told you when I came in, I am old and grow easily weary. Also there is one waiting without who must be admitted, but I can only say to you that before any other person is allowed to speak you must give your medium a rest for she is tired. You use her too much and expect too much of her under difficult circumstances, which we will not do, so make sure she rests before receiving another contact. I say to you Soskris, my children, Soskris dear brothers and sisters. I love you, for I can see you are good and holy people. Farewell. I shall bring her back.

SOLOMON
(Present Civilisation BC Earth)

---

13 November 1990

I have been with you before – long, long, ago. I do not think I have used this method of speech before. I used to contact you on what you called the board.

Yes. The ouija board.

My name is Solomon.

Not our great father Solomon?

Yes.

And you came in like an ordinary person.

I am an ordinary person. I am old. Ancient. Just another person. Just another spirit. It was many years since I was a living person so I have forgotten many things. I can remember all that you have taught me. It is so many years since I last contacted you and those others of your circle. I am to greet you all for you were my children. My household. But I do not see many here now. I see many spirits in your spiritual congregation but not many people like you used to have when you were in another building. Some have passed on I have been told. It is only a short few years that we are allotted. Not ever long enough to do all the things we wish to do. We are but playthings of the gods and I should not say that for it is wrong. It is from my day that we always said such things and it has been handed down to you.

Solomon, I would like to say, as you know, we were at loggerheads at the start of our research, but you have always had a special place in our hearts. Our affections and our love for you is unchanged and it was a day of great joy when you came on our side.

I must really admit I thought you were taking the path to the devil. Now I know there is no devil. Your path is good, white and clear and I am proud to walk it with you. I am proud that my children have found the light that I

161

could not in my living day find. I sought it. Yes, I sought it, as did all of my people. As did you in those days. My music girl (**reference to Nita**). An old woman now. Older than I when I passed from my life. I will come for her when she will die. I will not see her perhaps, but I will hope that perhaps we shall be reunited.

I believe I was Master of the Baths?

That is right and an honoured position it was. For only a very trusted servant can be in such a position. Only a very trusted soul who is essentially close to his king . . . I have learnt much since the old days when I spoke with you on the board when we made – passed messages of writing. I have tried to learn your ways and forget my old – what was it that you said I was? Obstinate perhaps.

Yes, obstinate, but you believed in what you were doing was for the good. For right, which is understandable.

We all have our own beliefs.

Do you receive any tuition from Jeculins?

No. It comes in various ways, but not direct. I have never been able to open myself sufficiently to receive these people that you call planet people.

It will come in time.

No, I do not think I will alter now. I think I am set in my ways for I am ancient, but not so ancient as my little Tethri, my little music lady.

Is her spirit older than yours?

No. Perhaps not, but her living years are. I suppose her spirit is much the same as mine. I think she came in my times, as did you. You may have had lives before. I do not know. Someone once told me that they thought you came from other planets. And perhaps she also came from another planet. I mean Tethri.

That would be before those times. The times of Tethri.

Yes, I think so.

Do you recall what my name was?

No, I do not, but then I only know because she was my child and also the little one that you call Teresi. Yes, a beautiful life from long ago, but so misled in our beliefs. So dogmatic in our ways.

There are still many people like that in present day Earth.

I see in you, I see the brightness of your lights, therefore I know that you must be good and I am proud to be with you. I am proud to walk where you walk, that I may be as you are. For although once I was called King, I am now nothing but a spirit. No King.

You are the leader of your people surely.

162

What people?

The spirit people of your age.

They've all been born again as you have. Only I do not get born again.

Would you like to have been?

No. I don't think I would. I have had to learn your new language, you know that don't you?

Yes, I realise that. You speak it well.

I have been studying it a long time. The language is so different to that which we had. But that is understandable – the world changes. The people change. The lives change. The desires and the content changes. People no longer revere the same things as we did, but they have perhaps better things to look to although many of your times would not look to anything. They are almost lost people. Lost in the wilderness of unknowing. Not knowing where they are going. Only the wise ones such as yourselves who have helped me to find the right path. You know. She knows. And the dear old one. He's gone. He was of my fighting men. Oh yes, in the ranks of my protectors.

Was he of your household personal guard?

Oh yes, yes and I am sorry that he has left you, but I think perhaps he is in a better life. I have not found him, but then I am not likely to find him, I am from another time. Another age.

Do you yourself require permission to leave your plane?

No. I am still sufficiently in control to be able to say I can do what I want. But I am no longer King. Once a King, but not always. I must leave you now for I am tired. I am grateful for this opportunity to speak with you instead of to write to you (*reference to ouija*). But it was mostly guessing what I was trying to say, but this is different. This is very kind of my Tethri to allow me to utilise her voice. I hear your friend has gone to sleep.

Sounds as though he's dropped off

Yes. Bless him. He was not of my people. I must leave you. Keep forever to your beautiful white path and do not forget to tell my Tethri I am grateful.

Your voice is recorded and she will hear it played again.

I do not know what you mean by recorded.

A recording machine recording your words.

I do not know there was such a thing. Well, there are many things I do not understand. I do know you have some things which you call wireless, television, which I do not understand at all. I think it is very, very frightening . . . and voices and pictures can go like that through the air. To me it is unnatural, but I suppose you understand it.

163

It's unnatural to your times, but natural to ours. The difference of ages.

I suppose because of that I must accept it, as you have accepted it.

Yes. You are born to it and you grow up with it and then it's part of your life.

And now I have to go from you.

We have been honoured by your visit, Solomon.

I hope you will let me come another time, but it will be some long while before I will be able to return again for it takes me a very long time to get here. Remember I come from over the centuries. You may not understand now, but it is a lot of travelling.

Perhaps another dimension is involved?

I cannot answer that question. I am not yet sufficiently knowledgeable to answer any questions of that nature. May God be always with you blessed children. Blessed, blessed children.

And may the love of The Almighty help you on your return.

I thank you. I thank you, my son . . .

CILLATONE

(Female Spirit of Wol, Second Civilisation of Earth)

21 November 1978

Do you remember me? I came long ago, when you were beginners in this exciting experience. I am called Cillatone. Soskris. I love you all, as I know does dear Athena and also the others of earlier times, such as dear Mené. We come often to watch you and listen to your words, and we are excited at some of the things you have learned, as your visitors teach you of their own planets. I am of this Earth, of course, but not as you know it, so therefore when you ask if I am of this Earth ... Yes and no. No, I am not of your time. I am of Wol. It is so long ago, during the Second Civilisation of this world, and it is such a long time to be a spirit.

It is such a long time since we have contacted you, but we are told that you must give way to new spirits that come from the other worlds, other planets, for there is not enough time for you to receive all that come. Therefore we must not intrude, or prevent any from being able to speak. At this moment I was informed by your protector, Peter, that there were no important visitors from other planets waiting to make contact, and so I am permitted to speak with you for a short while and tell you how we all still love you and miss the contacts we used to be able to have with you, when it was free for anyone to jump in on the board. It is different now there are speech contacts, for there were many who could not spell, so did not attempt to use the board, and there are still many who do not know the language very explicitly. Indeed, it is easier to speak a language than to write it – I find it so, and I am sure that most of your other contacts do also, though a lot of your words are very misleading, and would be greatly preferred by most people if they were pronounced exactly as they look if you see the writing, or if we are speaking and wish to write what we have said, it is difficult for us to be able to spell the words. It has never been easy, making contact with you, but now it is!

165

I am speaking through dear Nitesi and she is wide awake, although she is standing aside and allowing me to use all of her being, as well as her voice, and I can if I wish use her eyes. I find the light is too brilliant for me, and would prefer it if it were not so brilliant, then I could open her eyes and look at you. That is much better! Now I will open the eyes and see. Yes, I see. Hello, Normesi, hello, Teresi. So few here, except the unseen ones. I can see them. There are many here. You may hold my hand if you wish. Take hands together – then will we have a circle. Now, Nitesi is here at the side of this seat and I wish to hold her hand. She will then be joined to you through me and through you to Normesi. Normesi, you may put your hand upon my arm, and we are all now joined as one. It is only her spirit that is here, you realise – she has stepped her spirit out of her body. She might be listening, but I am not sure of that.

I am looking at a new place, for I have not been here before. I have been to the big place, where there was a tall tower and a large, tall room, with high ceiling and a little more ornate than this room, but not so comfortably cosy. I am pleased to see this instrument is still here – I hope she still plays it frequently? I am glad of that. We used to smoke, but not in the same manner as you. There was a long tube and it had two bowls with water.

I have certain knowledge of the distress of Nitesi, for which I am very sorry. I am unhappy for you, for I feel your unhappiness, and I know you are taking care of Nitesi, Teresi. It is known to us and we are most sad and sorry. We wish we could help, but there is no way to help, for as you know, Athena suffered in much the same way for many thousands, perhaps a million years. But she kept her faith, and in the end they were together, not as husband and wife, but as true mated spirits. Spiritual love is greater than physical love. Physical love is necessary upon this Earth, but is not looked upon kindly by peoples of other planets, for they seem to observe and think it unclean. But then, other planets are so much more advanced and so much more able to achieve things that we have never been able to attempt. Such as the generations of people that have been born on other planets without the help of man or woman, except by the production of the seeds, which are put together and make the finest, choicest, almost perfect beings.

When I was very young I thought that physical love was the most beautiful thing, for it was the normal manner to go about things. We did not make quite such a fetish of it as you of this age seem to do. We were more restrained, and chiefly using our abilities to make our babies. We all loved our babies dearly and everyone, men and women, were never satisfied until they had made their babies. One was never enough. We had

166

many. I think I had eight – I seem to remember eight. Athena did not have any, for she loved so well, but could not be a queen with someone who was not of royal blood. She would not accept any other person to be her mate. We did not have marriage, as you conduct it, though we did have worship places, temples you would call them, where lived the sacred people, the high people who lived only for religion. They were both male and female and these were permitted to mate together, within the temple. We were permitted to go to the temple and have a type of ceremony which ended in a joining of bodies, whereupon were we as you would call married, and that took place in the temple before the assembled priests and priestesses and before the royalty of the time – the controllers and royal families. Then was a marriage complete, when the witnessing of the physical was over and recorded. After that, we would stay together for the rest of our lives. There was no such thing as divorce or separation, for you would be punished if you attempted to do such a wicked thing. Once you have mated with your perfect mate, you have made your choice for life, and only death can break it and it is ideal. Do not marry until you are certain that you have found the one that is perfect for you. No hurrying into mating, or mating behind trees, or in fields, or in houses or palaces even – the first mating must be in the temple, and witnessed by all those who are proper to be there. One does not mind this, for it is a great privilege to have them witness your mating. Usually with the first mating is a baby created, and if the baby is not created with the first mating, you will return to the temple, but not needing the royalty to be present – only a few of the high priests and priestesses, not the whole lot of them, but just a few to witness the making of a baby. The making of a baby is indeed a holy thing, for within each person lies the ability to create a child. There is the seed within the man that meets the seed within the woman, and that is surely holy, that those two seeds should come together to make a tiny baby. It is God's great design. It is the same with animals and flowers and trees, and anything you can name. Happy were we to be allowed to make our mates in that way and have it observed by the highest in the land.

There were many cities, but only one ruler. I was the chief attendant to our sweet and lovely queen. This language is a bastard language. It is a mixture of many languages of your new world. I say your new world, for it is nothing like our old world. If you could find our old world, such riches would be yours, for what we thought common stones you would now consider to be valuable, precious gems of immense wealth, which we did not need. We thought the things that you now think to be more common, such as iron, to be very valuable. It was worked most intricately, and was

167

made into beautiful objects, and into things so small that you could wear them on your fingers. How strange it is that it is now so common, and all those gems you think so precious we used for our building blocks, and all that gold and silver that we built our houses of and laid upon the roads for our chariots to pass over. It is true that iron rusts, whereas gold does not – that is why we built our houses of gold and silver, so they would not fall down. We had not thought of using things such as you use – we would not demolish a tree to build a house. Nor yet would we know or ever think of using what you call bricks and mortar. They did not exist for us.

I wish to bring you the love of all those you know. All those wish to be engulfed in your love, which once you gave us, and I think you are still giving us. They are certainly always remembering you all. I am sorry to see that there are not many of you here, although there are a number of unseen Spiritual and Astral people. I can see quite a number around, some wraith-like and others more solid. I think the wraith-like ones must be the Astrals.

I will not stay longer now. I was happy to find that you did remember me, and I must say that when I go back and tell our dear Athena, she is almost certain to want to come and speak with you, for it is so much nicer than writing out words that we hardly know how to spell upon your board. I like this much better. I want to thank you, Nita, and I will pray that you will be happy soon. Try to smile a little, try not to look so unhappy. Blessings upon you all. Much love. I bid you farewell. I love you all. Farewell, dear friends.

MINOA

(Male Spirit, Second Earth Civilisation)

27 May 1979

My name is Minoa, and I come from the Second Earth Civilisation, after Athena, after the banning of the battle games. I was a Sedlar (ruler) while I lived and am still a Sedlar in afterlife. I have my community around me, the peoples of my time. I do not have any contact with Mené, nor yet Athena. I know of them, but I do not meet with them due to the time barriers.

I have had much time to learn your language, for I commenced to listen to you at the time when you were living in another house. I have been sitting within your room on many occasions when you have had meetings and I have listened to your talk so I could learn your language, for ours was very different. I think that the language that was in use at the time of my ruling was different even from the time of Mené.

I had a great city which was not Mené's city. It was a great place with millions and millions of inhabitants and they were all very good, loving people, as we all have been throughout our whole civilisation. There were many Sedlars after I, there have been so many that I cannot name them for you. They will no doubt come to visit you at some time, for all are interested in your great beam. Your beam apparently cuts through the time barriers, or we could not come to you.

We had lighting, but it was produced by a method using gas and we had little lamps that hung here and there with shining blue light caused by this gas. The gas came from the ground and we piped it. It was discovered during my reign and brought to great use throughout my large country for heating and lighting and for making of materials and objects, earthenware and varying things. What happened after my time is not for me to relate – it is for another, after my time. We had much beautiful pottery which was mined from clay in the earth and it was highly painted and decorated and

169

much treasured. Gold was plentiful and was used for building, for paving stones. Silver was also used. Iron was scarce and became very precious. Very delicate ironwork was wrought and treasured highly by the people who possessed it. It was treated with a certain manner of painting to prevent rusting, with certain preservatives in the paint that would keep the iron restored. I know that you now have a lack of precious stones, whereas we used them to build with, for they were not precious to us.

We had very happy lives and were quite learned people. We very much enjoyed our books which were made of vellum, but were handwritten and loaned or passed one to the other, that education might not be lacking and that one might share one's treasure with one's dearest friends. That friend would then share it with another dear friend and perhaps you might get it back eventually and perhaps not. It did not matter, for we loved each other dearly and what was mine was yours and vice versa. This is the happy way to live – we had a happy world, a happy time.

There were, in my time, other people coming of other races. I know not whence they came – they might have come from the skies. We never saw any craft, but these were strangers to us. We made them happy and welcome within our life-circle. They wore silver suits, and some of them could not remove their suits without they disappear for a while and they would return with ordinary flesh, such as you or I. We accepted such miracles because many miracles happened in our time. Anything that came that was a miracle, we would bow down before God and give thanks that such a miracle had been presented to us. There is only one God of the universe and there has only ever been one God. We know also that the stars hold other people.

Sedlars are usually men, although there have been some lady Sedlars. Athena was one of the greatest Sedlars and was a very fine lady no doubt, for in our history she goes down very highly rated. A beautiful lady of a beautiful time, but a sad lady, for she loved and her love could not be consummated.

Our cities were not buried until long after my time. The lost cities of the world – they are now lost for ever. You could never mine so low that you could reach them. It was over a long and gradual period that more and more of the world got eaten up with this rock, earth and sand. There were many, many mountains near to us, impossible to climb. There are many deserts upon this world and none knows what lies beneath them. Perhaps some day, one will come to teach you of this.

I will not stay longer with you on this occasion, but I thank you for receiving me in this manner. I will again come. It might not be telepathically but spiritually, when I will come through the medium and use my own voice instead of hers. I would like to say the word you always say. Soskris, dear brothers and sisters, for I know this means a blessing. God be with you, and I will leave my love with you. Goodbye for now.

MENÉ

(Great King of Wol, the Second Civilisation of Earth)

---

17 February 1980

For so long we have known each other. I take this opportunity to speak. I wish to convey many things to you. I am your old friend and brother Mené. I thank you for your welcome for I love you well. You are indeed my beloved friends and, as I said originally, my very precious ones for you are my only contact with this your present time. This medium, now Nitesi as you call her. She is what we call God-sent for we cannot operate or speak with you without her for you have trained no other to complement her uses or to take over from her should she not be able to continue for any reason. So you too should be thankful that you have her. I am going to speak to you now on something I have just been listening to. I have heard you speak of God. How He may have many guises. How He may wear many different types of clothing. Do you not realise as I now realise there is no guise for God Almighty, no clothes for God Almighty for God Almighty is a great and magnificent power and not a person. Speak now of The Holy Flocen for he can appear in any shape or form at any time and in many places at one time, which is an ability which is beyond any other spirit. I have come to learn all these things through your intervention when you taught me to know the truth of our true God. You remember how you taught me and I have listened well and learned much since that perhaps even you do not know. I have had from the blessed Icla much, much information and many, many long hours of tuition and help and instruction. We have bridged that great gap between my time and hers. To her it means nothing. She can go anywhere into any time. I now also can go, not anywhere altogether but many places and in many times. This I have found has taught me much and much that I will not have the time to tell you all about. I have progressed forward, not right to your time, but near to your time, and have learned much of my own Earth civilisation that

172

I had not realised. I am trying to be emphatic in my speech although as a general rule I am gentle of tongue, but I feel I must make you understand and only by emphasis can I do this. Yes, it is strange that I speak this tongue that you now have, so well. Whereas our tongue was so different when I lived. It has been a joyful duty to learn to speak your language properly and also to be able to speak with the great Icla. It has been a link between us that she can use your language and has helped me to use your language so much more fluently than I used when I have been with you before. I have been with you many times and you have guessed many of my words before they were ever spoken and sometimes I have said 'yes' meaning somewhere near right and sometimes, because I have not known the right word to correct you, I have allowed you to assume that what you said was correct.

You are referring to the inconsistencies of the ouija board.

I am and I am so happy you have discarded it, as are all those who make contact with you now. For it is far better to be able to utilise this body and this voice of our dear friend to whom we owe so much, all of us. Not just you here in this room, but us who utilise her. All of those from other planets are all grateful that you have such a fine medium. Such a rare-type medium. Still I am talking to you about God, Almighty God. I know you have taught me about Almighty God which I did not know then. You remember, no doubt, that we were Sun Followers. We still love the sun, so we realise in your present day how much you need the sun and you too must love the sun. For without the sun your many sowings would never come to fruit. You would be without much that you so greatly need. But there must come a time for you in the future, maybe sooner than you think, when you will learn that you can eat quite comfortably without any killing and without taking living growing things to cook and put within your stomachs to feed your bodies and keep them, as you think, healthy. There are far healthier ways and this will come to you in time and as I have said maybe before you really expect it. There will be a great movement and you are the beginning of that great movement, this I have learned. And because you are the beginning I bow to you and I realise that you are the holy people that were chosen to become the leaders and you could not have been given such a wondrous name as 'Children of Light' if you had not earned and deserved such a name. It is not for me to preach to you. King I may be, or was, yet are you in so many ways far above me, though you call yourselves little people, for you have advanced in ways that I could not advance. Were I to be born again I would indeed advance with you and would like to be born again. As it seems I have been too good in

173

my life and when you have been too good you cannot get born again. Sometimes I feel it to be a pity, for I feel there is much I could do more than I did in my own lifetime. In your sort of time I could do much to help, not maybe as a king, just as a person like yourselves.

Aren't you a free spirit now?

I am not yet free.

We understand that a free spirit can request to be born again.

When I have been made an entirely free spirit then may I ask to be born again, but that time is not yet. I must still wait a while and continue to take and make many more conversions as well as receive much more instruction. There is a new lady Icla now.

Yes, we know.

Not like our sweet, beloved old Icla, but clever and just and helpul, if not so loving as our sweet old Icla.

She gave me the impression of being a little more proper, formal.

I know what you mean. Yes, that is the correct word and with people such as I, that she knows to have been a king, although I would say perhaps, I was a chieftan. She will treat me very formally as will anyone who is under her command and I would rather they were as you and speak normally in friendly, kindly, loving ways, for that is my nature just as it is the nature of this good medium that I have. Friendly, kindly and very loving. So we must try to conform to the way they have set for us and behave in a manner they obviously desire us to behave in, but it is not entirely to my liking or for that matter friends of ours, like Athena. We know that some formality should be used with past kings or queens.

(Tape ran out)

THE AFTER DEATH EXPERIENCE

The greatest fear for living people throughout every generation has always been the fear of death – death of the body they inhabit. For far too many their body is the absolute be-all. When the time comes for that body to die, they assume a fatalistic attitude and hope and pray for their continuance as was promised by a religion some had only half believed in.

Both Christian and Moslem religions have sprung up from the Seeds of Truth so liberally scattered first by Jesus then the prophet Mohammed so many centuries ago, but instead of being cultivated in order to find the Greater Truth, the Church has allowed the seedlings to wither and become jaded, while the mosque has turned the flower into a weed. The result is that religion has become dull and boring to many in the West who would rather seek after more exciting bodily pursuits. In the East, Muslim extremist perverts seek to inflict their own bitter, twisted version of a bountiful, loving God's will on what they consider to be a dissolute West. By virtue of their religious indoctrination they appear to face death with a certain equanimity which is sadly lacking in the West.

In an attempt to redress the balance, part of Circle research was dedicated to asking spirits what happened to them after they 'died'. Inevitably, while some were offended and others were unable to recall or did not want to, there were enough who spoke readily of what they could remember.

The following group of selected transcripts are dedicated with gratitude to all those bold spirits who were unafraid of baring the personal secret of their own entry into the spiritual dimension.

HAROLD WATKINS
(Male Earth Spirit)

---

5 October 1982

Thank you for allowing me to use this body, this person. Thank you for sitting to wait for such as I to speak to you. Greetings to you all. Let me say I ask a blessing upon you. I ask that God's love be ever with you. I think you are already known as holy people, but I am a stranger here. I am only here because I find warmth in entering this zone. I think you call zone. Once was told of it. Big bright zone, but not any longer. I cannot describe the way it is, no longer – it is wavering. It is no longer this solid thing which was described to me and I do not see all those people I was told I would find here. There are no people here but you. There is a man hovering nearby.

Peter, our guardian.

Perhaps that is him, I do not know for sure. I think I talk with you only short while because I have no real message.

Did you come from another planet?

No, I am from – what planet?

We receive many people from other planets throughout the galaxies.

What planets? Where are they?

You must have looked at the night sky during your lifetime. All the stars you see are planets. This is what we are taught by our friends.

And you believe them? I think someone is hoaxing you. You don't think so?

When you go have a word with Peter who probably let you through.

He didn't let me through, I came.

He has seen and witnessed much of our meetings over the years. Have a chat with him.

Well, I will try to keep an open mind, but I cannot honestly say I believe in other planets.

176

How long is it since you passed over?
20 years.
What is your name?
Harold Watkins.
Are you local to the area?
No. Nottingham. I was quite old when I passed on. When I say quite old, I was 78 which is a fair age for anyone. I feel stronger now than I felt when I was alive. As a spirit I have a stronger life than I had as a living person. We do not suffer here like we used to suffer on Earth. Healthwise I was poorly – I'm not poorly now. I feel younger than 78.
Did you pass in your sleep?
Yes, I did, but my health wasn't too good. Chesty troubles and rheumaticky.
They say it's a lovely way to pass over, in your sleep. Do you have any recall of that?
No. None at all.
What was the first thing you became aware of?
Somebody finding me. Somebody meeting me and leading me off. Somebody saying, 'Come along, we're ready for you. We're waiting for you.' I didn't really bother about leaving my body. The only trouble was when I looked back and saw those that I had left behind. I was allowed to see them. I think you can if you ask. I had a look at the old body lying there and thought 'poor old feller' then laughed because it was me. I'm just a Nosy Parker really. I came around here and didn't know I was going to talk to anybody, although I have heard about you people. I thought I'd have a look at this wonderful zone I'd been told about.
Is our circle known throughout many planes?
Well, some people talk about it. I expect it is people that have been here.
You see, through various reasons, illness and suchlike, this is only our third meeting in about the last three months and through this we have lost our spirit congregation.
I have to go.

WILHELMINA

(Female Spirit, Earth)

---

2 October 1990

I am called Wilhelmina and I am an Earth person. I come with a message from the brother of Nita. Not the one who passed most recently. That is right, the one who is called Thomas. He is not here with us, but he has asked that a place be kept here for him as he always used to have. I am presuming that he had a special place to sit. He said he wishes for all of you to know that he loves you well. All of you and in particular his dear sister. He is quite happy and very active and no longer old, for we are not old when we get here. We are young again and vibrant, capable and busy. I also give you much love. I have been here before, but not to speak. I have been passed for quite some while.

Since the Second World War?

Oh yes, after that. It's pretty hard to guess time here. It's quite different here, there's no need to count time, but remembering, it seems to me it must be perhaps nearly 40 years ago that I passed away. I was just an ordinary housewife. I wasn't anything very special, but I did not live in the area which you now are. I lived in a town called Winchester. I had illness – a long illness and really was quite pleased to pass. I was quite ageing when I passed, but I am not aged now.

Can you recall when you left your body?

Yes, I do just remember looking down.

What did you have to do then to really get away?

I was taken away.

You were met by somebody?

Yes, by you call – we call – angels.

Winged persons.

Yes. I was escorted.

There was no tunnel?

No. What tunnel?

Well, some people have experienced that they have to go through a tunnel.

Oh, you're talking of the blackness. It isn't really a tunnel. Some may think it is a tunnel, but it isn't.

What the Bible calls the valley of the shadow of death.

Perhaps that is what it is. I passed through it quickly, buoyed on beautiful wings of others – and I was quite pleased to leave that poor old body.

(Transcript abridged)

HELEN
(Female Spirit, Earth)

---

9 October 1990

I greet you with love. That was a very, very interesting reading. I have listened to it before I came into Nita's body. It must be beautiful to go there. Of course, I suppose we of this planet are very backward compared to those who come to talk to you. I do not know when you had that person to talk to, but what a beautiful – I suppose – spirit person. It was an astral person, ah! I cannot see Astrals of course, but I do know that there are such things. I do know when Nita goes out of her body she goes astrally somewhere. It is very wonderful. I have never done an astral projection myself when I was alive. I wish I could have done. I would have liked to have gone some other place. I can go some other place now, but not very far. We're not allowed to go beyond one plane above us.

One below you as well, can't you?

Well, we don't want to go below but then I suppose there are other planes. Many planes, some of them very thin, some of them quite deep. You can go one higher if you're very good. Maybe two higher. Some people go up several higher straight away. What we call the special ones. We all do some wrong in our lifetimes, you know that, most of us from quite an early age, but some who die early never do any wrong. Some are meant to die early. Because of their short lease of life they don't have a long life expectancy. Though some have very long life expectancy. I had a good life, although I was not all that old when I passed over. We don't like to say dying. I was a wife and a mother. A young wife and a young mother and I had unfortunate birth and I did not survive it and my baby did not survive it.

So you passed over in childbirth?

Yes, and I was quite young, well not quite young, but not very old.

In your twenties I suppose.

180

No, thirties. I had three young children. I lived in a place not far from here called Wimborne and I passed away some many years ago. It was, I think, before the war started.

The Second World War?

Yes.

That's more than half a century.

Yes, it seems all of that to me, but I'm quite happy here. I'm used to it now and it's a life. It's a better life, but not enough to do. That is the only trouble.

Can you not study if you want to?

Yes, but I am not really a studying type. I never was very much of a studious person when I was alive and I don't think I am now. You don't change much you know. Whatever you were before you passed over, that is more-or-less what you are when you pass over. It's up to you.

The most fascinating thing that I would think to study is the true religion. The true religion is the most exciting thing in all life – because it is life.

You are talking about what you have learned over the past years and I know that you have been learning for many years now. Not as many years as I have been passed over, but for a lot of years.

Is there any glimmer of our knowledge on your plane?

No. We all know we are children of God. We know that. We are not as knowledgeable as you are for you have gained great knowledge, but I think you have been specially selected for that knowledge.

We are told this.

You've been told that. I thought you must have been, because it isn't everybody that has the privilege to learn all the wonderful things that you have learnt and I do know that you have learnt some wonderful things because I have been coming here to your circle over a great many years although I have never spoken to you before. One takes the opportunity when it arises. If nobody else was coming in and you really want to, you come in. But mostly, they're all too scared. You do have to pluck up your courage to come in and use someone else's body.

Could I ask you – you needn't answer if you don't want to – what you remember when you did pass over in childbirth?

I think I knew before I left the body that I would have to go. I think it was my time to go, but I don't think it was the time for my baby to go. My baby was born and lived a matter of some few minutes. So it did actually live.

It would have been better if it had been stillborn.

Yes. It would have been better if it had not have lived. But it passed with me. Round about the same time. It didn't come with me when I passed. It was received by some angelic people and I saw them bear my little boy away.

Did they speak to you?

No.

What did you do then?

I went in a long dark journey.

Was it like a tunnel?

No, it was like a big black cloud and then somebody came from somewhere – I don't know where – and helped me through.

When you were in the middle of it somebody came to you?

Yes. Somebody helped me through. I would like to have gone back, but they said, 'No, you can't go back.' I wanted to go back really to my body. I did not want to leave my husband. I did not want to leave my other children. My little boy and my little girl. I was only quite young, in my early thirties.

Can you recall what happened when you came out of the black cloud?

I came into the great brilliance of – I don't know how to describe it. It's like a most glorious light and gardens . . . so . . . so . . . I cannot explain them . . . It was like going into a beautiful . . . and then lots and lots of people started to gather around and some started to talk to me and to make me feel more comfortable, more wanted. And gradually I settled in there and I found I had quite a good life to lead, but I still don't think I ever had enough to do.

And that where you settled there – that was your present plane?

Yes.

Thank you very much, Helen. Quite absorbing really.

Well, I am trying to be as forthright as possible and I am trying to enlighten you because I know you are still inquisitive, though you are no longer called inquisitives. You are called The Children of Light now. But once you were called The Inquisitive Ones – and I knew you then. I also remember your friend Madcap Molly.

Is she still about?

Yes.

Does she come to this meeting?

No. She's not wanting to be involved in your learning of what you call Jeculin. There's lots don't want to be involved in that, although lots more who do. More do than don't. I am interested. I am very, very interested in anything that's appertaining to The Almighty and anything that's appertaining to being better than I am now. I think I am going to have another journey, but I've had a long time over here now. I hope I have a bit longer next time. Well, if it's a nice life I would like it to be longer. I think your medium is here, which means she will want to come in. So I will leave you.

Go with our love, Helen.

My thanks to the medium.

She will hear it on tape.

My thanks.

MARY
(Female Earth Spirit)

30 October 1990

I greet you in love and I must say it is nice to be here again. You don't recognise my voice? I have been before. My name is Mary. You do not remember Mary? I have come from quite some way. I do not stay here. I was a nurse in a London hospital. It was called St Mary's, Paddington. I don't stay here, I visit here. I go back to London.

To your old haunts, if you'll pardon the expression?

Oh yes, quite right. Good word, good word. I do remember you – you used to make funny remarks before. I think I was 42 when I passed on. I was a nurse still.

Did you pass naturally?

No, I didn't. I was run over. How many people get run over. It's a shame really isn't it, because we haven't done our full term of life. Accidental death. We're not meant to go then. It's not our time.

Can you remember what happened as you left your body?

No, too long ago. It's a long time ago now that I was run over. It's all right over here you know. Plenty of amusement – no not exactly amusement – interesting things. Only thing is you can't find your relatives. You know you've got relatives around who have passed on, but you never can find them.

Have you been on the plane above to look?

You're not allowed on the plane above. No, no. You have to earn the right. Well, I was a nurse, that's doing a good life's work isn't it. It's a hard life's work I can tell you that and I helped many, many poor old souls and young ones to pass on. I didn't realise what happens – I do now, of course. When you're still living you don't realise. Well, a few do like you people here. It's different after you pass on of course, you learn a lot. You gain knowledge that you don't know how you gain it. You don't necessarily

184

have to go anywhere to learn it. You just acquire it into your spiritual brain. There's a lot of unexplained things even after you pass on, my friend. I passed over and didn't realise anything at all about anything different, but it gradually came to me after time passed. You don't count time as we did on Earth and day and night doesn't mean anything. Hours don't mean anything. The thing is that once you've passed from one life to another you've got to start to live the new life fully and forget what the old life did or didn't do for you because it doesn't matter any more. There are some people who have passed over and they think they haven't done their job of work, so they have to keep on clinging to Earth for that reason, to try and keep coming back, which is silly of them because they can't do anything about it. It's their own spiritual mind or brain that keeps them earthbound. They feel they haven't achieved what they ought to have achieved in their lifetime, so they have to keep hanging on. They can't achieve it once they've passed over, so why hang on? They won't be told. It doesn't matter who tells them, they won't listen. Back they come. Do their haunting. Haunting. Silly word isn't it? Visiting is a better way of saying it.

Do you visit your relatives?

Well, I've not many left now. I think I must have been dead for about 40 years. There's nobody where I used to live that I could go to. Most of my friends were about my age and most of them are passed on now.

Have you seen any of them since?

No. I've got a lot of other friends, but not the ones I used to have when I was alive. I don't find many people to come and speak like this, I don't think there are many people that do this sort of receiving. There are lots of people who sit in circles with their hands touching and the lights all out. A little glimmer of red light somewhere or other. I don't like those places. They're eerie.

They're eerie to you?

Oh yeah, I don't like them at all. I have been to them before I passed on. I have been in one of those circles and you pay the woman ten bob or a pound. Ten bob as a rule. I don't think you have ten bob any more, do you?

No, fifty pence.

And you don't have half-crowns anymore. Ah well, I wouldn't know what to do if I was back, would I? I think I'm going to have another life, though. They say that you can go 50 Earth years, counting time.

Between lives?

Yes. I don't know where or what or when, but I've got a feeling it's coming on to me. Some people get born almost straight away again. There have been people who have passed over and not even had time to settle themselves into their new passed-on life before they've been escorted away to another life in another body. Hard going that is because you've got to start as a baby again.

So you're escorted to your new body as well as escorted from it?

Oh yes. Didn't you know that? Perhaps you never asked it. I'm glad you've learned something from me. I thought mine was a useless talk. I'm only filling in because there's nobody else that's got the gumption to come in and speak.

Do you remember what your surname was?

Yes. I was Miss Mary Wright, but I became married and I became Mary Sudan and my man, he lived quite a long time after me, but he's gone now and I haven't found him either. We're not so cliquey up here as we were on Earth.

When you pass over and it's not your time, do you feel the need to go and say goodbye?

You'd like to, but you can't.

You haven't the time?

No. It's not possible.

Someone waiting for you?

Usually, yes. They call them guides. They are very special people. They are highly trained and they are the kindliest of kindly people. We're not all alike. All spirits are different. Like categories. Some go to one place and some go to another. People like me – I'm just intermediary. I've got belief all right, but that's not it. It's what sort of life you've been living.

If you're a nasty person you go to a nasty plane where there are nasty people.

There aren't any nasty planes.

Well very low plane.

Yes, and those that belong to those planes will never see another plane unless they can be improved by very intensive teaching. These are the people that have to get born and born and born and born.

There's an incredible number of planes, you know Mary.

Yes, I do know this. I haven't been away from my own plane that I'm in now, but I do know there are a great many. I've got to leave you. She's coming back. Thanks for having me. Thank you. Lots of love and thank her too. Bye-bye.

WALTER
(Male Earth Spirit)

---

14 December 1993

Are you prepared for me?
You are an Earth person like us?
I was, yes. I was an old person. My name is Walter. I passed many years now. I have long rested. The spirit lives on, the soul is in the spirit, or the spirit is in the soul, whichever you wish to say and there is no death for the spirit. The soul is a little bit of The Almighty which we all have. We pass on to a new way of being, a new life or we just exist on another plane, some of us. I do but I can come back to this plane if I want. I was sad to hear of these people who live so long and to have such bad manners. (*Reference to a reading about Kari-Naris*). It is against the will of God.
It is all over now because that transcript I was reading was from 1979 and it is now 1993.
Is it indeed? That is news to me. I did not know. We have no time.
Well it's 1993 on the physical plane now.
If I was still alive I would be very old. (Chuckle.)
How old were you when your body ran out of power?
I was not quite so old as this medium, but she is a young old. She is young for her age although her health is not very good. I was 72 when I passed over and I was pretty worn out by that time.
Can you remember on your actual passing, sort of leaving the body. Did you have to go through a tunnel? We have asked different people this and different people have different experiences.
I think everybody has a different experience. I will try to tell you if it is any use to you. There was a time when my passing was to happen and they sat near and mourned before I was gone and then suddenly I was out of my body. I could see them there sitting round me and mourning but I wasn't there.
You were a little above them, were you?

Yes. The body was there. But you see the body is only a vessel to carry the spirit and the soul and when the spirit leaves, the soul leaves. Together they go and the body is no more. It has no further use and will decay in no time. It turns to worms if you leave it.

Did you recall what you did then, after looking down on yourself and your relatives?

I waited a while and I watched them for a while. Only a short while and then I thought well at last I am free and I can leave this place and leave this body behind, that I have no further use for it. I'm quite free and quite able to move without it and I travelled somewhere, I do not know. I'm not sure where.

Did you go through clouds or anything like that?

No. I went through an aperture and it was very dark and hollow.

You knew you had to go through there?

Yes. I knew it was my destination and did not hesitate to follow what I knew to be my destination. I don't think you have a choice. So I went into this place and I remained in this place for quite some while. I don't know how long. It might have been a year, or even more. Another year, I do not know because we do not count time. Now, I do not count time. You understand?

Yes, we know that.

And then eventually there was a great light came into this dark place and I flew towards it very swiftly. I didn't run, I flew. Because when you become a spirit you can fly. And when I finally reached – it took some while to reach – I think you might call it the exit. And when I finally got there it was so glorious I cannot possibly explain it to you. It was beyond any words and filled with the feeling of love. Filled with a great welcoming feel of love.

There were flowers, scenery?

No. There was bright light which you could not see anything in but the brightness, but you knew that it was welcoming you and that you could go into it and become part.

It wasn't the Hall of Time, was it?

It could be.

What did you do then, in this place?

I didn't do anything. I was free. I was happy. I was released. I was . . . I'd forgotten everything from my . . . the life I had just left. I could remember it now but then I did not remember anything. I just looked forward and not backward. I looked forward to become, to be with and of this great light. Is that making any sense to you?

188

Yes, it's making plenty of sense.

And then there were people come to me. Then I began to see that it was another place to live. Not exactly beyond the light, but encompassed in the light, but you don't see it immediately.

No, because you'd been in the dark.

Yes. And eventually, after some while you go beyond the impossible brightness and in the bearable brightness you can see people and a place to live. A place to be. And there are angels.

With wings?

Yes, and some of them come to you and they talk to you and question. And they decide where you have to go. But this was for me. I do not say it is like this for everyone.

It seems like some kind of reception centre.

Yes, it could be, but I cannot say that it is so for everyone.

We have heard different stories.

Because there are different people that I have met that have never even seen that beautiful light.

Perhaps they had the long tunnel or other things.

Yes. They did. But I had had this. When I went into the great brilliant light I felt buoyant and loved and welcomed and not ever afraid. Nothing, nothing feared me. And then there were the beautiful angels and they examined me verbally.

Did they ask you your beliefs?

Yes, and I told them and they said we will lead you to the place where you will go to rest. Which is like a renewal of the spirit.

Where did they take you, was it another sort of reception?

They are called planes.

Yes. Planes of existence. We know of them.

Yes, and one person will go to one and another person will go to another. It depends on what you have done with your life largely. If you have been a good and caring person. If you had been a kind and considerate person. If you had been a person who would help other people when they needed help, then there is a special place for you and those who have not done these things cannot go to those...

They go to low planes

Yes, and they are not so comfortable as where I was taken.

From what you tell me, I think you have been a good and kind person.

I was considered, I think, to be a good person. I was not to do with the Church, but I was a believer in God. I did not know God was love when I lived in my life, but I know now that God is in everything and is love, in everything. And when I went into that great blinding light, that was love and I felt the beauty of it and was sanctified and grateful. I cannot stay any longer because I am only allowed a certain length of time. I have to tell you that it's a great pleasure to come and speak through this very good person's body. Very grateful.

We are very pleased you did. We are very glad to talk to you. Are there many people on this wind-blown night, here?

No, not a great many, only a few were brave enough to. Perhaps those who stay around you more permanently. I am not a permanent one here. I have been before, but I have not stayed.

Are there some of them actually within the room?

I think there are, yes, but not many. Not many came.

We're holding another meeting next Tuesday, we hope.

Ah. Then I will tell everybody and ask them to tell everybody else that they find.

Thank you. Let's hope it's a nicer night.

I will say God bless you all, dear people. Thank you very much. It's a great and very exhilarating experience for me. I did not realise when I came that it would be so interesting.

You've made it very interesting for us too, Walter.

Oh thank you.

Thank you for talking to us.

May I come again?

You're welcome. Every spirit is welcome.

Ah. I have to bring you very good wishes from your friend. I think you call him Maurie. He told me when I was coming, 'Don't forget to say this.'

Mind the winds, Walter.

I will. I'll stay in your cone until the winds drop.

We know spirits can get blown around by them.

I don't want to be blown around. I'm a bit frail. Bye-bye.

FRANK
(Male Earth Spirit)

21 December 1993

Are you ready? Then I'll begin. You say that in one of your programmes.
Do you listen to the radio sometimes? Do you watch television?
I have plenty of time to watch television. It is an occupation for me and an entertainment. Don't like all the killing ones. I am not very young, so I don't move about a great deal. Having settled here I'm quite happy to be able to really keep her company (the medium) although she doesn't know I keep her company. My name is Frank. My real name is Francis, but nobody ever calls me Francis. They call me Frank. I passed over several years ago. I passed over when I had pneumonia.
Can you remember what happened to you when you passed over?
I don't really remember it very well. I'm not young you know I'm quite ancient although when – if I were to appear to you, which I can't because I'm doing this. If I were to appear and not do this, I would be as I was in my prime, when I first enjoyed my life. That is the way I would appear, not as I was when I passed on. When I passed on I was really decrepit and feeble. Useless to everybody. Good job I got the pneumonia so that I could pass on, because everybody found me a burden. Because I was 92 years of age, which is no young chicken. You feel better once you've passed over because you don't feel 92. You go back to the time when you thought it was the prime of your time. I can't really remember what happened to me, it was a long time ago and I was very ill. When you're very ill not much sinks in, but it was nice to be free and not to be ill any more. She's 82 and I think she thinks she'll be better off when she passes on (*reference to the medium*) and I expect she will be. She might have a long rest time, I don't know, but she won't have any repentance to do, for she's quite a good person. She's very well respected because of this work you do. And you have and she has

191

been doing for so long now. Without her you would not be able to have any contacts.

We have been given the name, the Children of Light has been bestowed on us.

I have heard this. I've been having a long talk with your good friend Maurie. He's not anywhere near my age. He's only a whippersnapper to me. He is Maurice Morris and he does like to be called Maurie though sometimes some people call him Mo. I don't get called anything but Old Frank.

Nita thought she saw some little figures walking she told me earlier.

I have heard there are little people, but I never saw any. But some people see them. I never ever saw one, but I have heard a lot about them. I do think they are about. Perhaps I would have been disbelieving when I was living. I didn't even think I would have an afterlife. I thought that was a lot of nonsense.

If you'd known what you do now, you would have liked to go over quicker?

Yes, because that last few years I was a nuisance to everybody. And to myself. And not so intelligent as I seem to feel now. I feel that my ability to think dropped away from me for the last few years of my living days. Her brain is as active now as when she was a young person. Her brain is very good but her body is wearing out although she is a lot better than she used to be. When I first came here and did not speak but came and sat and listened, 'cause I've learned a lot from listening here.

Yes, you will learn a lot.

Yes. Because you speak to people from other planets and it's wonderful to learn about them. That's something we could never learn about in our present life.

Can you see the Astrals – we have a lot of Astrals?

No. Spirits can't see Astrals. You have a lot of Earth spirits here who call this their home. Their place to be. They have, like me, grasped at something which is different as it's unusual. You see there are mediums and mediums we could go to. There are plenty of mediums we could go to, but I don't trust them.

Not much good then?

No, and they don't speak like you do to other people of other planets and that is the most interesting thing that could ever happen. It makes this place a special place.

You know why we speak to people of other planets?

Curiosity, I think.

192

Oh yes indeed. And love.

I think you must have what I didn't have when I was alive. You must have a great belief in the people of other planets.

We have. This is why they come to us.

I never had that. Never, never.

When they first came to us, we made them welcome with love and we believed them because spirits do not lie.

No. No spirit from any place whatsoever will ever lie.

Only an evil entity will lie.

I don't think there are such things, truly.

We don't have them round here. It's not a suitable place for them.

No. I think you are well protected from them. You are God's special children.

They (contacts) come to us because we believe them. They've told us they've tried other mediums and they do not believe that they are from other planets. They think it is Earth spirits, mischievous and lying.

Do they know that spirits cannot lie?

Apparently they do not know that. To us that's a basic fact.

I can tell you that spirits cannot lie and I'm a very humble, very poor educated person, but I'm better educated since I passed on, through being here in your Circle, than I ever was when I was alive, for I did not believe in an afterlife. I did not believe in people from other planets. Now I know I was wrong. My life was wasted by not believing.

On your plane –

It is not very high.

No, because you still have much to learn.

And because I was a non-believer.

Is the knowledge of people of other planets widespread on your plane, or would you go back to your plane and say about that and people would be amazed?

Well they might think I was playing a game. A hoax.

I think it's the higher planes where – when we started even on the higher planes there was not knowledge of people from other planets.

It is to me a great revelation and I am sorry for the way I was when I was alive, for I denied even the existence of God and now I know how wicked it was to do that. I am forgiven, but I regret that I had carried that through my 92 years. I was not a good person. I was not intentionally bad, but I just didn't believe and I didn't believe in an afterlife and I didn't believe in the churches. And I don't, even now, know that I was wrong in that. In their own way they are trying to be good people, they're not really following the

193

truth. The truth and the beauty of Almighty God. Almighty God is Love and that is the most tremendous power of all. In all this universe and any other universe that there might be.

The Almighty Power is throughout the whole of the universe.

Everywhere, but I did not know that until after I passed over, and I have learnt a lot from listening in your lovely Circle and in this great haven for us. For people like me to come and learn and live here. There are many like me who have learnt with me. There were many others who come here who were non-believers. There are many evil, evil, evil people, but when they turn into spirits, which they all must do, they either get consumed by their own evil, or they will earn their way out of it. I have earned my way out.

You keep going Frank and you'll get to a higher plane

I have got quite a nice niche in your cone. It is mine and none other will use it. It is there for me. I have repented my sins. I have seen the wrong of my ways and because I have been able to admit that I have been permitted to come to your particular niche.

You had to have permission?

Oh yes. I couldn't come without. None can come here without permission, except those from other planets.

Is it given to you verbally by another spirit?

Yes, and that might be under the direction of the great and holy Flocen, the great spirit of this universe. And if I say to you 'God be with you' I feel now that I am clean enough to be able to say such words. I thank you very much for establishing a place for me where I can come and rest and learn. I live here with you. I live in the cone. I could go to my plane, but I don't want to. I want to stay here where I learn so much. I learn from every different one that comes to you. I knew the medium and her husband when I lived on the Isle of Sheppy. I was a hotelier. She lived nearby.

(Transcript abridged)

HAROLD
(Male Earth Spirit)

5 April 1994

You don't know me. I know you. I know you well. I am come as a friend and I am very glad to be able to speak with you. She's good you know. She lets any old person come in if she – but then everybody has to pass Maurie and he is very particular as to who shall come and speak through her. I don't come from this town, but I am visiting here now and I have been visiting here several times. Many, many times. I actually come from London and my name is Harold. I'm very pleased that you're lucky enough to have all these people that come to visit you from other planets. In my day when I was in life we didn't believe in such things.

There's plenty that don't now.

I agree there are plenty who don't. But I know. You know. It's time the world knew there are other planets filled with people such as ourselves. Cleverer than us, mostly and they've got more love than we ever had. They know how to express love, we don't. We do, quietly, when we have love affairs between lovers, express love, but not giving it freely in the way it should be given. I realise now that the way I lived was quite ridiculous. I suppose toffee-nosed if you like.

How long have you been passed?

Quite some while now, about 40.

40-odd years?

Oh yes. I was 40-odd, 50 maybe. I can't remember exactly how old I was. I passed in a natural way. I had this heart trouble. I knew it would carry me off one day. One of the turns would take me. I was interested in anything to do with theatre and films. I was an entrepreneur, anything and everything.

Sounds as though you could have been fairly well-heeled.

Yes. I was. Money was not scarce. I come from a considerably well-

195

heeled family. I'd say, 'Pater old chap, how about it? Can I have so-and-so' and he'd say, 'Jolly good, yes rather' and then I'd have it. My Pater was a very, very kind man. Very generous, not only to his family but to many other people.

What do you remember when you passed over, when you came out of your body? Some don't like to talk about it.

I don't care. It's something we've all got to do. It doesn't hurt. Heart people go quite quickly when they do go, you know and it isn't painful.

Did you find yourself looking down –

Yes, I did. I saw my inert body and I thought that's an uncomfortable-looking position to be in. I couldn't do anything about it, you understand. When I did realise I had passed over I thought, 'I haven't done a lot of things that I ought to have done,' but there wasn't anything I could do about that either. It's too late.

You were still within the room?

Yes, I was and I thought how do I get away from here? I've got to get out of the room away from this incongruous-looking body before somebody comes in the room and sees me, but now I realise, of course, they wouldn't. I could see them, but they wouldn't see me. So I made for the window and the window was closed and I suddenly realised it didn't matter if the window was closed, I could go through anyway, which I did. It didn't hurt. And when I got outside there was a chap standing there. Well no, not standing – sort of hovering. He took hold of me and he said, 'Come on, I'm waiting for you. You can't keep me waiting. I've got other people to see to besides you.'

How was he dressed – a long white robe?

No. He was an ordinary-looking fellow and he had a bright brown tweedy sort of suit and he had a nice round smiling shiny face. Plenty of hair and he was quite a jolly chap. But he was quite stern with me because I kept him hanging about a bit and he said, 'Come on. We've got to get going.'

He took your arm?

Yes. And away we went. Through the air. (*Harold made a swishing noise.*)

Like Superman.

Yes, something like that. I don't know what happened after that. I'm not quite sure where he took me to.

Did it seem as though you were going through cloud, like in the atmosphere?

We went through atmosphere most certainly, but I don't know where we went to, or what happened after that. I think that's the time when he put me to sleep. I think I had to go to sleep. I don't know how long.

When you woke up, do you recall what happened then?

Yes. When I woke up I was in a place which was like a dormitory. Lots of other people were there.

Sleeping?

Yes, and I was the only one who was awake and a voice called me by my name and I went from that place. I went to where the voice was calling ... I've been told I'm not to tell you anything. I have just been told I've said too much. I was not aware I was not supposed to tell you. I think I have been sleeping for about 30 years, but I can't say any more ... Oh. Oh. Oh ...

Norman.

Maurie?

Yes.

I hope I haven't got Harold into trouble.

I think you have. I think you were a bit impertinent, asking too many ...

But this is the sort of questions I've asked for a quarter of a century.

And never had any answers. -

Oh, some answers. Tunnels and all sorts ...

Not many. I think you've overshot the mark with our friend. What was his name – Hawkins or Watson or something.

Harold Watson. Well, I ask The Almighty to please forgive if he over – and I accept the responsibility. I am truly sorry.

You have to be a bit guarded with some of these fellows, you know. I think you got him into a bit of trouble. He was dragged off very suddenly. That's how I managed to get in.

[Abridged Transcript]

GEORGE
(Male Earth Spirit)

13 November 1990

My name is George. Hi everybody. You've got a lot of visitors here. A lot of them sitting around in the room and there's a blackbird with bright yellow feathers around its neck and an orange beak and it keeps saying, 'I don't know'. I think that belongs to her. I think it's her bird. It's sitting on her shoulder. Well, it's my shoulder for the time I'm in here, isn't it? Yes. It's a nice bird. I don't know whether you can hear it, but I can hear it.

No, we can't hear it.

What a pity. It's got a funny voice. Oh yes, it's saying, 'Hello Minnie.' It's called Minnie. I've just been having a bit of fun. I have been to a meeting in another place where there were several people gathered together in a dark room.

A seance

Yes. I hate them. I went there – well – I was told that there was one of these things going on and I thought I'd have a go at it. I thought I'd get in there, but the person that's supposed to be a medium couldn't receive me. Couldn't hear me. I tried telepathic. I tried shouting in her ear. I tried to get her out and let me in, but she wouldn't have it. And then I found . . . it was a bit of fun I might tell you – I found there was a young girl there. She was about 16 and she was very fickle, but she was part of the circle and she was in a sort of state of – well, I don't know what you'd call it. Semi-trance and she was in some sort of fright trance, if you know what I mean.

Fright trance?

Yes, she was frightened. She was definitely a simple type of girl, but I had a bit of fun because I got in there and I shook them to the core. I had a wonderful time. I told them that the medium was a whole lot of rubbish and that she wasn't any good at all and the girl of course didn't know she was saying it. It wasn't her really, it was me, but they felt it was her. Do you understand? Oh, it was such fun.

They didn't realise, or accept that a spirit was actually speaking through her?

No. Not at all, not at all, and the person who called herself a medium – she's got a funny name – I can't remember what she's called, but she's got a funny name.

What kind of aura did she have? Mediums usually have a large aura.

She had a grey sort of . . . no, it wasn't a good aura. A greyish sort of aura. She wasn't a genuine medium. She's certainly taking money off people. But she wouldn't listen to me and I was shouting in her ear and telling her if she'd only listen to me I'd tell her what to say, but she wouldn't listen. She couldn't hear me. She was not in any way psychic, but the girl let me get into her and she didn't know I'd got into her and she's speaking and she's saying all these things and they're all going berserk. It was very funny.

Did you stay around to see what was said after that?

Oh yes.

What did they say?

Well, they started getting on to her and told her not to be so rude to the medium, but it wasn't her of course, it was me. I will be rude to her. She's a fake. She doesn't know what she's doing. It was so funny. I reckon those people realised they'd paid their money for nothing in the end. I don't know whether they did or not, but I certainly had a good bit of fun out of it. I stayed a good five minutes inside this girl and I gave her a whole mouthful. I really let off steam. Anyway I had the best fun I've had in a long time.

It serves the medium right for being a charlatan.

That's exactly what she was. She wasn't a medium. She's just a person taking money on false pretences and I think they were paying her fairly high sums of money to be there. There were about four men and three women and this girl. I don't know whether the girl paid. I expect somebody paid for her, don't you. I expect that's what happened. She was about 15 or 16, but she was simple. I had been hanging about there for some time. I was hanging about there for 10 or 15 minutes before I discovered I might be able to utilise the girl. It was no good trying to utilise the medium because she just wasn't acceptable.

Did you see any other spirits there?

No.

You were the only one.

Yes. But it was fun – oh it was good fun. And then I knew that you were sitting here because you always do and I thought, well, I'll get back there by the time you get started and I know you don't get started till you've had a bit of a yap first. So I got back here and – ha, ha, ha, I'm full of beans. I told all your friends in the room, you know all the – ha, ha, ha. Yes, I told them what had happened. They were having a good laugh. They've all been having a good laugh. A bit of hilarity going on. I told your keeper, or whatever he's called.

Maurie.

Yes, he had a good laugh too. Yes, serve her right, that's what he said.

The only one I feel the slightest sympathy for is the girl.

Yes. I don't think she realised what was happening because she was in a sort of shock state.

Wondering why everybody was on to her, I expect.

Afterwards she would wonder, yes. Although I think she's so simple that it wouldn't really have much effect on her. I wouldn't do anybody any harm, you know that. No, I wouldn't. I had a good joke out of it though, a good laugh – it was very funny. You never saw anything like the medium's face. And the men. I think one man was a solicitor. Their mouths were hanging open. Their mouths were like big round Os. Ha, ha, ha – it was funny.

Was it somewhere in this area, Parkstone, Poole?

Well, I don't know. Not here quite. Not near this place. I think it's further away.

It might have been somewhere like Wareham.

Well, it could easily be, it might be Wimborne, I don't know.

When you're going to a place, you only pay rough attention to physical buildings I suppose.

I don't pay any attention to them really. You just have a destination and you get there. If you know where you're going it's all right. If you're just wandering around aimlessly you might pay a bit more attention.

How did you get there – did you wish yourself there?

I heard there was going to be this meeting and I thought I'll go to the meeting.

Did another spirit tell you that?

Yes. Somebody told me there was going to be a meeting there, but I didn't think there's any address or anything.

So what did you do?

I just thought I better go there and then I suddenly found myself there. It was quite good really. Well, it was so funny. You would have laughed if

200

you'd been there. Well, if you'd been there and you'd paid money to go in, you wouldn't laugh would you? I think they all had to pay to get in there and that was eight people and the medium woman who wasn't a medium. And she had somebody who was another woman who led everybody in, but she wasn't in the meeting. She didn't sit down at the meeting. She made herself scarce somewhere. I don't know where she went. I didn't look. There's a funny feeling in this leg. I don't know what it is.

A touch of cramp, maybe.

I don't know what it is. It's like something sharp inside the – running around in the veins, or something.

Well, I think you did a good job of work there, George.

Ha, ha, ha, ha. It isn't very often we get a good old laugh like that. I wish you could have seen them and, in particular, that woman. I can't think what she's called. I'm trying to think what she's called. I did know what her name is but I can't think of it now. It was something like Belinda – but that's not the name. Oh well, I think I better go off I've had my laugh and I've told you about it.

Thank you for talking to us.

There's lots of people up here having a good laugh about it too. It's really quite amusing, isn't it? I'll come and see you again if you like. Another day. There's lots of people here, by the way. And I have been told you've got lots of what you call . . .

Space people?

Yes. I think there's a lot of them about. So you've got a good meeting even though there's not many of yourselves. You've got lots of other people here as well that you can't see, but I can. I can't see them all.

Can't see the Astrals.

I can't. I can't. I don't know which are space people, which aren't. Don't know anything about space people.

There won't be so many space spirits here.

They'd be astral-like and you can't see Astrals.

You see Astrals get a sort of advanced electronic boost to get here.

Are they electronic?

Not electronic – it's beyond that. They go in a sort of chamber when they want to go on an astral projection. They're from advanced planets. They're far more advanced than us in every way.

Well, that's interesting. Thank you for telling me. I'm going to have a chat to Maurie about it. See what he's got to say. He probably knows a bit, does he? I met a fellow the other day who says he used to be with you for years, years ago. His name is Peter.

201

Yes. He did Maurie's job.

I think that's so, but he said it wasn't at this house. He said it was when you lived in another house and I believe that house was a haunted house and it doesn't stand any more, it's been pulled down. I wonder what happened to the spirit that lived there.

There was a resident spirit there, or ghost as they call them.

I don't like that word.

We of the Circle don't like the term ghost because the first thing we learned is that a spirit on passing over is exactly the same as before passing over except he hasn't got a physical body.

No, but you can have a body that although it's ethereal is still a body. It can look solid. The only trouble is you can walk through it if you came towards me. I don't look solid all of the time. I don't have to, do I?

Physical people can't see you unless a spirit makes a tremendous effort to appear.

If you do one thing you can't do the other.

You can't talk.

No, I couldn't come in and use this medium if I wanted to stand in front of you. I'd rather use the medium. She's a good medium you know. I think you're very lucky, there aren't many like this because I've been lots of places and you can't get them. They aren't there. I've been studying this business a bit. I've been studying this business about your medium. It would seem that right from a very early age she was designated to do this but she fought against it for a long time and would not accept it. Would not permit it to happen. Would not allow herself to be used and then there came a time when she suddenly realised that it wasn't going to hurt her.

It started with the ouija board.

Yes, I heard this. I don't want anything to do with that. It's not a game.

We used the ouija board for a spell and Nita found she was able to receive people and so we stopped the ouija board.

I think before she started allowing herself to be used as a full-blown medium, as she does now, I think she started getting mental – what we call mind-talking. She started getting messages that way. I was told that she had a very long contact giving her some information.

That must be the Kari-Naris one.

I think it was people from another planet that found her able to receive them and made her do what she had to do. And that would be when she was in an open trance, not an astral trance like she's in now. I was very receptive when I was alive. I was able to get spirit messages. Thanks for having me. Thank you very much for listening and thank your medium

202

when she comes home. I think she is coming home now. Maurie's calling me. Bye-bye everybody and God be with you.

NURSE EDITH CAVELL
(Earth Spirit)

12 December 1978

Dear friends, dear brothers and sisters, I greet you in love. I know not the meaning of the word 'Soskris'. I have heard it spoken, but do not fully understand the meaning. Is it the language of other worlds? Of course, in my lifetime I did not believe in such things – did not, in fact, believe in an afterlife, but I know different now, for I am in a different life, which *is* the afterlife. I have always believed in Almighty God. I have always believed in the Holy Ghost and in Blessed Jesus, the Son of God. Now have I come to realise that those of the churches that teach us to call Jesus a God are teaching us wrongly. It is unforgivable that so many should be made to follow their instructions upon believing in Jesus as God. Jesus is a great, great person, a great prophet, and has spoken the words given to him by either the Holy Ghost or The Great Father, Almighty God. Now I do know, in this afterlife, that Jesus, Blessed Jesus is as a brother to all spirits, is as a brother to living or dead, for all have spirits.

I was a deeply religious woman in my earlier time. As a young woman I was foolishly religious and followed the teachings of the pastors, parsons and others who presented themselves as leaders of churches, wherein I would kneel and pray. I see now that they did not know any better – they taught what they thought to be right. I have listened here on many occasions and have heard other spirits who are visitors of yours talk of what is known to be truth concerning Blessed Jesus, whom I still reverence and always will. It is The Almighty Father who is in all and of all – the Almighty Father that lives within each living being and in all that lives and grows – this also I have learnt.

I am called Edith. You might know of me, for I am written about. Yes, I am Nurse Edith Cavell and I was a friend of Queen Victoria. John Brown was the Scottish gentleman friend of the Queen. I wish not to speak of my many troubles that I endured, and the great sacrifices that were made, not by me, but by those poor men whom I tended and helped. Many who died in my arms cried out to some holy spirit or other that they could see as they passed. Some even called to dear, blessed Jesus, believing as I then believed that Jesus was God. Times are changing and the truth must come out at last. Holy as he is, beautiful and kindly as he was, a great leader of men, a great preacher upon the hillsides, still did he speak the words that were given to him, for he was a man of no education and could not have spoken the words he spoke unless they were put into his mouth to speak. This I have been informed.

I was here on the night (*Sunday*) when you received what your good medium has called a monstrosity. Indeed, it *was* a monstrosity! We saw it not, but felt it, and it frightened us all from this place and all from the cone, including your good friend and helper, called Peter. It was so very, very powerful that all fled in terror. She was right to want to fight it on her own. She has been made a priestess of the First Earth Jeculin Associates. She was right to fight it on her own, to test her power – perhaps it was even sent to test her power. However, I could feel that she and the younger one were filled with dread and much fear, though each was trying to buoy the other up, so as not to display any fear to the creature, who was so revolting that we fled in terror. Even Jeculins fled in terror! I know not what he looked like – I know it was a male entity. I know that it was revolting and that it brought a revulsion into the inner part of each soul that was in this room, each spirit and even the Astrals. It was (though unseen) felt to be slimy and of many, many legs and arms. We flew away in much terror and she overcame it with her strength of goodness. When she offered it love, we who had the courage to remain within hearing, could realise that it didn't just disappear – it dissolved into a much smaller thing, whereas when it first arrived it was massive and all of us felt and fled in terror. I do believe that it preyed upon our fear and she was strong and brave and true to The Almighty, for first she prayed, then she ordered it away – no, first she ordered it away, but it would not go, and then she prayed for protection. Then she stood and defied it, and said, 'I defy you! You shall not enter my body! I will not permit it!' We who waited, who had enough courage to remain nearby, not in this place but above, dared not come nearer. After it received love it shrank and seemed no more to be like a beastly, slimy octopus. Somebody told her to count to ten and it would be gone. It might have been the Holy Ghost, or it might have been God himself! I do not agree that it would have gone had it been the Holy Flocen, for as I have already stated I think it was a test of her power, a testing of her ability to control even an evil entity. Control she did!

I am only here to tell you of this. Almost I dared not return to this place, yet on drawing near I saw that the cone is bright and beautiful, and her soul is bright and beautiful, as is that of her granddaughter, and yours, Norman. There are not so many here tonight – just a few, for the hard winds are difficult to battle against and we are apt to be swept away in another direction and cannot control, for after all, we are only wisps. Do you understand? When I am inside this body I am safe and I dread to leave it and go out again, into the heavy winds. Those who sit in the room with you are also protected, although the cone is blowing in all directions, but it is bright. The spirits are banding together and they are holding each other close so that if one is blown, all are blown and they will not be parted that way. They are stronger by banding together and they are waiting for me to return that I may be banded into their strength. There are only four people other than myself in this room.

I do believe you are to receive a visit from the holiest, the highest Holy Ghost. I think you shall receive Him very shortly and therefore I shall not remain. He is not within sight, but I do not think the winds will interfere with Him. As we journeyed here, we journeyed many together, to fight the great winds, others who are beyond the great winds are singing and they sing that the Holy Flocen shall visit the holy medium of His choice upon this Earth. There is only one that I know of and that is she whose body I occupy and whose spirit is floating just here beside me. We understand what they are singing, although their language is their own – it implies what it means. It could be a form of telepathy, but to hear the singing is so beautiful. You could not misunderstand that they are so joyously singing that He, who is the All-Highest, shall be coming to Earth and there is only one whom He shall visit. There is only this one that we know of and she sits here and allows me to speak. Bless her! I do not have any special powers of blessing, but I say 'bless her' with spiritual love, although I am considered to be quite holy, for I have helped so many people in the past, long ago when I was alive. We will not speak of my manner of passing, for it pleases me not to remember.

I love you all. Love is the whole and sole meaning of life. You have learned this great truth and must speak it with all people that come within your reach that you may pass the word to. Teach them and lead them gently, for they are the children, not knowing the great truths that have been taught to you of this Circle and to her who is now considered to be a blessed and holy person. I am most sorry for the hurt that she has endured, through the Earth man she chose as her mate. I pray she will get over it, but sometimes these hurts remain on throughout our lives.

206

I am going to continue to pray for her, that she may feel less hurt and less rejection.

I say to you all, as I came in love, I leave in love. God bless you all. God be with you. I do not wish to leave, but perhaps she should rest a while before He comes, the great and holy one who speaks for God. My friends are waiting above. Blessed people, farewell.

FEELAM

(Male Astral, Self-Appointed Tutor, Planet – Cincea)

---

10 October 1978

Due to your medium's condition, I am using the voice, but she has not passed into trance though she is permitting me to speak without interference. There is a reason that this is being done – it is not good to pass into trance whilst on a strong drug. It could be possible that it might be difficult to return and this we could not permit. She is wide awake, are you not, my dear?

Yes, of course I am. Continue – I don't mind you using my voice.

I am your friend and tutor, Feelam. I am pleased she will be able to hear most of this, though she is in a somewhat distant state, caused by the drugs. A build-up of drugs can cause this. A teaching night, if you so desire. I have no special teaching to give you, unless you ask me. You can travel into the past under hypnosis, a million years or more, but it must be done with guidance and by someone in a highly responsible position. No time travel is physical. It is spiritual and is only permitted in certain cases. It *must* be done under guidance. You cannot do it yourself and it will only be done for a reason. I think that time-travel machines must be the invention of someone's fertile brain who cannot conceive any other way to do it. The one who guides and directs during your journey to the past will also help you to return. You could appear to be a solid person, but would in fact be a spiritual person. You might even be an ancient representation of yourself in an earlier life. You would go to a spiritual past, not your mind. Under the right guidance you can go back and live another life for a very short period of time. During that time it's as real as if it were that same time, but it is, in fact, being guided back to that time. You cannot go forward. You could not go back to a period you had not lived in. You could talk to people on your journey and some might say, 'I have not seen you for a long time.' Others will say, 'It can't be him – he died two years ago' or something like that.

I have never been through this experience and have no wish to do so, though I would like to travel forward in time, but I know it to be impossible. I think we have reached the conclusion in this discussion. Is there anything else you wish to ask? Not being an Earth person, I am unable to reply concerning your inner-dwellers. You would do better to ask an Earth spirit. Dolphins are highly intelligent, but have difficulty communicating. They are full of love. It exudes from them and they have very large and beautiful auras. Auras surround the entire person. They are like transparent cotton wool, wrapping around the figure, and of different colours, depending on the person. The colours indicate levels of goodness and love.

I will now say Soskris to you all and especially to you, Nitesi. I am going to go now and visit Teresi, for she had laid herself open to concentrate upon this meeting and is regretful that she cannot be here. Although she may not be able to speak with me I will go just to comfort her. My love to you all, and thank you, Nitesi, for letting me speak, without going into trance.

That's all right. I'm glad I could do it – didn't know I could, actually.

Soskris. Remember, Feelam loves you.

LE-BOS
(Male Astral, from planet Wool-Bi)

22 October 1978

Soskris. I come to you with love, and my heart brings all that it is possible for a heart to give to you people of this Earth. You are the chosen ones, selected for the purpose of being a circle of true Jeculin believers. You may not remember my name for it is long since when I came to you in the early days when you were just learners. My name is Le-Bos. I thank you for those sweet and kind words of welcome. The planet from which I originate and which is my home and place of birth is called Wool-Bi. I do not know that you have had any others from my home planet, but I know much of you, whereas you know little of me, for I have studied throughout your long years of learning. Long for you, though not for us. There are reasons why it should seem a long while to you, one being that you live by counting time, which on most other planets is not necessary. Another reason is that, like most Earthly churches, you have a meeting on the day you call Sunday. Why do you call it Sunday? Is it because of your Sun, which once you worshipped? However, it is not important. What is important is that you choose only this day to meet together to offer your prayers, although I have now come to understand that you do also meet on one other day of your week to offer prayers and receive contacts. It would be far better for you if you could do this more frequently for the more often you could do it, the more you would be able to learn of life in the outer worlds in the great Universe – the endless, never-ending space that lies high and low and, besides, any way you look at it, space is immeasurable. This is one reason we do not understand your attempts to measure it. I know you have attempted to measure the distance between yourselves and the once-world called Moon. Once it was a world, a planet such as yours, with living beautiful people, but rather smaller than of your breed. Many other planets have people larger than you on them. Many

210

planets are much larger than yours in size and therefore have larger people. Some planets are a little larger than you and have people your own size. Then again, there are some very small planets which have very, very small people. There is a planet which is as a ball of fire and the people are just as little balls of light. Those people are all pure energy, not bodily figures as you have, but souls and spirits contained in small balls of pure energy. That is a good, good planet, as are most other planets which you know of and certainly all the planets that follow the Jeculins, whom you have called the Jeculin Brotherhood and called yourselves associates, which has been accepted into all the libraries on all the planets who are Jeculins. You have also established many other words, which have been incorporated into the Usietan language. Many words that you have invented have been taken into our language of Usietan and therefore those planets who can speak your language accept those words as words of your learning, but some of us know that they are not words that would be found in your libraries, for *you* have invented them.

I know all of you by name except Brian and Robin. You have not yet received ASIs? Brian, if the time came, as it most likely will at Tarset, would you then be prepared to accept the title? You cannot, in fact, argue against it. If the Almighty God wishes that you should be called an ASI or an ESI it is not really for you to refuse. You are now upon the path of light, which leads you directly to The Almighty and as such do not need to seek other directions to find your way to your God. You had found it when you entered this place, where resides this good woman, who gives herself not only to you people, but to us of other planets, who *need* someone able to accept us and allow us to speak. This is a good and holy person who will permit herself to be used in this manner. I do hope that you all realise that you are fortunate to have this person. I will speak now to you, my friend Robin. We have known you long, long ago. You are not a stranger in this Circle, for when you came to this circle you came to your home spiritually. You can look forward, through your spiritual feeling, to follow this path that these good people have been given. They did not find it – it was placed here for them to follow.

I am sorry for the old one (Tomesi) who sleeps, but he is quite old, though not in mind or in heart. In spirit he is very old indeed, from many, many millions of years, and his Earthly body grows tired. I am sorry also for this one that we call Nita, for I know she suffers from an Earthly emotional and very painful disturbance, which causes her ill health to be even worse, or can we say, to deteriorate? All of you who love her, as I can feel you do, and believe in her, as I *know* you must – do your very best to

211

look after her and try to keep her as happy as it is possible for her to be under very difficult circumstances which only apply to Earth people. No, forgive me, there are other planets in your dark corner of the universe where this same sort of emotion is the natural way of living. If we could eradicate that, and let love be for everything and everyone, without anyone needing someone to be personally theirs, then there would not be the suffering that exists in your world. In some cases people call themselves married and say that marriage is made in heaven. We know that marriages are not made in heaven, although The Almighty has, on many occasions, designed one person to suit another. There's no argument against that, yet do they so rarely meet that it has become a better way of living to avoid that contact, yet it cannot be avoided on your Earth. Your Earth has got its established way of many hundreds of thousands of years and it will take many hundreds or even thousands of years to bring it up to the level of other planets. The time will come when such suffering as I feel here will not be necessary, but we of other planets cannot help in this respect. All we can do is to wrap our love around the one who suffers and in that way help them as best we can, but we cannot arrange your lives for you – you arrange them for yourselves and if you go wrong it is only yourselves who are to blame, although frequently there is one who is more to blame than the other, as in this case with Nita. I beg her pardon – she is Nitesi. I hope I have helped to explain a lot of things that perhaps have not been understood. If I have, then I have not wasted my journey here to you, for my galaxy is far away. I am happy to come to you and happy to instruct you in anything you can ask me, if I know the answer and am permitted to give you the answer to what you want to know. There are some things to which there are no answers, because that is the way The Almighty has designed it and there are some things we cannot answer because we are told that it is classified information. However, if you wish to ask me questions I will help all I can, and if I am blamed for it afterwards when I return, then I will take such punishment as may be meted out to me. I am offering my help, if you wish to take advantage of this. I will tell you what I feel about you, Brian, and this may help you to adjust yourself. You are a very holy-minded person. You believe deeply in The Great Almighty and you believe deeply in the people of other planets. This is good. It is a fine start and perhaps you have not yet been long enough and received sufficient instruction, or maybe have not read enough of the instructions that have been given to this Circle for you to feel that you are suitable or even humble enough to receive the gift of an ASI or ESI. First you must have an ASI, then if you are lucky you will get an ESI. You must remember that if Almighty God wishes you to have it, how can you say, 'I don't want it'? You will get it whether you want it or not. I feel you are pure. You are, if anything, a little over-dogmatic that everything is guided for you to do, or not to do by certain high-up spirits. Perhaps you feel that God wants you to do this or that. If you think at all, think of The Holy Flocen who wants you to do this or that. In not all cases is this so – in some you may be misleading yourself. You say that everything is meant to be – NO! my son. Everything is meant to be one way that The Almighty and The Holy Flocen wish it to be, but you of this Earth, and sometimes of other planets, do not always do as intended, maybe not knowing they are wrong, but still they do not always do as was intended. They can feel, 'I have done as was intended, so I am good.' But they might not have done what they should have done, they might have done something of a different nature, perhaps something more appropriate and helpful to whoever they were attempting to help. Everybody's purpose in life on all planets is to help each other, never thinking physically, but always thinking mentally and spiritually. Think twice about everything and if both thoughts come up the same, then go ahead and do it, but if the second thought gives you a doubt, then you know there is something else you ought to do.

Now you, Robin, are very advanced. You have been a spiritualist and a believer in The Almighty, maybe not knowing of The Flocen, but thinking of him as the Holy Ghost, or even Jesus, a very holy person, but not God. There is only one God – God Almighty, the Father of all. You will go far in your belief and you will benefit greatly by your beliefs, for goodness is always repaid with goodness. No matter who you be, you or any other person you know, or even do not know, if you do good things as you *do*, then you will find good things are done for you. If you always remember that you will know you are doing what The Holy Flocen wishes of you. It is clean, simple and a straightforward path; no need to deviate. Go forward and you will eventually come to your spiritual home when the time is right. This is your spiritual home for now, but there is the time when you pass and you have still to find your spiritual home. Many never do because they have not behaved in the right way while they have been living upon this little blue Earth. You know why we call it the little blue one? It is because it has more sea than any other planet. It is a great waste of land, particularly as you have a great number of people upon your planet, and of a great number of nationalities, which is partly the fault of those high-up who tried to get a mixture of people to blend together. It seems as though they have forgotten the purpose for which they were put here and instead of blending together they fight together to gain each other's property and land. That is very wicked, for they have forgotten that once they were people who were given a very great opportunity. They forget their origin.

Who calls for help? The old man is in pain? (*Mr Smith, the next-door neighbour*) Let us put our hands together and say a small prayer for an old man, possibly nearing his time to pass. I will lead you in a prayer if you so desire.

'Almighty God, Blessed Father of all, we pray that you will help this aged person, and make his last days more comfortable, and also make it easier for the wife, who has a difficult task to cope with a man in pain who sounds fractious. Please God, listen to our prayer. Holy Jesus, wherever you are, repeat our prayer that it may be strengthened. We give our love to the old people who live in this building and suffer. Amen and Soskris.'

Robin, dear friend, no stranger – speak with me. Why should there be a dividing line between the animate and the inanimate? All are part of The Almighty, high or low. The things that made this seat came chiefly from living things. There is wood in here – once it lived. If there is fibre in here, once it lived. Whatever you can think of, once it has lived. Nothing is ever dead, not even things that you pull from the ground, or things that you melt in pots upon your stove, nor gold or silver or steel or iron – nothing is inanimate. To you it may appear so, but it all is part of God, created for your use, and slowly taught to you how to accomplish the different arts and work forces that you need to utilise these things. On other planets there are emplinadors and they do the work that you human beings do for yourselves. Everything has a spirit; even the sound that this organ makes, or the sounds that come from this tape machine. On here you have voices and music, your own voices, planetaire voices – even the voice of The Holy Flocen, which is the most marvellous thing to be able to make a record of. The spirit is there – ever rising, full of love and full of beauty, and every time you hear The Holy Flocen's voice you should go to your knees and thank The Almighty that you have been allowed to hear it! It is a good, great gift for you all. Even in your churches they do not hear the voice of the one they call The Holy Ghost, yet they know The Holy Ghost exists, but they think that God Almighty is a dear old gentleman who sits upon a throne in a place they call Heaven, with pearly gates, which is a fallacy. The great Almighty exists everywhere, in everything, in the spirit of every person, in the contents of all places where people live, in everything you can think of, in what you call electricity, in gas. It is out there for you to use. Do not think you are burning The Almighty when you burn the gas. Oh no! It is there to help you. It was given in love for The Almighty *is* love. Even when you go to your places you call 'loo', even

214

that excretion or water that you pass, it all has the love of The Almighty. Do not despise it – it helps to keep the body healthy.

When this planet has reached the same stage concerning eating habits as other planets, then they will become true followers of the Jeculin people. It will take a long time, but you are the leaders who are to spread the word. I am afraid I cannot stay longer – there is little power left, for I have talked much and for a long period.

Only the chosen ones of The Holy Flocen are permitted to hear his voice. It is imperative to remind you of this. I must return now. I ask you to give me your love, to help me to return, to build up my energy to return. Soskris to you all. I leave my love with you – some of my love *must* stay with you and I will always love you, for I have felt during the short time that I have been here all the love that comes towards me and towards the person who allows me to use her voice and her body. Soskris. Goodbye.

HILLY-HOCK

(Animal Spirit from distant planet)

---

31 October 1978

Soskris. I am unable to stay for more than a fleeting moment or so, for I am too big for this body to contain comfortably. I am a very large person, and do not wish to cause this good person discomfort, who gives herself into this condition of trance which permits others to occupy and speak through her. I am not as you; I am of a different species. You could say that I am similar to those animals you call bison but I am even larger than they and therefore must not extend this precious medium beyond her powers of endurance. My message to you all – you, young person (Teresi), and you spirits who are in this place, my message to you is of love and that although we have bodies as you would refer to as being animals, we have as high intelligence as you have yourselves. We have to adapt ourselves and learn various languages, not all easy to remember, for we do not have schools as you have on Earth, or as on other planets they have training centres. No one thinks of giving training centres to those of the animal breeds, except to those who are the leaders of the animal breeds and in all cases we are taught in groups. It is a slow process and requires much concentration for we cannot write as you write or read as you read for we cannot write. Therefore all has to be retained within the memory, when once told, we must remember and use the words we have been taught as best we can fit them together. My visit to you is in love but also to tell you that the many planets that contain animal people (this would be your term, not ours) are all able and anxious to convey their love to you, who are the chosen people of our Great Almighty, who is our Almighty, as well as yours. I could communicate to the bisons of your fields and maybe the bulls and cows also could understand me in my natural manner of speech. It is not speech at all but a method of grunts and growls and mooing noises, but other than that we use what you term telepathy. My people are

216

the occupiers of the planet and we are the people of the planet. We have our controllers, or teachers. It would be pointless for us to have a school when we have no hands to hold pencils or crayons or use paper or slate, for we have very horny hooves; we could not control the use of a pencil although a few have tried to do so by grasping the writing utensil between their teeth. This has proved disastrous because, our teeth being very strong and white, they break through whatever is held between them so that was a failure.

I fear I must not stay for I fear I am exhausting this body. This body is so loved and respected by all peoples of all planets, including your own, that we must not permit any damage to occur to such a good person – a holy person, who speaks for The Holy Flocen. We do not have any High Council as is the same on any planet whose sole occupants are four-legged or more-legged. I mean large insects as you term them; spiders and other such creatures – there are even planets that are occupied by cat-people and dog-people and horse-people – there are even crocodile-people, but they are all loving and follow the code of our Great Almighty. They are helped in their manner of living that they may not and *shall* not destroy or kill any living thing. They, as we, are attended by the wonderful and clever emplinadors presented to us so long ago, we know not by whom. These mechanical creatures or computerised beings are programmed to care for, and feed and keep in order the occupants of our planet; we, being obedient to the will of Almighty God, are happy to have their help and grateful that they were given to us. Before we were tearing up beautiful shrubs and lovely grasses and growing things like corn – even trees we have destroyed by eating the bark or the gentle small boughs and the green leaves, but not now; not for many, many thousands of your years. I am happy to have spoken to you, to have brought you this message of love from not only my people but from those peoples who communicate with us in the telepathic manner upon other planets – long-distance telepathy.

I am pleased that you have received me so gently and well and sorry if I have distended the body of this dear, sweet and kind person, who permits any and all who would do so to utilise her body and voice. I find great pleasure in being able to clasp these fingers together in this manner for we have no fingers – only horny old hooves! I would like to say, 'God be with you.' We are Jeculin believers but we are not permitted to be Jeculins because we are not as you humans are. Where on most planets you will find that the people stand up on two legs, we cannot. Yet we know that Almighty God and Holy Flocen love us and we regularly receive blessings and telepathic messages which are encouraging to us and help us keep our beliefs true and our paths straight – to do no wrong to each other or to any living thing or being. We welcome any space travellers who would come to take a look at us, for we have had several. We do not always understand their language but if they speak English it is very good for *I* can speak it fairly well. Some others of our planet are quite learned in that respect, including our Father-Leader. This is like you say King. I am a spirit and quite large! I do not find it easy to condense myself to the right size to fit inside this medium.

I will go now. I will say: God be with you and God bless you. May I have a blessing from you for I know you are holy people. I shall ask her now; place your blessing upon me, good Nitesi, that I may take it back to my people. You promise not to laugh if I tell you my name? I am called Hilly-Hock. My friends think it is foolish – they say it is like a flower and I am nothing like a flower! I am quite sure I am nothing like a flower! Pray allow me to leave. I leave my love and the love of my people and love from all those of other planets of a similar nature to me. I can say Soskris, because I understand it, although I am not a Jeculin. I know you use the word as you are followers of the Jeculins. I can feel the love from all of you. I go.

BELLON

(Planetary Leader of Planet Belloni)

12 November 1978

Soskris to you all and to those who sit within your Circle to make it complete. You cannot have a Circle of fewer than five people. You are sadly depleted. My name is Bellon. I have not spoken before, but I believe I came to you long ago, in fact, I know I came, but whether you actually received my messages I do not recall, for you were in use of a board, of which we do not approve, and wrong things were written down on many occasions, as were wrong names given to wrong people. Bellon you should remember: do you remember that name from the past? It may have been in the early days, before you joined (Teresi) and before there were so many who used to be in the other building, where the young ones were. I came long before that time but I have sat with you, even when you had the long period with the young ones. I am Bellon, as I tell you, and the name of my planet is Belloni, which is my name with ni on the end. I am the leader of the people on my planet and have learnt your language accordingly that I may converse with you as fluently as most who visit you. I hope not use wrong words, or to make mistakes as I transfer my language into yours. It is not so easy to do, unless one has much practice. I say to you, Soskris to you all and to all you other people, Spirits and Astrals who sit within this place forming for you a Circle where no Circle of live people exists. The number of three is insufficient – must have five to call a Circle. Try soon to get others who will make it come to five at least, if not more. I must thank, on your behalf, all those who sit here and that listen to the words and help to complete the Circle, to hold up the medium, and give her the strength to permit us, whoever we be, to use her voice. She is not absent from her person; she is within her person but is allowing me, without thought or voice interference, to utilise the voice and speak the words to you. As I speak, I feel pain passing through her head. I think it must be an effort for

219

her to restrain herself from speaking as I speak. If she wishes to speak I will withdraw from the voice box, so that she may utilise it if she desires. I withdraw ... No, she does not wish to use the voice. She seems to be sleeping, or half-sleeping, which is perhaps better for me, for in that way I will get no interruptions. If you wish to know anything about my planet I will give you such information as you desire and I would like to know something about the inner-life of you people on this planet for we only know what we observe from afar and very little of your personal lives. We are very much the same as other planets that you have made contact with. We have communal residence combines and we live most happily in close love, without the need for physical love or need to show any physical leanings towards any one person. We do not practise in that manner but there is much love in the spiritual love which is far greater than any other love that you could possibly experience through physical love; that is purely sensation which we have learned to do without and you should also try to do the same although it will no doubt take a long time. You have as yet no factories where you can manufacture people and you have no emplinadors to help you so you must work. We have these and have no need to work, though most of us wish to have some particular job to do which we do without needing or requiring or receiving any manner of payment. All we do, we do for love of each other. We have the general belt system of inner travel and outer travel and we have space ships and what you term hoppers which are the personal craft owned by two or three people or loaned to people as they require them for such purposes as visiting another establishment which may be too far for them to travel on the line circuit. It is all Vitrik controlled. We have the same eating habits as other planets. The difference with us to other planets is chiefly that we wear no clothes. We do not consider that our beauty needs hiding, nor does it disturb either sex with the vision of beauty of each body, for that desire has been eliminated long ago and beauty is the most wonderful thing when you can appreciate it without having to desire to mutilate it. That is what we consider you do when you perform the sex act, unless it be necessary to produce children, for you have no other ways. I would point out to you that your animals do not run wildly after the same excitement, except in the time of creating the replica of themselves. All your animals are of this habit but all you humans are very different, for you have made a fetish of what you call sexual desire which hurts us to know about and we hope that soon you will find the way to control yourselves sufficiently. I do not speak to you in this room personally; I am speaking generally of all the people of your planet who all seem to have this same driving desire which forces them into the act which displeases The Great Almighty unless it is intended for the begetting of children as each family desires. Our houses are not houses. They are large communes which are mostly built of stone, but in some cases, although not many, they are built in what you call precious gems which are plentiful on most planets but not on ours. We have a few palaces, a good word to describe them, which are built of these precious gems but not little, small gems such as you use but very large, boulder-size gems which are placed somewhat like a jigsaw puzzle together and made into a beautiful, shiny palace of many colours. Our ordinary communes are made of large stones which are cleansed by much scraping and glisten through much polishing, after they have been scraped smooth and cleaned but they also are made in the jigsaw fashion for there are no two stones the same size or shape. Therefore they must be built in this manner for we do not like to cut the stone as they are also a part of The Almighty. We can find large stones and smaller stones to form passages. Your language is the hardest of all languages, for so many words sound the same but are spelt in a different manner. If we see the spelling, as we can see in our picture learning houses, we do not always know how to make the sound come out right for they are not consistent as they are on other planets where everything sounds as it looks that it should sound, even though the shape of our letters and figures are quite different from yours. Those who wish to come learn your language and there are more than I who wish to come. I am the leader and there are some you would perhaps call my governmental people or councillors. They also are attempting to come and speak with you in due course and just socially make themselves known and help to keep friends with you for it is a wonder in the great universe ... I am feeling her nose for we have different noses and I am trying to establish the shape of this one so that I may tell them when I return that your noses are a little different from ours. I think that the only other difference between us is that our ladies do not have these things (*breasts*); the ladies and the males are all flat. There is a difference between the sexes in the genital organs. They are different but of course they are not used as you use them for we have the newer method whereby the seeds are taken from the best people and mated together to produce the best people. We hope to become a really perfect race of people. There is slight damage to the female's body when the eggs are removed but it is instantly healed by the healing chamber. A slight operation is performed but before the donor leaves the healing chamber the wound has already been healed in such a way that there is no mark left and we have no clothes to wear to hide anything and no need of things like you use on cuts – plasters.

Now, would you be kind enough to tell me a little more of your inner lives that I do not know of, that I may tell my people when I return for it is useless for me to come such a long journey if I cannot take back some news to my people, as well as some message from you. There are many questions. I know that you have to work for you have no emplinadors to do this for you.

Yes, work is very necessary on our planet but there are very many people who are termed unemployed.

How do they feed? Do your governmental officials supply them with it?

Not exactly. They supply us with that which we call money and is really quite an evil thing.

For you it is not evil – it is good, for you need it.

That does not make it good for lack of money can cause very many problems. It is not really a necessary thing but it is the system.

You have a system and you cannot help it and it is only time that will make you like other planets and that will take a very long time. We do not count time as you do for we do not go to work. You have to count time for you *do* have to go to work. We do count time to come here to you else we would come on the wrong day or at the wrong time of the day when nobody sits in the circle.

I can use her eyes and look about and it is different here – not unpleasant, but different from our communes where the rooms are so immense that maybe 100 people will be in a room at one time and in the next part of the commune could be another 100 people or more. I like this small, personal sort of place and I very much like to see the things that we never have such as pictures and these pretty lights I see. Those points of light are entrancing – I have never seen that before. This one by the head dances like fairies dance and is also entrancing. I shall tell them when I return of these things that are so pretty and ask if we may not have some things that are just as pretty as some of these things I see here. I am a great lover of prettiness, especially pretty things. I see many pretty people but I do so like these ornaments. To see so many beautiful plants. We do not have plants growing indoors – they are all outside. You probably would not like our pets. They are not dogs or cats, or rats or mice but they are a combination. I suppose in a way they are nearer to your rats than any other creature and almost as large as your dog but not quite. Some are furry and fluffy while some have long hair which you can smooth and make to look sleek and some have no hair at all or very, very short hair almost what you would call bald! But we do not mind what they look like. They are not vicious, they would not bite you. I understand that you have creatures on

222

your Earth that will bite you if they get the opportunity. I have not read far enough back in your history to know of the plagues spread by rats that you tell me of. I have only studied for this time that you call now, not going back in years. We do not store old memories of your Earth, although we do store old memories of our planet. We have more brightly-coloured trees and grass than you, but that seems to be normal throughout the galaxies. For some unknown reason all yours are less bright and less colourful, more indefinite in colour. We do not go to other places on this world, we only come to see you so we do not know how the Earth looks in other places. I am sorry – we had thought that this place was typical of the entire planet. Of course people who have light all the time do not think of the fact that you have night as well as day. Now I am not surprised but when I first came I was most surprised and not a little frightened to find myself in sudden darkness which to us means evilness. Yet I do not think this to be an evil place; indeed, I find it a holy place in spite of the darkness that surrounds you. I know of your weather conditions such as frost, fog and rain and I have heard of this thing you call snow. It will be better when you have Vitrik travelling as we have. Mostly our vehicles pass just below the surface in a tube-like system. Your underground travel sounds very much like ours. Do you have as we have leap carriages? You must run fast and jump on only if it is not a stopping place. We are quite able to do it – we are trained from quite early in life to be able to catch our vehicles. Of course, they do slow down a little when they reach each by-station but some only stop for the main stations and there anybody may get on without running or may get off without jumping.

We have much love, much happiness and content, and we are great followers of the Jeculin peoples and are of the Jeculin peoples. We have great celebrations at the periods when Jeculins all celebrate and you are also lucky and are able to join in these times with us and all the other planets where Jeculin is the leading religion, the only religion on most planets; not on yours, for you have so many we cannot count them all. There should only be one, wherever you are. There is only one path to The Almighty – there is no secondary way.

I have been here a long time and I have been waiting to speak a long time. I think that I ought to vacate so that she may again use her voice, or if she wishes to listen to my words. I know you are using this old-fashioned machine which to you is new-fashioned; to us, it is ancient and only kept in our archives to show that we once had them. We keep records of all the machines we once used, including things like this box (*television*) which we no longer need. Ours are huge, and take up a whole wall – more than a wall in this room, much bigger, or else we wear them on our wrists and some people wear them on a belt affair around their waist and just pick it up to look at it. We also have little by-stations wherever you go. If you are travelling and want to see something you only have to go and press a little button and there is a large screen for you to see whatever you want to see. You pick your proper button and get the direction you need, whichever station you wish to tune into. Then there are other places where you can go which you would call theatres and there is a big screen all the way around the wall and then all the seats are all the way round and you can sit down and watch everything going on in this place or that place. But you cannot have a definite choice in there, as you have to see what is being produced for you – that is, when you go into the SPURNINOGS that you call theatres. We have lovely hoppers – they are like bubbles. They take off from the ground and go up and up and up, something like you would call a balloon but of course they do not have people hanging beneath in a basket. We know of your recent attempt in a balloon to cross your Atlantic Ocean and they are followed the whole way – not by us but by a spacecraft belonging to another planet. I am not permitted to tell you which planet. We are not allowed to discuss anything concerning any other planet. That is one of the ethics of our code – that you may discuss your own planet but not anything that takes place on other planets. They are followed for observation and also it was doubtful that this thing could reach its destination with no power at all except the hot air they made which also is quite dangerous, for it is made by a strange sort of burner which shoots flame up into the balloon. It was thought that they could come to great harm and if they had done they might well have been rescued by the spacecraft that was overlooking them and might even have been taken to another planet. I do not know if they were aware that they were being followed and it is not allowed for me to discuss it for it was not our spacecraft.

I will have to leave you now for I have been in here too long. I have been in here for nearly one of your hours. I do not want to tire this good, generous lady who gives herself to us with never any kind of thought of recompense. Some day some of us must find some way to give her some recompense for all she has done, not only for you but for all of us, and even The Holy Flocen says that without her He could not come and speak with you all until one of you others learns to do what she is doing. I think now the thoughts are becoming disturbed in her mind, therefore she is wishing to return. I thank you for listening and I bring you love from my people and love from myself. Love particularly for this good medium lady and I

224

wish her well and better soon and to soothe her troubled heart and mind and spirit. Although she tries not to show it, she is still in a very distressed state but I can do nothing to help. Soskris. I would like to touch your hand. I am not a priest – I am a leader. Soskris, dear child. Soskris.

MASTER OF SPACE CRAFT
(Astral, our Galaxy)

---

7 January 1979

Normesi, as principal Circle question-master, called to the skies (words go on forever) asking for a contact from one of the space ships that were currently showing themselves in various places around the world and said that they would welcome them in love. The person who answered the call did not give his name, but said that he was the captain of his craft, or Master, as he called it.

You called me? I am here. I am from one of the space craft. I am a friend.

We welcome you in love.

And I come in love. You wish to ask me questions. I am prepared to answer, if I can.

We are very thankful that you have come and, basically, we would like to know why you have been paying so much attention to our planet.

There are many of us. We are mostly from this galaxy. We come because we wish to observe and we wish you to observe us, so that you can finally realise that there is life on other planets, not only in this galaxy, but in all the far galaxies above and below and around us all. We wish to be seen so that you may realise and stop being so arrogant in assuming you are the only life that exists. We come and we will bring you no aggression, unless aggression is shown to us. If that be so, then would we be forced to release our powers, which could destroy in seconds that place from whence aggression came. This we do not wish – it is against the will of the great Almighty God. We are not Jeculin peoples, but we are strong believers in Almighty God. Of course we know of the Jeculins – who does not? Perhaps there are some who do not, poor ignorant fools. We are not Jeculins, yet would we like to be, but first we need to learn, and know not where to go.

Why do you not come here?
Are you able to teach of the Jeculin faith?
We have had very many people come to us to learn, and they have been passed on to the Jeculins for further training. There is a planet called Wesoly in our galaxy and they have been converted to the Jeculin faith and this was due to two of their leaders coming and speaking with us.
We can go to them then, to be converted? Or can we come to you of this small Circle? You can teach? I will acquaint my many brothers and sisters who are travelling upon our space craft which are encircling your Earth in many places and showing themselves many times. I will acquaint them that here we can learn, and here we will come, or to Wesoly. I know of it, but I have not been there.
The planetary leader is called Wobley.
I know not of that name, but I will try to remember. I think perhaps that here we should come, for here we find this fine, bright beam which must mean something, and here is this person who seems to be a priestess of some kind – a holy person, for she wears a great halo around her head.
She is the priestess of this Circle and we are Jeculin Associates, the First Earth Jeculin Associates Church.
This I did not know. Why does she wear the halo?
She is a holy person who has been blessed by The Holy Flocen.
Is she able to bless us?
Yes, she has that power.
So my being inside her body is as a blessing from Almighty God? I do not know a Holy Flocen.
The Flocen is The Holy Ghost, the messenger of The Almighty.
Ah yes! This I know. We shall come. I shall bring my brothers and sisters, for we are not all males who travel upon space crafts. I use the words 'space crafts' because that is what you call us, or flying saucers, but we are not using such names, for we have names of our own. They are not important, as you would not understand. Each craft comes from a different planet, so each craft has a different name.
We are people from your galaxy, our galaxy, and we have a federation. We have a controller of the federation, who tells us how and when and where we shall go, to view whichever planet is to be under supervision at that time. At this time it is this Earth planet that we are examining, and hoping to receive joyful welcome from. Yours is the first welcome that we have received, indeed, the first call. I am very happy. I feel that I have made a great step forward in answering your call, which was brought to me by a messenger, I know not who, but who appears to be not of our galaxy.

I think it was a Jeculin messenger.

Then I am a fortunate man. We are people as yourselves. We differ very slightly, but not a great deal. We have pointed ears and slanted eyes, and high eyebrows which are just a little different from yours. We have slightly different emotional feelings to yours, but we are very happy people upon our own planet. Those others in the space crafts which are travelling together with us in one large fleet, they are also happy people. Mostly they are as you, as we, with very slight differences, but not enough to frighten anyone, should we ever land upon your Earth. This we cannot do, unless we are invited by someone of high authority. It is political authority we need, for we understand the politics of your world. They are rather frightening, for there are so many different conceptions of what is right and what is wrong. We fear that you have so much disintegration through wicked attackings and killings and warring – we do not wish to take part in such a thing unless we are attacked ourselves and provoked into defending ourselves. We come in love. I am a master space man, you would call astronaut, and I am a master of a ship, as you have on your veletision.

No, television!

Ah, yes. You have the Captain of Kirk – I am like the Captain of Kirk, but I am more like to look at the Mr Spock. I do not come from Valkarie, but there is a craft within our flight which does come from there. Their craft is maybe 1,000 miles in distance from ours, but that is nothing in space, for it can be passed in a matter of seconds or minutes at the speed at which we can fly. When you see us above your world we are hovering, otherwise we would be gone like a streak across your skies. You have already seen our craft – she has! She has looked out of her window and we know she has seen us, for we have very great telescopic powers. She has seen what we wanted her to see, for she is a medium person, and we have shown her the shape of our dome. We have lit it with lights, so that she might see the shape of the dome. We were there for at least four of your nights and on each occasion did she look and say, 'I see it!' There was also a smaller one, further back, and we sent out some small shuttle craft. They were not allowed to land, only to do reconnaissance. There is a fine landing space very near to you here, where there is sea on one side and much green, but I am afraid if we were to land upon it we would burn it and you would not like your green to be burned. Flames come out from underneath as we come down.

Have you any special questions to ask me, for I must return? I am master of the ship and I must go back. Would you like that some other from another craft should come at your next time of meeting? I shall try to arrange it for you, and I will indeed try to show us to you again, but not on this particular night. You may see another craft show itself to you, for we are trying to make you see us so that you can believe we do exist. We know that you, of this Circle believe it – that we *do* know. Now you have told us there is this Wesoly, that we also know of; and we shall go there and make ourselves known to the leader, Wobley. Here we will come to learn, if you will teach us.

Are there no more living people to your circle than those I see here now? It is sad that they cannot be here, for when we come we would like to find many here. We would like to be able to speak with many, and maybe even ... No, I suppose we could not take you aboard our craft. It would mean destroying your *craft* to land here (*probable reference to the close proximity of cars and boats*), and we cannot land without proper permission. Perhaps a baby shuttle would not cause too much damage, but that would only take one person at a time. No, I do not think it will be possible. Do not, please, think too deeply on this matter. Just watch for us, and we will try make ourselves obvious to you and then we will come in and talk with you – maybe more than me, perhaps a lot of us will come to talk with you, if you will let us. Are there others besides this good medium who can take a reception? Can you take a reception, young girl?

I could try.

It would be wonderful if you could, but there need to be more people here – a bigger, more congregational service. Can you try to do this? When do you meet? I know today is Sunday. I will try, if not to come myself, then to send another. Maybe you would care for one from Valkarie? Mr Spock is one from that planet, or if not, he certainly looks like one. I have looked in upon your picture veletision ... I am sorry – I have made this word come backwards every time! He looks like one from Valkarie, and his father too. You know, I cannot stay. There is someone here – a singing person, a gentleman. He tells me I am overusing the medium and he says to protect her he must, for she is his love. I must go, for he tells me I must go, that she may return to her own body, and I am sure he must be right.

May I touch your hand?

With pleasure! Do you feel any electricity? We carry it with us, but it is not called electricity. That is an Earth word. It is called Vitrik power and you are experiencing Vitrik power. Now, take your fingers from mine and hold them several inches away and you will still feel the power. Can you feel it? It is far greatly in advance of your electricity, which is so old-fashioned. Another touch, then I will leave you charged with Vitrik power. I am not Jeculin, so I cannot say the words, but God be with you, for we love Almighty God. Farewell. Thank the medium for us. Thank her and bless her. I thank her for her blessing. Farewell! Farewell!

Author's Footnote: *The claim of some Earth galaxy Space Masters to have Vitrik powered space craft is received with extreme scepticism. They had never been outside of our galaxy at that time (1979) and could only have heard of Vitrik. Their craft may have Cosmic Ray propulsion – a power which is impressive in itself and when eventually harnessed by Earth can solve all our power and energy problems – although Jeculin tutors have stated categorically that to their knowledge there are no planets in this galaxy utilising Cosmic or Vitrik. They believe the claim to be using Vitrik is either boasting or a genuine misbelief that the power they are using is Vitrik. The unique darkness of our galaxy bears witness to this. The degree of technological sophistication that is required to harness Vitrik is way beyond that which is necessary to acquire Cosmic power. So this great holy power will lie dormant in this galaxy until some of the peoples within it have evolved both spiritually and technologically to the very high level which will enable them to discover the means of harnessing it.*

SMITHY

(Male Astral, Captain of Space Craft from our galaxy)

---

9 January 1979

Hail to you all, friends of the Earth. Hail, and a blessing from Almighty God be upon you. I greet you also with love, with love from my own heart. The heart which beats within her belongs to the medium, but while I occupy the body it belongs to me, for this short period. Your medium, a goodly person, a holy person, has gone to visit my space craft. Perhaps she might remember it, perhaps she might not, for as I am Astral, so is she astrally visiting, but our memories are greater than yours, for we use all of our brains. You only use a very small portion, within the front part of your head. All the rest, which has so many compartments, is unused, therefore your memories cannot contain as much as ours do.

I am the captain of a space craft which is above your Earth at this time. I have been instructed to come and speak with you by he who spoke with you last and promised he would send another. I do not know the names of the captain of each ship, for each ship comes from a different planet. We are sent out together by the Federation, but we do not pass from ship to ship, therefore we do not know each other's names. You may, if you so desire, know my name. It is a simple name and one that you will no doubt recognise very well, for it is known upon your Earth and utilised by many people. My name is Smithy. I come from a planet which is in this galaxy, as do all the craft that are now visiting your world, of which there are a great many. The planet I come from you will not know the name of; for you have strange names for planets upon your Earth, which mean nothing to us. We are called XY ZEE 19570. That is our number translated into your language. We do not speak your language, but all captains have to learn the language of each planet that we are sent to see, to overlook upon our reconnaissance visits. I am come here tonight because I was requested to do so by the captain of the craft who came to visit you on your last

231

meeting evening. If you have any questions you wish to ask me I am ready to answer if I am able to do so, or if they are not classified information.

The questions have been set by a member of our Circle who is not present. The first is this: would it be objected to by your people if a member of our media, such as the newspapers, were to be present at one of our meetings?

There would be no objection by my people. I cannot speak for the other planets, but certainly not by mine!

You would be prepared to speak with them and answer any questions, for Tomesi feels that this would be a good opportunity to publicise your words.

Yes, I would speak, but I would not be allowed to disclose any technical knowledge which we possess that you are not yet in possession of; nor are you sufficiently advanced to understand. We are here in love. We wish to show you we are your friends, but if you show us you are not our friends we will be forced, if you make any move against us, any attempt to destroy any of our craft, we must retaliate, which would be of great damage to your earth. We would, of course, put our rays anywhere we wished them to go. We are not Jeculin, but we wish to learn. We have spoken together with the captain, who has passed word through to us by other channels and through other space ships, that it is possible for us to learn to become followers of the Jeculin faith and this we wish to do! Truly we wish to be better than we are. We believe in God Almighty, as you do, but we know no facts that lead us toward God Almighty except our great belief that there is a God Almighty. If you can help us, we are happy to learn what you have to teach us.

First, let me tell you we are different, very slightly, from you. We have the strange ears of the people that you watch on your space programmes, which are not so far from true. I am talking now of the great ship called *Enterprise*. There is no ship which resembles that in size or shape, but there are many ships that resemble the great ring of that ship and the dome which rises above. All our modern ships are built in what you would call the shape of a Mexican hat, except those that carry people of very high authority and they are more like mushrooms with short stalks. On top of the mushrooms are very black markings which indicate they carry people of very high authority, perhaps from the Federation, maybe not even from this galaxy. The Jeculins also have this method of marking their ships. There is no need for flame and heat in our ships, except in taking off and landing. Then must we expel that which turns to fire, but does not harm our ship – it purely harms the place in which it lands.

232

Tomesi would also like to know if you were to land exactly how big an area would be damaged?

That is a rather difficult question, for I am not particularly familiar with your measurements. I can only say that it would take a large expanse of open space, which would not matter, should it be destroyed to the depth of maybe two feet into the earth, but it would be a very large expanse that would be destroyed. Let me explain as far as I am permitted to do so. Our ships are of the appearance of round saucers, if you like, but on the top of the saucer is a dome. Between the dome and the outer edge of the circle are the corridors where all the workers are found – the scientists and the electronic experts. They are not really electronics, for we are much more advanced than you and we use Vitric power, and must have very highly trained scientists to cope with all the equipment which keeps our large space craft moving. We carry anything up to 500 people, or even 600. To keep it operating we need at least 100 high technicians. We have others for what you call crew. Some of the people on the space craft are purely crew and some are viewers, some are high-up people from our own planet who wish to view, who wish to take the journey, and some are old people who wish to pass their final time in a space ship. The outer edge of our saucer (as you call it) is what moves. This propels us through the air and all the mechanics are in the outer rim. The dome is stationary, and also the corridors where all the instrumentation that works the outer rim is situated, and also provides the air which we require to keep us in good condition. Our air is not quite the same, but I think we could breathe your atmosphere, as I think you could breathe ours.

Now, let me go a little further, though I must not reveal too much. On the under part of our craft (and this applies to all the craft that are in the fleet presently circling your Earth and displaying itself at various times) there is a central part, which is approximately the same size as the outer passages and the dome and it is from there that the flames come down. When we release the gasses to come down, it bursts into flame as we hit the atmosphere and, as we land, it burns a large hole. I say gasses for you have nothing to compare them with. The burning can even destroy rock. It is our only way of landing and we have special equipment to stop ourselves being thrown at the time of landing or taking off, otherwise we could be exterminated by the very act of taking off or of landing down. We are carefully placed into compartments that are protective to us and still give us sufficient air to breathe during the time all this takes place, which is a very short time. It all happens very quickly and a lot happens in that short time. You must be strapped down by iron clamps. They are not iron, but that is your nearest metal to that which we use. The clamps are put upon your body – your legs and your feet and your head and your neck – absolutely fixed firmly, so that you cannot be thrown at all. Then, of course, you must proceed to release yourselves. It is going up on take-off and coming down on landing, no matter how slowly we try to do it, that causes this great impact. The shuttles do not have the same effect, for they are much lighter, but they do make a burn as they land. One space ship of a similar size to mine can have as many as 50 craft that can go out at any time, to go to another ship, or to go closer to the planet they are circling. Their carrying capacity is two persons, or at a pinch three – not usually permitted. We have some craft that open up underneath, in a similar manner to some of your aeroplanes, and could magnetically take a vehicle, together with the people in it straight into the craft. It has been done. The people have not been harmed and have been returned. The only thing is that they will be disbelieved when they return. They are frightened, for it is an unusual occurrence, but we have tried to assure them that we wish them no harm, only love, and to show them that we are good and loving people who will not harm them in any way. None have ever complained of being harmed. A space man such as myself could easily go down in a shuttle and drop out of the shuttle without it ever landing, for we can jump quite high and we can jump down quite steeply without harming ourselves. It is our natural ability that we can do this if we so desire. You have got somebody that you call a bionic man – that is imaginary, we are not! We can do it, but we do not have all electrical things inside us to make us do it.

We do not live as long as the Jeculins, not in this galaxy. I would say approximately 200 of your years. There are three on my craft who wish to pass their last days in space and this is their general age. This is a fairly common age-span for the advanced planets of this galaxy. We are informed that those of other galaxies are able to live considerably longer and therefore we wish to have their resuscitation chambers, which we do not so far have. We have not yet acquired the knowledge which is necessary for this.

You will pardon me if I have to remind you that I am the captain of this craft and I must return, for I should not leave it for very long. If you have any more questions, please be quick, before my time expires. It would be possible for one of us to be dropped off from a shuttle, but we would have to have federation permission for such a thing to happen; and we would have to possibly send first an emplinador. I do not know that they would allow one of us to come – I think they would say that it would have to be many to come. If we came from our space craft or shuttle we would not look like you, for we would be dressed in silver skins, with no outer clothing, and we would appear to be silver people. Underneath those silver skins we have pink skins as you have but these are our travelling costumes. Therefore, should one of us come from out of a shuttle, which we could do, it would cause much consternation amongst your people to see a glowing silver creature, completely silver – face, head, hands, body and feet. The trouble with you, my friend, is that you are too impatient. You may have been hoping for many years to meet a space person and I quite understand this. But do you not realise that every time you sit in this Circle and someone from another planet speaks with you, you meet a space person? Shake my hand, my friend. How do you do? Or as I say in my language, '*Colly tunapar?*' So you see, you meet a lot of space people every time you have one of your meetings, whether it be from your own galaxy or from a far galaxy where the great Jeculins are.

Before I leave you I must ask you this most important question – will you undertake to give us lessons, that we may learn how to become Jeculins? I know we cannot become full Jeculins, but we wish to be as you are, associated, and we wish to have the greater advantages that you possess, the greater knowledge that you possess. We would come in great numbers to sit within this walled ... *palady* we would call it, you call it room, and we would crush into here to listen and learn and go back and tell others and even tell others on other craft, to spread the word more quickly. I did not realise that every living thing contains a part of The Almighty. Is this the beginning of our learning? This is a revelation which is to me astounding, that I can contain a portion of God, that great man of heaven! You see how you are advanced in some ways and backwards in others? We are advanced in other ways and so backwards in this necessary thing. Let us make this galaxy so that it is not a spiritual backwater, as you call it.

We do have day and night on my planet, plenty nights, and your sun is our sun. I do not think that the heat is diminished when it reaches us, though we have inner resources, as you have. You have inner fires and that helps to keep you warm. Ours are channelled to make sure that at no time shall we be cold. Why have you not done this, on your Earth? You are drawing oil and gasses from deep down in your world. It is old and considered backward on our planet. If you have the technology to do that, why can you not go further and get to the middle fires? But then, of course, you have not the equipment, nor have you the necessary metals that will not melt or explode in the heat – you have not found these technologies yet. You should learn! If only some of us could come to teach you, but we are not allowed to teach you that. Each world has to find out for itself

Nobody is allowed to teach their technology to another world. It is good that you have Jeculins to help you to find these things – I wish we had some to help us. Perhaps we have and I do not know it. Our emplinadors, as you call them, are called automatons by us.

There is a great deal of truth in your *Star Trek* programme in the things they say and do and the way they are able to do them. Much is very near to truth, such as their transportation. This is possible, where they go into their transportation room. We have discarded it, because sometimes the people cannot be assembled in the same way. It has been done, and has been used on many planets, but has ceased to be used by our planet and I think on many other planets as well, for the reason that sometimes, instead of their own head, a person might quite easily have the head of an over-sized fly. For that reason, it was discontinued.

We use our shuttles if we wish to land a small party. The bright red light that you saw tonight could have been one of our shuttles, but the light colour is actually orange. You know, your medium has very good vision for distance viewing, not for seeing here in this room, but to see long ways out, and she sees so clearly – she has beautiful vision for long distance. She was able to see the space craft that followed your ballooning people from one side of your world to the other. I will try, when I reach this vicinity, to give you some idea, that you might watch out and look for me. I will display our lights so that you will see more or less a green interior with brilliant white lights around it. Will you look for that? I have no idea when it will be – it depends on when I am sent to this vicinity, if I am sent to this vicinity. May we start our learning of the Jeculins next week? I shall pass the word. Do not be surprised if your walls are stretched out! I will bid you farewell. I leave you with love and I pray that the love of The Almighty be ever with you, for I feel you to be blessed people and because she wears this big halo she must be a holy woman. I bless you as far as I am allowed to do so and I say thank you for this very fine reception I have received, for although we have been circling your world for at least four weeks, no one has called to us, as you have done. For this, we thank you.

It is possible that if we were on the right frequency we could pick up Earth radio messages, but there are none but myself who speak your language on my ship. Therefore, it would be useless to send any others here and I could not leave my ship. We in the federation have a method of signalling which we can pass from ship, which all operators can take and pass on to the captain, and the captain will then decipher. Then we can make out what the message is, no matter how far away the other ship is. It could be thousands of your miles from us, but we can give them an answer through the code.

Who can say how many planets there are between your world and mine? We are all dotted around the galaxy – above, below, beside, around – everywhere. Do not think that you are the middle of the universe, for you are not. You are just one small planet, in one small corner. You call some of our planets the Milky Way – it is really very silly, but that is what you call it. Are your astronomers not foolish people? They think they are very clever, but they are like children playing with bricks and they do not know which brick fits where.

I must leave you now. I do thank you for receiving me with such great welcome. I feel the love you are offering and I give you love in return. I wish to thank most of all the good, holy medium who has allowed me the use of her body and I hope that she has enjoyed her visit to my space craft.* She was conducted there. She would not have been allowed to go there alone. We could not allow such a thing – she could be lost in space! She will be conducted back. Now I am returning she must be within call and she will be escorted by my second-in-command. Therefore must I return to my craft. Vitrik for you – feel it, keep it, let it charge your bodies. Bring her back.

————

Footnote: Nitesi did have a hazy dream-like recollection of being on a space craft, but that was all. This was a bonus, considering the contact speaking through her was using her physical brain, making it almost impossible for her to relay her experience back to her brain for recollection when she returned to her body.

HOGAR

(Male Astral, Master of Space Craft, Planet – Vulcanie)

---

14 January 1979

We are here in great numbers. We thank you for the welcome you offer to us. Each one of us who is present from our fleet are all Masters. There are five male Masters and three female Masters. There are other Astrals and Spirits within this room and to them also we say greetings, for we bring to all of you our love and the love of our people. I can feel that we are received in love and I am sure that my brothers and sisters can also feel this, as do the spiritual people and the astral people who are listening in this meeting. Truly, yours is more of an astral meeting than a living meeting and a few spirits are here to back you up. There are also many in your cone, which is controlled at the little gate by one called Peter, who has vetted us well before allowing us through. We understand this to be a duty which he must perform, for you must not be allowed to receive any evil ones, which we know there are within our own galaxy, but we would not let them hurt you, if we could help it.

My knowledge of your language is limited, but sufficient for me to deliver my speech to you. You can call me by the name of Hogar, if you wish. My planet is that which you know as Valkarie. I am a Vulcan. You have made one that looks like us and calls himself by our name (*Mr Spock, Star Trek*). A Vulcan he says he is, a Vulcan he looks like, so someone has influenced your people who have made this programme.

We will be glad to learn from you, for this is the purpose of this great meeting this night. We wish to become followers of the holy Jeculin People and we know you to be the Earth followers. Therefore, we know you can teach us. I would like you to give us the opportunity, whilst we are all banded together, to learn the beginnings, that we may return later to have our second and third and later lessons. If you will proceed, we will listen. Each Master here has a certain knowledge of your language and

238

will be able to interpret into their own languages upon returning to their own ships. They will be taking notes. Proceed, if you may, for our time is limited as we must return to our ships. It would be marvellous if we could meet with the Jeculins, but you must remember that we are of this galaxy and that we have never ever been outside this galaxy. There is a belief that between each galaxy there is a barrier which we cannot pass. Is there then no barrier to prevent you from entering the next galaxy? This is great news to us, for we have always believed we must remain in this galaxy and not venture forth into any other, believing it to be breaking a code of etiquette. We know we cannot land upon any planet without special permission – we must have the permission of the highest-ranking people of that planet before we would dare to get sufficiently close to make any sort of landing. Also, we do not wish to frighten the occupants of any other planet by appearing within their vicinity without being pre-warned so that they come to a state of panic and wreak havoc upon us with their atomic resources. They could destroy us, just as we could destroy them with our Vitric power, which you do not have and some planets near to you also do not have it. Perhaps those planets you call dead and incapable of supporting life have inner dwellers, for there are many planets where this is the case. We have amongst our Federation and in our fleet at least a dozen craft manned by inner dweller people who have the power of space flight.

It *was* right that we look upon God as being a superhuman person, until we had the word passed to us in these past few days. You believe that Almighty God is the Power of Love – this we understand, since you have told us and as she has told us. We must accept her word, for she is holy, or she would not wear the halo. If the Jeculins do not kill anything, then how do they eat? You mean that when the corn is ripe, and the ears hang with the weight of the fruit, it has a spirit and it would be killing it to pick it then? The thought is frightening, but I see what you mean the spirit is still living and therefore you are committing a crime by killing it. Even the grain that we use to feed our animals must not be used until it has died of its own volition? If the grain were to remain upon the ground, even though you think it is dead, it would grow again the next season, therefore it is not dead. What of the animals? We eat animals. I like it near raw – very good! If we did not do this, what would we have instead? If you believe in the Jeculin method of reprocessing food, then why do you not do that? You say that we are more advanced than you because of our space craft. It is true that we have space travel where you do not. We build very large craft – mine has 600 aboard. We make our power as we go, we do not carry fuel. There are the machines that do this.

Is this for consumption? (A glass of lemonade) May I have it? It is non-nectarial? No! No like it!

Would you like some nectar in it?

Ooh, nectar, yes! Lots, lots of nectar! It is make you happy drink. We do not have cigarettes. We have hoky-poky – a long pipe with bubbles. I would like one of your cigarettes. It is good! See? Look everybody! Is good! Are you not jealous? Look – good nectar, good hoky-poky! I am glad I came – will come again, yes!

We have monitored your planet because we are very inquisitive people and we have a method of catching your television pictures and, instead of making it come on a box, we can make it come on a big screen, as big as one of your walls. That way we can learn a lot about you and also we learn about your politics, which we find quite disgusting. You have many terrible fightings and killings for no purpose whatsoever. This is barbaric and you must realise that you are in great need of help to overcome these terrible things. Yet you must understand that no other planet can in any way interfere with anything that goes on upon another planet. We are not permitted to poke noses into what does not concern us. It is almost a universal code, and we would expect you to do the same, but we do not feel that you truly believe in occupants of other planets. Only a very few, such as yourselves, and a few highly intelligent scientists who believe that Almighty God has made beings upon other planets. Most other planets have only one people. We Vulcans have only one people and the other planets that have their ships in our fleet have only one people, who are all wishing to learn, to get out of this dark corner of the universe and become those who follow the path of light – this is very important. You understand, of course, that we are not very emotional, but we are very logical people and when we devote ourselves to a certain cause, nothing will deter us from that cause and we will follow that or die in the attempt.

For your benefit I have called my planet Valkarie, but it is in fact called Vulcanie, which is close, but not quite the same. We do not mind if you call it Valkarie – I do not know what the word means, but it sounds quite pleasant. Maybe the reason for Mr Spock's amazing likeness to us is that someone has received contact in the same way as you have. A good medium can always receive contact from any planet – it matters not whether it be this galaxy or any other, or even from your own Earth, where you have a spirit world.

Our method of astral projection is different from that used by the Jeculins. We have a method of suspended animation, wherein the body

240

becomes a frozen entity and the spirit goes forth. It gives the spirit time to make a very long journey – we can go anywhere within this galaxy, which is a very large galaxy and holds millions of planets. We search for the love that you say exists in the other galaxies. Not physical love. Physical love is a near impossibility for us, because we do not feel emotion of that kind for each other. We feel sisterly and brotherly love, but that does not contain any physical love. We are of those that reproduce mechanically.

Will you excuse me a moment? I will have a private telepathic conversation with my friends who are here. They all feel it is time we made the return journeys to our ships, for they are without Masters, and only our second-in-commands in charge, which they are not truly trained to do. I am to tell you that we are encircling your Earth for the period of four weeks and we are not in close formation, but are travelling at a distance of 600 to 1,000 of your miles behind each other. Your question of the possibility of us showing ourselves at a given time and place I can answer here and now very briefly. Over a certain portion of your planet a group of space ships have shown themselves and been photographed by some of your people. They have taken various pictures, in various stages and of various numbers of craft. In addition, this has happened in another part of your planet, where a good viewing has been seen during the past period of four weeks. Also in this vicinity, this good medium has viewed one of our space ships, in fact, the one who is the leader of our mission, and she has viewed this ship on at least three occasions and has reported it to you other people. We are no longer to encircle your Earth, for we have now to go on to another planet, where we will also spend four weeks of your time. We are leaving your vicinity now, and will not return for at least six of your months, or maybe one year. I can promise you nothing concerning any sightings, for it is a different craft that is sighted on each occasion and we must follow our instructions and only show ourselves when commanded to do so by the Federation. In the case where several were observed over on the other side of your planet it was instructed that 20 or 30 craft should be visible. We have the power to make ourselves visible, but we are normally invisible. We can only make ourselves visible by illuminating our dome to such an extent that you cannot help but see them. We can also send small shuttle craft from our larger craft, of which we carry 50, sometimes 60, and we can send them out on reconnaissance. They may be sighted and could be termed to be what are considered to look like cigar-shaped objects, but they are in fact our small craft that leave the Mother ship, and are really only used for telescopic reports.

None are there for the purpose of harming anyone on any planet – all are love, all carry love, come in love and would help if they can, but are not permitted. Each planet must make their own struggle alone, to reach its own culmination of success. We can only occasionally (unbeknown to you) loan one or another of our good scientists, who can help you without being known to you as coming from another planet, but who will not take the credit for anything he teaches. I can tell you nothing more and I can make you no promises. We will be back in this vicinity in either six or twelve months. We will come again to be seen. Never fail to watch the skies, for it may not be our fleet out there, but there could be another fleet from another group of planets that have been chosen to go out by the Federation. Believe me, they all come in love and friendship, and they will call to you if you could only hear them – 'We are your friends!'

Our Federation is a large proportion of the planets in this galaxy, with the exception that we do not allow in the Federation those planets that we consider to be very evil. We do not have any of the animal types in the Federation, but there is a special Federation for the animal types, including the insect types. The insect types are of no comparison to those you have on your Earth, for they are larger than men and in many cases they are very, very dangerous, venomous and evil – those are not permitted in our Federation. We would never dare to even try to make friends with such as them and nor must you. They are not for you, for you are human people and must only be in contact with human people. I am telling you – from this galaxy, do not have contact with those types. Do not have them, for they would do you harm and hurt and should they enter the good body of this holy person who is allowing me to utilise this whole body, I am afraid great harm would come should you permit such an evil entity to enter her. I do not think your Peter would allow it – we were well vetted before we were allowed to come in, ears and all! I will come again, if you so desire when I return to this vicinity. I will ask that our conversation be put into the records of our Federation, for we would like that to happen. We would be very happy to send astrally to you, for we must continue this learning, now it has started. Even I may be able to come astrally, but it means that my body goes into what you call suspended animation. It is very cold, as if life has been withdrawn altogether.

Thank you for your hoky, thank you for your nectar, thank you for your hospitality and thank you for the use of this beautiful and kindly lady, who has permitted me to use her body and voice and even scratch her ears! I love her and I feel that she loves me. The leader of our fleet is called Hosanna. I must leave you now, for I feel I am over-using the medium. I have learned something, and I have taught you something. I say the Jeculin word – Soskris. Come, my brothers and sisters. We go.

———

Footnote: Later it was learned that there was a force field around the perimeter of every galaxy regardless of its shape. Subsequently prayers were said that the misinformation given to Hogar would be rectified.

TINKLE

(Male Astral, Captain of Jeculin Spaceship, Planet – Mobil)

16 January 1979

Soskris I say unto you, brothers and sisters, children of the blessed Almighty, you whom we know as the chosen ones. We greet you in great love and respect, for you have many conversions to your names. There are spiritual conversions, worldly conversions and many, many more over the past aeons of time in your Earth spirit worlds.

I am what you would term an astronaut. I am not from the fleet that has been encircling your Earth in the past few weeks of your time. I am from a Jeculin ship which has been overlooking those craft to make sure that they were not about to offer you any harm. We are also a fleet, but you would never be able to see us from your Earth unless we came nearer, which at this moment we have no intention of doing. I am a ship's Captain and I am a friend of another great astronaut, Cebia, whom you all have met. I do not come from Cincea. I come from a planet called Mobil. We are like yourselves, with the exception of the colour of our blood, which tints our skin slightly blue. It is a pale, pinkish blue, but our blood is blue and therefore the colour shines through our skin and makes it have a bluish glow. It would be nothing to frighten you if you were to see us, for we look like you. We do not speak your language unless we have learned it, as I have done, and many others you have met. It is in all of our visual libraries and many are interested to learn this queer language you speak, which contains so many unnecessary words. However, we understand and are happy to try to communicate our thoughts to you through your own manner of speech.

I am not here to teach you anything, only to socially visit you. It is my personal wish to visit in this manner and I have left my sleeping body upon my ship. It is my allotted sleep time, so I am not depriving anyone else of their time, for they would have to be on duty anyway, whilst I am on sleep

244

time. I have taken this opportunity to come to offer my love and the love of my people upon the ship and also the people on my planet. I have informed my people that I would be visiting you and was not deterred in any manner from making this journey. If you wish to know, I will tell you my name, but it is a funny name and you will probably laugh. I cannot speak it in my own language, as you would not even be able to get your tongues around it. To translate, it would sound like Tinkle-Tinkle. I do not know of any other that has my name. For you, I will be Tinkle and I will try to visit upon another occasion, if you wish. I am far away from you, a very long way away, so my visit this time will be short, for I must return to my body in time to awaken, to take my own time of duty in command.

Upon our ships, we have four commanders. They are all responsible for different functions of the vessel, but one must be the complete commander, and that is me, so that although I have commanders, they are under my jurisdiction and we are working accordingly very happily together. Nobody has resented this journey that I am making. All would have liked to have been the first to come. I am also the commander of our fleet and I have four commanders upon each vessel. Mine is what you would call the flagship. Mine is the leading, overall command, and the other ships in the fleet must obey such orders as are given from my ship. I believe you have the same system functioning with the air-travelling vessels that you use. They are very frail and expendable. You have tried with these rockets and made the journey to your moon, which was quite an enterprising thing for you to do upon your small blue Earth. I think that you will understand that we have given assistance to some of your rocket people, which perhaps has not been released as news to the general public, but I know that those who were in that space rocket or module were able to communicate through a sign language with people from another planet, who assisted with love. I do not think this has been revealed to your people. The astronauts might have been in fear of revealing what they had seen. They may have been too afraid to admit that they had actually met with and been helped by what are termed upon your Earth as aliens, although we object to this word very strongly. Nevertheless, those people that have been helped, and there have been more than one set of astronauts that have been assisted, have all become very religious people, for they believe they have been helped by God. In a manner of speaking they have, for we are all God's children and we follow the great Code of Love, which we cannot, under any circumstances, break. Nor can we harm any people of any planet unless we are first attacked. Then we are forced to defend ourselves and our methods of defence are so much in advance of yours that it is only natural that some destruction should occur, if we have to defend. We try not to destroy. I think our craft are much in advance of those of your galaxy.

I know there is a fleet that has been encircling your Earth and we have been overlooking them. I do not think they were aware of us, but it was our job to overlook them to see that they were not going to do you any damage or harm. I think their mission was a peaceful one and was an effort on their part to reveal themselves to you so as to prove there are other people such as yourselves on other planets. I think that was their sole mission and we are in agreement that this should be done, for your Earth should not be so arrogant as to believe that you are the only people that God Almighty has placed upon a planet. It is so childish and immature that we wonder at such stupidity. I am glad to hear that their commander came to you. If only your people could realise that when these people come to you they are coming in love and in peace, even those of your own galaxy who are not Jeculin, but are still believers in The Almighty. With the exception of a very few planets this is the case and they are not the ones who would have space travel, for they would be animal peoples who can still be God-fearing and God-loving. I know of one planet in your galaxy where the people are scaled, almost like reptiles, but with very good brains, yet they are warrior people who fight between themselves. We understand that the reason for this is that the chief who can gain the most land will be the highest, but always will come another chief who feels himself stronger and will try to overcome the first chief and become the strongest. I think they will not harm you, for they have no space travel and are not likely to have, unless they have been given emplinadors. This I greatly doubt, for emplinadors are usually only given to those who are great lovers of The Almighty and can be trusted not to misuse them, such as your friends the cat people from Jorpoa. These warrior people have long and very vicious tails, which they use as weapons, swinging them round and they are very agile in using it.

I am sorry – I am not eager to leave you, but I have to return before my duty time arrives and I have yet to return to my sleeping body before I can go on duty and it is a long journey. I was pleased to be able to come, for I am pleased to be able to report to you that those space craft we have been observing were not here to do you any harm. Of that we are fully convinced and will inform the Great Council. If you can teach them of the Jeculins as we have heard they have asked to be taught, it will be a wonderful thing.

I am as you all. This is of course a lady person, and she has a beautiful halo and a very great aura, and there is a very great aura for the young lady here (*Teresi*), and yours is blending very well with these auras, my friend (*Normesi*), together with the other visitors in this room. There is one who stands very close here who has a very fine aura and also one over there who has a fine aura. (*Joshua and Mow-Bar from Alphar.*) These people seem to be protectively taking care of you. Whoever they are, they would seem to be very good people who are undoubtedly believers in the Great Almighty and Holy Flocen. It is my time to leave you and I believe your medium is getting tired, for this good person here (*Joshua*) tells me it is so. Soskris. I journey now.

LEDAN

(Male Astral, Historian, of Planet Ocena)

15 April 1979

I am here on this occasion because I am following the high glow of Nigel and I welcome him, because he has not been in this house before. You remember me, Nigel? I have spoken with you before on many of the times when you came to the meetings. I am so happy to see you returned once more, for here you will find nothing but love and grace and goodness and you will leave feeling a better man for having made this contact. There is a time coming that will be a time of trial to all of you. If it is a trial for you you must ask The Flocen for help and He will give it to you. You will understand that you must do your best to be lenient and kind to those you find to be arrogant. If they are to you too arrogant, try to find the love in your hearts that will help them to overcome their own arrogance. Try to lead them gently to the path of light. You are the Children of Light. I speak now of the boy, man, the child that is everything, almost an impossibility. I speak also of Tom. His arrogance is growing worse and with each day increases. You must be lenient with him and try to lead him upon the path he must follow; try to guide him away from his silly ideas and try to make him understand that he cannot make money from religion. There is no money to be made for you personally; if there is to be money at all, it must be for the Circle and not for anyone's personal wishes. The boy Marc – he is an incredible creature. Whence comes his knowledge I know not. Is he from your Earth? who knows? Neither does he know himself. He will come to you, I know this. He is thinking of you constantly. I have been near to him – he is in another country. His aura colour is peculiar. It is not bright as yours are. It is dull, but it has a yellow tone in it. It is an old gold shade, tarnished almost. It varies according to how he behaves, but then everyone's aura changes depending on their mood or thoughts or way of being. If you go into the church and kneel and fervently pray, then your

248

aura will grow bright immediately. Yours have grown to be very beautiful, and so tremendous that they reach so far up into the heavens that you will soon need another gatekeeper. Perhaps it can be organised for you. The cone has grown enormously – it now accommodates a great number of people. It is the belief that grows and makes the cone greater. The cone comes from Nitesi and is added by your own strength. You have cast a light, here, within this Circle – the pathway that leads to Almighty God and you are upon it. That is why you are called the Children of Light; for you there should be no night, no sadness, no unhappiness, but we cannot help it if these things come into your lives. It is only you who can deal with them, not us for it is against our code to interfere in the running of any human being's life.

I will go back to the subject of brother Tom. You must be forbearing with him; it is old age that makes him turn his thoughts to one track and he cannot get away from it. You must be lenient with him and lead him away from that track, for he will not get what he wants. I think he might not come any more to the meetings which is sad because he has a true belief, but allows other things to override it. It is this wanting to contact what he calls aliens, which is a term we very much object to. To you there are no aliens, but to him we are aliens, not brothers from another planet. He is used to talking with these people as if they were of the same standing as himself when in reality most of them are of very much higher standing and should be treated with respect and not demanded of to do this, that or the other.

Your beam is visible to everybody but yourselves. People of other planets have more developed spirits than you have. Everything of them is so much in advance of you. I have heard you say before the meeting that you might be bringing another medium into the Circle. I am anxious to meet this person and I hope he will be able to receive us. Let him know that if he comes here he is protected. Maybe it will not be myself or any that you know who will speak through him – maybe some new ones that have never been before, but whoever it be, accept them as you accept all your friends.

Our love is with you and we pray that the love of The Almighty may ever be with you. We love you dearly. I will pass your love on to your many friends on my planet. Soskris.

ICLA

(Female, Jeculin Supervisor of Circle Tutorage.
Planet Cincea)

---

22 April 1979

Holy Children of Light, I am so happy to come on this occasion. I bless
you all with all the power I have and I wish you to know that I love you
now as I always have done. I am of course your very old friend Icla whom
you have known throughout your long years of learning and studying and
patiently working our will as we would have you do. Soskris to you all and
to all you new ones that I have not seen before. I give great welcome and
dear, dear love. It is for you four that are new to the Circle that I give an
extra wrapping of love, to enclose you in the warmth of love and the safety
that comes around you all.

We are strongly against all killing of any kind, even in as much as we
will not kill animals to eat nor take anything living from the ground until
they have fallen and they are recycled as you have been taught in the past.
We must have no killings and we must have no member of this Circle who
is interested in weaponry that might be the cause of this terrible deed, this
terrible killing which is a wicked act of this Earth.

I love you all and I leave my love with you to keep you safe and guard
you from harm. I will be with you on your journey, Patresi. Soskris to you
all.

JENNY (Little Girl. Earth spirit)

Hello everybody. I am glad to be here and I am glad that the dear, beautiful
Icla would let me in to speak with you. Have you ever seen her? She's so
gorgeous, so beautiful and so glowing with light. I'm not allowed to stay
very long because Icla said there is another waiting to visit on the other
side of the room. I wanted to say that I love you and I did not steal any

250

chocolates and I did not use any perfume. I can't eat any chocolate!

I love you all. You know, you who are strangers here, I live here with Nan. I sleep on her wardrobe. I am the little girl who always stays here. I only go away when I am called. I am called now – goodbye.

Footnote: Jenny used to live in one of the adjacent row of cottages long since demolished to make room for council redevelopment She often spoke briefly through the medium if the chance occurred. She loved playing with Nitesi's perfume bottles and had mastered the art of making them spray, admitting she was responsible for a bedroom smelling strongly of perfume and a noticeable drop in the perfume level of the bottle used. Apparently on this occasion she had also got the blame for missing chocolates! Although not having met in life or being in any way related, she looked on Nitesi as her granny.

NESTIA
(Female Spirit from Fincia)

24 April 1979

Holy Children of Light, so recently called by this new name yet the news of it has passed through the galaxies. Children of Light; so beautiful to be called so for a wayward planet such as Earth. How happy we are that you of this planet have learned at last to see the light which is leading you towards The Almighty. You have been taken by the hand by The Holy Flocen and led on to your path and that is why you are now called holy Children of Light. It is, as you must realise, a great and impossibly high honour that has been put upon you, to give you this title, for it is only the very closest to The Almighty that are called the Children of Light; therefore must you be considered to be so close to The Almighty and if not The Almighty at least so dear to The Flocen, who is the hand, the voice and the will of The Almighty. You do not know my name. I am Nestia and I come from Fincia. Our group of planets are all in Holy guidance, for it is a very select area. Without appearing to be arrogant I can tell you that the Cincean group of planets is considered to be most holy. I am a woman of medium advanced age, halfway through my journey. It is good to speak to you through this good person. There are not many mediums who permit this – most of them stay to quarrel with us or fight even to prevent us from coming in. I am halfway through my lifetime, but I am passed over. I was lost from a space craft six or seven years ago in your time and it does not distress me to speak of it now. Several people have been lost when they attempt to leave the space craft and walk the skies. We have a lifeline and if it breaks we are lost forever. My spirit is whole as my soul is, but my body is disintegrated in space. They couldn't catch me – I went too fast. It was my own foolish misadventure that I went where I was told I should not and was not prepared for what would happen to me. I was indeed a precocious lady and at 170 or more of your years one can still be precocious and

252

perhaps a little wilful, which I admit, to my own disappointment. I was one of the scientists and I was responsible for certain equipment upon my ship. There were two others ready to take my place when I ventured forth from my ship. You do not have to ask the captain; you see, there are exits from our level and the captain is on a much higher level. Everyone on my level knew I had taken this great step and advised me against it. I cannot say exactly what happened to cause my loss of life; all I know is I belong to Fincia and I returned to Fincia. Our spirit world is not overcrowded. We have levels such as you have, but they are according to the knowledge you possess and the occupation you were in when you passed, so I have passed to the scientific plane. I can receive much teaching on subjects such as yourselves. You are heard of all over the galaxies as the holy Children of Light, the protégées of The Holy Flocen. We can go back and do other journeys if we wish, but I have not been long enough in my present state. After about 100 of your years we are asked to make the decision; do you wish to remain a spirit or do you wish to have another life? Most people choose to have another life. We can have stress and strife in our lives as well as you. For instance, if we become argumentative with each other, as some are inclined to do. These are not a great many, but there are those you will come across that you cannot possibly speak with without getting into some sort of argumentative trouble and that can cause great strife throughout the whole portion of the community you live in or within a space ship, if that is where you are. Personalities are screened before we leave, but then personalities can change, particularly in the torrid atmosphere of high and fast-speed travel. It brings out facets of the personality that were not apparent before, as it did in my case – it made me wilful, so I was not complacent and was keen to be adventurous and do things other people were not doing. I said, 'Why should I not do it if I wish to? If I do not come back, that is my own fault.' And so I took the journey, the walk into space and was lost accordingly. It is not done as a habit – very few people do it, though some do with success. Mine was without success and was not a necessary trip, but a wilful one. External maintenance is a necessity and in such cases harnesses are used. In my wilful trip out into the atmosphere no harnesses were used, only the one retaining lifeline, which snapped. I was brought back to Fincia and now I can travel how, where and when I will, so my wilfulness need not now be curbed! If I wish to come I can come. It was the speed and stress of travel that turned my mind a little. Those who were under me had to take my place and sadly report to the Master that I was no longer within my body. It is quite usual for the female astronauts to outnumber the men. We are quite

253

well built and the men are the smaller of the species. We do not use them for copulation, it is not necessary any more. We use them for ordinary love play, but not the other thing. There are many planets where the women are larger than the men – the women are the overbearing leaders of the planets – I mean they bear the brunt of all the decisions and are responsible for what takes place upon the craft, especially when we have female masters. If we were to land on your planet our ships would make a superficial burn upon your Earth. If we do land through accident and cannot get ourselves repaired, before it is likely there will be any capture of any one or any part of our vehicle, we have to destroy our ship. It is a necessary prevention. If the occupants of the ship could speak the language and strip themselves of their apparel, which is moulded on to them and has to be unmoulded to be removed, unless they could do that they could not be loose in any world that was not their own and this applies to any planet, not only yours. A Jeculin planet might be less agitated by the appearance, but unless they were invited they would certainly be agitated. I have been an astronaut from the time when I was a little over twelve years of age. I learnt my trade aboard a craft – that is the best way to teach, far better than going into schools. You are put into a ship and probably you are only picking up little pieces of paper the scientists are dropping on the floor, but you are still learning all the time and gradually you become able to manipulate first one thing then another and finally you become a scientist yourself. I am glad you find my conversation interesting and I will endeavour to come again, but I must give precedence to those more important than myself, for I am not at all important now. I bid you Soskris and I leave my love with you and I hope I may take your love with me, for if I leave and deplete my own love I must have some back to replace it. You send your love with me and I go in love in the same way as I came. Soskris to you all.

TINSIE
(Female Astral from Opea)

24 April 1979

I say Soskris to you. I come in love and I greet you, oh blessed, holy and righteous Children of Light. Such a great title to have. You do not know me although I have sat within your Circle many, many times. I am a person, an astral projection, and I come from a far distant planet that is called Opea. My name is difficult to translate and too long for you to remember, so you may call me Tinsie. I am happy to be with you and I have a prepared speech which I am likely to forget if you interrupt before I have finished. I am a lady, tall lady with very long, pointed nails. I am a leader person and I bring you love from my people. I am not in control of the whole planet, but only a part of it. We have bodies such as yours but with tall ears and we have uplifted brows for the eyes, which are also uplifted like your oriental ladies. The gentlemen look the same, but they are not so tall as the ladies. We walk with a little shuffle, not as you walk striding out. It is like a small movement that carries us forward but only a few inches at a time. This is because we have very small feet and we walk almost upon our toes. It is considered very elegant and is perhaps the reason for the gentlemen being smaller, for they walk upon their heels as well as their toes, but they still walk in a totter manner. We are highly praised for our intelligence by other planets. We have inter-visitations with other planets in our area, always by invitation of course, for no planet persons will visit another planet persons without first being invited. I live in a palace. There are other people who are not so high up who live in communities and are as one large family living in one large building together. We do not have sexual intercourse, but we have instant breeding in the inoculation chambers. All are sterilised at birth whereby they cannot make intercourse between man and woman with any breeding resulting. So we can have intercourse if we wish, but it is not thought very ladylike or gentlemanly. It is done occasionally, but we know with it we cannot breed children, for we are all sterilised so that we cannot produce any children; they are done in incubators. We have many rules of etiquette in our society. Sometimes we are not observing the rules and are reprimanded for not behaving in a discreet manner; we are crossly spoken to, even myself. Even though I am a leader I have a co-leader who is my spouse – we are of one family, yet we live together as spouse and spouse as did your kings of long ago. We are associates, not actual Jeculins. As a leader of the people in my area I am also astronautic, for it is necessary for leaders to go quickly from place to place to settle problems and calm matters down if necessary. Our planet is divided into four portions, each with its own leader and leaderess. Different places have different rules. There is one who is the supreme leader – he is my father and we leaders are all of the same family. My brother is my spouse, and we are permitted to cohabit if we wish to, and nothing is seen to be wrong in this. But then, we are not Jeculin people, we are only followers. We are only brothers and sisters in that we come from the same batch and although we all have the same father we do not share a mother in common – many, many mothers, but one father. The leader of the planet is the father of all leaders. The leadership is hereditary. The next supreme leader will be the eldest, not necessarily son. The first to be born in the batch is designated to be the leader if and when our father passes on. I have many sons of my spouse. I have been in a space craft to visit your planet. Your planet is much smaller than ours – that is why you are smaller people. I will leave now and will come again when I have another prepared speech to give to you. I love you dearly. I bring you love of my people and hopes that we will all sometime be able to meet together. I am now the spokesperson for all my people and have been instructed by my father to say these things to you. I leave you in great love and will be returning to you soon. Soskris.

OODGIE
(Male Astral, Captain of Space Craft, Planet – Issiko)

24 June 1979

Soskris. A blessing be upon you all. I am come to speak with you again. You know my name and think it funny, but I do not mind. My name is Oodgie. So you looked for my craft and could not see and you were regretful. Yet you looked straight at me and failed to recognise that my craft was other than a star. We were stationary, but the Earth moves, giving the illusion that we were moving. There was no reason for us to move with the Earth, for we were out of Earth's atmosphere. Maybe I am not visible to your eye, for you mistake me for a star. We have certain instructions which means that we follow a course and we are not permitted to go against those instructions. It is like your air lanes. You must pass upon a certain level in order not to collide with any other vehicle which may be in the same orbit. We have been trying to signal you with our lights by putting them on for about three seconds and off for three seconds. At this time, we are directly overhead of this portion of your planet. Within one hour we will no longer be directly overhead because your planet will have moved a fractional amount. You must wait until it is quite, quite dark in your atmosphere and then endeavour to view not only my craft, but three others that are in your vicinity. I cannot speak for them on the matter of flashing lights, for they do not belong to my group. You must not be disappointed if you cannot see, but remember that if you are able to open your eyes, try to see with naked eye for better vision, for it is difficult for you to train your magnifiers on one particular space and they are no help over a long distance.

The fact that you say light travels is a fallacy. It is an unproven theory and no matter how many times you think it has been proved, light does *not* travel. Light is either there or not there. If I flash my lights tonight you will either see it or not see it, otherwise you could look for me three weeks

257

from today and then see me. It is not sensible. I am there and if you have the seeing eye, you will see; and if you have not the seeing eye, you will not see. I will tell you this; if you look at my craft from a certain angle it will appear as a large round hat with a small domed centre, which is in fact very large. Around the perimeter are the illuminations and around the shape of the dome are the illuminations, according to the angle you are looking from. If you were underneath you would not see the dome and if you were looking at it sideways you would see half the perimeter and all the dome. We can fly in any way. There are other types of craft which are more like mushrooms, wherein the large part of the dome is the perimeter and the small part underneath is like the stalk, which is where the legs come from when it is going to land, if it is going to do so. The mushroom-type craft is usually heavily marked, for it carries, as a rule, important people, as I do myself, but I do not have that marking. I am carrying people from High Councils. I am able to tell you that they are all anxious that you should be aware of their love and that they are here in this vicinity at this particular moment in time to observe your Earth, through our own telescopic type of viewing windows. With our kind of beam viewing we can penetrate bricks and mortar as you call it, like your X-ray.

We are also able to hear all that you say. We have what you would call an electronic gadget that can seize sound out of space and tune in to it. We get a wavelength on you and dissect that which we want and obliterate that which we do not require. Sound never dies, therefore it would be possible to pick up sounds made a million years ago, if the equipment were invented to cope with this. The sounds would not stay in the place where they were uttered, but would travel into deep space. They would, however, bounce back eventually to their place of origin, for everything goes in circles. Everything that exists in time or space goes in circles and must return eventually to continue again upon its way. These words that I utter now will never end. Blessings. I leave. I am called away. A blessing upon you all and my deepest thanks that I have been permitted again to use the body and to speak with you in this direct manner. Please convey my gratitude to the medium. Soskris to you all.

258

OODGIE

(Male Astral, Captain of Space Craft, Planet – Issiko)

---

3 July 1979

Brothers and sisters, I have been with you before and I come again. I am still in your vicinity. I am Oodgie and I am sorry that you could not see me when I promised that if you looked you could possibly see. Perhaps I was too high for human eye to visualise. We are a little closer to you this time, for we have come to realise that you cannot see us, that you cannot distinguish us from the stars, although we are not so far away as stars. We can glow as brightly as a star, and often do, particularly if we wish to draw your attention to us, which we have tried to do. I am come to you astrally – my body sleeps within my craft.

I will try to flash my lights to you and hope that you will visualise them. We have been in orbit, but we are hovering at this time. I have been flashing my lights for periods of two to three minutes at a time and if you have not been looking out at these times you would not have seen me. I have not got multi-coloured lights as some other craft have. Mine are white, and very brilliant, more like searchlights. If you do not see, do not be discouraged, for at least you have made the effort to try and I have at least made the effort to try to display myself to your eyes.

We cannot move from our lane. We have to have special permission to move closer to your Earth. The lanes which you use for your aircraft are much lower than those we are able to occupy and we must not interfere with any of your flying arrangements, which go on all the time. If people in your area have claimed to see a space craft so close it could not have been an actual ship, but a shuttle craft, which is supplementary to the mother ship. If we had permission we could do this also, but we do not have any permission, so we cannot send any shuttles. We have no reason to send a shuttle. A shuttle is usually sent when someone is to be put down or picked up from your planet. No Space Master may disobey

259

his instructions and you would not wish me to do this thing that could possibly interfere with your flying lanes, as it is your prerogative to use these lanes, it being your planet. The shuttles are usually illuminated, unless they are coming secretly to pick someone up. On this I can give you no further information for there is not one that I have been instructed to pick up. We are only upon a reconnaissance flight and must keep our distance from the surface of this planet. We are happy to be able to try to make contact with you and are more than happy to have the use of this medium and to be able to talk with you so openly about what we want and do not want to do.

I will leave you now and ask you to look at me later this night. I will be there, flashing my lights and hoping that you have the all-seeing eye that can see that which is there to be seen. I am quite sure that your medium will be able to see this time, unless there are low clouds, in which case we can do nothing to make you see us. I am bringing love to you from all those upon my craft. Soskris, brothers and sisters, holy Children of Light, and I say to you in your own words, may God's love be with you. Farewell.

ATINAR

(Female Astral, Space Craft Group Leader from Suklar)

11 May 1980

I am not known to you. I am called Atinar. Soskris my friend, my brother. Dear ones, Soskris to all of you here, spiritual, astral and living. I come from a planet in a galaxy adjoining. It is called Suklar. The galaxy which is adjoining yours in an upper position is called Cereal. It is the name of that galaxy from which I am coming and it adjoins your own galaxy. Above the position where you are now placed is I. It is like the continuation of your sky, your space, but there is of course as with all galaxies a division. A force field which separates each galaxy. All craft can pass without difficulty. They have the means of passing all force fields, but it is to keep each galaxy separate. It is not put there by anyone – it is there, just as space is there, just as planets are there in space. I will give you a little information about myself. I am senior space craft leader. Group leader as you would call amongst your Earth planes I think.

Group Captain?

Group Captain to lead all craft coming in formation through space travel to visit other planets. Sometimes in other galaxies and sometimes within our own.

You are a formation leader as well then.

Yes. Yes. I am a lady senior craft leader.

Have you come down from your craft now?

Yes. I am come because I am wishing to meet those of the great light which is renowned throughout all galaxies and is now so clearly seen shining into space and which has this extra special holy beam which joins it. If one could only get to the other end of that holy beam, then would we indeed find something wondrous there.

Does the end go as far as the eye can see? There is no end that you can see?

261

No end at all. We can see where yours ends, but where it is high, high in your atmosphere, but that which comes to meet it seems to go forever and must pass through many galaxies.

It goes out beyond the galaxy? You're telling us things we didn't know.
It must go through, not through the extremities of the galaxies, but right through the middle of many galaxies. If you would understand that a galaxy might be, in case you do not know, we will say for example an oval shape and another perhaps oval shape above it and another one which would be oval maybe going that way and then still something underneath it and another one lacing in there like that ... (*Atinar was using the medium's arms to demonstrate her words. She continued talking and gesticulating to emphasise the closeness of the galaxies to each other and how each galaxy is bordered on all sides by other galaxies, which meant the beam of holy light must go through many galaxies to reach us*) ... right through the middle of all of those comes this great and holy light.

So this special beam can be seen in another galaxy?
Oh yes indeed. Do you not understand that you are much discussed upon other galaxies and upon other planets because of your great beam and the great holy light which meets your beam. They say it is Almighty God's Earth Jeculin beam which He has given to you to meet your beam and your beam has been given to you. To prove who you are. To show who you are. To lead us that would know you easily to you. But if one could go to the end of that other wonderful beam ... Not that yours is not wonderful, for it is, but this other holy beam must go straight to The Almighty. And there is where you must put your feet and we who are already Jeculin peoples would do all in our power to help you to put your feet upon that beam that you can climb to The Almighty. Eventually you will do so. So we come from far and wide to see you who are talked of so much because of this great, great thing that has happened. This spot where you sit which I recognise to be only a very small and humble place. Not a manger like where child Christ was born. Oh no, but in its own way equally humble, as you are equally humble people. Are you blessed people? – or you would not have your own beam and certainly you would not have the holy beam that comes down to guide us all to you. To show us where you are. Perhaps no one has taken the trouble to explain all this to you before.

We knew of the holy beam coming down and we were grateful that astronauts used it. Space people do come and talk to us, but I had no idea that it went way outside the galaxy.
We do not go into the beam. We must not go into the beam, but it guides

262

us for we can see it. It is like a lighthouse going through galaxy upon galaxy. Of course there is, as you know, no great black holes in space as your people teach or claim. But perhaps what they imagine is a black hole in space is not a black hole at all for there are no holes in space.

What do you think it could be then?

I think it must be the place where the source of power lies. The source of power is the great and wondrous blessed Almighty. I do not say it is though, but we know there are no holes in space. No black holes that you could drop through and be lost forever, this is not true.

Our scientists bounce radio beams off the stars with radio telescopes and they get signals from some stars that give far more powerful signals and they cannot explain them. Are those they get those extra powerful signals from possibly the suns of each galaxy?

Not necessarily. It is possible that the planet which you are trying to bounce your radio waves upon are receiving your waves and trying to notify you that they have received them and are returning their own waves back to you. Trying to tell you, 'Yes, we know you are trying to contact us. We are trying to contact you.' All will tell you of all that I know, all the planets that I know and I do know many in more galaxies than I care to count, all will tell you, 'We are your friends'. And you write a song which says, 'We would like to make a contact with you.' We would like to make a contact with you. Yes, there are some people that get some knowledge into their heads which tells them what is going on and they speak of it and speak with actual knowledge, but few believe them, so they think them to be fictional work. But it is not all fictional, some as yourselves are receiving information. Just as we of other planets also receive information concerning you. But do always remember that when you get contacts come to you through your medium they are not coming out of idle curiosity. It is because there is such ... such ... a big talking point throughout different planets and different galaxies concerning this new thing that is like a new life beam born, a new world being created where your beam . . .

(The recorder clicked as first side finished and after explaining to Atinar the tape would be turned to second side, she said she would have to leave anyway.)

263

RIKKA
(Male Astral from Cincea)

June 1980

You who are from far places, Soskris, I come in love. It is a pleasure to visit here. A pleasure much longed for, much dreamed about by many people who would visit this blessed place wherein sit those that were chosen by The Holy Flocen. Chosen and taught. Chosen to be Almighty God's emissaries. Chosen to be called The Children of Light. Not until you had earned it could that name become yours. Yet earned it you have. And all who visit here come in reverence and listen eagerly with bated breath to those who would speak through this good and kind medium. This woman who has given her very soul to the work that she does, not only for you but for us. For without her we could not be with you and with her we can ever be with you. You do not know my name. It is in fact unimportant, but since you like to know the names of those that visit, I will acquaint you, both name and planet. My name is Rikka. You do not know me. I am from Cincea.

You are male Astral?

I am and you have had many from Cincea. I am yet another who comes to speak. To be as one with you. To join with you in your Circle and to be able, with you, to become known as one of The Children of Light. For me it is a privilege. One I could not obtain in my own planet, but in yours, here in your Circle, this I can be. One of The Children of Light and will return to tell others of my experience here and how big is the love that welcomes me and all others into this Circle and there are many here. Many that speak not, but many that devote their time and listen to all that do speak and give their love, freely, not only to us, who come to speak, but to you who sit here listening. You are indeed loved. Do not ever forget that and give your love out, so that they also may feel loved. I would wish that I could be here with you more times, more frequently, but I am informed that one must not

264

usurp the space wherein others would speak. Once you have been and there are others who have not been, then must you refrain from coming again to speak. For you must allow those that have not had that chance, to be able to speak through her, this blessed person who gives herself and the use of herself. Neither ever remembering what she does, or where she goes, while she permits herself to be utilised. You must surely realise what a great service she does for you as well as for us. You must surely feel grateful that you have such a person, as we feel grateful. For we could never speak to you without her. You could, of course, go back to your old method of using a board, but too much guesswork goes on with a board, whereas with the spoken word there is no guesswork. You can hear what is needed to be said and it will register and remain in your brains providing you are not fickle minded. We do not come for fun. We come to know you, to love you and to be loved by you. We come to strengthen you. We come to help you to be more sure of what you believe. And each one that comes is another peg pinning your Circle together and each one that sits here, as part of your Circle, is helping to bind your Circle together and make you all as one. A great offering soul, going up in love to The Holy Flocen and Almighty God. There is much beauty in such a service. Much beauty that cannot be found in your other religions. This is a personal thing. Every one of you must feel personally your response to all you have learned and all those who come to speak to you. Remembering that none come this long journey just for the sake of coming. They come because they wish to be part of you. To be one with you and probably to teach you something. In love I come. In love I spread my warmth around you. The strength of my love around you and around these Astrals and Spirituals both in this place and up there in your cone. I am indeed able to give much love and I am also able to receive much love. If you have any questions you wish to ask and I am able, I will answer.

Are you a religious leader?

No, I am not. I am a very loving personality. I love deeply and dearly all my friends. All my people, brothers and sisters and you included, but most of all I love The Holy Flocen and the blessed, wondrous Almighty. We of course do not call our God as you call The Almighty. But The Almighty is a fine way to call our Immortal God.

How do you call our Great Father?

Each planet has another name.

There is no Usietan name?

No. Each planet – yes. The Power, translated into your language. The Power. But there is no other name for The Holy Flocen. That is one name and one only in all planets that understand the Jeculin claim. It is for everybody and The Holy Spirit is for everybody. A father to everybody. Not only you with bodies, or I with a body, but all things that live and breathe and grow. For everything that grows, breathes. All is filled with the joy of love. All things, all trees and plants, grasses and seeds of flowers, all things that you can think of, all imbued with the love, the warmth, the power. Only people of this small blue, backward Earth, so few of them, realise that love is everywhere, all around you. Love is in everything and in everyone. Even your animals and birds. Your beasts of fields, all are imbued with the same beautiful love. Look in the eyes and see love in any animal you care to look at, or any bird. The eyes, you rightly say, are the mirrors of the soul. And if you look in the eyes and see love, you have seen Almighty God. That is a wonderful thing to be able to see. For you will never see the immenseness of Almighty God, you will only see the tiny portions that are permitted to you. But look in eyes that show you love and you are looking at a part of The Holy Power and think always The Holy Power is not only The Almighty as you call him, but also The Flocen is the spirit of that Holy Power. The blessed Flocen, your father and my father. The holy being who helps so graciously with no expectations of anything in return. Only love. But only love. Love is what makes any world, any planet. It's only love that keeps that planet in light. No, I am not a religious leader. I am a person filled with love. I am come to you in love, to talk to you in love, as did your dear mother Icla talk to you many times. Perhaps will come to you and talk again. I feel I have the power to do this, just as this good medium of yours has the power to receive us. A power she has been given. Not one that you can actually foster or encourage, but one that you can use, once it has been given to you and it has been given to her to use and therefore she, being a good child of God, uses it as it was intended to be used. You should bless her for it, for she blesses you with the power that has been given to her to do so. You must love her. You must indeed be grateful that you have such a one and you must always remember there will come a time when you must find another. Maybe not yet, but you should be prepared. It has been said to you before and it will be said to you again. But it is not in her hands, or yours when the time comes. You will need someone, for you must not let this Circle drift apart for lack of a medium. You must stay together even if it is only for the purpose of prayer meetings though she must continue until such time as you can find a medium with enough power to help you as she does. I leave you now...

266

GRANAD

(Male Spirit from Planet Fu-Lieu)

October 1980

Granad.

Is that your name?

Yes, Granad. I greet you with love also. The name of the planet that I am from is Fu-Lieu. As you would say in lieu of something. It is not very far from your galaxy. It is adjacent to what I think you call perimeter of your galaxy and we are consequently not needing to travel very far as some of your visitors who come through many galaxies.

You are in the adjoining galaxy.

Oh yes. Not of your galaxy, of the next galaxy. Well, one of the next galaxies, for there are many that adjoin you, as you must realise, and there are many galaxies that adjoin our galaxy.

Are you an Astral, Granad?

You call Astral one who is sleeping on planet?

One whose body lives.

No. I have no body now. I am spirit from other planet in other galaxy.

You are male?

Yes. I am fine big fellow. Was and still am much interested in this type of meeting Circle. Is interesting to visit such places and become acquainted with people concerned to find out their reasons for forming Circles such as yours. Many are for curiosity, some are, as you, for serious research. And some are for good sport, but is not good sport to play with spiritual people. You were eager to know what becomes of you when you have finished with the body and now you are aware that you live another life. The same as you're living now, but in another sphere, on another level. You will be in a world of spiritual people. It is not just going into space you know, it is a place that you are going. It is like a shadow of your world. If this is of any interest to you, I tell you. You find to go from this

267

life into another life like going to sleep and waking up and there is all of your new life ahead of you and when you are going ahead you still have much to learn. It is best if you can forget your old life, but most spirits, particularly Earth spirits, have an unfortunate habit of wanting only to remember their Earth life and not to look forward to the new life which they have to learn as from beginning again. For if a new life going forward and must forget old life going backward. Does make sense yes, no? I have life ahead because not long passed to this new spirit life. I have life behind and do not want to say I must not speak of it, but I know I must learn new life ahead and not try to relive old life over again because old life was not good enough. New life will be better. Try to remember what I tell you now because you can make this big mistake. I hear many people make this big mistake.

I think so, on our planet. You said passing into the next life like waking up after a short sleep, but I believe there can be many cases, can there not, of passing over with complete awareness of leaving the body.

Oh yes, you can be aware you leave the body. Try to imagine little sleep. Not big, little. Come end time little sleep. Have to be little time between. Then you can say, 'O-ho. I am up here and I am down there, but I am down there no good not alive any more.' Yes? So I am now up here. It seems like up here. It might not be up here, but it seems like up here and down there is the old me, now no good any more. I just go a little while. Only a little while – short – quick. I am starting new life.

You passed over quite recently on your world?

Yes and I am still remembering other life, but I have got to forget other life and not try to live that life over again, but find new life to live and go forward to much better things than I had before. You go forward and make a new life with new people and perhaps sometime soon you go and make yet another journey. It depends on how good you have been in your life you have left. I am new to this sort of contact. I have been where there are others on other planets, but have not yet been to speak with people as I am speaking with you. Is like experimental journey for me. If one wants to cling to old life one cannot go forward.

And if one wants to cling too severely to old life one is earthbound.

Yes – or any other planet-bound, wherever you come from.

But surely cases like that would be very rare on your advanced world?

I do not think so. No, I think people could be just as your people can be. The more you hang on to old life the less chance you have of beginning new life, because onwards is good and backwards is bad. And so you see this lady here, over here.

You mean Nan, the queen lady.

Yes. From many, many centuries and clinging still to her beautiful gown. Her thoughts of the life she leads. Yes I am speaking about you. Never mind, never mind. Yes, all right I don't mind who you were. So, why don't you go forward? [*These words were directed to Ann Boleyn, who was present at the meeting. While transcribing the tape a strange high-pitched sound like a one-sided garbled telephone conversation could be heard briefly in the background to Granad's words. The tape had picked up something which was not audible to Circle members at the time. Could it have been the English queen's protestations to Granad over his criticism of her obsession with her former life and untimely death? Unlike Granad, she did not have the luxury of the medium's voicebox to make her views heard.*] You go forward. I tell you forget the old one. Come, be a new one like me. Come forward and learn. As a little child learns. There is plenty to learn. You listen to me please, you living ones and you others who are spirituals. Learn that you can go forward and you can make much more of a new life than you ever made in the old life. So don't think about the old life. Try to tell these people (*the Circle*) when you come to speak to them through this good medium that there is more to come to. More for us to have than we ever had when we were as they are now. I mean as you are now. I'm talking to her (*Ann Boleyn*) and these others, spiritual people. I want them to come forward with me and when it is your time I want you to think like this. To come forward and learn as a little child learns. Slowly I know, but you will have more greater, bigger, finer life than you had before, but you have to work for it for yourselves. You've got to learn. So if you just sit back and dream about what your past life has been, you will get nowhere at all.

I think there is one thing we have learned in this Circle, Granad, that is that the gates of the universe are open to us.

Yes and there are others like me who are working to help you to come forward and so long as you will remember that what is past is passed and is not possible to live it again. Come, find the new life and then you will find something worth having. I am giving you good advice. Am not very good at this language, but I think you understand me well.

I hope Nan will take notice of your words.

I am hoping she will because to cry for what is so long past. It is a waste of tears, my dear. Come forward and smile and be happy and see that the great light that lies ahead of you is to belong to you if you will only reach out for it. I will take your hand if you so desire and lead you towards it. Oh, you think you cannot leave your own spirit world. Perhaps you cannot, I

269

do not know, but there must be something in your spirit world that is better than the past. This I am certain of.

Yes. Nan could have had five lifetimes – five journeys in the time since and it would be completely forgotten –

She must be quite good or she would have had more journeys, I think. She could not have been such bad person as she says they say she was.

I think it would have been a service to Nan if she had had another journey in a pleasant environment, a good environment.

I think I have to go. I think this medium is very tired and I have talked rather a lot.

(Tape abridged)

BO
(Male Astral from Planet Wesoly on Far Edge of Our Galaxy)

October 1980

I am a friend of Wobley and I come from Wesoly. You know of course that we have recently become Followers of the Jeculin belief or as you would have it, the Jeculin Brotherhood. I know that you like to know a person's name when they speak through this good medium. I have a very ordinary name. It is so simple that you could not possibly forget it. It is just plain 'Bo'. Oh yes, I am Astral.

Male Astral?

I am. Our planetary language is different from yours and different from Usietan naturally, for we have not yet learned Usietan. We have a few words, as you have, but there is plenty of time, we are but newly-formed Jeculin Followers as you know. I say newly because we have a longer life than you have, therefore the period of years that we have been associating and learning with the Jeculin people is perhaps to you quite a few years, but to us it goes very quickly. You understand we don't call it a long time. We think of it differently from you for our time is quite different. You know what we are like.

Like us.

You are the same as we are. We are people as you with the exception that we do not wear so many clothes and we do not have this cold atmosphere that you have. It is quite chilled here, but perhaps that is because it is growing into your winter time. However, I understand from those that are here who talked to me that you have not yet had your summer. Whether you will have one or not I do not know.

We won't have one this year that's for certain.

What a shame.

What they mean of course was the summer was very disappointing.

271

The time when it should have been warm and sunny, it wasn't.

I find it a little uncomfortable for I am used to a warm atmosphere and I do not really like so many clothes upon the body, but then of course she must have them for she is of this planet where you need more clothes. Our limbs are free of clothing, they are not encased in these sort of things. Legs are bare and arms are bare and bodies are largely bare, with the exception of little draperies shall we call them? or diaphanous veils if you like. We are not ashamed to show our bodies. Our bodies are to us quite beautiful. It is too hot if you put too many swarthings upon them, so we wear the very least it is possible to wear.

How does the sun of our galaxy appear to you?

A long way off.

It must shine far brightly than any other planet.

Oh yes. It is as a sun, but far, far away. Our heat is not from the sun. Our heat is from the next galaxy. I don't know if this has already been told to you.

Yes, it has. I wondered how much of the Vitrik heat, light was lost in coming through the ...

The force barrier.

Between the galaxies, yes.

Yes, some of it is lost, but not altogether and also the light is there most of the time although as we turn, as you turn, as the planet turns, we will some of the time be ...

Darker?

Yes, because we will be facing the night. As we turn half of our world faces the night and the other half faces the Vitrik warmth.

The night side of your planet, surely that would be the side the sun would be visible in the night sky? Does it shine as a very, very ...

No. No. You have it wrong When it is night you cannot see sun.

Can you see the sun in the Vitrik light, through the Vitrik light?

Yes, but it is not through the Vitrik light. The Vitrik is coming from one side of us, the sun is coming from another. So you see one half of our planet will see the Vitrik and the sun at the same time and the other half will see no sun, lots of stars and night-time.

And it changes on a daily basis – your days.

Yes it does change on a time period.

How long is the time period compared to our 24 hour day?

We do not have 24 hour day. We have a time period of approximately – well no. This does not apply to everybody, for everybody adjusts their time to suit themselves.

You don't keep a basic time?

No, because we do not have to work. The light period is longer than the dark period and this goes on throughout the entire time. Not as you when your night period gets to be longer than your day period and another time your day period gets to be longer than your night period. We can sleep for periods up to two, four or six hours if we so desire. The normal person stays awake approximately six hours and then has to have a sleeping period. This is reckoned in your time. We do not count time as you do. Two hours of sleeping period we find to be long enough at one time. We do not have to work. We do not expend our energies except by desire.

How far is Wesoly advanced – I know you have space craft – I mean emplinadors, sophisticated android type emplinadors?

We do not have any android types. We have the mechanical type. Yes, the very big ones and we have some movable ones, but they are not what you call android types. They do not look like humans. They are metal men. Something like when you used to have knights in armour and our metal men look something like that with the masks and headpieces. Visors that will come up and go down as necessary, but of course behind there are the – what you would call – computerised tapes.

Can your metal men sustain a conversation?

Ah! Only what they are programmed to say. They do not speak in a human voice. It is a metallic voice. More monotonous than a person speaking. Not so melodious. I like particularly the speaking voice of your medium, although it is nowhere near my voice. My voice is considerably more what you would call deeper and more resonant. But I like this speaking voice, it is a good tone and easy to use. It would be too difficult if I tried to speak in my own tone of voice.

Are you personally associated with Wobley in any way?

Ah! I have met him. Not out of habit of course for he is planetary leader and I have met him on a couple of occasions, but it is of course a very great honour. Just as it would be for you if you had one supreme leader over your entire planet, it would for you be a very great honour if you ever got to speak to him. Because you see he is the supreme leader of the entire planet and you are lucky to have him for a friend. I call him a friend, but I do not associate with him as a general rule. Largely speaking I am way below him, beneath him. I am of course not forced to do any menial or manual work. I only do that, as we all do, which most interests me and I find myself most drawn to the what you would call medical profession. Where we have these very large, you would call them hospitals, we do not, but they are more like factories than hospitals. Where people are renewed and also I am interested in where emplinadors are made. I do other things beside these. I do lecture on what I know to those who are interested enough to attend lectures, which is like a voluntary university where people come not because they have to, but because they wish to know about these things. And people such as I who have already passed through a long period of learning are now in the position to give a long period of teaching.

Are the emplinadors made largely by emplinadors?

They were originally made by people, but they are now made by emplinadors. You understand the emplinador is almost replacing what you would call workers. With the exception of those who do voluntary work, they do replace all workers. All land work and building work is done by them. There is no need for any man ever to soil his hands, but if he wishes to do so that is a different matter – he would find himself outnumbered wherever he went to do this sort of work by emplinadors. These, of course, performing their functions to replace the manual labour that man would normally have done some hundreds of thousands of years ago. It is not only us that has this. This is pretty general. I do not know about some of the planets in your part of the galaxy, because they are away from us. You are not close to us. We are in the same galaxy, but the galaxy is an enormous place. Do you realise how many planets there are in one galaxy?

It has been estimated 100,000,000,000.

That's about right.

And there are some galaxies with more in them.

Yes indeed.

Have you any really large wild animals on Wesoly?

Well, they're not wild anymore. They're not wild. They're not killers anymore. They are all well cared for by emplinadors and all have their normal – just as all peoples – have their normal distribution of food in the same way that we do. So are the animals fed. They have no need – there is no sort of killing of any sort upon our planet and has not been for a long time before we became introduced to the Jeculin practice. For we have always believed it wrong to kill and we have always believed that animals should not kill each other. And if they are given sufficient food why should they kill each other? Killing is wicked. It is against the Code of Love and we have believed this long before we met with you and came to know of the Jeculin peoples.

We knew from Wobley that you were very nearly Jeculins in everything but name.

Yes and still in everything but name for we are only permitted to be called Followers. We cannot actually be Jeculin peoples. I do not know how long it will take, but because we have not been of the Jeculins until we met up with you through Wobley and you got us really for the Jeculins to take us over. When I say take us over, they do not really take us over. They have taught us many things in addition to what we already believed. But of course we did believe in God, but we didn't know what God really was. That is the great advantage that you have brought to us. Because we thought of God as a superhuman person and we certainly didn't believe or know anything about the one you call Christ, but we did believe in the Holy Spirit. Yes indeed we did believe in God, but we didn't know well enough. We thought God was some superhuman elderly gentleman the same as your churches still teach on your planet. There have been people who have said upon our planet, 'God is an astronaut.'

That's been said on Earth before.

I know. I have heard that it's been said upon your Earth that God is an astronaut. But there are millions of astronauts – that's what you call them. There are millions of them. Every planet has them. Can you imagine the confusion in the minds before we came to know the truth through your intervention when you first met Wobley.

I would have thought that you believed in a divine power. I am surprised you had the same idea as Earth people of there being a superhuman.

We thought it was a divine power. We thought he was a divine person. As we are, only divine and we're not divine. That's what we thought and I believe it's what your people believe upon your planet. Well, gradually they will learn. The Almighty Power is The Almighty God and God is The Almighty Power. But then who am I to tell you, when you first told us. I feel I have to leave you. Yes, yes. It's Peter here called. He says the medium wants to return . . .

LUKI
(Female Astral from Floating City 'Karrigotta' from Planet Gotta)

---

21 October 1980

I come from the magnificent floating city which you know as Karrigotta. We belong of course to the planet Gotta and I am not related to Fury who has already spoken with you, but I know of him. I am astral person of the female sex and I am called Luki. I do not come from Fury's – what you call – I cannot make any word – he lives below me. I am higher than he. Upon a level that is higher than his. I come to you and would speak love with you for we are indeed very loving people as no doubt you have already been informed. We are for you great friends and are happy that you are interested in our planet. I have for you a little news which you may or may not be aware of and that is to tell you that because you were once – many people on your planet – that now exist upon your planet were once from other planets and other galaxies. We are of course interested in your planet because of this thing that was done so many millions of years ago when all different types of people were put upon your planet and those people have now forgotten why they were sent to your planet and what their mission was. They have unfortunately gone far from the road of truth and forgotten the path of love. Although they love in their own way they do not love universally as we are all intended to do. You know of course that I speak of many different nationalities upon your planet and of the many different countries which exist upon your planet and I am not sure that you yourselves were not people from outer space. I mean you of this Circle. Originally you could easily have been so.

We were in the First Earth Civilisation some of us.'

I think this is true. I think it is true. I am sure you will understand because of the fact that people from so many planets have been placed upon your small planet, it was really like rehabitation – rehabilitation of

276

your planet. Because of that - that they originally have come from other planets in different galaxies, of course all peoples of other galaxies and of your own are very interested in your small planet that contains so many people from space. It makes you a point of interest that other planets do not have and apart from that of course we are always observing. Not necessarily you alone, but many planets. In your particular case, on your planet, we are interested especially because you have these people who originally were from other planets and are no longer remembering what the purpose of their being put upon your planet was - to start and create the great religion. I am not sure that Gotta has any people upon your Earth, but we are very interested in you, particularly in our what you call laboratories where we have long sight. You call telescopic sight. Like Vitrik eye. You understand? And now I have one more thing which I must remember to tell you before it goes, because we are excited when we come in here and it is very easy to forget. I have to tell you that your Tomesi has asked why can we not come and put our pictures upon your television screens to bring for you direct messages. Yes, we would love to do this, but first you must learn how to harness Vitrik, for we can only broadcast with Vitrik and not what you use and Vitrik would not be suitable to be received upon electronic equipment.

I think Fury said it would blow it to pieces.

I am told I must give you this message – it is important that you understand that we cannot do this thing, for we would dearly love to do it, as would many other people from many other planets I am sure, but since they do not use what you use it would not be possible for your equipment to receive. Even if we attempted to do this would cause much damage to your equipment for Vitrik is quite different to electricity. You understand that? I have now given the messages I was asked to give and I can now talk to you socially, as a social call, if you so desire. Perhaps you will like to speak with me now. I am listening . . . Oh, you have nothing to say. You are what they call tongue-tied.

How is the floating city?

It is great. It is a marvellous . . . It is something – do you not know of us? We have been here before.

Louis wasn't here on that occasion.

Ah! We have large planet, but too many people, so we have built a floating city. It is as many levels – like you would call storeys one upon the other. It is approximately ten miles in length and two miles across. This is supported by many space stations almost touching each other and joined by heavy girders over which is an entire rubberised, pressurised skin

277

which makes our air and atmosphere. And we all live within this commune which is one enormous commune holding a great many people in this space. We do not breed upon our floating city for there is not room to increase the inhabitants. If any are to pass away, which they will do, then we may go and collect others. To return to our own planet Gotta and get others to replace them, but it has been agreed we shall not breed upon the floating city.

You used the term space stations just now ...

Yes, because it is your term.

By that do you mean power points for the propulsion?

Yes. They are as space craft only they are doing a job of upholding a city between them.

And they are practically continuous all the way round the perimeter?

Pretty well. And these are joined by large girders to keep them together.

What are the girders made of?

You would not know if I told you for it is a metal of our own, which you do not have upon your planet. It would resemble – only much stronger – what you call steel. It is very light in weight as are all space craft very light in weight but very strong. It is miraculous that we have established this that can stay in space indefinitely and will not at any time need to land anywhere and is in perpetual motion. We have many levels. There are, I think, as many as twenty levels which are all the same lengths. The whole complex is of ten miles by two miles and each level accommodates many, many people and also animals. There are grass, plants sections where the animals are there more for ornamentation than any other reason for we do not eat them. They are there to make it homelike. There are nearly as many emplinadors as people. Not quite, but very nearly. Probably one to three. They do all the manual work and they do provide for everything and everybody. Also supporting work for making the space stations able to carry on without ceasing to function all time. It is a great stress and strain upon them. They are being reconditioned perpetually to allow them to remain working the whole time. We have been in space already a hundred or more of your years.

I suppose the emplinadors take the odd one out here and there for an overhaul.

No, not able to take a complete station away, but gradually overhaul each station. All the time there are a number of emplinadors who do nothing else, like there are a number of people who go around and do nothing else but cleaning windows, which are not made of glass as you have, but still need cleaning. Your breathing will make for some amount of sediment upon the transparencies which are our windows. We have something in place of glass – it is not what you use at all. You have glass and you have another thing called perspex and you have a thing called – I cannot think what it is called . . . vinyls thing. I do not know quite what you call it, but it is in much use upon your planet I know. We have not got exactly like this, but something similar, but more advanced and better.

Advanced plastics, do you know . . .

That is the word I was trying to think. I could not remember plastic.

Do you know what they are processed from? Some of our plastics come from oil.

A lot of it comes from our home planet Gotta and is manufactured there and passed on to us as we need it for renewal and sometimes big space ships will come and deliver a whole load to us.

Have you a landing bay for a space ship to pull into?

No, we have a means of getting out of our floating city. It is like a small force field which we must go through and also return through and it is self-sealing when we go in a small hopper or even a larger craft, for we have many craft attached to our floating city. We can go in those, but only the people who are specially trained are allowed to go into space craft. Not ordinary people. I am what you would call ordinary person, not permitted in space craft, although I could go in hopper. Which means I could go from one side to the other and it would only take a flash of time in a hopper to go from one side of this complex to the other. And if we wish to go up or down we use the same sort of system you call lifts. We could go up and down in a little hopper if we wished to, but we still might have a long distance to walk or to get on a little convey belt – a conveyer, you know? Which runs the whole length of each commune and upon each level there are about ten communes. Each one being approximately one mile in size. So you see with twenty floors or levels there are a great many people accommodated upon our magnificent floating city. It is really quite stupendous and as far as we understand the only one we know of. There may be others in other galaxies, but we do not know of them. We are an experimental city in space.

We have heard of other floating cities in the past – but not of your size.

No, I think this is quite unique in size.

Perhaps a mile square maybe, something like that.

Yes, this is quite unique in size, also because it has so many different levels whereby we can accommodate so many people. It is a masterpiece of ingenuity and is greatly thought of amongst many other planets of the galaxy.

It must have been many years in the building.

I think indeed it must have been and I've got a feeling that now it is in transit it cannot stop. It has got to go on and on, because I do not know where it could go to if it were to stop.

Well there's plenty of space anyway.

Well no, it won't stand – well it would I suppose – stand still in space providing the rotary arms were going round on each station, Yes, I suppose it could hover, but we do actually move the whole time and we have special plotted course where we may and may not go between the different portions of space reserved for each planet. We have to go between them.

But I thought there was no between. We were taught, that one area went up to another.

Oh yes, but you must understand that where your area ends the other one has to have a little space in between before the other one comes to it. And the same on the sides and up and down. There are mostly little force fields in between – not great big ones like you have in a galaxy, but little minor force fields which are created by some unknown power which we do not know of.

The planets do have their own gravitational pull.

Oh yes, everybody has that everywhere. That is essential and it differs so much on each different planet, this I have been informed. But then you see I am not permitted to go on a space craft so I could not visit another planet. I can only visit as I am visiting you, which is astrally. Have taken boost to come for we have fine good boosting chambers and can visit each other in the same way if we wish, to save travel.

The whole of your lives must be full of interest viewing different planets all the time and different galaxies.

Oh indeed and we have very fine – what you call . . .

Telescopes.

Yes. To look through and it brings a planet lovely and close to you so that you can look at it and see all the beauties. We are not allowed to travel very close to other planets, you understand that. We must stay at a distance whereby we could not come to any harm or bring them to any harm.

Can your telescopic equipment, from the distance you are, bring a planet so close that you have to pan all over the surface? That it is so large that you can see only one spot of it at a time?

That is it. That is it. And then when you have examined that spot you will move on and see what the next part is like. It is really playing I spy and is not really very kind for maybe they do not want to be observed, but we do not do them any harm and it is a great point of interest to us as we are perpetually moving.

280

And you can see actually down to buildings?

Yes. We have even seen people moving about in some cases. It depends on where the planet is when you attempt to view it in relation to where we are. When it is in the far corner of its airspace we would not be able to do that, but if it is in close proximity then we can indeed examine it quite closely and they can examine us.

You are in our galaxy at the moment?

No we are not. We are in our own galaxy. We have not yet been out of our galaxy. I do not know that we intend to go out of our galaxy. We are not anywhere near you. We are far, far away, but it is very interesting to come and talk with you and to tell you, as I have been asked to do, that there are reasons why we wish to be here with you and why we wish to talk to you.

You've come as far to us as if you'd come directly from Gotta, your planet.

Oh yes, indeed. Makes no difference. Once you get into a booster chamber and you transport away, it doesn't matter whether it's a little distance or a long distance. You just set course for where you wish to go and there you go very quickly and is really a marvellous manner of transport and we can go back in that way to Gotta if we so desire. But I do not think many people go back to Gotta. It is quite an exciting event to take an astral journey somewhere. It is no good taking an astral journey if you do not know there is somebody to receive you. It is a waste and you could be severely reprimanded for utilising a boost chamber if you have nowhere special to go. It is important that you give information as to where you intend to go.

Who do you give the information to?

To the emplinador in charge and that is all recorded and kept in a record. Everything that you do will be recorded and more or less what you say. What I am saying now can quite easily be recorded.

Not on your floating city, surely.

I think they are doing something about it. There is a method. I cannot give you this method because I am not permitted to. But as I am able to talk to you here, somebody else is able to listen to me talking to you here. It is highly probable that somebody is doing this because most things are monitored.

We know all our conversations are monitored by the very nature of our business here, but we didn't know it was possible to be monitored from a great distance.

Oh yes, yes. Most people have somebody else monitoring them whenever they go anywhere. This is almost without fail. There are only a few people who would not be monitored and they would be people like The Blessed Efun or The Holy Flocen. Which I bow my head. I will leave you now. I say thank you for receiving me so kindly and in such a gentle manner and many thanks to your good medium for the use of her body, also for you accepting the messages I have brought to you. I leave you with much love from my people, my friends, and I am hoping I take with me much love from you all. We are indeed very loving people who believe that love is universal and must be shared and in such a way do we serve Almighty God. You call Almighty God, but we do not, but it is the same thing. The Immortal Power is the same thing to whatever planet or whatever galaxy you come from. Is the same all over the universe for all eternity. So I leave you now. I am leaving much love and hopefully taking much love with me.

Please take our love with you.

And to return again if I may do so, or if not me some other person from our city will at some time or another come to contact you and renew the love bond that is between us. For love is a bond and shall never be broken.

We wish you much happy floating.

Thank you. I leave you in love and say unto you Soskris brothers and sisters and in Earth language God bless you all.

CHERRIK

(Astral, probably Female, from Planet Turpi)

11 November 1980

I say to you Soskris. Everybody here and all who are listening. I thank you for your kindly welcome. I come from a planet that is called Turpi. You have met (*contact*) a person from my planet who is a great musician, a great composer. He is called Selsey. He has made music through this your medium and that music has been put on a small tape with this tape machine that you have here and it has been listened to by several different people who have found it very interesting. We understand that he who is called Brian has taken this tape away and made a number of copies of this tape and given them to people. This he had no right to do without the medium's permission. That which was hers alone has now gone to other people. I do not complain as she has not complained, but I do not think it fair that this should have been done. If a great privilege is given to you by someone such as Selsey it should not be abused by others. I am not able to stay with you for very long for I have been told by he who minds the cone that I am not to remain. It is too late he says. I have been waiting for some time.

Are there many people here?

There are a few left but a lot have gone on. There are a few left, maybe half a dozen. One is a lady of your Earth after life, a queen lady.

That'll be Nan. (Ann Boleyn)

Yes. She stays here with you. She said she cannot bear to miss a single meeting. She must hear all that is said. She is learning from all she hears and is becoming more broad-minded, which is good for she came from a time when people were very bigoted and narrow.

Yes. Hundreds of years ago.

Yes and she has much now in learning. She has said that the many meetings she has attended has given her great insight into what you have been taught.

283

She must have taken to heart the lecture of a spirit contact we had several meetings back. He said a spirit must go forward and not look in the past which is finished.

This is true. All should realise that you must go forward and not look to the past. We know that those who come here who have passed on speak mostly of their lives as they existed before they passed on. That is because they cannot seem to look forward into what they now have and maybe do not appreciate what they now have and can only wish to remember what they had. One should accept the new life as it comes to you and forget the old and whatever happened in it. If you do not look forward you will never learn, you will never advance. You can only remain tied to the past which is not the right way to be in the new life that you will have when you pass over.

I think there are much wider horizons in the life of a person when they pass over.

Yes, if they will only look for them, but those who will only look backwards are defeating the object of the new life they now have. I have been told she has said that she has slept for what she termed to be several hundred years, but still her past is as yesterday and still she remembers that which was taking place in her lifetime, whereas she should be creating a new life for herself in this existence that she now has upon another level in another dimension. I wish that all spirits could take advantage of your learning as she is doing and try to forget their past. Try to live for the future and try to remember that they have a life to live after passing over and it will be theirs to live as a lifetime until they come to live again in a new body. It is useless to have an afterlife if you do not take pleasure in it or advantage of it. I ask you to remember and to try and remind any who come to you who are spirits that they must look forward and forget their Earth lives. If they have once related it to you let them there cease. Tell them not to continue to dwell on the past. This is a duty that you must establish to help them through this period to make them realise that they are indeed in a better life than the one that they had when they were in their old bodies.

In our early research most of them did seem to enjoy it better than their Earthly life because they had no worries, no troubles, no diseases.

And so they must have a better life. Once they have said who they are and what they were and briefly how it affected them, surely they can then start to tell you what there is for them now and how they should go forward. All must go forward. I am not a passed spirit so I cannot myself say what it is like, but it must be better than what they had before. I feel absolutely certain of this.

Well, what they have in front depends on how they have been on Earth. If they have been good people they go to a plane of good people.

This is so, but is no good for them to dwell on the past and try to relive what has happened in the past for it is usually detrimental. I am told again that I must not stay here.

(Abridged transcript)

285

HAB-BLU

(Male Astral, Inner Dweller of Earth)

---

2 December 1980

(On this tape the contact was already speaking before the machine was switched on.)

. . . outer habitation from my inner habitation. Am called Hab-Blu. Am person. Male person. Scale person.

You are an inner dweller.

Yes. You call water person.

You are Astral?

I am of course Astral. I could not come otherwise. I think – or perhaps I could were I spirit, but not as yet am I that. I am still hale and hearty and quite strong and virile and young in years. Not very young, but not old. Am, as I say, scaley male. No need of clothes. Scales are large and represent some illustrations you have of past types of apparel called by strange name such as chain mail. Scales will overlap as those. Not on face. Not on hands. Not on feet, but everywhere else are scales. Once we believe we had tails, but now we have feet. Tails of course separate at the end and could have been tails once, but are now feet and legs. You understand? Even for you this could have been so. It is quite possible this was so even for you in many distant past times beyond recollection of your historians. Perhaps long before the beginning of this your present civilisation. I say your present civilisation because we have not had more than one. We are as we were in the beginning. We do not live great many years. We do live of the same number of years that you could hope to attain, which is approximately 75, but we are indeed virile right up to the time of the end of our lives when we are as you would call stark dead. No, not quite right – stone dead. Yes because indeed we do become as stone dead. I do think that the spirit does leave the body, but the body itself will turn to stone, for we always leave the bodies in the water and they do fossilise and become like statues laying

286

upon the floor bed – no, the sea – water bed – I am getting lost for word. We do not have your language, you can tell that from my name. Our language is quite, quite different from yours. Were you to visit us you would indeed be astounded first at the great and magnificent caverns in which we live. For they are indeed most beautiful and most intricately carved by our people over many, many centuries and preserved because of the nature of the rock from which they are carved. They are not able to crumble with time as can brick buildings or cement buildings crumble with time. You understand we are as we were originally which is very, very far back into the past.

How have you evolved since the early days?

We have advanced I suppose, yet have we ever been advanced. We are not interested in your nuclear power. We are not interested in your airships or planes or space craft. We are not interested in people on other planets for they do not know we are in there.

Our people don't.

It is a pity you do not know, but I do not know how you could reach us. I only know we can reach you either telepathically or as I am now, on a visitation of spirit when body is resting without any means of having help to transport spirit. Spirit must come under its own power. There are many of us who are something Blu. I am Hab, you do not need to say Hab-Blu because Blu is another name. There are many different names, it might be something like Too-Blu, or Wel-Blu. I think you have had a Wol to see you. Did you not once have Wol to visit you from our people?

We had a waterman. I think he said we could call him Aquarius.

Ahh, that was your loving name for him and he liked it, but I think his proper name was Wol, but not Blu, something other than Blu of another tribe. I am big tall male person, many scales all variegated colours and iridescent and very beautiful – no clothes, we do not need. We do not wear clothes, but scales do not come on hands. Do not come on face, but do come all over head like cap. No hair. No hair anywhere. We are hairless people. We do not have eyebrows because we do not have hair. We do not have eyelash. We do not have whiskers on arms or fingers.

Do you know whether your seas lie on the outer crust of the Earth, or whether they are on the inside with the crust of the Earth as your heavens?

I will try to explain something to you. You live on the outer side of Earth You have beneath you much depth. Some of it is oil, some of it is mineral of great value to you. Gold and other metals that you might value. You have also deep seas and these seas must have a bottom as must the oil which might join to the seas must have a bottom. When you come to the

287

bottom is a thick layer of rock. Absolutely solid. Completely solid, impossible for you to penetrate. Impossible for us to penetrate to get up to you. On the other side is the same for us as you have on your side, the sea and the oil and the minerals and the gold and silver and all the things that you treasure, but we do not need them. So we do not cope with them. We have no motor cars. We do not want motor cars. We do not want aeroplanes or space craft. We could not fly them if we had them. We could fly little aeroplanes, but we do not want them.

So when you look to your sky you are looking towards the inner part of Earth?

Yes and it is actually a kind of artificial sky. It is a sky and it has an atmosphere, but it does not have any stars in it as you have and it does not have any sun or moon, but there is light in the sky. The sky is always light, but it is an artificial light and I cannot tell you from whence it comes. It is something that has been there from time immemorial that we ourselves do not fully understand, but we believe it to be a holy power which lights us.

It must come through from the molten very centre of the Earth.

We believe it to be a holy power that lights our skies and gives us warmth and gives us the things that one needs to survive in complacency and comfort.

What do you eat?

We eat whatever we fancy in the way of vegetation. Unfortunately we eat our brothers who swim in the sea.

The fish.

The small ones, not ourselves of course. Not our fellow brothers, but the little ones who are also our brothers, but there are some little ones and they are so plentiful that they must really be eaten to keep their numbers down otherwise they would overrun us. This is necessary for them to be controlled in this way, therefore they are part of our food, but a lot of our food is also from vegetation which is quite different to the vegetation that you have.

Is it water vegetation?

Yes, but it is very lovely to eat and you would find it most enjoyable.

You cultivate it, do you?

Yes, indeed we do and we process it and make the most delicious and desirable dishes that connoisseurs would be flabbergasted to taste.

And you manage to do all this under water?

Oh no, we have these great caverns.

They are above the water, some of them?

They are all above the water.

But Aquarius told us you could not stay very long out of the water.

We must go back to the water to revive ourselves at least every four of your hours, but it does not take more than a few minutes to revive yourself So that you do not have to stay in the water if you do not wish to, however if you do wish to you can stay there for as long as you desire.

Have you got more land than water?

No, more water than land and much space where there is what you call oil, but we do not require it. We do not venture there. No one could survive in the thickness of this glue.

It is like a lake of oil separated from the water?

Yes, by rock. It is separated by rock and if you wanted it you would have to drill for it just as you do, but we do not want it so we do not drill for it, but we know it is there.

How do you know it's there?

Well, it has at times leaked and spoiled our waters and if a hole comes through the rock it has to be repaired and the waters must be cleansed again with sterilising agents, detergents to cleanse the water so that we do not become all glued up and cannot move.

Do many of your people do astrals to the surface and watch our television?

Some do, but we do not stay very long because we have no means of sustaining ourselves, only by the power of our will and as I said to you, we go mostly in shoals as do all fish people. We do not go singly anywhere, but many of us together and there are here with you tonight a whole shoal of fish people, water people. I think there are about 25 of us. Only I am the one to speak because I am the one with good brain to have learned language and to have studied many historical records and to know about you and your several – too many – civilisations. And to know about the outer crust of the world, not liking it so much as us. We do not like your outer crust, we like the inner crust best.

I'm sure you're much cosier and warmer in there than we are out here.

Our sea is warm. It is not cold like yours. If we were to go in your sea we would freeze. I have taken much pains to learn the language and I have read many books and studied many historical works to know about your progress throughout the ages, but there are no historical books about your First and Second Civilisation.

You have books in your own world?

Oh yes, we have books. We are older than you. We are older than you by millions of years.

How have your people gleaned this information? By doing astral –

I presume that this is so. That many adventurous ones such as we are have come and got the information and taken it back and made records of it in our own language. We also have much written in your language, because after all you are part of Earth even if you are only outer crust. We feel we are the true inner dwellers and you are the interlopers on the surface and I suppose you think the same about us.

Well, apart from this Circle, there's nobody else on Earth that knows you even exist.

Oh yes there are. Oh yes. I think there are many people dotted about here and there who know of us. Who have heard at some time or other some telepathic or astral person come to speak to them at different periods. In fact I know there are many people, but I cannot name them and there are many people not only of your country but of other countries as well.

Has your race of people got a name?

We have only one race. No. Why should we have a name? There is no need for a name, we are THE people.

The Inner People.

No, we call ourselves the true people. We feel we are the prime people, but perhaps that is arrogant on our part. We do not know anything about your 'Soskris', but we do know of a holy – Hongla? Hongla?

That's your word I think.

Yes, but I cannot put it into your word.

The Holy Power.

Ya ya, power. Power yes. I have to tell you just to correct my – in case I have misinformed you. We have manlike faces, but we have got bottom lip which – (*the medium stuck out bottom lip*).

Protruding.

As all fish people have, with no chin, but the face itself is manlike with eyes and nose like this, but this lip or tongue at the bottom of the nose (*more facial distortion*). I cannot describe it any different, but we are considered to be very beautiful. In your style of beauty we are not, but your style of beauty is not beauty to us, you understand? To us it is what we are that is beautiful. We can look upon you as the interlopers. As the ones who have commandeered the outer crust. You are not like us in a lot of ways. We are not warlike. We are loving, gentle people, as are all fish people. As you know they go together and they do not fight each other. Very, very rarely, except the big fish will eat the little fish and that of course is wrong, but it is our only way of existence apart from the vegetation.

290

Have you any really big ones like whales?

Oh yes. They're brothers. They are not as yours. You have whales. Ours are not called whales, but we know what you mean. Ours are loving friendly. You can play with them and sit upon their noses or even climb inside their mouths and they will not mind. You can frolic with them as you can with dolphins. We have dolphins.

Are they very similar to ours?

Yes, They are not called dolphins, but they are just the same as what you call dolphins. They are of course very highly intelligent fish and closest to our intelligence and some say even more intelligent than we are, but of course they do not have the ability to build anything or create anything as we do. We have hands and feet whereas they only have tails still. Perhaps one day their tails will split up and they will have feet and legs and then their fins will become hands no doubt. You've got some fish with arms, you know that don't you? I think you call them seals. We are learning more to survive without returning to the water and as the time goes by you can manage to do it longer and longer every time.

Your present generation lasts longer than the previous ones on land.

We don't live any longer, but we can stay out of the water longer. We are determined that we will eventually be able to stay out of the water altogether. Then I expect our scales will drop off, but I do not know what will happen when our scales drop off because underneath each scale is a little breathing apparatus. They might heal up. We might get bigger lungs. We have scientists you know, but we do not make things like nuclear weapons and we do not make things like aeroplanes or trains or motors. We have no need for them. We have no need for any mechanical things really. We do not have any tellybox like you have.

Do you have any communication wiring?

We have some communication, but it is done in a different method to yours. It is done with machinery of a kind. For instance I can go into a chamber in one of the big – I call it cavern for your benefit – and I can go into a small chamber which has transparencies so that you can be seen inside it and in this small place you can talk to your friend who is perhaps a long way away, the other side in another sea altogether. We do not have electric, it is something else. Oh yes, it is a power and it has to do with the light in the sky and we believe it to be what you call holy.

Is the power used in other ways?

It is used in varying ways. It is used in preparation of food. It is used in the making of different things if you wish to have furniture.

Does machinery operate from the use of this power?

291

Sort of small instruments. Something like you might say do-it-yourself gear. Is that right word in right place? I have seen people with these things only yours are done with electricity and we do not have that.

Do people who are closely associated with this power all of the time become – appear – more luminous than the other members of your people?

I think you are coming on to classified information. I know what you are trying to determine and I do not think I am permitted to answer because the power source is very secret. Not only is it very secret but it is not understood by us, though there are some who understand it, but not I. I am losing my strength. I am getting weaker.

I was wondering if it was the same power used by our brothers from other planets to power their space craft.

It might be, but I cannot guarantee that it is so. I grow weak and very tired. I must go back to my body, it needs water. I think I have taken overlong getting here. My friends are agitating. They also need water. Yes, we go now.

Well, go with our love and thank you for talking to us.

We would like to know when we may come again and may we learn about Soskris please?

Go with our love and take our love to your friends.

Thank you.

HEMMERY

(Male Astral, Space Master from Trincea)

July 1981

Greetings to you all. I am come to you from upstairs, no, up above. I am hovering up above. High. Visible I think when lights on.

You'll have to put the lights on for us.

I will.

If you can do a blinking –

No – yes. It will mean manipulation.

Otherwise it will look like a star to us, you see.

No. There will be lots of light for we are big. They are multicoloured. Multi-light colours. Yes? You may call me Hemmery. I have not been before.

Are you Master of your ship?

I am.

Male Astral of course.

Of course. Usually only Masters learn the language unless for some special reason some other person of crew is likely to come to you, which I doubt.

What is your home planet?

Trincea.

Oh. That one I haven't heard of but of course I know the group very well.

Yes, you know the Cincean group. Is very famous. We are supposedly the good people. We specially, no, I have made wrong word. I was trying to find right word without boasting. We must be humble.

You are the pathfinders.

Yes, thank you. Good word. We must be humble. All must be humble. Arrogance is a sin. I think you call sin – wrongdoing. Simple word, covers much. Not got great control of your language. It's sufficient.

293

You have people by my name on your planet. I have got second name – it is Philby.

That is the sort of family or batch name?

Batch name.

Is yours a lone ship?

No, no. I am lead ship. There are four-O.

40. Oh you're a large formation of 41 altogether?

Yes, I am one. I am ahead of others by some miles, but we are spaced some miles, of your reckoning, distance apart. We are not close formation. You would not see other craft close behind. We are in big arrow shape and I am ahead of the others by a long way. We are passing through your galaxy. Not to visit your planet and not to take note of your planet at all. No. Not of interest at this time. Have other things to investigate and will be making return journey when investigation completed, but have to pass right through your galaxy. Will be returning through galaxy maybe some days – I do not know how many.

More than some days I would think because it will take you a few days to get to the edge of our galaxy surely.

Yes. And then further to go and then have to do our investigation and then return, perhaps at another time of meeting I hope, in which case can pop down. A quick hello.

Your ship is hovering at this time. Can it remain hovering for ...

Only because I have instructed that I shall not be here long. I've come down astrally.

Could it be possible that we could see the craft when we go out?

Yes. I am trying to tell you I will show many coloured lights. There are six different colours. All bright of course. I will try to make them – will have to manually operate when I return – to make them ...

Flash on and off.

Yes. I can put all on and then all off. When all alight is very colourful. Variegated. Like you call fairground.

The only trouble is you may be so high that it appears just like another speck of light.

How high can you see?

How big is your ship.

Very big.

How many people?

We have roughly 700 counting, but not all crew. Some are passengers. Some are to be delivered. Some to be left behind.

Do you carry High Council markings?

No. We are not that high. We have got 41 craft. One – me, ours, my craft. Each craft carrying 400, 300 some and the very last pair are quite small. Only 150 each craft.

How many planets are involved in this operation?

Each craft – there are two craft per planet. Twenty and mine, Trincea. There is only one from mine. My big one. You know our shape no doubt?

Disc with a dome.

And revolving outer rim. You know about our craft bodies?

We know the central part, living quarters, are stationary and the outer rim revolves.

We have the super-ultra revolving outer rim which are revolvers upon revolvers.

Ah, you've got the new experimental type with the individual –

Yes, I have. Discs spinning on a spinner, that is the drive. This is super-ultra spinning. I cannot find other words for it. It is central stationary. Central upper and lower. The main body of the craft is in the upper and lower domes.

You carry your own power?

We make it as we go and expel it and use it again. Do you not know of this?

We've heard of Vitrik power.

This is right. It is drawn from the universe as we go.

I was told that when you come into our galaxy you use stored Vitrik.

We do. Because you have not yet harnessed it and we must not take what belongs to you.

But you're not really taking, you're only borrowing it if it's expelled again.

Oh yes, we would dispel it, but we will not take it before you have found it.

A great pity. It would lighten our darkness you know. A little bit.

Yes, you could say that we could make your darkness light.

I wish you would. If all your craft that came through used our Vitrik it wouldn't half lighten our darkness.

We could make your darkness light. It is a dream for you, is it not? You are so unfortunately retarded. It is not your fault, it is because you have had more than one Earth civilisation. Your planet is called Earth and you call civilisation your growth upon it.

I think everybody in this galaxy would consider it a favour if you used our Vitrik to lighten our darkness.

But there are certain codes which must be observed and this is not allowed. We must not assist you in any way until you have assisted yourselves and have then asked for assistance. It cannot be given to you under any other circumstances, even though some of us – myself included – would like to help. Would be like mother or father to help you climb your obstacles. To help you create that which you have never found the way to as yet, but which one day will happen for you. But as long as you remain as you are, a turbulent planet, you will not be able to ask for help, or you could not receive it unless it was a request from the entire population of the whole planet, not just of a country as you call the segregated parts.

We've been told this many times.

We are sorry this is so, but it is part of the ethical code which must be observed at all times. It is a great pity that these things cannot be vaulted over. Yet we understand that they are just rules that must never be broken or mutilated and such assistance as we could give you must be withheld because of the condition of your planet. The conditions are not favourable upon your planet. We are sorry. It is not the fault of you who are the good people in this Circle. The people who have been called the holy ones. It is not your fault, it is the fault of the peoples of your planet as a general conglomeration. The entire force is at war with itself and therefore must be at war with outer forces. You understand. These things cannot be overcome until you have overcome them yourselves.

Maybe hundreds of years in our case.

Maybe, yes. Maybe you will not be living. I might still be for I am quite young yet. In your counting of years I am under 32, which is young for me. It is young to be a commander. Of course, we do have a few young commanders, but not as I am – an overseer. A high lord. I am rather young for my position I was trying to say.

Sort of admiral of the fleet. Equivalent to.

I think that might cover the position, yes. I am not wishing to be arrogant, but I am young for my position. But I was chosen for it and trained from a very early age. My training did start when I was of the age of – laying in the sleeping training where we have . . .

When you were in the cot, as you might say in the cradle.

Yes, yes. We do not call it that, of course. I understand what you mean There is training which starts from the moment of birth. As soon as the brain is able to receive the training, the training will start for some people. The selected ones.

Is there no way that we can communicate with you?

I do not know of any way, for you do not know how to do astral projections for a start. You cannot do that and you have no booster chambers.

296

There are people on Earth who do astral projections.

But you have no boosting chambers. How can you get beyond your own Earth without a boosting chamber? You cannot get beyond your own Earth. We have boosting chambers. My body sleeps temporarily – is that the right word? – my body sleeps while my spirit comes avisiting and uses the body of your lady.

Of course, you've only come a short hop though. You've come from your ship.

Oh yes, this is quick, but I could have come from my planet the same way, which is quite some distance for it is several galaxies away.

Do you look like us?

Oh yes, except that our hair is very fair. We are all fair people. We do not have dark ones, but some have pink skin and some have pale skin.

I expect the hair is probably due to being bleached by the Vitrik rays all the time.

Many planets have all fair people, particularly planets that are high in Jeculin training. It is the favoured colour. We feel it is unfortunate if we were anything else. If we know of anyone else we feel them to be unfortunate people. Any other colours I think. Yes, we are like you in most respects although perhaps a little more, to our mind, more beautiful.

You are probably more uniform in appearance, there are many different facial features on Earth.

There are many different facial features for us as well, but we are batches of course, you understand.

Not all the batches look alike?

No, but all still have same colouring and I think something to do with that is the manner of breeding and the cleansing performances. I cannot tell you much about that for that is not my – I have not been into that part of it.

What speed is your craft doing?

What speed? It isn't doing any at the moment, it is what you call hover.

What speed will it do? The top speed.

I cannot put it into your language, I'm sorry. It is very fast.

How many days would it take you to cross our galaxy from one edge to the far edge?

I think perhaps a ship of my size will take four of your ...

Days, weeks?

Weeks. From one side of galaxy to other and then we have yet another galaxy to pass into and we have already passed through several. Four galaxies I think, we have passed through.

297

And the average time for galaxies is about four weeks.

Well, I am rather a large craft you understand and a large craft is not capable of such high speeds as the very small craft.

Oh, the smaller ones are faster?

Oh, much. The large ones are more cumbersome and more majestic.

This is why your small craft are in the rear?

Yes. They can come and do scouting if we need them. That is my position, if I feel any need for them they will come forward – for they have twice the speed that I have.

So they could cross our galaxy in two weeks?

Oh yes. Let us try to come to some arrangement concerning my endeavouring to let you visualise. You will wait until your sky is quite dark. Then you will look – I will try to remain for half of one hour in near vicinity, which will be over water and I am about one and a half of your miles ...

One and half miles above the surface?

Yes.

We should see you at one and a half.

Yes, I think perhaps you could see now. You must remember lights will come on and stay on and then will go off a little at a time and then will come on a little until they are all on. That is the only way it can be done. I will have to use other hands besides mine to get it to work as fast as possible. All lights are for special purposes you understand. At this time we are approximately one and a half miles above your Earth's surface – no, above your Earth's atmosphere.

Oh. Now this is a different matter, because the atmosphere goes up many miles. We will not see you.

If you think it's likely you cannot see me I will not do this thing for it is strictly against rules really. I will be using lights that are for special purposes to signal. To put them all on at once is not truthfully the correct thing to do. I must leave you now. I must go back to resume my duties. I came because of your cone and I have made the effort before to learn your language. I knew if I ever came here I was going to look for the cone to come to speak to the people who are called Children of Light.

And in your turn you have made us acquainted with another planet of the Cincean group which we did not know of.

I feel for you. Yes, so will you now say for me to leave in love. Thank you and I bring you much love from all my people. I cannot speak for the peoples of the other ships for I have not told them I was making this journey, but I will tell you now that I am sure that they all would be interested to know – and I will when I return tell them that I have made the journey to see you – but I will say now Soskris to you all. Also I would ask very humbly if I may call you my friends.

Yes, indeed. We are honoured to have you.

I say thank you for receiving me in such kindly manner and for the use of this good mediumistic person.

ODELL
(Female Astral from Ocena)

July 1981

In love I come to you and greet you all and I bring to you the love of my people. To us you are known as The Holy Flocen's chosen children and we know that you, although are only few are still greatly talked of throughout the universe. The great experiment. You are the great experiment. You realise that you have been taught so much for the purpose of starting the new religion upon your small blue planet. I hope you realise this is your purpose. I have not spoken with you before, although I know of you very well. My name is Odell. I am from a planet that you all know. It is called Ocena. You have many from Ocena. I am a woman.

Female Astral?

Yes. I am pleased to be with you and I come in love as we all do knowing that I will be received in love as you all receive your visitors. We know you are inquiring people and that you wish to have information. We cannot always bring you information and yet each new person that comes to you is a new entity for you to study and will bring you some word that you have not heard before I am sure. Will bring you some information that is strange to you and of course you may ask questions. This you are undoubtedly already aware. We do not mind you asking questions and will always answer them if it is possible. There are some questions which must remain unanswered for even we cannot know everything. If we know we will answer, if we are permitted to do so, without causing any trouble. Have you any questions to ask?

Do you do anything in particular?

I do not have to do anything. As you know we are a very forward planet and all is prepared for us. There is no need for any person to work, but there also is no need for any person to be lazy and most of us like to do things although we do not have to do them. I am one of many skills. I have

300

mastered many different types of skills. I do not call myself fully proficient in any one, so I cannot say I am a – whatever you like to think of – but I am one who knows much of many things, but never enough of everything, for there is always more to learn. I have told you nothing in actual fact in that answer, but I am sorry I cannot call myself any particular type of person for I am not specially trained.

Is this your first astral projection to another planet?

Oh no. I have been here many times.

To our meetings to listen?

Yes. I have done many astral projections and to other planets as well as to yours. I usually go to visit someone that I know. Perhaps I will go and make friends with someone and then return to visit them again.

How do they know you're there?

Oh, because we have people such as you have.

You visit a spiritual circle?

Oh yes, how else would an Astral be able to make contact with living people. There is no other means. But many more people upon other planets are capable of receiving than you seem to have upon your planet. This is one of the things that is much advanced on most planets, particularly Jeculin planets you understand.

When you go to these other meetings do you meet other Astrals from other planets?

Quite frequently, yes. It is always interesting to listen to what other people from other planets have to say. Some have nothing to say. Some are really just conversationalists, but many have got something special to say. I have nothing special to say. I come to you with love. I come to you as – surely it was my turn to come to you for I have been here so many times and not had the opportunity of speaking. But I do not have any special message except that I bring you much love as we all do.

We know your planet well.

I know you do and you have had important people, much more important than I am.

Is there any news of Hedda lately? (Hedda is a universally famous Ocenan sculptor who created a colossus, the marble figure of a man which was so high that a person standing upright at its base would only be level with its toes. When the marble split in a crucial area, he left the statue part finished and went into seclusion believing it to be a judgment of The Almighty upon him.)

No. All is quiet. He is no longer in seclusion. The last I heard of him he was working on a large group and I believe he used you as the models.

This is the last I have heard. I do not suppose he has finished that group yet, for I believe he was intent upon doing all the work himself.

How about the colossus, does it still stand?

Oh yes.

A landmark, no doubt.

Yes. One does not discuss that. I would not dare to criticise. I know my own opinion, but I would not voice it.

My personal view is that he is a little over critical of himself but perhaps that is good, I don't know.

No, I would not say that. I know that he has been in seclusion and has spent much time in prayer. I think to regain his confidence in himself.

Your great historian who has now passed on, Ledan, is there somebody to finish his work?

He has been instructing somebody, but that was a great disadvantage, for the person he was instructing was not following him closely enough and was utilising his own . . .

We know of this because he came to us after he passed over.

Oh you do. Well now he is instructing someone else, but I do not know with what result.

You are quite well versed in general knowledge though.

Well, I suppose I am. You are speaking of the very famous ones. There are many of these very famous people from Ocena. It is a planet which is favoured with very many people of great talent.

And you have a neighbouring planet which is very forward in technical matters haven't you? – Docena.

Oh yes. Yes indeed.

We learned from them of the work to produce bodies for people that need bodies . . . to culture bodies.

I'm afraid I cannot discuss this subject. Perhaps you know more than I do.

There are four planets in our galaxy that were devastated by nuclear misuse and they have large head and very tiny bodies.

Oh yes, I do know of those people and I also know of the brain people that have no bodies at all.

We know of them as well because one of those visited us. They lie on cushions . . .

Yes, but now they have having made . . . they have emplinadors which are producing for them mobile means of propulsion.

Mobility. They had their monkeys which helped them a lot, didn't they.

Yes. Specially trained – as servants – very intelligent.

Their servants in love, not as slaves.

Oh yes. Servants in love, of course. We do not consider anyone as slaves, not even an emplinador. Even they are not slaves.

We believe you have on Ocena and Docena the latest type of what we call android emplinadors. Very like people. So much so they cannot be...

It is very difficult to tell them from people, although they do have a bounden duty to declare themselves if you ask them.

Ah, they don't declare themselves unless you ask them.

No. If you ask them they say ah, they must declare themselves. They are not really people, but they are so near to it that it is very difficult for anyone to discern. You were asking about the slight whirring noise which is very difficult to mask.

But some have done this, we understand.

Yes, a very few. They're not in very large quantity. They are of course still workers and because they are workers you almost automatically imagine that they must be emplinadors.

The word emplinador is a Jeculin word I believe, or is it universal?

It's universal now, because even where there are no Jeculins they still have emplinadors and call them that.

The word emplinador actually covers any kind of robot from an android type to a thing as big as a great factory building, doesn't it?

Well, yes, I suppose it does. An emplinador can be as small as a mouse.

Are there any that small?

No, not really, but it could be. Small as a small animal, or as large as a large person, or as large as a room, or as large as a building. It is all mechanical and mostly computerised. Computers are what drives these things really. You are on to a subject now that I do not particularly understand. It is very technical and I have not in any way trained in any technical sense. What I know – I have a smattering of everything that I have picked up from time and place because I am, as perhaps you are, inquisitive.

Do you have any interest in the histories of older planets?

Yes, but it is not very easy to obtain histories of other planets. It is easy to obtain the history of your own planet, but not of other planets.

Are you well versed in the history of your own planet?

Mmm ... medium.

Have you any idea how long it is since the transition from cosmic energy to Vitrik?

303

No, no, this is way, way beyond anyone's memory. We know of cosmic but we do not any longer know how it functions.

It's a lost science.

Yes I suppose once there was for us what you have. It is called electricity. I have been here many times. I have listened to you. I know you are chiefly interested – well no, not chiefly – but you are extremely interested in people from space craft. I have met some of these people, they are very fine people, but of course they go away for long periods.

You've met them at home, you mean?

Yes, but they do go away for long periods.

Do space personnel when they go back home mix freely with other people or are they segregated?

Oh they are free mixers. They are always very willing to visit, or in their rest periods will discuss their journeys.

Do you have any discussion groups on Ocena where you're actually debating?

Oh yes, it is a favourite pastime and also it is good to go to these learning groups which if you're interested in many other things, matters, learning, not necessarily school learning, discussion groups where you will learn something. These are always interesting. These I like very much. It passes much time away, you see we must do something. We must interest ourselves in something and if we are not creative then we must go to as you say discussion groups, or to learning groups, which is not necessarily in school.

It's rather ironical that people on the Jeculin planets have such a rather nice long span, which at times they may have a little difficulty filling out and Earth people with so much to learn, so ignorant and so much to learn have virtually no time at all to learn it in.

It's the other way isn't it? One extreme to the other. Too much time or not enough time. Oh we have plenty to do. We can make plenty to do, but we do not have to work. I know you are forced to go to work to make what you call money to earn money for supplying your needs, but we do not have to have money. What we need is given to us.

But you do have a communal service which is compulsory very early in your lives.

Oh, early in life. Early in life.

Which is a good idea because it is a form of discipline and everybody needs a certain amount of discipline.

It is rather like the continuation of your school time.

Does it follow on directly after school?

Yes it does. That is compulsory. Everybody has whatever they want and there are so many emplinadors there is no need for any of us to work. Everything is done for us, but if we wish to do it we can do it. I like to do lots of voluntary work and in particular I like to go into medical places, which pleases me. I am not trained as a medical person but I like to go and assist wherever possible. We do not have illnesses as you have them. We have accidental things yes and replacement of limbs. We have limb banks, but we do not have things like you have common colds and influenza and another funny one that I cannot remember its name, which people do not now die from but used to die from a lot.

Tuberculosis.

Yes, that is a funny one. We don't have these.

We've got much worse ones now.

We don't have cancer illness. It is all adverse.

You don't have cancer problems at all?

No, because at birth all children before they leave the medical centre are all thoroughly checked and anything that is wrong with them, if there is anything wrong with them which is very rare, is all put right before they are released.

I think I was taught that you – when I say you I mean all the Jeculin advanced civilisations – changed the blood of all babies at birth.

If necessary, yes.

Ah, it's not necessarily changed on every child? It's just if they find some kind of possible defect it's changed completely?

Yes. I suppose we are very fortunate that we do not have these, what you call illnesses.

When you put people down on a planet like Earth – and I know many planets put people down to help us, technicians – you must have great difficulty impregnating them against the variety of diseases we've got.

I don't know that we do.

Perhaps Ocena hasn't put any on Earth, but there are many planets which do.

No, you misunderstand me. I do not know that we do impregnate them against the diseases that they might contact on Earth. I think we allow them to proceed exactly as an Earth person would.

(Transcript abridged)

305

WILLIAM JOHN SPENCE
(Male Astral Originally from Oxford, Now Living on Planet Curlieu)

28 July 1981

My friends No, I have not been to you so I am not truly entitled to call you my friends, but I feel you are my friends, for I have taken much pains to learn about you and all that goes on in this your holy Circle where you are called The Flocen's chosen Children of Light. You will be surprised when I tell you who I am, but I must warn you before we proceed any further, there will be many things that I am not and I emphasise 'not' permitted to reveal to you. However, I have been permitted to come to you and to acquaint you with the fact that people such as I can come back to you and speak to you upon occasions given the rightful permission by the rightful people. I am a person such as you. A person of this Earth, but – and here is the but – I do not live upon your Earth anymore. Our Earth, my Earth as it was. I am living upon another planet.

You've been taken away?

I have.

Voluntarily of course.

Yes. I did volunteer to be taken and I was taken. I will tell how I was taken, this I am permitted to do, but certain things I am not permitted to tell you. Yes, I will give you my name. My name is William John Spence. I was a person from the town of Oxford. I have a brother who still resides in Oxford. His name is Joseph Spence and he is a doctor. He may have retired, I'm not sure. He could have retired. He may not now live in Oxford, but he is an Oxonian as I was. I was taken from my home at a prearranged time. I was asked to leave my home and walk to the edge of some cliffs. We do not have cliffs in Oxford, so I was not able to be taken from the town of Oxford you understand. I was asked to go to a town which is called – it is in Kent – it is called Sheppey and there are cliffs

306

there at the point which is called Eastcliff. I was told to stay in this place for a while, which I did, as if on holiday. I was told to walk to the edge of the cliffs on a moonless night where there are no street lamps only grassland and cliffs going down to the sands. I was told there to lay down and to consume a sleeping pill, which I did. When I woke it was a long time afterwards and I was not upon our planet. I was upon another planet. I have no knowledge of the journey. I went into a sleep caused by the sleeping pill and during the time I was asleep someone must have come and taken me. I do not know anything of the journey. Nothing at all.

How did you receive instructions to go there?

I was told as you are being told now, through a person.

Were you a member of a psychic meeting – circle?

Yes, and people did not believe. Those that were present did not believe that it was true. Yet, when I disappeared they obviously must have known that it was true. Now this is some years ago. No, I cannot give you the exact year, I am sorry. I think perhaps it was early in the reign of this queen that you now have. Very early.

Probably in the 1950s.

I think yes. Some years have passed. I do not look any older. I do not feel any older. I live upon another planet in a home, a commune, with lots of other people. I have been what you would call acclimatised. I am not allowed to give you any particular details of that process, nor can I tell you anything about the journey for I was not aware of it. When I first came to realise I was upon another planet was after I had arrived there, which might have taken some either weeks or months, I do not know and after I had been what is known as acclimatised.

They probably did that while you were unconscious.

I think they must have done this. Now I live in a commune with many people. I am told that I will live many more years than I could live in an Earth life. I am told I will live to be perhaps 150 or even 200 years of age whereas some of the people who are upon this planet, which is called Curlieu ...

That name sounds familiar. I don't know whether we've had someone from there.

I'm not sure, I can't answer that question. It is called Curlieu and here they do live to 300 or even more years, but since I was already in my fifties when I was taken, they say I will live perhaps 150 or even 200. But I will not live as long as some of those or if I had been taken earlier I could have had a longer ...

Is it a Jeculin planet?

307

Yes, it is Jeculin. We are Jeculins.

It's not in our galaxy then.

No, it is not in the galaxy of Earth. I say it is not in our galaxy because it was my galaxy and I suppose in some ways I still feel it is, but I know now it isn't. I know of course that I am a highly-favoured person.

Are you the only Earth person?

No, there are many others here. There are many of both sexes, but we have of course been – I don't know the word to use – it is like remade.

Sterilised?

No, I don't think so. This is such a different life to the life we lived upon – there's no work to go to. No money to earn. No possessions. Well, I say no possessions, there are some possessions, but not as we had when I was a young man. Not that sort of possessions. No working for it anyway, but of course you can work if you want to, but you don't have to. Because I am a person that does not like to be unoccupied I do anything that I can. Anything that I am permitted to do I will do and there are very few things that they won't let you do, but there is nothing that you have to do. Now because I am an Earth person and really I think we Earth people who are upon this planet Curlieu are here for – well, we are like curiosities to them.

They must surely have taught you the true religion now though?

Yes, we do know all this. This we know, but there are many things that we do not know although we are already very much more advanced than we were upon Earth. There are many things we have not learned. We are sort of curiosities to them and they like to examine our behaviour. They watch us really under a microscope almost and I am quite surprised that I have been permitted to make this astral journey to visit you and that I was allowed to use a boost chamber. I do not know any other person of my nature, or any other...

Earth people?

Yes. who have been permitted to use a boost chamber. This is a breakthrough for us and we hope that now one has been permitted perhaps others will be.

You knew of our group?

Oh yes, because it is much talked of. And also of course I know of Vitrik power. I don't know what it is, but I know it's there and I know it's wonderful. It's cleansing. I tell you that it's beautiful and it's not killing like electricity.

It charges the body doesn't it?

Yes, but it won't kill you like electricity does. If you take a shot of electricity, you just die and shrivel up wouldn't you, but you don't with Vitrik.

It's a holy power as well as being –

Oh yes, it's wonderful. It's wonderful and this for me is, is – I don't know why I've been permitted to come to you. I really do not know.

Well it's a great experience for us.

It's a great experience for me and to me it's almost beyond comprehension because I know that we're kept under, under –

It shows that they have faith in you and in us as well.

Yes, I think this must be so, but you see the thing that surprises me is that I and those others who are like me – there are others of both sexes like me upon Curlieu and they're all voluntary people. They've all volunteered to go.

Did you leave your family as well?

Yes, but then I didn't have a very close – I was 52 I think – I didn't have a very close family connection at that time, although I did have my brother, but that didn't matter. He had his own family and we weren't that close. I told you his name, Joseph, yes, but although his name was Joseph I used to call him Jim. I suppose everybody thought when I left that it was an extraordinary thing. Where did I disappear to? They thought perhaps I fell down a cliff and got lost in the sea, but of course this is not true. Many people have been taken. Many people. Not only to Curlieu, but to other planets.

You weren't taken against your will?

No, no. I agreed that I would go.

And you were the only one?

Yes, at that time. I don't know any of the other people, not from my Earth life, but it is most interesting and of course the most extraordinary thing is that we are really their – we're like toys to them – do you know what I mean? But they're wonderful people. They're really wonderful people and of course it's a wonderful life, but it can be if you don't make yourself some interest, it can be very boring, but of course if you've got much of a brain you force yourself to do something.

I expect you spend much time in their film libraries, don't you?

Well, I try to, but they don't seem to want me to stay there too long at a time. They say the reason for this is that my brain will not accept too much and they say this to all of us, that our brains will not accept too much at a time and they don't wish to stress us, but I think there are things that they don't really want us to know.

But it is fact that their brains are larger than ours.

309

Oh yes. And of course they have the most stupendous memories.

It's not that their brains are larger. It's that they use all their brains whereas we use only about a third of ours.

I think this is so, but of course I have a better memory now than I used to have but I still have not got the same capacity that they have for remembering things.

Do you miss anything on our planet?

No, no. what is there to miss. I would have missed companionship if I had had any close and necessary companions at that time, but I had reached a stage in my life where there weren't any people that really mattered.

(End of tape)

FEDA
(Female Astral from Planet Ocena)

March 1982

I come to you to bring you love from those who you know. You may not know my name, but I know many people who know you. I come from the planet Ocena. There are many from this planet who have visited you. My name is Feda. I am female astral person. I am not a religious teacher although I am a religious follower. I am in fact artistic person and I paint many pictures, or make music and dance. We have many very beautiful arranged dances upon our planet. It is a form of entertainment you understand, which we do for each other and this I love doing very much for it expresses love and gives much pleasure to those who watch. In addition to this I make music on instruments occasionally, but my chief interest is with painting of pictures and these are quite well known upon my planet. I have done some fairly famous ones. They tell me I am quite proficient and I have decided I will paint a picture, just as Hedda (*famous Ocenan sculptor*) has made the statues of you, I would like to paint a picture of you, but I would like more people than I see here. I do not want to have spirit people, or if I had spirit people they must be ethereal in the background. I want to have you living people, but I would like more living people than I see here.

So would we, Feda.

Perhaps sometime some more will come then I may come and view them and then I can put them all in the picture. I know you have had many more people than there are here, but I cannot say that I know what they look like, although I do know Teresi. I also know one who came here who is called Lindesi, but she no longer comes.

She is married and lives –

Where are the others, Jinder - Jindesi and Christo? These I remember. Lovely people, but I cannot put them because I cannot see them anymore. I

311

do not remember well enough the exact features, unless you have pictures of them which I could perhaps view and memorise. But it is not a project I have yet started so there is no great hurry about it. I can come again and hope that there will be others here. I would dearly like to see Teresi again. Perhaps you will tell her that I wish to paint her picture and then perhaps she will come so that I can view her. This is all something to happen in the future. I must see you all a number of times before any of it can happen. Perhaps I have to go further afield to find some of the older ones that I wish to paint.

Perhaps you can sniff them out.

Do you think I could follow them? No, that is it I do not know their scent. When you know a scent you can follow quite easily the person's aura, but you have to know it first. If you have made a note of it you will never forget it, but you do not automatically make a note of it, not unless it is for some special reason. I have also when I was here before seen the big black dog and the little spirit girl who used to mind the big black dog. I am making a picture of the black dog with the little spirit girl. I can remember what she looks like you see. She's not here now. I do not see her. I believe the dog is a spirit dog now, but I still need to make him as he was when he was here with the little spirit girl minding him. It will make a beautiful picture. That will be the living with the spirit – you see what I wish to paint? I like to create the unusual and it is always good to be able to create something that someone else has not done.

Are there many people here tonight, Feda?

There are a fair amount. I have seen many more. I have indeed seen very many more. There are not so many Astrals as usual and I have been told there are not so many Spirituals, but there are a lot in the cone. The cone is very full. People use your cone as a shelter place.

So we are told.

They rest there and keep themselves comfortable and make it a sort of a home instead of going to their proper plane where they really ought to belong.

Do the words from the proceedings of this meeting filter up into the cone and they can hear?

Oh yes, it all goes through. Even if they are not in the room it does not matter, it all goes to them and they are all sending love down to you. Some are Spirits and some are Astrals. The Astrals I can see, but Spirits I am only told about. If they want to show themselves to me I am able to see them, but only if they wish to disclose themselves. Some do not wish to and some do not mind.

It's always an enigma to me that a passed over Spirit really should be more substantial than the Astral because there's a soul in the Spirit. The Astral theoretically should be more ethereal.

I will try and point out to you that Astrals and Spirituals are actually in two different dimensions, but they can come together if they so desire. It is a question of choice between them and if they are in agreement to do this they can do so, but the spiritual person cannot see the astral person for the Astral cannot display whereas the Spiritual can display. I cannot display, my body is asleep with my soul. It is impossible for any Astral to display, but it is very possible for any Spirit to display if they have sufficient power. If they wish to reveal themselves to an Astral they can do so, even although they cannot see the Astral they can feel and sense the Astral and know what the astral is like. You understand? It is very easy, but we are definitely in two different dimensions. They are one part and we are another part. When our soul comes to join our spirit then we will be like them and be Spirituals. Then we will be able to display if we wish, but as long as we are Astrals we cannot display. Is very essential for you to understand, is it?

Yes, we knew of the facts, but that of course does explain it. They are in different dimensions.

Another life. They're in another life. I'm in my own life still. My body lies back upon my planet, Ocena and in my body is my soul. Here is my spirit speaking to you and all my intelligence is here.

When you go back to your body you know what –

Oh yes, because my intelligence comes here with me. There are few of these mediums. There are not a great many upon any planet. They are always very, very scarce, perhaps for each planet only half a dozen with special powers to be able to do as she does. There are many who do other sorts of spiritual contact, many other methods of spiritual contact, but this is by far the most, the most efficient and the quickest and the most – can we dare to say – the most truthful. Because, you see, if you speak your words through a person's mind and that person has got to repeat them, they are not going to repeat them exactly as you want it and perhaps we are too polite to correct them. Very often they will speak words perhaps we had not even suggested to them, perhaps because they think they should say them. This happens in what you call spiritualist churches upon your planet, but not upon other planets for there are no pretending mediums upon other planets, whereas upon your planet there seems to be quite a large quantity of semi-mediums. Only able to receive a little, but pretending to receive a lot and semi-mediums only able to know a little and pretending to know a lot. It is best if they do not pretend to know it all

313

or else they do not claim to know it all, because so few of them really do know.

Does your planet have communes right round the whole surface of the planet?

Oh yes. We have large beautiful gardens. They are attached to the communes. And we do not have a lot of sea like you have. We have some sea, but only very small, not very deep either. Not big enough to sail great ocean-going liners on like you have.

They would run aground, would they?

No, not necessarily. It wouldn't be far enough for them to go, unless they went round and round and round the one sea. We do not have ships as you have them. We do have craft for air. We do have what you call hoppers, the little bubble cars. The transparent ones that you can see through and hold two to six people.

They can travel on water as well?

No, no, no. Over. Over water. As low as you like over water but not on water, not in water. Although we have got some small boats – you call them boats – which are transparent. You can see the sea creatures. They are quite transparent and you go in them for the purpose of viewing those creatures that live within the waters, and it is very beautiful. And of course some of us go, as your people do, what you call scuba dive to be able to view the marine life and to go into the marine caves which are very beautiful. But the extent of water is small. Small in comparison to yours.

Yes, we have an unusually large amount of water.

I would say the largest amount upon Ocena is the amount of water you have between your little country and the next country which I think you call France. That would be the largest amount of water we have.

In one place you mean?

Yes.

Is there any tide on the water?

A little. Just lapping.

Do you know the cause of the lapping, is it air currents?

I think yes, air currents, but most of our water I believe is what you would term man-produced. We have rain only in very slight quantities. Not like you would call heavy rain, but just very fine thrust like down upon your face. Like little cold needles on your face.

Can you tell when it's going to rain?

Yes, usually you can.

Is there a darkening of the sky?

A slight darkening, although of course we have Vitrik light as you know, but it can become slightly darker and then – it's so gentle and it will not make you soppy wet because there is not sufficient of it to do that. It is very beautiful. We do not mind it, but it does not happen very often. When it comes everybody goes out in it. They enjoy it.

How about growing things – they are artificially irrigated?
Oh yes, yes.

How about trees, or do they get down into underground waterways?
I think they do, but you know of course our colour is red not green.

Your foliage is red, yes.
Yes. That is because we do not have so much water. Water makes green and without water you get red. You know that trees make their own liquid. Did you know?

I thought they had to have water.
Yes they do, to the roots in what you call the earth, which is also red. There is liquid in the earth. Moisture in the earth. It is always there. It is in the earth. It comes from beneath the earth somewhere. I cannot really go into the details of this because I do not fully understand it as I have not studied this aspect. We just accept it as it is.

Underground water.
I think yes. Which would be drawn up into the earth, through the earth, for the trees and what you would call the flowers and grass, the plant life and of course the fine vaporised rain that comes occasionally, but we all go out when we get that vaporised rain. All go out to feel it on ourselves.

Do you have any mountains?
No, we have no mountains. We have no ice either. No snow, no ice.

Is it fairly flat?
No we have little hills, not very big ones. Little bits, just undulating.

Have you any mines or underground workings that you know of?
Well yes, because the buildings are made from stone that is mined from the earth. The stones are very beautiful colours and most of them quite clear, but variegated colours. They are see-throughable.

Transparent
Sorry – I could not think of that word.

(Tape slightly abridged)

PELO

(Male Astral, Space Master from Docena)

---

8 June 1982

I am here on this occasion with no special message, just curiosity brings me here. Curiosity to see what you are doing, what you are like, who you are. I know of you. I know of your light. I know of the light that comes to meet your beam, as you call it. I know of the many spirits that have visited you and will continue to visit you, though there are many who would like to talk to you, from many different planets and I am but one. I come from a planet you may know. It is called Docena.

Yes, we know of Docena.

I am what you would say astronaut. My name is Pelo.

You are from a craft in transit?

I am. We are above you at this time but you cannot see us for there is much cloud. You would not be able to see us unless the clouds clear and that is not likely at this time.

From past experience we do find that usually your craft are too high for us to see.

You have to have the long sight. I do not think you have it, but she has it. She has the long sight. She has many times, we have been told, viewed different craft.

Are you a lone craft?

We are on our own. We are 250 people upon one craft.

Are you the Master?

I am the Master. It is usually only the Master who learns to speak the language though others who may have some smattering of your language would not have sufficient knowledge to be able to hold any conversation or to give any long diatribe. Of course it is necessary to learn the language of any planet we are going to visit and it is always the Space Master who must undertake this work of love and although others may try in the

316

learning, they will not become as proficient as the one who is the one who shall speak for them all.

Yes, as with anyone you are putting down on the planet.

Ah that is a different matter. In that case they must be entirely proficient. They must be completely able to talk on any given subject at any given time and mostly so that they will not be detected from an Earth person for we do not wish it known when we put people down. They would be dissected if we did allow them to become known. That we do not want. Though the whole of the people we have put down on different planets have returned to us in due course in the same manner in which they left us. If they were to be discovered on a planet such as yours, which is a warlike planet, which we do not approve of. A warring planet where people kill. Wicked killing. And this would mean that any person that you would term alien, and that is the term you use, or would use for anything you did not understand. And you would take that person to pieces. Examine them. Dissect them. See what makes them tick, that is the expression. See how they work, and find out if they are mechanical or human. They are of course human, although we do have mechanical beings and they are quite free existing. Well-programmed ones. Advanced ones, but we do not put them upon your planet.

Your 250 crew are all people?

They're not all crew.

But they're all people?

All people, yes.

So any robots you carry –

We do not carry any, only what you would call rigid. They are working all the time, but they are stationary within the ship.

Part of the craft?

Yes, part of it. They could not be put down on your Earth, if we wanted to. It is not possible.

Is yours one of the newer experimental craft, with the separate rotaries?

Yes, there are the discs, yes. You know of this, do you?

Yes, but I do not remember if it was a Docenan astronaut who told us.

There is more than one planet using them.

They are becoming quite widespread?

Yes, yes.

I know the tests were very successful. They found they could go faster.

Yes. They are far more manoeuvrable and can go in any direction at any time. This is good, a great advance. We can go backwards or forwards, if you understand me.

317

But you could go backwards on the other craft as well, couldn't you?
No. You must turn the craft.
That's really quite a step forward.
Oh yes. You know the principle, I take it? The outer rim with the overlapping – I do not know what you would term them – for want of a better word, in your language I would call them plaques.
Yes.
They are overlapping.
And they are set on top of the main disc which also rotates?
Yes.
They rotate individually on top of the large rotating disc?
That's right and under this is a 'batafray' that you can walk round, they are above the passageway and there are passages to take you into the belly of the ship.
Where the crew's quarters are?
Yes.
And also you have a passage all the way round the perimeter of the ship?
Oh yes, yes. It's underneath.
So actually the top of the disc goes over the outer perimeter passage?
That's right. They're not all like that, some have a further addition on the outer rim, but we do not have that on ours.
You do not exchange a lot of space technology?
No we do not, but we are becoming more universal.
It wasn't a Docenan craft I first learnt it from.
Or Ocenan. They have them as well. They are a near planet, a sister planet.
I think it was from a ship from a planet in the Cincea galaxy.
Oh that's another galaxy. It's not our galaxy. That's CINCE-AH. We call us Docean.
You mean for things pertaining to Docena?
Yes. However, there are other planets close to us that have similar names which you probably know. There are ten or twelve. I think twelve in all with similar names.
I think we've only had Docena and Ocena from that group.
Ocena is very famous.
I think, of that group they were definitely the first to make contact with us. Among the people we have been fortunate to receive, Hedda, the famous sculptor.
Oh yes. Who has not heard of Hedda. He is known universally, not just on our planet or his planet. He is known universally.

And Ledan.

That's another famous name. A great scholar. A very great scholar.

Did you know he has passed away?

Yes, I believe he has. He has passed on to the afterlife.

He came to us astrally and after he had passed, he came to us as a spirit.

Certainly. I can do that for you myself. If anything happened to me I could come back to you as a spirit. Why not? The travelling would be harder because there are no booster chambers. Nothing to help you on your way. Only willpower. Spirit power.

I wonder if you could ever get to a state where you can produce Vitrik to help boost spirits.

I think not. It would probably burn them. It could quite easily do that. I do not think that would be viable.

Yet there is a strange quality about Vitrik. It is a holy power.

Oh yes indeed, it is a holy power, but on the other hand it can only be used in certain ways for certain purposes and cannot be used for everything.

Can you give me an instance for what it couldn't be used for?

I can't. No, no. I expect there must be things. We know what it can be used for, but there are not too many things it cannot be used for.

It can be used to power a space craft. It does provide natural light.

Yes, indeed, yes.

You do not need heat because it provides heat with the light.

Yes, and the skies are always light and we do not have dark night where Vitrik power is in force. Firstly you use electricity and instead of electricity we use Vitrik, which is a great power and not nearly so much required. We do not need very much Vitrik power against where you need a lot of electricity.

To do the same job.

Yes, to do the same job. We broadcast with Vitrik and it only takes a very little bit whereas you use tremendous amounts of electricity to broadcast. There will come a time when you won't be able to afford to use it in the way you use it now. There will come a time when you cannot. I do not know if you know this.

Somebody hinted to us that electricity is not endless.

It is not. It is not endless. The fact that you are using now the wrong things to create your electricity is a step down for you instead of a step up.

You're referring to nuclear?

I am, yes. It is a step backward instead of a step up. For you know you have destroyed your own planet with the early civilisation with the misuse of this same power that you are now meddling with and this is going to happen to you again if you are not very, very careful. I am quite adamant when I tell you you are going on the wrong track – by utilising this power that we call evil. Evil power. Devil power. We do not believe in the devil, but we can use it as a word for something bad. And bad it is.

It is bad because it destroys life?

Anything that destroys life is evil and anything that is evil must be devil. They say there is no devil. There is devil. There is devil in this wicked thing. This atomic. Come the time when you can perhaps ... perhaps you can use it in a different way, then it might lose its evil portent. There will be, one day, a possibility of fusion.

Oh that is clean.

But fission is terrible. Is very terrible.

They are working on atomic fusion.

It is still atomic power that is being used. If only you could get through to the cosmic power and then through cosmic to get to Vitrik power. Then you would be up. Then there would be no need for this atomic power, this nuclear that you call it. It is bad.

Our scientists know of cosmic power, but have no idea how they can harness it.

If only they would be friends with people from other planets, some of us could easily help them.

We understand that the very advanced planets like your own can't help us because it is so far back in your own technology –

That we've forgotten how to do it. Just as we don't know how to make electricity. We don't know how to make gas.

(Abridged Transcript)

KERSHAW

(Male Astral, Teacher, Planet – Kari-Naris)

---

22 May 1979

I greet you in love. I am a Kari-Narian and I will tell you of things that have happened. I am living on Kari-Naris and am astrally projected as I have been before to bring you messages of our life on Kari-Naris. We have had great turmoil. We have had battles and many have been killed. There has been a great revolution and The Father is defeated at last. Now will we have peace in our land. Now may we perhaps earn our souls. We are all desirous of learning more of your ways, knowing the truths that you know, learning what you have learnt, that perhaps we may be granted our souls and no longer have to go below to die and wither away into ashes. If Vinnette and her people have souls, then blessed be your Almighty God – I hope that I may also call him my Almighty God. I am not able to until I have learnt all you have to teach me. I must know, that I may teach the others. I am a teacher and therefore was not involved in the fighting part of the revolution, but was a director nevertheless and many deaths I fear me are because of orders I have given. Yet it had to be done, for we could not continue under the old leadership in the way we were going, for all brothers and sisters were becoming as brainless creatures with too much inter-breeding. We have now to segregate those who are from one part of a family and get the females away from them so that they do not continue in the way they have been accustomed to. We have black and white and we do not mind them mixing, but what we do object to and want to cease altogether is brother begetting child upon sister and father upon daughter etc. This must all end from now. Now is the time when our revolution has finally finished. Now is the time when we must make our new rules. Now is the time when we need help and guidance. Can you not give it to us? We need you. We need help to overcome all the wrong that has been done. We need a way to get them segregated so that they may no longer cohabit as

321

they have in the past. Laws must be made. We have a leader – Paul. If he has a soul, when he begets children perhaps they will have souls, but we wish to have souls also. Will we not be in disgrace for having committed so much killing? We have spirits of a kind, but spirits that wither with us when we die. Also we do not wish to live for so many long years. How can we overcome this long time that we are forced to exist? We want to live like other planets for a few hundred years, not thousands of years as we now live. We are very overcrowded even though there has been much killing.

The first law you should make is that cohabiting between brother and sister, father and daughter etc., must cease immediately. Perhaps you should also make it law that only planned breeding should take place.

Do you mean that copulation should cease?

Perhaps sterilisation would solve the problem.

Oh no, I do not think that would be the answer. If some were to come forward and volunteer to be sterilised, then that might help, but we surely could not sterilise anyone without their consent? We could pass a law that after the production of one child a female must be sterilised, and this would help to adjust the population problem. There are, of course many going below all the time and even there they have overcrowding. We wish to do away with this, but we do not know how to do it unless it is that we cease to have our baths, in which case we will quickly pass over. But then, if we have no souls, we will be gone for ever. They are sent below because they become unsightly for they are no longer allowed baths because they have had too much treatment already. What can we do with them if they do not go below? Do you think we could advise mercy killings, for they do suffer when they go below. They gradually get eaten away.

Have you any drugs that can make them feel well and happy until they pass?

Not at this moment, but we have scientists who could produce this. Many have said they would rather be put to death than go below. I have fear of going below myself. What of those who are already below? Could we not seal up the caves so that they will die quicker? If we were to go and offer to terminate their lives there and then, they would all say yes. They, poor souls, will have no chance of gaining their souls. No more shall go below – I promise you that. I know this opium drug you speak of. It causes madness within the brain.

I wish to find some law that we can use to put an end to these long lives of ours and I feel it shall be done through the baths. I shall return to you regularly, if you will allow me, for it is religious instruction we badly need. What we need is souls. Let us be forgiven for the sins that have been committed upon our planet, for we are trying to make a new generation, a new way of living. We know there is one Almighty God, and we know now it is not our Father. He is dead – he was among the first to be killed, but he had many supporters. Half of the people were for him and half against him, but we were stronger than they or perhaps we were more clever than they.

I do not think your Jeculin friends know of our situation, for they do not come to us, not to view us even. I say thank you for all your good advice, your counsel, and I will act upon what you have told me and put it to my fellow law officers who are trying to form a government. We would gladly accept anyone from any other planet. You may take that as a formal invitation, for I have been given permission to utter these words. In love I leave, and I take with me the precious memory of all you have said, and I thank you very deeply and sincerely. Farewell, my friends.

PAUL
(of Kari-Naris)

---

25 March 1980

You know me I have been to you before. I am the young Paul.
Kari-Naris?
I am. Thank you for welcoming me. Loving greetings to you. I have now many children. I have fathered many children, but none have been from those who are close relatives and I will not beget any children from those who are closely related, nor will I allow of any others to do this. I am being greatly helped by a council of Jeculin people who have settled upon my planet and are helping me to control and reorganise it into a whirl-less way of being and complete love. We have always been loving, very, very loving people, but we have not known this direct love which we must address to The Almighty. Now we do know and there are many churches that have been erected so that we may gather the people together and teach them of the new religion. And they are loving it, for those that are left alive are all the good ones. All the bad ones were fortunately destroyed. I say fortunately because we could not have managed to resurrect our world if they had not been destroyed. I do not believe that it was right to destroy them, but it was the only way to save ourselves and to save our planet. To make a new start with the cleanly people.
Was there a clear division between the two sides, or was there a portion neutral?
I suppose there were a few neutrals, but mostly there were us who did not hold with the way of things and those that did hold with the way of things and it had to be that we should have to make this great resolution to decide which of the two beliefs were to govern our world. And with the help of the Great Almighty we have succeeded. I feel that although The Almighty detests any form of killing, we have been helped to overcome evil. I feel certain this help has been given to us to overcome the evil. We

shall atone for what we have done wrong. We shall atone for the killing. Those who are relatives left behind of those that have been destroyed shall be given the greatest care and the kindest treatment and the greatest and deepest love to bring them forward to be as us. I mean the young ones who knew not which path to follow, except the path that their own parents and elders followed. Now we are their parents and elders and they shall follow us and we shall make them good people. This is like adopting an enormous family, but it is a duty that we must care for those who are left behind by those who were destroyed and they are coming now to be as good and believing as we are and also to realise the wrongness of the intermingling and cohabitation.

You do great honour to our little planet, the fact that you, who have done so much to bring about a new world on Kari-Naris, were born on our little planet.

I am more than honoured to say that I am proud, if it is permitted to be proud, that I was born on Earth. I feel myself to be an Earthman. I feel myself to be as much an Earthman as you are, for my mother very wisely took to your world and adopted its ways and was indeed one of you while she was with you.

Is she still alive?

Oh yes.

Is she aged?

She is approximately 2,000 and some years and of course she has many children other than I. She did not have to bring them up, you realise that? It does not happen that way and still it does not happen that way, but perhaps one day it might. I do not know how near we could come to the Earth way of being. We do not want to get to the point where you have to work for everything, nor do we want to come to this bad thing that you have upon your planet which is called communism. We do not want that. I, now a young man but the leader of this planet, am not boasting of what I have done, but I am extraordinarily glad to be able to say I have done a tremendous amount not only with the help of the peoples who have come to the High Council from other planets. I have done a great deal on my own. I am not old, I am young. I think in your counting I will be 30 years of age.

So you were born in our year 1950.

My mother was already then of 2,000 years, but because of her appearance no one would know that. I do not fully understand how she manages to retain her youthful looks having stayed upon Earth for that period of time.

How many years was she on Earth?

I think it was 60 years.

Without any rejuvenation?

Yes and still she retains her beauty and I do not know how for the baths have always been three-monthly. Now she is still a glorious young woman in appearance.

What was your father's Christian name, was he a Paul as well?

I do not think so. I think he must have been a John, but I am not certain. My mother and I do not meet to discuss this matter. I see her sometimes upon the vision sets, but I do not meet with her. It is not that I do not wish to meet with her, but it is considered at this point that we of my age should stay together meeting with people of my age and she of her age should stay together with people of her age. I have not got time to travel or to journey forth and give time to those older ones.

Have you seen the superb Jeculin space ships? How fast they are.

Of course I have seen them for they have brought Jeculins to us. They do not remain with us. The Jeculin people remain with us, but not the great moving craft.

What were your craft powered by? Your motion-machines. Is it cosmic power?

No it is not cosmic power. It is a power. It is not anything that you have on Earth. It is a sort of a heat power. It does have fire in it like when you blast off a rocket there is much fire beneath.

Does it burn fuel that has to be stored?

Yes it does. We do not make it as do the craft that visit us. I do not know if we have Vitrik in our region.

Is your galaxy a light galaxy? Does it have daylight all the time?

Oh yes.

Well, you've got Vitrik.

I am at this moment having a beautiful sleep upon my planet and I decided I would come to pay you a little visit to tell you how we are progressing for there is much that has advanced considerably since I spoke to you last and all on the lines that you yourselves have originally suggested. There are no underground caves anymore. They are there but they are not in use. They have been cleaned and all bones and bodies removed and buried in a communal grave. Such remains as were there from millions of years was a colossal amount of wasted material which we now know should not be wasted, but those who had died beneath were left in peace. They have not taken their bones or such flesh as remained for clarification. They have left them in peace to be buried in a beautiful communal grave in an enormous mound and although the caves are still there, it is forbidden to go anywhere near to them for they are considered to be infested with evil and with creatures who are ferocious and voracious creatures.

Living creatures?

Yes, but they are considered evil and although we know that all life belongs to The Almighty, we still believe that these man-eating creatures are evil.

They feasted on the bodies I suppose.

And some not really dead.

Were they large creatures, like our lions?

No, they are not large creatures. They are a little larger than rats of Earth, but not so large as a dog.

You've sealed the caves, have you?

No we haven't sealed them. They are still there, but no one will venture near to them for to start with there is a terrible odour which comes from that area. We have erected barriers which are also vapour cleansing to prevent this obnoxious smell from travelling forth and pervading the rest of our planet. It is the smell of millions of years of death. Bloated creatures have lived off the dead, yet we are told we must not destroy them and I am as a part Earthman in agreement that they must not be destroyed, but they will not be fed by the bodies of men and women anymore. They will indeed be thrown food from time to time so that they can feed off that which is given to them which is not putrefied flesh.

Have our Jeculin brothers left any advanced emplinadors?

Oh yes we have many. They have given us the most modern equipment that you can possibly imagine.

Including food producers?

Oh yes and food production is absolutely wonderful. It is certainly a great surprise to us all and a great innovation in our way of life. We are indeed most happy that so much help has been given to us voluntarily from these marvellous people from other planets and they are not all from one planet. There is one or two from each planet in the High Council and they order what it is that is required from their own planets and it comes. Absolutely free of charge and without obligation. They ask nothing from us but that we shall learn the truth of the universe and the true belief and love Almighty God as indeed I did from the very early time of my life when I lived upon Earth I loved Almighty God. It is to me not an obligation. I do it of my own volition because I want to do it. I feel myself to be a part of the great religion.

And now your whole planet is beginning to belong.

Yes, it is not only beginning, it is progressing. They are now having great preachers already who have been trained by the Jeculin people to go and speak to masses of people to teach them.

The old people who are suffering with their great age, are you giving them happy drugs to keep them happy?

Yes, because we have given them now the choice – and they have the choice – to die naturally or they may ask for the goodnight sleep.

But are you giving them the halfway choice where they can live with the aid of drugs that will shorten their lives, but die happily?

Yes this is so, but perhaps all, with the exception of very few, have chosen the way of the goodnight sleep. They choose it sooner than rot away. You see once the baths stop they start very quickly to deteriorate. I can see that this will happen to me one day, but not for many years. We do of course speak more or less your language, you know this don't you?

No. I hadn't thought about this.

That is why when our old father was alive he thought when you prayed 'Our Father which art in Heaven' you were praying to us or to him because it was considered that our planet was Heaven. It's the only known Heaven that I know, but we do not now call it Heaven any more.

Tell me, the heat on your planet. Are you near your sun? Does it come from the sun or does it just come from space?

It comes from space and also there's great internal heat.

Can you feel that coming through the surface?

Yes. There's great internal heat which really we have to do something to subdue. I'm not very technically-minded. I can't really give you the details but it is vast and also there is also almost perpetual running water for cooling purposes. We have reservoirs of water. Some of it comes from what you call the skies.

So you do get rain.

Yes, but it is always warm even when it is raining for the rain itself is quite warm.

Surely those deep caverns must have been unbearably hot?

Yes indeed and it must have been the most terrible way to go, to be forced to go into those caverns for in there the deterioration process would go that much faster.

Is there any volcanic activity on Kari-Naris?

Yes there has been. Not recently, but there has been. I have not seen it as yet, but there are volcanoes although you will be surprised to know the volcanoes are covered practically to the lip of the volcano with brightly-coloured trees of all variegated colours, chiefly red, but other colours like purple, mauve, pink, in between, but the predominant colour is red. There is more than one volcano, but I have only seen one.

Have you any areas of forest on Kari-Naris?

Yes, but again it is red not green. The leaves are more yellow colour not like the beautiful sweet soft green of Earth, although we have made a green by sowing different plants and colouring them and watering them with coloured water which makes them come up and grow green. These we like very much for our bowers, but the bowers are only used now as summerhouses. We have built ourselves proper – not closed houses like you have for it is too hot for them – and also we do build of what you on Earth treasure as jewels, jewellery. We do have gems, large stones, tremendous stones. If we wear them they are like baubles for they are worthless. We have the problem of how to keep cool. We have of course invented things that make artificial winds to help to cool us and utilising water for a swilling elba process to cool the ground.

Can you make clouds rain?

No, we cannot make clouds in the sky rain. They come of their own accord, but when they come they are quite warm.

The rain is warm?

Yes. It never strikes you cold as it does upon your Earth and we do not ever have snow.

And your planet is not anywhere near the sun in your galaxy?

Not extraordinarily near. No. Most of the heat comes from the sky and from the internal fire. I would love to stay longer. I am very much enjoying our conversation and would like indeed to continue, but I feel that my power is growing less and therefore I will have to get on my way before I have not got enough power left to take the long journey. For it is indeed a long journey, but it is very quick, for like other planets we do have the boost chamber as well as the rejuvenation baths. The baths are only in use for a certain length of time now for we are aiming to cut down the length of our living to 300 – not 3,000. We have had people up to 4,000 years of age. Our years are different to yours. Our time period is much faster than yours.

What is it based on, do you know?

Frankly I have not gone into it yet. You must remember I am still quite a young person and very involved with many important tasks and things that have to be completely altered, but there are many things that I haven't had time yet to learn about and one of them is to take Kari-Narian education. It seems that from the time I came back from Earth I was already – claimed if you like – to be trained as a leader. That's one good thing the old father did. I've never been like the other boys or fellows of my planet. I can't really mix with them very well. I'm getting better at it now, but it is not a happy thing for me. I would like to have someone like myself to marry with who would be like I am half and half.

In comparison to yourself do you find the other boys rather effeminate?

Yes indeed they are and I am not. I am extremely manly and they do not understand me. Of course they can't chide me because I am the leader and because I am the leader they all show civility and I suppose in a way they kowtow to me. That is an Earth word I learnt when I was a little boy. What I am really anxious about at the moment is finding someone compatible to myself that I may marry with. I haven't found anyone yet. I don't want a Kari-Narian young girl.

Perhaps you ought to honour the Earth with a quiet visit and select somebody.

That would be the answer. Perhaps with the help of the Jeculins I might just be able to do that, but it wouldn't be right to steal a girl away. I would like to have a wife. A proper wife, not the many I cohabit with because of the production line which must be kept going, for every one I father has a soul. And so I must keep working at it – it is almost like an abhorrent duty. You must believe me I do not enjoy what I am having to do.

The Jeculins can help you there because they can take the seed...

It can be done, but not yet. They are not ready yet. We are not ready yet for that type of breeding, but it will come. We have been promised it will come. In the meantime I have got to work almost day and night and I'm given many fertility drugs to keep me functioning and I am afraid they are going to kill me off very early if they don't stop it soon. I would like to be more as it used to be on Earth. There are certain things that were on Earth that I will never be able to establish upon my planet. There will never be work like you have on your planet. Here we only have hobby work, but we have got apart from the new emplinadors, which are beautiful and efficient –

Have you any android type emplinadors?

Oh yes. They're very beautiful and we've got some great big roomful type of emplinadors. They are really huge computers. I was trying to say something – oh – we have a whole breed of people who are workers, but they don't get paid for it. They're forced to work just for their keep. They are really the less intelligent ones. Now this is something I would like to alter. I think if they are forced to work they should be given a certain standing and they should be able to earn money that they can get for themselves what they desire, not what is given out to them automatically. For they don't get everything they need even though they have to work all the time.

With emplinadors gradually taking over the workload it would be a good idea that no more of these people are bred. That they slowly die out.

How can we do this? We know, we have learned we cannot kill them. They are not intellectual people.

They must have been bred for the purpose from non-intelligent people.

This full purpose is to do exactly what they are told to do and nothing else.

As the workload decreases you must stop the breeding of non-intellectuals so they will slowly decrease in numbers through natural wastage and the emplinadors will do the work

That is a good suggestion. I shall have to talk upon this to the council. I would like that we should have an upper and a lower class. I don't see how everybody can be upper and no just menial. We don't have money although we do have exchange, but when I was living on Earth I can remember my mother and my father had money and they bought what they could afford which was beautiful and great excitement. We never had that great excitement. Now I don't get pleasure in what I have, because it just all appears before me which gives you no choice and no pleasure in what you have.

To an Earth person that would seem like absolute heaven.

No I do not think it would. After a little while you would become as bored with it as I am and of course my greatest boredom is not being able to find anybody who is like me. When I can find somebody to be a companion, then I will be much happier than I am now. At the moment I will freely admit I am discontented because I have no close companions and no one I can mate with as a real mate. Plenty of women, yes. I want somebody who is like me that I can love and give all myself to. That I can spoil and pet and who will spoil and pet me. It is necessary to my way of being because I am after all fundamentally an Earth person. I am very masculine. I'm sure my father must have been a most masculine man and that is why I can find nobody who really is compatible with me for they are all very effeminate on my planet.

You can forgive women for being effeminate.

Well yes, but the women are sometimes more manly than the men. More dominant. I really will have to leave you. My power is going quite low now and I think your medium must surely be wanting to come back.

PAUL
(of Kari-Naris)

Tuesday 15 June 1982

I am Paul. You have prayed in your prayer and mentioned my people. I am come to you now as I have done before to report to you, for you have been so helpful to us. It was through your intervention that any good has finally come to my planet. For we were indeed a wicked planet before we were taken over; as we now are. I am becoming more of a man now. I am more subdued. Of course it is several years now since I became the leader as you know. I am also glad that we have Jeculin control and I do not have really very much control myself, but I am quite satisfied to be the figurehead and to do more or less as I am told for I am not a person who minds being controlled if I am to be controlled by such wonderful people as the Jeculins. If it were others I would object, but I do not object to them. We have a marvellous committee now who are taking us very far forward in time. We have many innovations that did not exist before. We have also abolished many things that did exist before, which I think you were aware were going to be abolished.

The underground caves.

Yes, and of course the resuscitation baths are no longer in use, but there are some other of a lesser nature to sustain those who would need them. Who had already been in the old baths and could not remain alive without some help. If they are still useful to us, on the word of the Jeculins, they are being kept alive with other baths, but not so drastic as the ones which we usually had. This will be something that will die out eventually. Perhaps it will be a great loss. I do not know, but I do not object. I have never had a bath myself – not of the renewal baths. I have ordinary bathing of course, but do not misunderstand me. I am not a dirty person, but I do not wish to go into those resuscitation baths at all, ever. I only wish to live an ordinary span of life.

How many of our years do you think you'll make without the resuscitation baths?

Perhaps like you, for I am never going to go into a resuscitation bath. I will prefer that others shall take over from me and I will go my way as The Almighty has intended. There are many who feel like I feel. The younger ones I mean, of my age, but they do not go to the baths until they are older than I am. Once having been to the baths they must continue or disintegrate. They start at what you would say about 30. Yes, that is right. I have got a friend, an adviser, who has travelled here with me and he is speaking to me. He is Jeculin. He is a controller. I am now well-controlled. I have no objections. I do not in the least mind that I am not permitted to make any decisions. They do listen to me, but if their decision is different to mine I will submit.

When a decision is finalised it is proclaimed in your name?

Oh, yes, yes.

You're like our Queen really.

I am. She is a figurehead, a mother to the people, as I am a father to my people. Although I am young I am their father. They think of me as their father, young as I am. Of course, he was called 'Our Father' – you remember? And always they believed in your Earth prayers, that you were praying to him. He believed that. We believed that.

How did they hear of our Earth prayers?

We know a lot. Always have known a lot about your Earth. That's why we used your Earth as a place to send people like my mother. For a punishment. Yes, as a penal colony, because we thought . . .

We were barbaric.

And you still are barbaric. Because we know that you are, even at this time, in the throes of much evil war. Much evil war. Not altogether yours, but upon your planet.

We've just finished that one fortunately.

But you have yet to review and reclaim and rebuild and repair and the lives you cannot replace. We did feel this sadly for you, for as you know I am half – half a person as you. Half of an Earth person. I am very close to you because I am half of an Earth person.

Do you remember your Earth Father?

No. I just vaguely know that he was dearly loved by my mother and by myself and reverenced and looked up to. I believe he was only a working man. Perhaps, I think a university man, but still what you term a working man. To earn – as we do not need to earn money for we do not have money. But I would love to come back to Earth. Now I did tell you that I am

333

looking for a wife and that I would like to come to Earth to find a wife and bring her, but they tell me I cannot do this. They say an Earth person – entirely Earth – it would not be suitable upon our planet. Only if I were to return to you and stay would it be suitable. That I cannot do for I am king. I am father to a planet, so I cannot do that. So I yet have no wife, but I long for a wife. I have hundreds of thousands of brothers and sisters as you know, created by 'our father'. I do not feel for them as they feel for each other, for I am not entirely like them. But they do feel for each other very deeply mostly with the exception that some rebel. As you know, they have rebelled, but that is all behind now. None are rebelling at this time, for we would not rebel against the Jeculins and they are in control.

They are only there because you asked – or I think we asked.

You asked for help for us. You were the saviours. You did not cause the revolution – but you were the saviours. We have emplinadors also now.

Have you the human-type emplinadors?

They look human, but they make a whirring noise. They are distinguishable by the sound as they move. We have not yet found a way to obliterate that sound.

Some planets have, but they're very advanced.

Yes, but I do not know how they have done it. I like them. They have names of course and they have numbers, because they are modelled on people. You know? So you will get perhaps 100 that look like one person and they will have numbers. They wear them in a little disc upon the chest area and there is a little flap that you lift to see what the number is, though they can tell you their number if you ask them. The name is the same name as the person which was used as the model. If you were to know that person, except for the sound, you wouldn't know it wasn't that person because they do look alike, but I think they are a little more not quite smooth in their movements, as people are. Not so graceful, particularly if they dance. Dancing isn't so graceful, but they can dance. I often have one as a partner. Quite good fun. Enjoyable. That made you smile.

Yes. Are there any female-type emplinador robots?

Oh yes. Chiefly they are female. The bigger ones are male, but the ordinary-sized ones are female. Some are male, but mostly female. The females are prettier than males you see.

They're made prettier.

Yes and we like pretty things round us. Particularly we love pretty clothes and jewellery. We love jewellery. I suppose I don't love it as much as the others, but that is possible because I am half-Earth person.

All the buildings, we learned a long time ago, shine –

334

Oh yes, very pretty. Very pretty. All made of beautiful jewelleries. Gems. But then, you see, they're not very valuable to us. We have so much of it. So it does not count as being of great value.

They are probably what we call semi-precious stones, because really precious stones would be very hard and difficult to build with, like diamonds, one of the hardest things known to man.

Well, in some cases. Of course they never ever wear out. Our houses don't fall down. Your houses fall down, or my house back on Earth has possibly fallen down now. I don't know. But our houses never fall down. They will endure for ever because they are made of stones.

How are the stones bound together?

There is a special – like cement – sort of joining. A fusion. Do you understand what I mean?

Between the atoms of the stone?

Yes, yes. So they cannot be parted. I suppose they could if you dropped a gigantic and horrible, terrible bomb on them, but then we don't believe in those things. We are still playing those man games you know.

Man games?

Yes, we have man games – didn't I tell you?

Running?

Yes, all those things. These ball games and man games. We call them man games.

Did you have them before, in the time of the old father?

No.

It's a more recent innovation?

Yes, yes. We started them. I think my mother must have brought them. Must have told them they come from Earth. They're man games. Earthman games.

Football. Do you play football?

Yes, I love it. I love it, yes.

The World Cup is in progress on Earth.

Well, we are football crazy. Yes, very much so – and I particularly like boxing.

I don't think the Jeculins like that.

No they don't, but we like it. I like it, so long as nobody does it on my nose, because I wouldn't like my nose broken. But we do wear protective shields when we do it. We are using head shields to protect the heads. So we don't hit on the heads, you see and if we were to damage our bodies there is now this new method of repairing bodies which didn't exist before.

Which the Jeculins brought?

Which the Jeculins have built. When they brought us emplinadors they built us these beautiful factories. Repairing factories. But only for young people. Not for ones who have ever been in the baths. Those who have been in the baths cannot have these sort of attentions. I understand on other planets they don't have any illness, but we do have illness.

What kind of illness do you have?

Varying illnesses.

Do you have colds like we have and influenza?

Running noses?

Yes.

Yes. Nasty. Making loud noises. (Paul made coughing sounds.)

Oh, bronchial. On the chest.

Yes, yes and pains in the head and aches in the back and arms and legs. Mostly for older people. Young ones aren't having it much. They get pains in the head and they go (Paul coughed) and running noses.

Oh well, that's some of our favourite plagues on Earth.

We have not got the one you call cancer, although they tell me that I might have it because I'm Earth. I'm Earthy they say. I might have it. I don't think there is a cure for that.

There's no cure for leukaemia, cancer of the blood.

I don't think there's any cure for that at all. Any of it. You could have all sorts of it. I don't like it. I don't like to think I might have it. They say everybody born on Earth is born with it in them, only it lies dormant. Well, I was born on Earth, so perhaps I have got it.

If it lies dormant, it is no matter.

No. I just don't know what to do, or what not to do so as not to disturb it. I like smoking and drinking. I like mild – you call drugs. Not heavy drugs. I don't like what you call hard drugs. I like mild drugs, smoking is a drug. It makes happy. Happy Smoke we call.

Like marijuana.

I don't know what marijuana is.

A kind of tobacco that makes you feel happy.

Well, I suppose that's what we have then. We call it Happy Smoke. That's a good translation.

It's non-addictive. No more than a cigarette.

I think I'm pretty addicted to it. I couldn't give it up. You see I've got a lot of vices because I am half-Earth person and you know I like sex.

Well, I understand you had quite enough of that when . . .

Yes, I don't want any more. That's all stopped now. I objected. I told

336

you I was going to. I had the Jeculins on my side because they hate it. They don't like it at all.

Yes, they prefer clinical methods.

I do like it, but not when forced to, you understand.

There's a difference between duty and pleasure.

Ah. A great difference. When you do it because you want to is one thing. When you do it because you're forced to do it – that's nasty.

Anyway I think my time has come now. I want to come again as I like to keep you informed as to what is happening and we are coming very far forward now. We are also having a space craft now. We were before. We've more modern ones. We're having now – there're not quite ready – the same as they have on other planets. They are coming from a planet called Docena. They are making them specially for us and there's going to be fleets and fleets of them. I think we have got to do something back, but I don't know yet what. I'm excited about it because, I know I am a bit old to say, I would like to learn to be a space traveller. I don't know if they will let me though. They say, being the Master and the Father, I might not be allowed. You know what I'd do if I was. I'd come to Earth and find me a wife and see what I could do.

There are no Earth people but yourself on Kari-Naris?

Yes there are.

How did they come to be there?

They're not full Earth people, they're half-Earth people.

From people like your mother?

Yes. There were several came when I came.

On the same pick-up?

Yes. I have to leave you now. I am very happy to have had this chance to talk with you again and I always am. My love is here with you and I say may the love of The Almighty be ever with you and Soskris to you all.

337

FILIA

(Male Astral from planet Grocenia)

---

22 April 1982

I have been informed by those here present that there have been no meetings for some time. This we are all sorry because many come long journeys to visit you. Many come with messages for you or just to speak to you and make themselves known to you, or because they are from another planet and you have not yet received anyone from that particular planet. Such as mine. You do not know me. I have been here before, but not to speak. I have been here before to speak and have not been able to speak for there was no meeting. You like to know the names of those who come to you so I will tell you I am called Filia. I come from a planet which is known to you through the sister planets concerned and the name of the planet from which I come is Grocenia. We are multiple – many of us (planets) with similar names I am trying to say. We are come to you in love because you are interested to hear from people of other planets and each one who comes to you is an emissary from their own planet to, as it were, be a spokesman for those others of his or her planet to make contact with you and speak for those other people who are not able to come. I am male. I am Astral. I am a teacher. A teacher of many different classified matters, but chiefly in the matter of medical. We do not have illness such as you have upon your planet. We are more fortunate, it has been mostly eradicated. I am trying to use correct words. I have prepared speech. We have much medical learning, but not much practice. In case we should need it there are many of us who must know. There might come one day a time when we will be needed, but as it is we are chiefly unnecessary. Am I making myself understood? And because our work is essential in case of accidents, we must of course be fully prepared. Yet knowing full well that we will not have the use to practise unless such a contingency occurs. We hope it will never occur for we do not wish to be as you are upon your

Earth with much sickness, as there is sickness in this body I am now occupying and there is sickness in two other people in this room. And there is sickness also among some of your spiritual visitors. They are not actually suffering now. They had in their past lives been sufferers as they carried it in their souls. It is unfortunate that I cannot assist any of them. Cannot help them. I would like to do so, but it is beyond my powers because I come from so far away and I have no means of giving help though I would dearly love to do so. For it is the wish of anyone who learns to be proficient that they should be able to exploit their abilities if necessary. And I feel that it is necessary, but not possible. I come to you in love and I bring you the love of many people from my planet. I am coming as spokesman, having made special learning and design prepared speech to greet you. So far I have said all I wanted to say and I'm only now able to try to reply if you wish to ask any questions.

Are you in the Cincean galaxy?

Cincea is another galaxy altogether and there are many in that galaxy.

We've had representatives from about five planets in that galaxy.

As you have no doubt had many from the galaxy which I represent.

We know Ocena and Docena.

There are many others. Many, many others with similar sounds.

Do you engage much in research?

Oh yes. To know and not to be able to see whether it is suitable is hard. For the lack of illness is good for people such as I but strange not to be needed.

(Remaining tape spoiled by malfunction)

TARAN

(Male Astral, Space Master from Ocena Two)

---

21 December 1982

I do not recall how long it is since my last visit, but I have been before to speak and then you were surrounded by many thousands of good well-wishers and supporting spirits which gave added strength to the meeting. I am called Taran and I am come from Ocena. I am Ocena Two.

Ocena Two? As opposed to Ocena.

Ocena One, Ocena Two, Ocena Three.

'You are male Astral?

I am and I have been before but you may have forgotten. Long ago. There were many Spirits here, many loving countenances, many Astrals and many, many spirits. Now there are few. A wisp here or there. I am more feeling than seeing.

We have been decimated through sickness and a variety of reasons.

Although the light which emanates from the medium is still visible it is only a thin pale light and the light that comes down to meet it is still there, so bright and beautiful, but it does not really meet the light of the medium. This place was packed with Astrals and Spirits when I was here before. It might take you some while to rebuild that strength which you have had. You really need more people to be sitting. I am very happy to be able to say 'Happy Tarset'. We have been making a little celebrations ourselves – it is the end of Tarset almost – there will be one more day. There must be others such as I who are travelling, but we must of course continue to travel.

You are from a craft in transit?

Yes and we are happy to be able to make contact with you.

You are the Master?

I am. I could not pass you by if there was any possibility of speaking to you. You are still well spoken of upon our planet – upon our planets – and

340

we all refer to you as The Children of Light although the light has gone dim it is not through lack of belief I am not a very religious person myself, but I am a loving person and extend my love to you in the way no doubt that you would like to extend yours to me as you have done in the past.

Are you on a mission in our galaxy?

I am not permitted to discuss my mission. Most of us are not permitted to discuss our missions. I am passing near to your sphere. I come in to speak because I was aware that suddenly the welcome was coming for me.

This last year has been bad and of course we did lose Tom – Nita's brother Tomesi. He passed on.

Oh I remember him. Yes, the one with many questions. The oldish man. Yes, I remember Tomesi.

He was a little bit obsessed with getting a craft to put down an artifact

Yes, yes, I remember that too. There was much discussion about that. Much discussion. It is a number of years back. I will tell you something that I am permitted to tell you. It is no longer classified secret and that is that your people of your planet had got one of our space vehicles and they have also had our space people, but they have unfortunately been the cause of their demise. They did not understand the needs of our people and they did make them as prisoners to examine them and while holding them as prisoners were not able to satisfy their critical requirements.

Were the captors of these people English-speaking like ourselves?

Yes.

They were Americans then.

They were English-speaking people of our planet too – Ocena Two – that were taken. This is no longer classified information. It is something which we have greatly – we have been greatly dismayed by this happening for – it is some while back –

A number of years?

Yes. But because of it we will never allow any other space craft to come near enough, when anyone is aware of it, to be captured. We cannot permit these things to be done and nor will other planets permit it to be done if their people come. We are only trying to help when we put people down upon your planet. We do not expect them to be put to death when they come to help.

Of course not. Was it unintentional – the putting to death?

We presume it was unintentional. We can only hope that it was unintentional, but nevertheless it happened. It was done. We were putting down helpers for you. To give you people to teach you the ways of improving your manner of living and improving your use of your sciences.

341

You are very backward and if we did not help you with an individual here and there you still would not be progressing. We have to keep doing this to you, but you do not know we put them. They come singly usually. Then we send a batch as that has happened and you have captured the craft and the people. They did not stand a chance.

How on earth did they manage to stop the craft taking off?

Because they got the people when they were all out of the craft. It was quite a small craft with I think five individuals. The five were never returned or the craft was never returned.

Of course they wanted to find out how it works.

They will never find out for they have not got the use of our power.

Vitrik

That is right. Until they find out how to use Vitrik they will never make that craft anything but a toy.

They can't use cosmic yet. They know of cosmic, but can't harness it.

If they had kept our people alive perhaps they would have helped you find Vitrik, but we are not supposed to help you find Vitrik. You are supposed to find it yourselves. It is your task.

I think we have been told we must go through cosmic first.

This is true, but you are on the verge of cosmic. When you come to laser you are coming to cosmic.

We've been told this before and I asked the speaker if laser is used in connection with drawing in cosmic and the person was unable to . . .

Because he was not a technician any more than I am in that respect. You would need to speak to somebody who has knowledge of cosmic power and would be able to tell you. Who knows what cosmic power is anymore. It is long-forgotten. It is to you a word, to us it is something from the distant past. Laser too is something from the distant past. But you are approaching on to something when you come to laser. We do not call it laser. We do not have it anymore. It is no good to us.

Of course Vitrik does everything, doesn't it?

It does indeed. I'm sorry my time is expiring and my strength is growing very weak.

Please go with our love, Taran. Thank you for coming.

SON-RA
(Female Astral from Planet Welis)

---

12 March 1985

I am here because you belong to The Holy Flocen and you meet together ever in the hopes of making contact with The All Highest. I am more than pleased to be able to make your acquaintance. I am sure that you are giving me the same welcome that you have given to others before me. Soskris. Soskris to you all. I am called Son-Ra and I come from a distant planet which is known as Welis. It is of the adjoining galaxy to the one in which your planet resides. We are as you appear to be. You call human beings. We do not call human beings, but we are as you. Nearly as you. I am a person of integrity and I am highly trained in my profession. I am female and in middle years and what you call observer in what you call space craft. I am working, not at this moment.

You are a female astronaut?

Ah! That is the word. Yes, I am trying to speak in your language and it is not as easy as mine. But you would think mine difficult because always your Earth language is the easy one and any other is the hard one. I am trying to establish myself conversationally with you. I bring you good happy love, good spirits and much regard from all who are upon my craft. It is not my craft but the craft where I am.

So you came down from the craft to us.

Because I am now resting on the craft and another is doing my duty. The craft is overhead, still hover. High, high, high. You call sky.

Are there many females in your crew?

No, there are few females. More male, but we are specialist people who are female and we are not breeders. We do not breed. You understand my meaning? Some females are breeders, we are not breeders, we are specialists and therefore must not and do not want to and I am not allowed to do breeding.

343

Does your planet have marriage like ours?
No marriage. No. We have close association.
Friendships?
No, more. More friendship. More, deeper. Love of course is the prime way of being for all. All peoples. Breeders as well. Love is important. It is – without this you cannot live. You must have love and you must give, give much love. Is most efficacious, not. Oh I am lost again. I am forgetting my prepared speech. I have no more speech – all gone.
Is your galaxy a light galaxy?
Yes.
Vitrik light?
Vitrik, of course.
You are Jeculin?
Oh, of course. You are children of The Holy Flocen. How would I know if I were not Jeculin.
We do receive star people who are not Jeculins, usually from this galaxy.
I am not from this galaxy. Ask me more questions. I have forgot speech.
So your space craft will be Vitrik-powered as well?
Is there any doubt – there is nothing else.
For you, but we are rather a long way from that.
You are backward. You are sadly forlorn. We are sad for you – we pity. We are sorry. Once you had much power. Once you had more power than now – in another civilisation. Long, long ago.
Many millions of years, I believe.
Yes, yes. More questions.
You said you were an observer. You observe the planets you view?
Yes, and recording them, and is most interesting for there are millions of planets in every galaxy. All must be recorded.
Do you catalogue the geographical features of the planets?
Oh yes, yes and the appropriate position to its neighbours. I am very advanced in my learning of this, so that I can be the responsible person to record these very important matters.
Have you been observing the planets close to Earth?
Yes.
Could you tell us if the planet Mars has inner dwellers?
No. I do not know. I cannot tell you. I do not have knowledge to tell you this. Sorry. I regret cannot make comment on your galaxy. As yet have not studied sufficiently to be able to. There are so many millions of planets that you call stars. You must not expect me to have this knowledge

so soon. We have only just recently entered your galaxy. It is too soon for me.

How many days is it since you entered our galaxy?

We do not count. Not days. We have no days. I do not know what is days.

It is a 24-hour time period.

Is hit on head days?

Ah that is daze. This is days, plural of day.

What is day?

A 24-hour period from sunrise until the next sunrise.

I have not yet learned this thing. Have got much yet to assimilate. Will learn soon perhaps. Sorry to forget prepared speech.

Do you observe placement of cities on other planets?

Not really. We have to utilise certain instruments and ascertain if and which of these planets have different minerals that could or would be useful and in some cases to find out if there is life, but not necessarily this. We do not have to find this out. Chiefly it is to ascertain the minerals of each planet. And some have other sorts of assets, perhaps gas.

You can detect this beneath the surface?

Oh yes, we have instruments and it must all be recorded. I have much work to do in this new galaxy. In this, that is your galaxy. We have been other galaxies, but not this one yet.

Is this kind of work a speciality of your planet?

No. Other planets do it as well. I think there are other space people who do this work. This is the purpose of our mission.

Are you a lone craft?

No. We are one – then five, six more. Six I think you call. I must go now. I bring you much love and for all your peoples here who want it I give love. Love from the people of the craft of which I am observer.

We thank you for talking to us and please give the love of our meeting to the people on your craft. We wish you well on your mission and to the people of your planet

I thank you. I was told that I would be able to make contact if I find the light. I found the light and I am here. I came down following the big light which comes above to below and then I found the light that comes up but it is not so big as I was told it would be. It is a good guide. I am guided by the light. It is called your beam. Soskris to you all.

FREEDY

(Male Astral, Young Teacher, Planet Ocena)

---

26 March 1985

I greet you in love. I come to you in love. For we all love you and many from far places come in love to you. You have been known these many years as The Holy Flocen's experimental children. You now are known as the Children of Light. This is universally known. Many, many planets know of you, speak of you, tell of the things you have tried to achieve and have indeed achieved. For you have in the past been very instrumental in helping peoples of other planets to find their ways when they were lost and teaching many peoples possibly never having been able to find the way of the light until you taught it to them. There are many people who can bow down and thank you. Remember this when you think of yourselves. I know and we all know that you have somehow lost a grip on what you were doing. But it is not your fault entirely. It is through a force of circumstance that you cannot alter. It is because you have had those who were staunchly with you drawn away from you and because they were drawn away from you it has weakened the links of your chain, but it has not weakened your faith. Your faith is still great and we recognise you as the Children of Light. The Holy Flocen's special Children of Light. You do not know me by name, although I know you well. I have been here many times but I have not spoken to you before. I am much practised in your language. Over several years I have been learning and I am pleased with my attempts now to muster as much as she (the medium) is aware of in your language for it is through her that we learn. She does not know this. She often speaks with us during her sleep hours. She does not recall this in her wake hours, but we do hold converse with her and sometimes teach her things during those hours of sleep and it has been so throughout all the years you have been together. We try to come to you others as well, but you are not always receptive to us. If you would open your hearts we could

346

help you in the same way. I have been here in the room with you. You call this a room. I have been here with you many, many times. I know you so well. I know you and love you well. My name is Freedy. You do not know me by name because I have not spoken before. I am Astral. The name of my planet is well known to you. It is called Ocena. And you have many people from my planet come to speak with you. I am male Astral, young, in teaching and young in teaching, but I have much time to go before me, and will learn much more to teach and I will learn much from you, and from her. It is easy to learn from her for she is so open. She is ready to open her mind and heart even in sleep. This is a nice place to be and there are nice people here with you, good people, some Earth spirits and many Astrals who come from other planets. All are giving you love just as we know you are giving love to them. I am sorry but I have forced myself upon her but my time was drawing near for me to leave again so I had to hurry in and get her to hurry out. She is not far away. She has informed me mentally that she does not recall any of her outward trips. She does not know who she speaks to or where she goes, but I will tell you now she is still here in this room and she often is still here in this room, and she listens just as you listen. I will have to say Soskris to you now. Soskris and the love of The Almighty will ever be with you. I love you all. Blessed children I will come again. Goodbye.

ROSHA
(Male Astral of Sudicarmus)

---

13 February 1990

This is for me experiment because normally we do not use our voices. We are telepathic people and speak telepathically to each other and only use our voices if we are broadcasting or singing. I have made special effort to learn your language. Do not understand all of your words but have simple conversation to hold with you and have much to tell you, if you are interested. I am called Rosha and the name of the planet that I am from, Sudicarmus. It is actually a number, but you would not understand our language.

Nowhere near Kari-Naris?

No, no, no, although I have heard of the famous Kari-Naris. It is much improved of recent years.

You are Astral?

I am and I had to have energy boost to bring me across the distance from my planet. Vitrik, of course.

You are Jeculin?

Of course and we are teaching. Tutors, that better. Not all, but most of us, go very different places to teach. To make our ways known to other peoples.

Is there a religious aspect to your teaching?

Oh yes, yes. We are as you. We are favoured by The Holy Flocen and we also know of your Earth Lord.

Jesus.

Yes. Who is a Jeculin spirit. He came to you to save your world. He was a great teacher. He is reputed to be God's son. He is as are we all God's sons. I am come because you do not know telepathic peoples.

Only Kari-Naris, who are famous for their telepathy.

348

This I have not heard. They have a language of their own. We have language of our own, which all planets have their own, but it is for other planets we must learn wherever is always different. Must tell you about where we are on our planet. We live under the ground. You know if you have a flap – two flaps, come together, two flaps, open wide.

You're talking of the surface of the planet?

Yes.

You go down . . .

No, not go down, we go up, up, but when we have done what we wish to do we go down and close up.

Why do you live on the inside of the planet – is there no atmosphere?

No, no. You are not right. It is because the surface is dusty ruck formation and not possible to build and we have elaborate buildings, but they are within and everything is controlled by Vitrik and rises mechanically using power of Vitrik. God's own power. Your God. We have God too, but we don't call God. We have God, we bow down.

The Immortal Power.

I bow my head because I am a religious body and in awe of the Power. This is difficult for me because I am not clever, no not . . .

Sufficiently expert with our language?

Thank you, thank you. Correct. I have tried to learn. I listen to your waves in the air.

Radio waves, television?

Yes, yes, yes. Pictures in the air.

Where do you monitor these pictures – not from your own planet?

Yes. We have power-assisted viewing building which drives up to the surface so that we can view other planets with our apparatus. Is not the best way to learn, but is all we have. We are keen for you to know of us. I have to leave. I have not finished my message. I will return another time and finish.

We thank you for talking to us.

Soskris. Subsoody.

Soskris, Krisselt et Salis.

Ahh. You are wise. Help me away.

349

BIKKEL
(Male Dolphin Spirit)

---

21 September 1993

I am different from you. I am friend and I love well you people. I am not able to stay very long for I have no means of ... I cannot find the word ... that is I am not able to have what you call boost. I am a passed over ... I guess I am a spirit. I have been like I am now for a long, long time and I am sweetly loving you. I have been here before. I am male. I am not like you.

You're not from this planet?

I am not from the earth. I am from the sea. I am what you call water-person. I am Bikkel, that is my name. I have difficulty with your language and also with this voice.

Have you a human-type body?

No. I have fish-type when I had body.

Perhaps a bit like our dolphins.

Yes. Similar. I think that is what I am.

But from another planet?

No, no from the sea.

You're from the seas of the Earth?

That is right.

We had dolphins years ago. One was called Waa- Waa.

I know Waa-Waa.

He still lives physically?

No. He is like me. Waa-Waa is Spirit long, long time. We do not call Spirit.

Perhaps you have another word for the same thing.

We are difficult with you, this ... this talk. Not easy. We have no book. Cannot read. Have to learn by sound only.

You're doing very well.

No. Very poor.

350

Very well for your difficulties.

I wish I could do more, but I love well and love you and love her and love all those that I have met around you. I cannot stay, I have no strength.

Perhaps our brethren will give you love.

But will talk some more if you would like to receive me. I was very pretty one when I was male you say dolphee.

Dolphin we say. We know they have great intelligence.

That is so. But they have to learn by listen.

We were told by a dolphin they have tremendous eyesight over distance.

Yes, this is so, but not so much now, when we are not living. I come and I go, but I leave you much big love.

Will you give our love to your spirit world?

Yes. Yes.

We love all living dolphins and all passed over dolphins.

And whales?

And whales too.

They are bigger than us. Very, very big. We are pink and grey and they are black and white.

And you have a curious little snout – front part.

If you say so.

Compared to fish.

Well most of them have big round mouths. We have long mouths. I must go. It is only for love I bring.

HEK

(Astral Surgeon, Jeculin, Planet Lacinea)

---

5 October 1993

Soskris everybody. I greet you in love. I will have to try to speak lower, because this is straining what you call the larynx.

It's not a dear dolphin again is it?

Oh no, no. I am a person, not a dolphin. I think you did have a dolphin when you met last time, and I was listening. How clever to be able to speak your language.

Wonderful, isn't it? You saw him did you?

Oh yes. Only spiritwise. I'm not Spirit myself I am Astral.

Are you of this planet?

No, no, no, no. Come from far galaxy. Many times come here.

Not from the cat-like people?

No, no. I am ordinary person like yourself. Not a doggy person, not a pussy person. You say cat. Not a catty person. I make my voice go lower because I am hurting her vocal cords. I do really have a very high voice. I come on what you call space craft. I am not a technician or astronaut. I do things medical. I am going from my planet to another planet to teach them how to make operation possible for removing and replacing limbs and replacing vital inner parts. They need to be taught because they are not yet clever enough to do it. You are not yet clever enough to do it on your planet, but I cannot come to you. I would come to you if I was – if we were invited. I am not very comfortable with this different voice, it's not natural to me.

I don't think we've had anybody from your planet before, with the high voices. The only real high voices we've had was the dolphins.

Ah, but that was different. That was a Spirit. I am not a Spirit, although I was able to observe when I came here before. The last time you meet I was here. That was because we were going to go to another place first and now

352

we have to retrace our steps a little to go in the opposite – no not opposite like 'L' shape. Like you make the letter 'L' and so we come back this way and I say please let me come here for just short visit. I like to come here. I have been here before in many long time.

Was that when you were on a craft or from your own planet?

No. On a craft. I have to travel to other planets quite frequently because I am what they call superior in my profession. I am wanted on other places but I only go when I am specially invited. Requested. For my help to teach them.

Are you in a lone craft?

Only one. Just one. I have got funny name, you will not pronounce, but my friends call me Hek and I am proud to tell you I come from Lacinea.

Is that in the Cincean group? Cincea, Bincia?

Oh yes, they are all in the same group. It is like grouped around each other with similar names. We are very special people.

I know. We have had people from Cincea, Bincia and I think Rincia.

Not mine, Lacinea?

No. Because of the voice you see?

Yes, but normally speaking I would prefer to talk in that – what you call high. We all speak like that. I am not comfortable in this voice. I come really just for experience and experiment because I have listened here before and I have heard so much in lots of other planets about this – these people called 'Children of Light'.

We are honoured to be so well known. We have been told before. It is difficult to comprehend. Unknown on this planet, that we should be known on so many other planets.

Because you are what we regard as a holy experiment. I think you understand. It was The Holy Flocen who first brought you together and made you learn what you now know. You should have been made into what you call a temple. That did not materialise for lack of people.

When you came in and I was reading, you disagreed with 'you can't have two spirits in one body...'

Oh yes you can. Yes, yes, yes. If she wishes to remain within her own body, I mean her spirit. If she wishes this, she has only got to squeeze herself small and then somebody else can squeeze themself small inside and join her, but, it has happened before now, but it is better if it is not like that. I have not tried it. I must go. Will you please accept the love I bring and not only from me, but from my people. I will be going now because the craft does not want to wait.

Give our love to your crew and to your planet.

353

Thank you. I am going to another planet beyond yours.

I hope you are successful in your mission.

I hope to be. I have not yet failed. So I say Soskris and in your language God be with you.

And I say in the universal language Soskris, Krisselt Et Salis.

Ahh. You are – just a little knowledge I see.

Just a little.

TONDELAYO

(Son of Crazy Horse, Great Chief of Apache Nation)

---

19 April 1994

I am Spirit person, not Astral. I am a guide person. I guide people like you or her if she died I will guide her. I am Indian. I am called Tondelayo.

North American Red Indian?

Yes. But I have the language and I am called Blondybum. That is cheeky name. My father is Crazy Horse. I expect you know of him. I am Tondelayo, son of Crazy Horse, and I am the guide to this good woman. I am very happy to take up this position. I may have to do another journey.

Is your nation Sioux?

No. Apache. Well, I am not an Apache, Sioux or any of that lot. I am one of God's children. I believed in God when I was a living person, because we were taught to believe when we lived in reservations. We were taught by people like yourselves.

Do you have wings?

No, I am just a person. A Spirit person and I am unable to display myself because I am a speaker not a displayer. We only have a certain amount of energy. You must use it for one thing or the other. I am using it now for speaking. Formerly I would use it just to be a protector as far as I possibly can, but you cannot prevent everything for some things are written long before and cannot be unsaid. You cannot undo what is to be. You must go with it and protect the person as far as possible. The planned destiny cannot be interfered with. It sometimes seems unfair that some of the best people must pass sometimes very early, but that is not for us to say, or for them to say. It is planned that way. There is a reason for all. For all who exist there is a reason for their style and for their being and for their time of passing.

Are you attached to Nita now – are you watching over her?

I am going to be watching over her. I'm not yet. I was not assigned – I

355

have selected. I am like your Maurie. I am making my own selection of what and where are jobs that do my service. This is a service which when you pass you will also have to find some way of being of service, not necessarily in this way, but this is a nice way. Not all can have it. Some can have it and some can't. It is the same with people like Maurie. They would all like to do that job, I think, but he has volunteered to do it and he has devoted his afterlife, his spirit life, to doing this great and very honourable thing and without him you could – no you would not be without him – you would be with somebody else, but he is very good at what he is doing. He is caring very carefully for all the people who await around you and all the people who wish to pass through the – shall we say a gateway – to come in to the medium and he will only let those through that he thinks will be right for her. And now I'm going to be here to make doubly sure that happens. I'm going to assist her.

You mean when she goes out of the body?

Yes. Somebody's got to do that.

Maurie was saying he's worried about that – particularly when our Circle is weak.

Somebody's got to do it, so I have got to do it.

That's very good, thank you for that.

And don't forget I am called Tondelayo. I didn't want you to call me Blondybum.

Not really – it is a bit cheeky isn't it? Do you have a blond bum?

Well it seems that my rear portion is much lighter skin than the rest of me and so they called me cheekily Blondybum.

The other Apaches called you that?

Yes, but it isn't part of the language, it's just the translation. I like it though, but it's cheeky.

I like some of the Indian names when they are translated because they are so colourful.

Oh, very. Yes. Like my father – that is a wonderful name. He was a great chief, my father, but we're not here to talk about that, are we. We are not here to talk about things that are long past. We are here to talk about what's going on now. What I'm going to do. She does need someone who will go with her when she goes astrally, because she doesn't know where she goes and she might go and get herself into endless trouble, but I shan't let her get into any trouble.

Thank you, Maurie was worried about that.

I knew it. I knew it. I heard of it and that's why I volunteered. Well, I've got to know you all quite well.

You've been quite a number of times?

Oh yes, I've been here a long time. I've been one of your permanent people that's always here for a long, long time, but until I was ready to take over the new duty, I wasn't ready to talk about it until now. I will come again if you want me to, but if she's gone off on a trip I really have to be with her. She's gone now and I ought to be out there after her. She can get into all sorts of mischief if somebody doesn't stop it. Well, I'm going to be the one who's alongside and make sure it's all right. So for now I'm going to say farewell to you. Thank you for receiving me. Thank you for being pleased that I'm going to undertake this duty.

Thank you for talking to us, Tondelayo.

Farewell.

MOL

(Female Astral from Cincea)

---

10 May 1994

I am come to speak with you. Soskris, little people.

Are you a big person?

Well, I come from a big planet.

You have a little lady-like voice for a big person.

I am a lady. I am a tall lady, about 2 feet taller. I am come to you in love, as we all do. To bring you love from those you have met already. I was listening and I was interested in the story of Miriam which is to your world very important. He was such a little miracle, but we have miracles too, upon our world. We do not call it world, I say world for your sake. There are many miracles that are not recorded in the same way as the one with Miriam. There are so many miracles that happen every day that people do not even notice. You take them for granted.

On our world?

Oh yes, and on ours. Our world is well known to you. It is called Cincea. Yours is a little planet. Little planets have little people. I am called Mol. It's really short for a very much longer name. We have a lot of history of your Earth. We have made many times contact with you from Cincea. Many people have made contact with you over many years and there are other peoples – not in your country – in other countries – that have also been contacted. We only have one language, but you've got so many countries on your planet. In the First Civilisation there was only one language and it wasn't yours. You have many countries on your planet and once they were all one country. So it was everywhere that you have other countries and your country, all the same.

Was it many millions of our years ago?

Oh yes.

358

Do you know anything about the dinosaurs that ruled our Earth for so long?

They didn't rule your Earth – they were the biggest creatures.

Were they before the First Civilisation?

No, they were after.

Were they before the Second Civilisation?

Yes.

You are very learned, you're like a history professor.

Well, I am a tutor.

Let's get that straight – the dinosaurs were between the two civilisations.

Yes, after the great explosions which destroyed all the people. Some were taken away to other planets, but some remained. And then there was a big and lifeless bit and then came dinosaurs.

Dinosaurs came after the radiation had faded away?

Yes, and nobody knows how they came or what they were. They came out of the sea.

Yes, possibly.

They did. They did come out of the sea and onto the land, and really they devoured everything. I will have to go. She has come back. Soskris.

FEELAM
(Astral, Space Master of Cincea)

24 October 1994

I am called Feelam and I come from Cincea. I bring you a message from Mol. She says she will come when she can. I am here purely to tell you that she will come, but you must be patient and wait, but when she comes she will bring you the help and the knowledge that you seek, for she is a very clever historian. She has been learning of Earth for many, many years. It is her forte to do this and she is only too pleased to be helping you. I am a Space Master. There might be other people called Feelam who have been to you because it is a very ordinary name, like you have ordinary names on your planet such as William, or Bill, or George, those sort of names. Feelam is an ordinary name but I am not an ordinary person because I am a Space Master and as a Space Master I have to have a lot of information and a lot of learning to get to where I am now. I am very happy to visit you, but I will not be able to stay with you very long because I have to conduct my craft across the galaxy and to where we are going. I have stopped here specially for Mol and she is very happy to tell you that whenever she can make the journey again she will and I hope she will come with me when I come back again because I do come quite frequently across this galaxy to visit other galaxies.

In my writings somebody told me that he crossed our galaxy in two weeks of our time.

No, no, no. Much, much sooner. That is a slow time. I could go across it faster. About five days. We do not have nights. Your days and nights count as days, but I cannot stop to discuss that matter. You know very well that we think you are backward. That you have much to learn and you don't seem to attempt to learn it. You of this Circle, yes, you have learnt a great deal. I cannot stay. I am sorry. I say Soskris to everybody. I say much love. I say let God take care of you all for God is the greatest power there ever has been known, the Power of Love.

360

HILSA
(Female Astral, Religious Teacher from Planet
Osirus-Osirus)

5 December 1994

Sorry to disturb you, I was adjusting the volume. You are called?

Hilsa.

Why did you say Osirus? It sounds like an Egyptian goddess or god.

Oh no. It is the name of my planet. Osirus-Osirus. I must tell you, you have too much arrogance. Not you personally. Your people. You say 'The World' as though you are the only people. That is wrong. It is not 'The World', it is your world, yes and you can call it your world, but you should never say 'The World' because that makes it that you think there are no other worlds and there are millions of which you are one of the most backward. We have many worlds in our galaxy. We do not call them worlds. They all have different names. Osirus-Osirus. We have named it twice – I do not know why. It is a beautiful planet. I wish to say that many people know of you, as your Circle, Children of Light. It is very famous throughout the galaxies. Not just one galaxy but lots of galaxies because you have been selected from all the peoples of your world to do the work you are doing and you have been taught by very important people like The Holy Flocen. It is an almost unheard of thing to happen. You are what they call an experiment.

Hilsa, are you Jeculin?

No, we are not. We are Followers. We cannot be Jeculins because we are not in that area.

All Jeculins and Associates have to be humanoid. You are humanoid I presume.

Oh yes, we are. We are pretty people. Pretty eyes and loving. We are quite tall, but not so tall as the people of Cincea.

You sound female.

I am.

What is the average height of your people?

We are near to your height, but a little bit more. A little bit slimmer.

Are your space vehicles circular?

Oh yes.

It seems the best design.

Yes it is an advanced design.

Vitrik powered?

Yes. We like to come to speak to you. Not just me or others of my planet, but from all the planets that I know of, like to come to speak with you in love because you are the special selected people. It is because of who you are that you get so many people from other planets. We know you get a lot of people from other planets because it all goes on record.

Is there communication between the worlds – a sort of broadcasting between them?

Oh yes. Except for you. We cannot talk to you and you have not got the equipment to do this.

So when any planet hears about us it's not just from space travellers?

No, it is all written up. It is very important what has happened to you. It is reckoned to be a miracle. A selective miracle. A special, special miracle.

It would be a miracle if you could get our world to sit up and take notice.

It doesn't matter about your world really. It is because you had done so well after being selected to do what you have done and because you have stayed with it that is the important thing. Even if you could not have the trance medium and you might have to go back to your board work, even so you are still unique. You have other spiritualist people on your planet, but they do not know what you know and they do not have the ability that you have. They don't listen if we speak to them.

They probably think that you're an Earth spirit.

They do and they also think that we are playing games on them and that is not true. No Spirit or Astral will play a game, not in this respect. Not where it is so important, so serious.

Did you come down to us from a craft?

Yes I did and I am on my way to another planet, not in this galaxy, in another galaxy and I am going to teach there. I shall remain there for a period of your time – you count time, we don't – I shall remain there for a period until I have done what I said. I am a teacher. I am very much with love for you and for your good medium, specially for your good medium. You have this beautiful cone which accommodates so many people. I say accommodate because a lot of them stay here all the time. Someone who thought he was very clever invented time and so you live by counting time. You live by numbers, do you know that? We do not want you to but you will never stop now.

What I find difficult to understand is how you and other advanced peoples can live without numbers.

Oh we have numbers, but not to live by them. We don't have mathematics, that's not necessary. It's an invented thing for your planet and some clever man or some clever men got together on your planet and invented it and now all you can do is live by it. Everything is controlled. You do realise it was invented by you and not by us.

Am I right in saying The Almighty wants us to understand what will happen to us when we pass over?

If you do not know that is completely true, I cannot say that that is so, but I think it might be a good thing if you were not afraid of passing over. Some people are afraid on your planet.

Have you seen a person actually pass over before your eyes?

In this planet, no.

On your planet?

Oh yes.

Were you able to see their soul?

No. I don't think anyone has ever seen a soul. The spirit can be seen but not the soul. I do not think you can see a soul. It's very tiny. The soul is part of The Almighty and every single living thing has that minute part of The Almighty in them. It is so infinitesimal that you cannot image how small it is.

You are a religious leader are you?

I am, yes. I am not very old. Not old like this medium.

What is the lifespan of your people in our years?

We have perhaps two and a half times more in years. I can live to 210 years; you can only live to 80 or maybe a little more, because I think your medium is a little more and she has been very good to continue to do this work since she has passed the age of doing it, but then her intellect is very high. If her intellect were not high she could not continue.

She continues because she knows we have a task and she is helping me.

And also because she has been taught and trained by The Holy Flocen to do what she is doing. The Almighty gave her a great gift of music and she must still go on and make the music. It is most important that she does because stored in her brain is the music that was given to her when she was

363

born. She has always been in other lifetimes a person of music. A maker of music. An important person of music. She may not be important in your lifetime now, but it is important what she is doing.

Both of us have been told that in most of our lifetimes we've been searchers.

You have been doing this work in other lifetimes. It is all part of the great plan, but until you come together it cannot happen. Although she had her ability long before she knew you and you probably had your ability long before you knew her, it could not come to fruition until you came together...

I am sorry but my time has expired. I am very happy to have come and made your acquaintance. I will try to come sometime in the future when I am free and ready to travel.

(Transcript slightly abridged)

PHILBERT
(Male Astral, Jeculin Space Captain, Bincia)

---

1 May 1995

I greet you with love. Soskris to you all. I am very honoured to be able to come here on this special occasion. I have got to conserve my strength because I have not had a boost. You call boost. I am come without.

You are an Astral, not a Spirit.

Astral, of course I am. I am captain of an aircraft.

What is your name my friend.

Ah. You are a nosey man.

Well, we like to know who we're talking to – you know our names.

Sometimes it is good for you to have mystery, but I will tell you my name. Philbert. I am called Phil. Some people call me Bert, but most people call me Phil.

Are you from our galaxy?

No. I am from a galaxy beyond – not far beyond – about a galaxy and a half away.

Are you Jeculin Followers?

Yes, we are. We have always been Jeculin Followers and we are travelling on a mercy mission to rescue some people. I do not know the circumstances until we arrive, but we know that there is some rescue necessary and this is my job to carry out such a mission. A mission of mercy.

Is it in our galaxy?

No. It is beyond. We have to pass through your galaxy, but because it is your big day for the medium (*reference to Nita's birthday*) and she might not have very long to do trance mediumship, that we have decided to rest a while and come in to speak to you for the space of a few minutes. It will not delay us very far. I am very happy to be here. I am very happy to make your acquaintance. I have not been here before, but my brother has been many times. He is not here now.

365

What is your brother's name?

I am not supposed to tell you, or what my brother is. He must speak only for himself, but I am allowed to say that he has been here. I think to talk to you.

What is the name of your planet?

It is called Bincia.

Oh, you're Jeculins. You're full Jeculins.

Yes, of course we are.

When I said Followers, I meant Followers.

Yes. I doubt whether there are very many full Jeculins as we are. We are very honoured to have this position. We are very grateful to have it and very humble that it has been bestowed upon us.

How many Jeculin planets are there? Twenty, more?

I am not able to answer that. I am not permitted. It is not for me to discuss. I can only tell you that there are quite a few in our vicinity. I mean the vicinity of Bincia. I have been here now since what you call seven o'clock.

You've had a bit of a wait.

I have, because she was having some treatment with her friend. He was aware of me and told her and she held conversation with me. I don't think she heard what I was saying, but she spoke to me as though she could hear. She's a very, very nice person. She is really good, good medium. She is a holy woman and deserves more than she has got in the way of sight for this time. For she has given very unstintingly of her services over many, many years as have you dear Norman, that we of our planet all look up to, for you are also a holy man. We are very happy to be able to speak to you, speak with you and we are very happy that she will allow us to utilise her body even if it is only with our assistance to get her into the trance position so that she can let us use the body unobstructed. I have not got long to stay because we must go on.

Chris said he felt you had a beard.

No. No hair on my face. I am tall. I am robust. You call well-built. I do not call myself captain.

Well, that's the translation.

Yes. I am the master of my ship.

It's a large one, is it?

Oh yes.

How many people aboard?

About five hundred.

How many shuttle craft do you carry?

About 30. I think we have 30 aboard this trip and we can carry up to 50. We do not bring them unless we think we need them.

They carry two or three people, don't they?

They can carry up to seven or eight at a pinch. Pinch, that is your word. At a pinch. We don't pinch. Oh no. That's not nice.

No, it's not. Are the shuttles circular like the mother craft?

Oh no, no. They're quite different. They're small – they're shaped like little boats, with hoods on. When we get in we're shut in and we can't get out until we get where we're going. Ha, ha.

You don't control the escape apparatus from inside the craft then?

No. There has to be a controller that goes with the craft. Even if there's only three people in the craft, it has to have a controller.

And he can't open the craft before …

No, but he will fly it.

Of course it would be dangerous to open it in the atmosphere.

Must not be done. Must be careful. We don't want debris all over the place. It would interfere with other flying objects.

Have you heard of a space craft that crashed in the American desert 20–30 years ago?

Oh many have crashed, many, many my friend. Many have crashed.

On our world?

Oh yes.

Chris: There was one at Roswell, 1947.

I don't know which year, what year – I don't count years. I don't count days or nights. We do not have it.

You have Vitrik light throughout your galaxies, don't you?

You mean what you call the sky?

Yes, and in space beyond the skies.

It's all sky just the same.

But it's bright all the time.

It's not bright from the light of the sun.

It's bright from the Vitrik, we understood.

That is already in the air, there waiting to be collected and used and again expelled and used again.

We were told when we start using Vitrik it will brighten our skies.

Yes, it will. It will, but you won't get Vitrik to come bright and white like we have it as long as you have balls of fire in your sky. We don't have any ball of fire.

We were told there was one sun in every galaxy, but your galaxy has no sun. Has died perhaps?

Perhaps. We call it sun. I do not know. I only know of your sun.

And the one ball of fire in your galaxy has died – gone – died out.

I don't know we ever had one. I only know we've always had Vitrik. But then it – like me – I haven't had the learning of any other – I haven't needed to ask about it. I didn't want to know about it anyway.

But you have had Vitrik for millions of years?

Oh yes. I can't tell you how long. Of course there are millions and millions of galaxies, you know that. There are so many galaxies it goes on forever. Nobody's ever come to the end of it. No one. It does boggle the mind and so does the power you call God. Great, wondrous, magnificent God. That great, great power. No old man as you have had imaginings and told in your Bible. Bible? Rubbish? Some of it is absolute child's rubbish.

Some of it is fairy stories and some of it is true.

Exaggerated truth. But you are a backward little planet. I'm not being rude you understand. I understand you are aware you are backward compared to other – although a lot of people on your planet don't believe there is any other and they are the mad ones. Who could think that your little planet was the only place where there was life forms. It is quite ludicrous. It is not clever. It is far from clever.

And some of those same people if they saw your space craft in the sky and recognised it for what it is – they would still say, 'It must be a trick of the light'.

Or a balloon. Crazy people.

You've heard some of the excuses and explanations?

Oh yes. I'm a down-to-earth person. I say down-to-earth because that's your expression. I like it, it's very descriptive. I like your language too.

Can you monitor our TV programmes quite easily?

Yes, yes. I watch it sometimes.

Really, by monitoring our news broadcasts that's going out all the time, you can know everything that's going on in the planet.

Oh yes, we do. We do. People such as I have to know all about these things – and we have to know your language. I have to know it. Happy, happy, I like it. It's a bit silly at times (*Philbert chuckled*). I make allowances for the fact that you are not an advanced planet like we are. Long, long ago it was quite different and people used to speak like (*Philbert gave a series of grunts*) and you called them cavemen. They were at the beginning of your present civilisation.

Did they develop on their own then? We understand our present people were put down from other planets.

Some were definitely put from other planets. Those that were taken away – their descendants were brought back.

They were brought back for which civilisation?

This one that you have now.

What about the Second Civilisation?

I don't know about that. I don't know about the First Civilisation or the Second. I know about this one. Not all of it, some of it.

So cavemen might well have been home-grown and developed.

They weren't really cave people, that's just an expression I think.

They were sort of apemen really.

No, they were men, but they didn't have a real language at that time. And then there were others in other parts that did have languages. Like you have now so many, many languages. I cannot learn them all. I could, but I won't. I'm only coming here so I'm not going to learn for places I'm not going to go.

English, the language you speak to us, is the language of space in this world largely because America which has done so much space work – there's so many English out there, that is their language as well.

They call themselves Americans, but they are not Americans they are English people that have grown into a people of their own.

They've taken in people from other countries.

You know of course that they were your riff-raff – is that a good word? Yes. They were the rubbish you got rid of and sent out there. (*Philbert chuckled.*)

There was another country. We sent criminals to Australia and they speak English as well.

You sent criminals to America as well.

I don't think they were all criminals.

No, no. Not all, but they were from your little land and your little land is quite a small land on your little planet.

And yet we ruled about half the planet when our empire was in flow.

Yes, and you let it go. You should not have let it go. It would be better one people all over the planet. One language, one people – like us, Bincia. We have only one language and it is the most perfect planet because of our beliefs. I cannot stay with you any longer, dear friends.

(Transcript abridged)

369

FRONTA
(Planet Colinsia)

4 August 1995

You do not know me, I am new to your language, but I am a friend and I come from the planet called Colinsia.

Does that belong to the Jeculin group?

No. It is not anywhere near to – they are in a different galaxy. I am called Fronta and sometimes I am called Billyboy because once I was Billyboy as an Earth person.

You are formerly from Earth?

No, I am a Star bod – I should not have said that – I am a Star Person just as you are a Star Person and she is a Star Person and she will have to go back very soon. She has done a very long stint on your world. It's not all that easy to say your manner of speaking, but I am trying to adapt myself because I have a message for you. It is to tell you that you must prepare yourselves for the going of this very wonderful medium who has been great service to you and to us, all of us from different planets, but we will welcome her home. She will come and you (*Normesi*) eventually will come also because you are twinned with her. And you other people will perhaps earn your way to come to her if you so desire.

You mean Nita when she goes will be going to another spirit world?

Will be going to a Star World because she came from a Star World. She is a Star Child as you are a Star Child.

But we both have had many Earth lives.

Oh yes, you have been here over many, many long periods. You have been loaned to this world and you have to be returned and she is going to be returned very soon. I do not know how soon. I don't think she minds. You have got a job to do here. You have always had a job to do here. That's what you were sent for, both of you and I think but I am not certain that the other male person here has been sent also, but perhaps not from the same

370

star. The lady here present has not been here very long. She's new spirit, not over many decades.

She's a young spirit, you mean?

No.

Has she come to Earth from another Star World?

I think, but not so long ago, maybe one life ago. Not many like you. Not many like your good medium. Not many like this healer – he has had many lives.

Chris (Healer): I believe I have encountered other lives in what we call dreams.

This is possible. You can recall sometimes and you think what a wonderful dream, but it was not a dream it was an experience from another life. This is very possible. She (*medium*) has many dreams. In fact I think she has so many dreams that she almost wearies of them. Some of them are from her other lives and some of them are out of her imagination. My strength is going. I've been waiting here too long. Normesi you will come back to us and you will find her then.

I'm sure your spirit world must be a wonderful place.

Oh yes. I cannot remain with you – my strength is going . . .

371

(Unidentified Earth Spirit)

11 August 1995

... you know where you come from. You were told.

Colinsia

That's right and that is where you are going back to.

***But Nita has been praying that she would like to wait in our spirit
world till my time comes.***

I know. I have heard and I think she is well within her rights to ask for
this privilege, for she has carried out all that has been asked of her to do
over a long number of years and now she asks a favour for herself which is
not really such a great request and I think she will get it. She wishes to stay
in our spirit world until you reach your time to pass also. She wants to go
with you and not alone and I agree that she should do this.

You said 'our spirit world', are you an Earth spirit?

Oh yes, I am.

Would you tell us who you are?

Does it matter? I am long passed, long dead. I have always been for
many years a Spirit, and I have not had to have another life. Earlier
perhaps I had more lives than one. Since I passed which is when she (*Nita*)
was a young person and you were a boy. You, Norman, were a boy. I am
not an English person.

What was your nationality?

I don't know why you want to know that. It won't help you at all.

You probably have something more important to say.

I have got some things to say to you. You have to go back to your other
world. It is called Colinsia, nothing to do with Cincea. In another galaxy
far away, but that's where you came from a long, long time past.

Was it millions of years?

Yes. You were here for the Earth Civilisation One. You were not here for
the Earth Civilisation Two, but you were here for Earth Civilisation Three
and you had many, many lifetimes. In the First Civilisation you didn't

have many lifetimes. I think you only had one, but that doesn't matter, you didn't want a lot then.

Did we go back to Colinsia after the First Civilisation?

I do not know. I think perhaps you might have. You have to earn what you are doing. You have done it before, but you won't have to do it again. You have been chosen to do this work because of who you are. Because of who she is. She is known throughout all the galaxies as a medium par excellence. She has always had this ability. This mediumistic ability and she has done it with the greatest – she has done it because it was expected of her. She knew it was her duty to do it and she will not have to do it anymore. But she may be granted this wish to wait for you before she returns to Colinsia. Colinsia is a wonderful place. I have not been there but I have heard of it. I am Earth spirit and therefore will not have to go because I did not come from there, but I wish I could go there with you.

Do they have physical lives on Colinsia?

Oh yes. I don't know whether you will have any more physical lives. You had such a lot here. I don't think it's necessary for you to keep on. Now then, we have this young man who is also not from this planet. He is a Star Person and he has had several lives on this planet since he came, but he didn't come from Colinsia. I can't tell you which one he came from, but it wasn't Colinsia. He came after you so he hasn't had so many lives as you have or she has, because however many lives you've had she's had the same amount. She's worn out really. Tired, tired, tired.

But one can receive spiritual rejuvenation in the spirit world.

Oh yes, you can and you can have a long rest in between. In fact I think you had a long rest between this life and the one you had before. The one you had before I don't think it counted very much but there have been earlier lives that counted a great deal.

Can you tell us if the lady present is a Star Person?

I don't know but I would like to find out for you and if I can I will come back and tell you. I am not able to stay with you for long because your medium is not too strong. She has what you call a dicky heart.

The soul doesn't leave the body till the brain is dead, does it?

The brain dies when the soul and spirit leaves. The brain doesn't go on after. There is nothing cruel about the matter of life and death. It's natural, it's what was intended. I didn't mind it. I don't even recall it now, it's too far back. Too long ago.

(End of tape)

373

MESSENGER

---

18 August 1995

She has asked for special privilege on passing. It is granted. She shall remain in Earth spirit world until you, Normesi, pass also when you will go and collect her and take her to whichever planet you have decided you shall go to. There is another special message for you. Colinsia is your home planet, but you do not have to go back there if you do not wish to. You can take the choice of Ocena or Cincea, or Colinsia. It is for both of you to decide and you have to let us know which you decide upon. I will not remain for I am only messenger here for special purpose. Soskris to you all and I go now.

Thank you messenger. We are honoured indeed. Soskris, go with our love.

MAURIE

What about that then?
Is that Maurie?
Yes.
Well what about it – Cincea?
Where are you going to decide? You and she between you.
Well we won't decide while we're still breathing down here, I don't think.
Yes, you will have to decide before you leave here.
Oh, did you get that impression?
Yes, I did. I most certainly did. You have got to decide and let them know. So you and she can go together either to Ocena or Cincea, or back to your home planet which is Colinsia, which is in another galaxy altogether. I think you should choose to go to Cincea, but you might like to go to Ocena – it's very modern.

Well, Cincea must be even more modern.

It is more holy but it might not be more modern – I don't know, I can't go there. I am only an Earth spirit and I cannot go there. You have been granted this special privilege because of the work you have done. It's in repayment for all your many years of doing what you're doing. I wish I could go with you.

I wish you could.

Ah yes, I do wish I could go with you, but I am only a poor old gatekeeper.

Well, your job has been very important for us Maurie.

Yes, I know it has and I have done it to the best of my ability and will go on doing it for you as long as it is possible for me to do it. As long as she is able to go into trance and allow this to happen.

She went off very quickly. Was she helped?

Yes, she was. The messenger was in a hurry and he could not wait. I will not remain because I don't think she is very far away.

We might take a break now anyway.

It would be a good idea, but there are lots of people here and I am glad to see you have got a new person to sit with you. I say welcome. He's very good aura – bright yellow. That's excellent and plenty of it. I won't stop now, I have not got the strength to stay anyway.

Well, it's always nice having a few words with you Maurie.

I don't suppose I will come back this evening again, but I hope you will get somebody later on and you might because there's a lot here.

More than usual?

Yes. There's a lot of strange Space people that I don't know. There are some people here from a space craft. There are a lot of them. I don't know which one is going to do the speaking, but one of them must have learned the language. Usually the man that controls the ship. Away I go now and I hope that you have a good meeting after you have your little break.

Thank you, Maurie. All our love to you all.

She's coming back now.

After a brief refreshment interval Wilton, one of the Space visitors Maurie mentioned, was the final contact of the evening

WILTON (Space Master, Planet 'Twenty-One')

I have helped her into trance and I have sent her with – I don't know who he is –

Tondelayo the Indian.

Yes, he is an Indian man with long, long hair and he is taking care of her. He is taking her away out of the room now. She has gone on a little journey with this Indian man. Now, normally speaking I am very strong. I will try and gain a bit of strength as we go along.

Are you one of the Space people?

Yes, I am a Space person.

You're probably a Space Master.

I am the one who had to learn the language.

Space Master, captain of the ship?

That is right and if you don't learn the language you can't visit the planet and if you don't learn the major language which seems to be your language. Other planets only have one language. You have many.

Other planets only have one people.

Yes. You have got too many peoples. You have got a conglomeration of – I don't know – not very clever.

But it's not our fault.

No, it is something that has developed through our fault in the early days when it was thought to be a great experiment to repeople this planet after I think you call it the Second Generation –

Civilisation.

Yes, that will do. And they came from all sorts of planets. Big planets and little planets and black planets and white planets. Even some animal planets. You've got them here as well. Animal people. Lots of animal people.

Can you give us a hint of one or two of them.

Well, you've got the things you call cows and you use them for milking and breeding – you shouldn't eat them, but you do. And then there're big things called hippos. There was no life on the planet when all of these were brought here and they were little when they first came but they've grown quite big. Do you know what I mean?

Yes. They've increased in size over the generations.

And in quantity – there's so many now.

What about the ancient mammoth with the long tusks, that's bigger than our elephants? That came originally from another planet?

I suppose so, but I can't name it. I don't really know. I don't know about the elephants either. I think perhaps they came from another planet. I'm sure they did, but they weren't as big then as they are now. They have increased. Man has increased. He was little when he first came here. When he was returned here, because he was taken away. A lot of them were taken away at the end of the First Earth Civilisation, when your wicked atomic power wiped out your world and nothing was here. Nothing grew. It took a long time...

Millions of years, we understand

Yes, before anything grew again. Then there was a Second Earth Civilisation that I can't tell you much about. There doesn't seem to be any library that can give you much information on that. I don't know anything about your Second Earth Civilisation. I do know that they did try this big experiment to bring people from different planets and animals from different planets to repeople this planet for the Third Civilisation which is now. But now it's beginning to look as though you'll have to do something more positive about finding cosmic power. You have got to find cosmic power before you can get to Vitrik. The Vitrik is there if you could only find it. Not only your planet needs to find it, all the other planets in your galaxy have got to modernise themselves because they want the Vitrik as well. Not any of them have the cosmic.

They haven't got cosmic either?

No, no, there's no cosmic in your galaxy. It is there, but it is not being used.

What do they use then – you probably know we use electricity as a basic workhorse.

You do and I expect they do too. I don't know. I haven't visited any other planet.

We have been told electricity is finite. That it could all be used.

I believe you could be right. I don't know for sure but I think it could happen and you also have got to modernise your ideas of what you call rocket ships. They're no good. They're like big toys and men risk their lives in them. Men are fools. Men need teaching.

Your craft is a circular one?

Oh yes – no, it is not exactly circular. It has a down part and an up part. The down part is transparent and the up part is opaque.

Would you tell me your name, my friend.

Oh yes. It is Wilton.

It sounds an English name.

No. There is no such thing as an English name – all your people came from other planets and they brought their names with them.

What is your planet my friend Wilton?

It's a number really, it's one of those. If I were to tell you, you wouldn't know what I said. Say number 21, that's the number you can give us.

Are you a Jeculin planet?

Followers. Yes and we are very happy that we are now permitted to be Followers. For many years we were not allowed to be Followers. It is now that we are considered to be rehabilitated, re-educated, rejuvenated – I can't think of the proper word for it. We were not in the first place as good as we are now and we have had to cleanse ourselves and become better people so that we could become Jeculin Followers. We would like to be Jeculin Associates, but we have not yet reached the stage where we are permitted to be. You are very fortunate that you have been given that title and you also have been given the title Children of Light which is beautiful because you walk the light path that leads only to the great Almighty. We know the great Almighty is not a person. Where are you?

I'm sitting next to you.

But I can't hear you.

I'm talking to you now.

Ah yes, I hear that, but when you go silent I think you have left me.

I was listening. I'm inclined to interrupt too often and I've been told off for it.

Oh well, I understand if you don't ask questions you don't know the answers. So you ask questions and if I can answer them I will, but if I can't you must be patient with me and understand there are some things I am not permitted to tell you.

Well, to return to your craft I presume it spins.

Oh yes, it does.

Can you tell me if the spin is instrumental in keeping the stability of the people inside, as we have the force of gravity. Does it provide you with a gravitational pull on your feet that you can walk about?

Oh we can. Most certainly we can.

Is it the spin that provides this?

I don't know. I really don't know. That's something I've never asked myself I will ask and perhaps I will return and tell you. Not this moment but another time. Because I think you should be entitled to have an answer to such a question and I can't help you, which seems ridiculous but it's one of the things that's never occurred to us.

Several years ago I was speaking to a Space Master and he was telling me about a new experimental craft that he had. It was quite new then, but he said other planets had them, with little revolving discs on top of the big one, overlapping one another.

378

I don't know about that.

Yours hasn't anything like that?

No, no, but we do spin. The whole thing.

How long would it take you to cross our galaxy at a fast cruising speed?

I would say maybe 13 days or nights. It is day and night isn't it?

When we say day it covers the 24-hour period which includes the night

Yes, of course you know that you live by these numbers. We don't.

We know that.

We have some numbers, but we don't live by them. You do in everything you do. You've got everything controlled by numbers. You call it mathematics, I think, but there's no such thing on other planets. Your people have invented this and they think they're very clever, but really they've got to alter their ideas. They have got to try and find cosmic.

Pity someone can't put a technician down to sort of point us in this direction.

Well, it has been done before, but secretly.

We know that people are put down to help with medicine and different things.

Yes, it has been done. I think it was done even with your atomic power, but we don't hold with atomic power. We don't hold, but some planets do. The Almighty of course does not hold with this terrible power because it is a killer power and The Almighty will not have anything appertaining to killing nor destroying – destruction of living things. The Code of Love is all-important. We go now on a mission of mercy so I will not stay with you very long for I am holding up that mission of mercy.

Is the planet you are visiting in this galaxy?

No, beyond. Quite near your home planet which I understand is Colinsia.

So we've learned in recent times.

Yes, but you haven't been told that until now. I understand the reason is that you were not ready to receive the information as yet, but now you have to be recalled to return to your real home planet.

Just recently, this evening, we received information giving us the choice of going to Ocena or possibly Cincea.

How fortunate you are. You will find if you want holiness go to Cincea. If you want advanced knowledge go to Ocena or Docena if it is offered to you. That is a very good planet also, not quite up to the standard of Ocena.

Docena is one of the planets with the craft that have the rotating discs on top of the big disc all the way round.

Well, I haven't seen those, I really haven't. I haven't seen any craft that is much different to ours, but then we don't travel all that much. We have got certain periods of travelling and distances to travel, but we don't really travel the whole time. We spend a lot of time 'in state' – I think I said that wrong.

In situ?

That might be it, yes. I'm not all that wonderful with your English but I'm doing fairly well.

You're doing very well.

I can only use what she knows. It's not good me saying things she doesn't know because it won't come out right. I have to use her brain. She's very good to let me do that. I think she is coming back so I won't be able to remain apart from the fact I must get back to my craft and get on.

Are you a lone craft?

Yes, only us. Very, very high, and I'm an astral projection from my craft, but we still have what you call a boost chamber to help us get quickly to where we want to go. My body is sleeping. My body is resting on the craft and I better get back now because I have been here too long.

Do all Space Masters speak Usietan?

Not all of them. A smattering of it. Where would we go to speak Usietan, unless we go to Cincea? Lots of people have a smattering of it. Just an exchange. Oh, oh, I must go. Soskris.

HALLODE (LODEY)
(Male Astral, Teacher of Religion, Ocena)

---

25 August 1995

We are friends of yours I am not alone, there are five of us. We are from another planet as you no doubt might have guessed. We are definitely your friends. We have always been glad to be called friends.

Ocena?

Yes, of course Ocena and I am glad to hear that you have chosen to come to us when it is your time to pass. She has said it loudly and clear, 'I choose Ocena'. She could have chosen Cincea.

I don't think either of us think we are holy enough to go to Cincea.

I have heard her say that and I agree that you have got some more progress to make before you are really suitable for such a place for it is the holiest of holies. Not a church, a world, but a world that is purely holy and I do not think I could ever go there or live there, for I, like you, must claim not to be holy enough for such a holy place. But I am a holy person really. I am a teacher. I have got my companions with me who came from Ocena. We came together, not in a craft.

Are you a spirit contact or Astrals?

Astrals. Our bodies sleep. It is a hard journey astrally. You probably realise how hard it is.

I thought your boosters would blast you here.

Yes, they do, but we still have to have much strength to come such a long, long way. It is not just round the corner you know, it's a long, long way.

So our dear planet is galaxies away?

Yes. I have been here before, you probably may remember me. I am called Hallode. I think you called me Lodey. It was not this house. Another house. A big, big house. A more spiritual house really.

There were spirits about in it.

381

I think so, yes. Lived there with her. She didn't mind. She got used to it. Don't you remember calling me Lodey?

It's my memory, I'm sorry. We've had so many contacts. Ocena was our first human-type contact planet.

We were early planet visitors.

Yes, the only one that beat you was the giant wasp planet – Quaslr.

That is quite right and they are beautiful people, but they are not humanoid. They are not like us. We are like you, but they are not like us or you. They are like creatures, but they have lovely spirits. Lovely natures and so loving, but then our people are very loving as you know. We are not ashamed to love each other openly. I do not mean sexually because we do not believe in that. Spiritual love. Open. Everybody loves each other.

But then you are all genetic brothers and sisters.

Oh yes, yes and you will be very happy when you come to us. If you come to us, you can you know. You can be very happy and we will teach you much that you have yet still to learn and you will perhaps have another lifetime on our planet. I do not say you will, but you could.

Tell me, do any of your people, like yourself when you are reincarnated have any recall of your previous life?

Very little. An occasional wisp, but like you when you think, 'I know that it has happened before' and you meet someone and you say, 'I know her, or I know him,' met him before, but you haven't really, it was in an earlier life. Not to worry. We do not worry. I have come specially to tell you that we are going to make you very welcome. I will not be in the spirit world which you will be in because it's not my time yet. I've got quite a long while to go before I reach passing over time, barring all accidents of course.

You've got an expectation of about 300 of our years, haven't you?

Oh yes, but I haven't got all that left. I've got half of it left.

It's a long time.

Yes and you will not come to us until you are spirit people. When you are spirit people I can assure you our spirit people will make you very, very welcome because you people of this Circle – it isn't a Circle, it's an association – you are so heavily discussed. Nicely, very nicely, because of all the things you have done. All that you have undertaken over these many years and all the things you are still trying to do. We admire you very greatly.

Do your people know that we are trying to get a book that will tell people...

Yes, we are well aware and we are most pleased that you are

progressing with it and would like if possible to give any help you might require. All you need do is ask and someone will come and help. Just as she had help with the Kari-Narian story.

There's a potted version in the book – will be – of the Kari-Narian story.

It's a very tragic planet, but it's better now than it ever was.

Terrible bloodshed, wasn't it?

Oh yes, dreadful. We do not believe in bloodshed, but it had to happen because of the one they called 'Our Father, who art in Heaven' because they called it Heaven. They did not realise it was blasphemy. They were cruel, cruel people and very immoral people.

We have a word for it, hedonistic – pleasure seekers at the expense of everything else.

Yes (*Lodey chuckled*) I shouldn't laugh at it. It is really disgusting. As a teacher I would never sanction any of that.

Are your companions also religious teachers?

Oh yes, we are a group. We are friends. I am not able to stay any longer. I was here before you had what you call 'the break'.

When she couldn't get off.

No, she couldn't. I did try but it didn't happen. I tried this time and it did, but I liked what you were reading. That was her prayers.

Yes, she wrote them.

Good prayers. You are all good people. This is your friend Lodey and I will come again if I can. I might come next time on a ship. A space craft.

Then you'll only have a short hop to make.

Maybe only have a little effort to make. Maybe no boost chambers at all.

How long does it take one of your space craft to go from Ocena to Earth in our time, approximately?

I don't know.

Would it be months of our time?

No. Weeks. A month, maybe two months. I don't know.

It's so far away.

Craft travel very fast. Each time some vessel takes off it goes a little faster than the one before, increasing the speed at which we go from galaxy to galaxy...

(*A Circle member sneezed. The sudden noise causing Lodey to vacate the medium more abruptly than he had intended.*)

ALICIA
(Female Spirit, Cincea)

27 October 1995

Soskris, my brothers and sisters. There are rnany people here who are not visible, but they are here just the same. Some are Spirits and some are Astral. All are here in love. None – none at all would say otherwise. I am a person from another planet and if you say hello, I say hello, because I have learnt to be alike. It is necessary for me to be as polite as possible, or you would think me very, very rude. I am your friend. I am friends to all the people who are here listening and waiting for someone to speak, but not many, they want mostly to learn from you people. My name is Alicia, but I come from another planet. You used to have a little girl called Alicia.

Nita's first Earth guide.

Yes, but you see the name comes from our planet and has passed to yours. My planet is called Cincea.

I might have guessed with such gentle speech – such politeness.

I am from a holy planet. I am come here to tell you that she is upset. She is deeply disturbed (*the medium*) about her friend. I heard what they talked of before and I am surprised that the friend – you, young friend – are not going to continue with your sacred job of healing. For healing is one of the most important things that anyone can do. While you live, surely you cannot give up such a great gift and let it be strewn upon the waters as though it did not matter. But she is upset for you, dear friend. She is afraid you might be following the wrong instructions. You must listen very carefully. You must try very hard to do whatever your conscience and your own spirit feels is the right thing to do. She cannot help you although she would like. She would dearly like, but it is not within her abilities. I will say no more. I have said enough.

Are you a spirit, Alicia?

Oh yes.

You've made a long journey then.

Yes, I did, but I love to come here. I've been before many times and I stay a long while when I get here, to get enough power to get back again. And those here are very good to me. They give me plenty boost to help me back again.

Can Spirits not get a lift on a space craft that's going in that direction?

Some can, yes, and some do, but they're not supposed to. They have to get in – go in secretly, and they become stowaways – that's what you call them. Even if they are discovered, nobody minds, but really and truly it is very hard for living persons to discern spirit persons, unless we care to show ourselves, which normally we do not. I don't want to show myself, although if I did you would think me quite pretty. I am pretty. I was pretty.

No one has ever showed themselves within our Circle, I don't know why.

Yes, they have. Her brother has shown himself many times. Not to you, to her.

But not during circle meeting times, that's what I mean.

Oh no. I don't think anyone ever will.

Why?

I don't know why.

Patrick: I saw The Holy Flocen once.

You have been very fortunate. You – and your wife, Mr Normesi. *[This was a reference to the experience of Normesi's wife, Marie, who is not psychic, after the amputation of her left leg due to bone cancer in 1977. Her painkillers had worn off and she was looking at the globe ceiling light in the ward as she fought the pain while awaiting the next dose of painkillers. As she watched, the globe slowly transformed into a wonderful smiling face and arms reached lovingly down towards her. When the night nurse arrived with her medication she was amazed to find her sleeping peacefully without the aid of drugs.]*

Oh, when she was in the hospital bed.

Yes, was very fortunate.

You know of that?

Yes, I do. It is well talked of throughout – not just our colony, but others. It is well known. She is a most favoured person, as is this young man here. This young – Patrick. I cannot stay much longer. I do not have the power to remain. This is not easy. When you are a Spirit you don't have a lot of power so you have to be very careful and use it very gently and very tenderly. And she is not feeling very well (*the medium*) for she has been greatly upset. Specially this evening and as she was early. I came earlier in the day and she was already upset about something. I don't know what.

We were told our original planet was Colinsia. It has a Jeculin sounding name.

It's in a different galaxy.

Is it Jeculin?

No. Followers, yes. We Cinceans are in another galaxy altogether and there are a few planets that are similarly based as ours around us, as you probably know, but this one that you originated from is long, long ways away. I cannot stay with you any longer. I would like to stay, but I'm afraid I do not have enough strength.

Are you planning to go back this evening?

Oh, no. I'm going to rest in the cone. I'm going to wait until I can build up enough strength and get enough help from all these others around me.

You feel the strength building as you rest?

Oh yes, but it will take time. I have already been up there about four days. Perhaps I will be another four days before I start to return. I will come again if you want me to when I can get enough energy to travel. It's a long way – a very long way. I must go. Soskris to you all. And I do love you. You are lovely people and she is lovely, lovely lady. She is a lot older then I was when I passed away. I have to go. Soskris. Farewell. Love, love, love. A cloak of love for all and for the little animals who are very good for you. Bless you all.

SEWAY
(Male Astral, Planet Longsin)

---

8 March 1996

I am a friend from afar. I am your friend. I am called Seway and I come from a planet that you may know of, then again you may not know. It is called Longsin. I am not a preacher. I am an ordinary person, but I have been brought to the High Council and they have asked me to act as their emissary and come and speak with you.

The Jeculin High Council?

No, our High Council.

Your own planetary council.

Yes. And on Longsin there are many very holy people. I am not one of them, but I am respected as being what you would call a good citizen. I am come on astral projection, not on a space craft, on the long trip from my planet to you which is many miles, because the distance is great and I had to have what is known as – you call – a boost to get me here. It is my happy duty to tell you that although you have not had any contacts for some considerable while, there are many who would still wish to make contact with you, because you are the experiment that was made all those years back. Your years – we do not have years, but you have years. And many years back the experiment was made to create a new type of believer and you are the leaders. The ones who were chosen. The Chosen Ones. You remember, you were called for a while The Chosen Ones. And you were chosen and you have done well, all of you. You and her, the medium. You and she – is that the right word? – have done well. You have been stalwart and you have been true. You have given of your lives to this work and tried to give to others the same feeling of complete belief that you yourselves possess and by doing this you have earned yourselves a great name, not on your planet, oh no, but on other planets, important planets and in important ways you have gone forward as great prophets and as you

387

should and you are highly, highly regarded because of your efforts in this manner. So therefore we are to tell you that your efforts will never be wasted. You'll go on and on and even if you cannot have further contacts through this medium, which is not easy for her now in her reduced state of health. Even if you cannot have that, still your prowess will go forward and you will get the credit for all you have done and all you are doing. So keep faith with what you do and believe in all the things you already know to be true. Give your true faith and it will be a reward for you in your time when your time comes and that applies to all of you here present. And those Astrals and Spirituals who are in keeping with you will also have the same blessings. I am able to tell you this because that is my sincere and true message. I love you all and I am happy to have made this journey, long though it was.

We thank you for your message which is very buoyant for us. Is your planet Jeculin Associate planet?

We are Followers. My name is Seway. I will try to come again, but I cannot promise and a lot depends on your medium who is no longer as strong as she was, but she is very willing and we do appreciate all that she has done and we do appreciate the fact that she is still willing to try. I will say bless you all. I will say that The Holy Flocen blesses you and it is with His permission I say bless you. Bless you.

And blessings upon you, Seway, and our love goes with you and our thanks for your message.

I am not a holy man and yet in a way I am, but I have great love for you. I'm not very old. I don't think I'm as old as you.

What is the lifespan expectancy in terms of our years?

On our planet?

Yes.

About three times your lifespan.

A bit short of 300 of our years.

Not quite.

250 years.

No. About three times, yes, about three times your lifespan. And your lifespan should be 75 – that is the normal length of time for Earthlings.

But I think it's getting longer as the generations go on.

Yes, perhaps, because maybe 200 of your years ago people were dying very much – half your ages. But I cannot stay now, so I cannot talk with you any more. I say Soskris. I say bless you all and I say thank you for receiving me and in particular I say thank you to the medium.

She will hear your thanks from the tape.

Goodbye.
Krisselt et Sails.
Thank you. Goodbye. Soskris.

HELGA
(Female Astral, Planet Wumpi)

19 July 1996

I am here in love and I come from a distant planet. You may have heard of it before. We call it Wumpi.

Can't remember it.

Perhaps you have, or maybe you have not been told that the person came from Wumpi. I come to speak to you. My name is Helga and I think there are other people called by this name, maybe not from my planet. I do not want to repeat myself if I can help it because I am not very sure of my ability to convey what I came to speak of. And I have been worried for I have been in the house where you, man, reside and I have been watching the little times when you sit and write your work. You call book and I come now to tell you, you must remember always that what your leader tells you must be taken note. If you do not, if you and the medium do not agree it will not be good for the book. Think and think well what I am telling you I hear her say this night. She does not quite agree. Yes. Think on it. I am friend and I know what you feel and having achieved what you have, you feel it right that it must be there like that, but she hears it for the first time and she says 'no'. So you must listen.

I have already agreed to modify it.

Ah. That is good. Now, I did not come for this purpose when I came. I came because I love you. I love her. I love you both (gesture to Patrick): I did not come to lecture.

That means you as well Patrick.

Oh yes. Oh yes. I am pleased that you are here for your strength helps her a great deal and she is so willing to do this work and we are all greedy and eager to have the use of her body when we can. So you must forgive me. I did not come to lecture. I only came to tell you, I love you.

We love you too.

Thank you, thank you. Two kind gentles – no, gentlemens.

Gentlemen.

Thank you, is it men or mens?

Men is the plural of gentleman.

Thank you. Now I understand. I will learn better if I come again and you will remember?

Yes, that's rather a Germanic name on Earth. The German races.

Is that so? I did not know.

We're told all our names come from space anyway.

Oh yes, I believe they do. Most of them, maybe not all, but most of them. Lots of names come from people's occupations, then long, long after, it is forgotten that there ever was somebody in the family who had that occupation. I am happy to be here and happy to talk with you and happy to be in this nice kind, very willing medium.

Your gentle voice suggests you are female.

I am.

Astrally of course, I presume.

Of course.

Did you come direct from Wumpi, or did you come from a craft?

I came from a passing craft. It was coming this way and I said please can I come too. I did not say quite that, but that is what it would be in your language.

You had a short trip instead of a long one.

Yes, a very short one. But I like it. I like to travel in one of our beautiful fly – fly-car.

We use the term for inter-planetary craft as space craft.

Space craft sounds nice. That sounds nice.

Are your space craft circular?

Some are and some are triangular, but when they are like that they have lots of lights all round perimeter, and they are in that position (Helga demonstrates with hands a horizontal triangle).

The triangle is lying flat in space.

Yes, and the middle is all the . . .

Machinery?

No, no. That is where the captain, master and his people are.

The control room.

Yes. Good. You read my thoughts.

And in between the perimeter is all solid?

No, no. It's occupational, – no, no, wrong word.

I don't mean solid like rock. I mean it's all part of the craft.

391

Yes. I have forgotten what I came to say. I have to go. Will I be able to come back another day?

If Nita is able to trance we love to have visitors from other worlds.

Oh I do like to come. I would like to come. When we come back, if you are here, I will come in.

We meet on this night every week.

I know. I know. I come again next week.

Patrick will be here next week so we will have strength.

I come again. I will remember what I came to say next time. Bye-bye, is that right?

Yes. English expression. Go with our love and take our love to your crew and our thanks and our best wishes on his mission.

He will be pleased. Thank you. He will be quite excited. Perhaps he will come too next time.

Bye-bye.

Soskris. Krisselt et salis.

Ahh, krisselt et salis. Thank you.

CY-BY
(Astral, Planet Wisbye)

23 August 1996

I have come to you from a far distant planet and I am grateful for the use of this excellent medium. She is not a well person, but she is very, very willing. She has given me, and others like me, the use of her body and her throat and her brain over many long years. Almost an impossibly long period for a medium to go on creating the opportunities that we need so that we can talk. We have to talk to you because that is the only way we can get to know you. Get to know what you think and let you know what we think. My name is Cy-By. The planet that I come from is far away. Very, very far away.

Another galaxy?

Oh yes. And I have travelled here on a space craft. You call a space craft or a flying saucer. I know a saucer is what you put your cup in to catch the drips. It is the shape that causes you to say that. They are not all that shape you know. Some are triangles and some are what we would call cigar-shape and you have some strange apparatus – is that the right word – that you call balloon. It has funny little baskets in some cases. They cannot go into space. They are not of any use to you really and you have not yet designed any rocket instrument which will go for any great distance. You have been to the moon, I know, but what good has it done you? It is just something you can write in your archives. I have heard that you have attempted to send a probe to Mars. I do not think you have managed to capture anything of its real abilities for Mars is a strong planet.

It has a lifeless surface. We wondered if you knew if there were internal dwellers?

I do not know. I am not here for that purpose to discuss such things. I am here because I want to tell you some things that are happening now that you should be aware of. It is important that you know your medium has

393

composed some very great pieces of music which we have stolen from her. I do not think she minds. She has written one which she calls 'Soskris' which is a beautiful piece of music and we have taken that piece of music and it is broadcast between planets. There is one other which is called – no two others – one is called 'Krisselt et Alcien' and that also is very beautiful and lastly she has done a piece she has called 'Krisselt et Salis' which also we have taken in the same manner. These three pieces of music we have taken. If you'd consider because they are named for us, that we have the right to do this. And they are being broadcast between worlds. It is a great honour for her, you do realise that? Now I want to ask a question. She has written a further piece of music which follows the piece she calls 'Krisselt et Salis'. I do not know what she calls it, but we would like to have that piece of music also. We have not got permission. It is not named for us.

She would be honoured if you do record it. You would like me to ask her to play it so that you can record it?

I want her to play it again and I want to know when she will play it again. She plays these pieces she has written sometimes at night, after she has gone to her bed.

Does a space craft have to be sent or can you pick it up at long distance?

We can pick it up over quite a distance, but we would prefer to send a recording machine.

In a space ship?

Yes. We have got already the three I have mentioned, but not the one I have asked to be able to appropriate.

And she recorded it on her tape following 'Krisselt et Salis'?

Yes. So that is the reason for my journey here. I want permission. We have taken the music that I have named because it is named for us, therefore we do not feel that we should not take it.

It is written for you, my friend.

Now I want to know for something that is not written for us, will she let us have it?

I say yes, she will be honoured.

Thank you very much and now can you tell me a time when it will be appropriate for me to have a recording machine but more adjacent than we have used at the moment?

I cannot say which evening it will be.

I will have to have a little time, say one week from today, or one week from yesterday.

I would say one of our weeks from yesterday, because tonight is a meeting night.

Yes, that is right and she can do the playing of the music any night, can she not?

Yes.

But we will say one week from yesterday.

Six days from today.

Yes, and you say yes she will do it. Thank you. That is why I have come so far, so far. We want to know that she has given her permission.

Are you Jeculin, or...

Followers, as you are yourself.

You have the circular craft of Ocena and Docena – we think they are Associates – I'm not sure.

I am not from Ocena or Docena.

You know of them?

Oh yes. They are not our galaxy. We are closer to you than that.

Did your craft make any other calls on its way here?

No. You are our aiming point. We have come here specially for this permission and to tell you we have utilised the other music that was named for us.

She will be highly honoured

I am so glad. I want really to let her enjoy a little for she has not got a lot of time left. You realise?

Yes. We know. I am racing to complete my writing works that she listens to and approves, while we have her. How long, in our time, did it take you, approximately, from your planet to reach Earth area?

To reach Earth area.

Yes, to where your ship is now located.

I will talk while I think. When I first heard the music and I put it forward that we should have it and it was agreed by the High Council that we should have it. (*Tape turned over.*)

I repeat the question that from your planet to reach our planet, and you're in another galaxy, it took you...

About four weeks.

Of our time?

Yes.

Thank you very much.

Now I have got to make telepathic or oral – is that the right word? – conversation back with my planet to get someone to be ready for next week with recording apparatus that will be sufficient.

395

Does that mean another craft has to be sent?

No. There isn't time is there?

How will you get it?

They will have to borrow from another planet.

A nearer one.

Yes. By where we can get here quickly.

The High Council must certainly be involved that you can do this.

They are involved. This music thing is the most important thing. Your medium is the most important medium we have contacted in many years past and we shall be so sorry when you lose her but she will be going to a far better place than she is now in.

We have been told Ocena.

Yes, and you will be going also. The one called Norman. Are you her brother?

No. We were told a long time ago we were twin spirits.

Ah not like twin people.

No not born twins, spiritual twins.

Thank you for the information, I'm very pleased. I am going now. Much love to you all and thank you for listening to me but I was told you must have this information and we must have the permission before we take it, her music. I go now in love, as I came and I leave my love wrapped around you. By the way the planet that I come from is called Wisbye. I go now, I cannot last another second.

FREDERIQUE

(Male Planetaire Spirit from our Galaxy)

---

1 November 1996

(Nita and Norman only)

I greet you in all sincerity. The deepest love possible for any person to bring you. I am a spirit person, not a living person. Do you understand my meaning? I am not of your world, but I am of your galaxy. There are many planets in our galaxy that speak almost identical language to this which I am using. They are well advanced as far as you are concerned. You are the baby and we are the fathers. I am a father, but I love you dearly and I forgive you that you have not advanced. You cannot help it. It is part of your upbringing and not the fault of the child. The fault of the fathers. The fathers are responsible and I am a father. I have come to talk to you about your medium. You have got indeed a very good and very reliable medium and a very scarce one. You will go a long way before you will find another like her. She has given her body, her mind, her thoughts. Everything that is necessary. Her voice. Her hands even, and she gives them freely. There are not many mediums who will not interfere, but she goes completely away, therefore you are most fortunate. And this medium is really a very special medium. Now, for your sake you have to try to find another medium, because her time has, or is, expiring. You will not perhaps be as fortunate in the next one, but you must take what you can get. You may try yourself, if you allow the thoughts to enter your mind, speak them aloud and you will find you are able to do it. I am talking to you, my man. My Normesi. Because there is no one else to talk to here except spirit people and they cannot help you. They do help you in any way they can, just as she does. She's helped by them, you know that don't you? And she is many times told of things when she doesn't go into trance and she tries to retain them in her mind and tell them to you when she sees you and this is good, but

397

not always quite authentic, if you follow my meaning. Little bits can get added of your own thoughts. It's not impossible to do that. It's not improbable that you will do it, but I do want you to try. Try to be able to get contacts. And if they come to you try to be able to receive them and don't be afraid to speak it, but you have got to have someone to speak it to, you realise that don't you. Failing all else you have got your little instruments that you were using here that you call recorders. You can use those and that will help you. Listen to what you think the spirit has told you and listen to the words that you have spoken and you will find gradually that you come to make sense and you won't have to think it out at all. It will happen for you. Am I being followed? Good. I know perhaps you don't want to do it, but you are in a position where you're really forced to do it. Unless you can find another medium, because you cannot rely on her very long. When I say not very long, I don't know how long. I have no idea how long. It might be today, it might be tomorrow. It might be next year. It might be in the year after, who knows? But help you need, because you're in the fortunate position of having been given all this information that has got to be passed in some way or another to the rest of the world.

This is what we are trying to do with the writing of a book.

This I hope for your sake will happen, not that you will be punished if it doesn't happen, for you will not. You are in such a position that there is only you left to tell it, when she's gone. Unless you can get back your strong members like the young Teresi. But I doubt you will get her back because the man will prevent her. It is not her fault. You must not blame her. She still believes and you have others who believe. They are far, far away including your own living daughter who is also a good believer. But she also is far, far away, but she could have been your medium. She could easily have been your medium. She has the power, but she might not have been with the same abilities as this present one. She has given herself so completely to it. I don't know any other person who could do that. But I am afraid she will have to leave us and she'll be like me then and probably coming and visiting you Normesi. You must be glad of that. I haven't got very much more to say to you and my time is running very short because her strength is running very short.

Is your planet very far from us?

Not in my way of reckoning, but in your way of reckoning yes.

Are there many planets in between?

Yes, there are. Some have names and some do not. Some have people and some do not.

What is your name?

My name – you will laugh. It is Frederique.

Frederick?

Well, we do not say it like that. It is Frederique. You have on your planet lots and lots of names exactly the same as the names on our planet.

Have people of ours from the First Civilisation been taken to your planet?

It is possible there are quite a lot of them still there, in which case they have come on through the ages and the language is practically the same.

Do you know as a fact that your planet was one of those who evacuated people from Satalle?

No, I do not know that as a fact. No, I cannot state that. It is possible because there are so many with your names. So many names the same, with mine as one, only we do not pronounce it as you would pronounce it. We have it Frederique. It really has the sound of French intellect.

You are male?

Oh yes, of course I am and I am a middle-aged male. I wish I was younger, but I am glad to be as I am. I am a spirit person, but not from your planet. We pass over just the same as you, only not quite so early. We last a little longer.

About how much longer? In our years if you can.

I was about 70 when I passed over and I was considered middle-aged.

So 140–150 years.

Yes, 200 perhaps if you're lucky, like you have the odd ones that make 100. I'm afraid I have to leave you.

Thanks for chatting to us.

I am glad I could come in. I am very, very pleased to have had the opportunity. I've been telling her all day please try tonight because I'm coming in.

Do you attend the meetings?

Oh yes. I've listened many, many times and if I don't get it directly I get it second-hand through somebody else.

Are there many here tonight?

Yes, there are a lot of people … and there's a big spotting light coming down to meet you.

It still comes down on us?

Oh, yes, yes, yes, yes, yes. Which shows there is something very special going on here. You are specially-trained people – you know that, don't you.

Yes, we have been indoctrinated.

You have. Yes, you have and you are so fortunate. But I really must go now. God be with you.

God be with you Frederique. Thank you for talking to us.
Thank you for receiving me and thank her please for allowing me to utilise her body. Good-bye, my friend.
Soskris.
Soskris.

NONI

(Female Spirit, Planet Merry)

8 November 1996

Soskris to you all. I thank you for the reading on the excellent and wonderful person that we all know, the one time Icla who now has left us, I am sorry to say. She no longer lives as a person, but lives as a spirit and it is possible that she could, if she so desires, come sometimes to visit you again, for she loves you dearly and nothing will quell that love and that by a woman who was indeed of great help to you in your early days.

But she was a spirit when she taught us, I thought.

I think not. She was a person. She used to be – she told you she went to a temple as a High Priestess. It is long ago. She has passed and you have forgotten, or if you have not forgotten perhaps no-one has ever told you. You do not know me for I am a stranger to you although I must say that you are not strangers to me, for I have been so many times and sat with you in your meetings, even if I did not speak, I was here and learned much with you as well as listened to what you had to learn. And you have been good and patient and you have taken it all very, very seriously and you do deserve great credit for the length of time you have devoted to this calling. For it is a calling. You were selected to do what you do, as you probably know. You, of course, are people –

May I just intercede –

and you want to know who I am.

Yes, because you have digressed. You were going to tell us.

Yes, I was, but something else came up. You don't know me at all because I have not spoken before. You may have heard of me from others, because my name is quite well known. I am called by a simple name of Noni. Noni is just a nickname. I can't tell you my full name, you would never remember it even if I did.

It sounds feminine.

401

Oh it is indeed feminine and I am a feminine person and I have been sitting here a long time waiting for this opportunity. Yes I did rustle round her.

Ah it was you then.

I wanted her to get on and let me come in. Well she's done it. Here she is and here I am. I haven't got any special message for you except to tell you that it is important that you keep these meetings going even if you can't get a reception because she isn't well enough. But you must try to keep the meetings going because you've got a whole host of people who live here with you and they want you to keep it going. I'm talking about the spirit people and the astral people who visit. I'm talking about the people of your own world, the spirit people of your own world and those that come from other worlds and astral people who come sometimes with the intention of speaking, sometimes not, sometimes finding no opportunity, or maybe she's not well enough. We will never do it if she's not well enough. It is unkind to her. We do know when she's well and when she's not and at the moment she's quite well and I'm very happy to be here.

Are you of our world?

Oh no. Surely you've already discovered that I couldn't be. I'm more advanced than you.

What is the name of your planet?

Ah the planet. Yes, you do know the planet, I think. It's called Merry. I think you've had somebody from Merry. It's Merry – like happy. Have you had someone from there? I think perhaps if you look in your little book you will find it. You have got a little book where you used to put everybody down who spoke to you. The important thing is to get the receptions. I believe you had somebody last week who was willing to help you to get reception; so that you yourself could have a go. You have to give yourself up to it. You have to allow it to happen. There's a young man sitting here – I don't know his name – and he hears voices. But he allows himself to hear voices. That's good. The doctor might say that's mad. But it is not. It is not. I promise you it is not mad.

We know it's not mad. The doctors think it's mad.

Your medium – she hears voices – she knows it's not mad. I do not blame you for not doing it, but I think you ought to try. You are in a position where you could try. Nobody would grumble at you if you didn't succeed, would they? I can't stay with you very long because the strength is not very great.

Are you astral?

No. I'm spiritual.

Ah I understand.

And spirit people don't have as much strength as astrals.

They can't get artificial boosts.

No, and also although she is very much better and much stronger, she hasn't been able to give me a lot of strength. So I must not misuse what strength I have and I need to get back.

The physical people of your advanced worlds ought to make it known that they can give lifts to spirits in their space craft when they're going a long way.

I have heard this is so. I haven't had one myself, but I think I might try. If there is one about anywhere that might be going somewhere that I have to go, but then how does one know where they go?

I suppose you have to eavesdrop.

I suppose, but I hadn't thought of it. We do eavesdrop. We all eavesdrop on you here.

We know that.

Well you don't mind do you?

You're very welcome. All of you.

Yes, yes. Thank you. Thank you for receiving me. Thank you for letting me come in and thank her for making a special effort and I'm sorry if my rustling upset her.

She will hear your words on tape.

Very good, very good and I might come again if you will let me. I have no special message. I am only a visitor. Perhaps she ought to wait for people who have more messages for you, or perhaps some stronger motive in coming. Mine is just plain curiosity and I'm proud of it.

We are the kings of curiosity, this circle is.

Yes, I think you are. I think you could be that. I will now say bless you all. Bless you, bless you. Soskris. Noni now leaves. Bye bye.

MAURIE: (Circle Gatekeeper)

I didn't know whether to let her in or not.

That's not our –

Yes it is.

I thought you'd emigrated old son.

No. No. No. No.

No. I knew you hadn't.

I'm always here. It's just that she hasn't been well enough to do any trancing and for that I'm extremely sorry. I don't know whether I ought to have let that one in because she didn't have a special message, but she was so sweet. I think perhaps she might have been before, but I don't know. Did she say she hadn't been before?

She's been eavesdropping.

I don't remember her myself, but she hasn't been sitting in your cone, I can tell you that. She might have been sitting in this room, but I don't know about up there. I don't think she's been up there – I would have seen her. They can't get by me. Not in a hurry.

Did you hear the conversation earlier about a group in Bournemouth that may be doing something similar to what we do?

I don't know. I honestly do not know.

Could you find a volunteer up there as a spy to sort of eavesdrop?

No, we don't do that.

Oh you don't do that. No MI5 stuff up there.

If you want to know you'll have to go yourself. I should think it might be a good idea. I do advise you to do it. It could help you considerably. I don't say it will. You might help them. Who knows? I've got something to say about the daisies. Tell her not to mind the daisies. (Nita had been seeing clumps of daisies through the mist that blinds her vision) It won't hurt her. I don't know who's causing it, but I know it's happening. She's not to worry about the daisies. She's seeing daisies. She can't see anything else, but she can see daisies where there are no daisies. I think it's spiritual, but I can't alter it. It's not harmful. Tell her that. Now I will say bless you all. Soskris.

Thank you for what you do for us Maurie.

Thank you for listening. Thank you for sitting so patiently when you can't get a contact. Bless you all. Soskris.

LOLAH

(Female probably Astral, Planet Wesoly)

---

15 November 1996

Soskris to you
Have you been to us before?
No. I am a stranger, but I am really more than that because I have been many times. Many times I have sat here when you come together to meet. Sometimes you do not get contacts. It all depends on how well she is. She is not well at the moment, but she has vacated and let me come in. I don't think she's gone anywhere. I think she's here. I think she's not well enough to go anywhere. I am glad to be here and to be able to speak to you, but I have come with a sort of complaint. It is something that people on other planets are distressed about. That she no longer makes that lovely music. We all miss it very much on other planets.
You are from space?
I am from space and I have come a long way, but then I do that quite frequently because I like to sit here in your room when you meet. Sometimes I come the day before and I stay the day after.
Do we know of your planet?
It is called Wesoly.
That's in our galaxy isn't it?
On the edge.
The far edge.
Yes.
What is your name?
It is Lolah. Not Lola, Lolah.
I think we may have had your planetary leader, long ago.
I don't know. I am here because I wanted to speak to you. So many different people are putting in to each other saying, 'Where is all the lovely music? Where's it gone? Why can't we have it?' I know that she's

405

been ill. Perhaps that has prevented her from making music, but at one time the music was so prolific and there were so many people saying, 'Listen, there's that music again.' It's so beautiful.

Do you mean people here, or people away?

People away. Nothing stops. Sound goes on forever. You cannot imagine how far it will reach. It doesn't stop. But when she doesn't make it, then it has stopped and we are sad. So it is really a request that she will start to do it again if she can. If she can't we will understand. She plays music on her tape recorder, but it's not the same as when she sits down and does it herself. We like to hear her making music.

Original music.

Yes, and if she can, please will she. Will she hear this?

Yes. She will listen to the tape.

Very well then. Listen to me, Nita. We really want you to make that lovely music again, if you can. So please try. Thank you dear. I am really a sitter, but this time I was told to speak and I have. I will not be able to stay because the strength is poor. Thank you for listening to me.

Thank you for being so kind. Bye-bye all of you. Thank you. Thank you. Thank her for permitting me. I think there is somebody else going to come in, but I don't know who. Bye now.

MAURIE

She was wrong, there isn't anybody else coming in.

Maurie?

Yes, this is Maurie.

Well, you're somebody else, but I know what you mean.

Ah, ha ha. Well I'm always here. Always just above your heads. Thank you for listening to Lolah.

She made a personal request which Nita will hear.

I heard. You've got to encourage her to do it. I don't know why she's not doing it. She seems to think she's lost the power to do it, but I don't think she has. She hasn't gone away this time. She's just here in the room. She's sitting there and she looks a bit despondent. Perhaps it's because of the new hurt she's got. She has got bad luck at the moment with these broken bones. She says she hears the bone go click, so I think it's a broken bone round the side.

The transcript I read when Lolah came in; from Nadia, does she...?

Very nice. Lovely lady.

Yes, well-spoken lady. Is she here tonight? Does she still come?

Lovely Russian lady. No, no, I don't think so. She has been quite recently. There's another one called Naomi. She sticks around very often. She doesn't seem to want to come in to talk.

How about Nan? We haven't heard of her lately.

You mean the queen. The great queen with the great dog.

Ann Boleyn.

No, she not here. Quite often she brings that great grey dog. Grey, shaggy, long-haired. She combs it. She makes it look smart.

When you go back to your planes do you see animals up there?

Yes, quite often. With people where they were strongly attached. I cannot stay any longer.

Thank you for the chat, Maurie.

Thank you for having me. I love talking to you. I go.

Thank you for what you do for us.

A pleasure. It's a pleasure.

Footnote: Being in the room, Nita (medium), would hear the conversation with Lolah, but would not be able to recall it. While a contact is using her brain she is unable to relay information to it for memory.

NOAH
(Male Spirit from Mars)

---

14 March 1997

I am not a person of great abilities. I cannot do clever things with my hands or make beautiful music with my mind. No, I am just an ordinary person, but from another planet. I come to be with you in a time when you feel bereft of people calling for you, or people calling on you. I'm glad that you have come and your good Nitesi has not gone away. She is here beside. She is afraid to go away. She has no guide any more. I heard her say some while back that she thought she had lost her guide. Yes, she has. That is because she hasn't been doing sufficient work. Not her fault. It's the fault of her health and she is not even now really ready to be doing this. But I wanted to come to speak to you. You don't know me, but I'm going to let you know me. I am from another planet and, as I said just now, I am not a very clever person, but I am very honest and trying to be even more so. Blessed peace, blessed aura. I want you to realise that by doing this she is risking her life. Do you hear me, you who listen? I do not want her to go out of my reach, out of my sight. I want her to stay here.

Is there someone else here who can stay by her?

Only your guard, Maurie, and he is already doing a very valiant job. I want to tell you that she has worked for you for long, long years. Never ever refusing and always accepting what was happening to her. Working her way closer to The Almighty by doing this. But now she must stay here, near her own shell. I call it shell because that's what we always have called it. My name is Noah.

As the biblical Noah?

Yes, you once had a very famous person of that name. And I come from a planet which is not very far from you in this galaxy. You call it Mars.

You're an internal dweller.

I am. But I am a person who cares very deeply and wants to help to

408

protect your good lady. My visit to you tonight is purely to help her. She deserves it.

It's so good of you. Are you humanoid, similar to us?

Like you. Just like you. No different. Maybe a little taller. Maybe a little rougher. But you need me and I need you. I will come again when I think she is well enough to do this. If she is not well enough I will not come in. You'll have to let it happen just the way it can. So don't ever try to force her. Remember, she is willing to give everything. Even her life if need be, but we don't want that. We want her to be here for us, with you. We want her to be with you and that is what she must do. If she comes again and allows me in, I will not refuse her offer. I will say God bless you, my daughter.

This is a big thing for us – you are the nearest space visitor that we've had.

You are kind to remark on it. I am glad that you appreciate it. I will not remain now because I do not want to strain where there is no strain needed. Her ability is very fragile. She has passed her time of doing this work.

We are aware of this.

But she will go on doing it if you let her. Sometimes you must say 'no', sometimes you must say 'yes'. I cannot stay with you because I haven't got much time or much strength.

Much love to you, Noah. Thank you.

I will come again if it becomes possible.

You haven't far to go. You are a spirit?

Oh, yes.

It's not too far for you to go, is it?

No. Quite near.

Neighbour.

I go now. Soskris to you all. Much love. Real love. Come back now Nitesi. Come in . . . come in.

409

PRAYERS

CODE OF LOVE
(Nitesi, Automatic Writing)

We love all things intensely – the dark night, the dawn, the day with all its hours of brightness. The large and small animals, the birds and leaves, trees and plants and all of life we love with a blinding sureness that the Almighty *is* and is all things for us to love and understand.

The simple things that happen from day to day are all designed by The Almighty for us to love and comprehend and believe in. We believe in all that is wondrous, all that is beautiful, all that is sad beyond human thought. We believe in the equality of all things, in the forgiveness of sins, in the life everlasting, in the purity of faith and justice, and in The Almighty, who guides us and leads us to salvation.

Through the Glory of The Almighty we exist and The Almighty is the Power of Love that carries us through life to the very portals of death, which is the beginning of a new life of wondrous beauty and sublime ecstasy for those who truly believe. For the word is the meaning of life, and death . . .? The beginning of the end, the end of the beginning, when the real life of the spirit will start.

We truly believe in all these colossal things, as truly as we believe we will draw breath tomorrow, will live tomorrow, in the coveted spirit afterlife, as we all eventually must. We believe in The Holy Flocen and that The Flocen is the voice of The Almighty.

AMEN

A PRAYER FOR TODAY
(Normesi, 1997)

Oh Great Father of all life please make us more aware of how Thou would have us be. Send thy message strongly to our souls that our hearts may show us the right path in today's world. Help us realise that by giving love to our fellow beings we are giving love to Thee also which in turn strengthens still further the great love Thou hast for us.

Open our eyes to Thy presence all around us at all times, in the eyes of our fellow humans and animals, in the beauty of growing things, in the majesty of trees and the scenic wonders of our native skies. When we are desolate give us confidence in knowing that if we make the effort Thou wilt not let us fall by the wayside. Help us to realise that where the only love is selfish love lies the downward path to a self-created hell on Earth.

We pray for our world leaders and all administrators everywhere that under Thy guidance their decisions will be fair and humane. Oh Immortal Power of the Universe, let our hearts overflow with love that it may spread to all with whom we come in contact and from them to others in an ever widening wave until the whole family of life is encompassed within the eternal warmth of Thy great power.

*　　*　　*

The following prayers are a small selection taken from those written by Circle members in earlier years which enabled their Jeculin tutors to assess how much of their teaching had been absorbed. They were all approved by them.

THE PRAYER OF THE CODE
(Tomesi)

Almighty of the eternal galaxies, we humbly beg that you will accept our prayers, our humility and our love. We give you thanks for having been privileged to learn the meaning of The Code, which is summed up in one wonderful word – Soskris.

We are contrite for having to partly transgress The Code, owing to the circumstances which surround us, and are grateful that you (who understand all things) do not hold us in fault for living as we live.

We ask that you guide us in the way of The Code, teach us the way of The Code, so that we may in time be gathered into the fraternity who live by The Code. We humbly thank you for the knowledge of the truth which you have allowed us to know. May we ever say the one word which not only symbolises but *is* The Code – Soskris!

AMEN

OUR DAILY PRAYER
(Normesi)

Almighty of the universe, we ask thy forgiveness because we do not pray as often as we should. We ask Thee to recognise that Thou art forever in our hearts. We ask that we may remain ever humble, always remembering how favoured we are to be allowed to share the knowledge of Thy wonder.

Lead us to the people, and them to us, whose souls are crying out for the knowledge we now possess, that we may sow the seeds of Thy holy word on fertile ground. Help us to assimilate and retain in our minds and to fully understand the true meaning of the great truths that have been explained to us with such great love and patience by our beloved Flocen and Efun.

We ask Thee to give us the words that will destroy lingering doubts among those who should be converted, according to Thy will. We earnestly pray that it be Thy will that we should eventually join the People of Light, that their further teaching will enable us to fully comprehend the wonder of Thy love.

In return, we pledge our life and love to Thee, that Thy way may be our way, Thy will be our will, Thy love be our love, that we may be encompassed by the warmth of Thy great love for all eternity.

AMEN

THOU ART THERE
(Colin)

Dear Almighty, when I look within, when I am quiet and still, thou art there.

When I look at the sea, large and moving, never still – all is change, yet ever returning to itself and complete, Thou art there.

When I look into space, no large or small – all relative, no fixed point beyond my worldly mind to grasp. Yet I can see, Thou art there.

A tiny spider on a thread which I cannot see or feel – alive as I am alive, yet so small a thing. What room in his heart for love? Yet Thou art there.

Almighty God, which art love itself, what room in my heart for Thee? I will find room in every part and be full of love, that I may ever give it generously. In giving love is my greatest fulfillment. In receiving Thy love is my greatest joy.

AMEN

PRAYER
(Normessi)

Dear Father Almighty, already resident in our souls, we offer our humble gratitude that we have been selected to be founders of the First Earth Jeculin Associate Church. We pray that our holy conquest of souls on Thy behalf may reach the same magnitude among the living as it has among our spirit brothers and sisters. Soskris.

We pray that Thy love, now inseparable from our hearts, will expand and blossom further to drive out the remaining vestiges of arrogance and the selfish fetishes that we know still reside therein. We realise that in this way Thou can curb our impatience, heal our wounds and soothe the distractions of our Earthly minds, thus making us more worthy servants of Thy will. Soskris.

Thou hast apparently given us a status in the universe that, though we do not fully comprehend it, we do realise we are not worthy of it. If this is humility, then perhaps in this one respect we can be humble without any difficulty, because it is a logical conclusion. It is an irony we must live with, at least for the present, that our holy work is better known throughout the universe than it is on our home planet. Soskris.

We beg the pardon of our Lord Protector, The Holy Flocen, that He understands that because His overwhelming love fills our simple hearts it leaves little room for the awe to which we know He must be entitled. Awe is akin to fear. But how can one fear such a perfect manifestation of the eternal love of our Almighty Father? Perhaps we are as spoilt children and, if this is so, please forgive us for we are not so sophisticated as our extraterrestrial brothers and sisters. Soskris.

AMEN

DAWN BREAKS

(Lindesi)

As words of love wing their way heavenward, light filters through the darkness, slowly bathing the new day in warmth and love. Dawn's chorus crescendoes in an arch of the victor's song, heralding the new day. Another day to pray to The Almighty and reverence The Flocen for the miracle of life of the spirit – the spiritual revolution, when a man awakens to his soul, the heart of his being.

He can say, 'Praise to The Almighty, for I have seen the light and felt the Power of Love that enfolds all living things, guarding us and guiding us, drawing the pattern of life into a spiral of love, peace and harmony – reaching ever upwards, lifting us from our lost being and captured heart, revealing a new way of freedom and love.'

We are children of the universe. As we look to the stars, every fibre of our being vibrates to the harmony of The Almighty's way of love and life. Our voices blend to resonate with love and ecstasy as we pray 'Soskris!' to The Almighty and the Holy Flocen.

Our being vibrates with flowing energy, pulsating with life's harmonious chord. Our cup runneth over with love.

AMEN

SERMONS

IF AT TIMES YOU AWAKE IN THE NIGHT...
(Nitesi)

If at times you awake in the night and find it hard to recapture sleep, this is a good time to try to commune with The Almighty. One thing is certain – if you speak your thoughts aloud, no matter how quietly, they will be heard and even possibly recorded, to be kept forever in the great Memory Bank of the Blessed Almighty. At times you may feel that your words fall on stony ground and lay there awasting, but this is not so, for if your heart sends out the love it contains and your brain reasons out the words to convey it, then you have made actual contact, if not with The Almighty One, then with The Holy Spirit who is our dear friend and guardian, of whom we must ever attempt to be worthy and must revere in our hearts with the deepest love possible, offered humbly and sincerely, in grateful thanks for all the gifts He has granted to us. One of these precious gifts is to realise that psychic phenomena are not only possible, but part of our inheritance. How fortunate are we who can open our eyes and see, if only for a second, a vision of The Holy Spirit, or the glow of any of our other friends who love us, as we love them. Such are the marvels of spirit communication, no matter what form it takes, whether visual, audible, mental or written – all are sacred gifts from the All Highest, for those who love enough to accept them! So when you can, take your quiet moments and dedicate them to prayer and communion, and feel the restful placidity enter into your being through the spirit, which offers love eternal to the All Highest, our Almighty One who has ever been and will ever be the only God in existence. You will find the effort will be repaid a millionfold by the peace which will be yours, and then sleep will come freely and easily, and you will awake to a new dawn, refreshed and glad in the knowledge that The Almighty cares for and loves you, as you care for and love The Almighty.

LIFE IS FOR LIVING ...
(Nitesi)

Life is for living, yet so few know how. So often drifting along on a seemingly even keel, knowing little or nothing of great joy, or even great sorrow, so that each day follows another with no depth of meaning and for lack of use our brains become more and more atrophied. One thing is certain – we are born to die! What we do with the time in between is our own business. So many people are afraid of death, yet all know that they have to go when the allotted time has expired. Most of us cast it from our minds whenever possible, imagining that by ignoring it we can make it go away, or put off that fateful day!

Strangely enough, many are content to live this way. Yet there are some who think a little deeper, who seek the greater truths, who long for the miracle touch to move within and open up the heart to starker emotions, the brain to greater knowledge, the soul to more perfect love and life to better living.

We have not lived until our hearts have cracked a little, until anguish has touched our souls and disappointment brought us low. Then (and only then) will we come to the truth. We will realise that life is never simple, that to reach the heights of happines we must first learn the depths of despair! That to attain grace, we must first know humility! In each living being, the spark of The Almighty lives and that love is inborn within all living creatures, all things great and small.

So that love to love may flow, and ever flowing onward may interlock all of life into one great whole – into The Almighty. When we have learnt all this, we have lived!

SERMONS

The Flocen has given us, the chosen few, a great responsibility to interpret our learning, to teach those who seek truth, be they living or passed over, yet we are humbly grateful to bear those responsibilities and accept the tasks gladly, knowing we do but carry out the will of The Holy Spirit. The greatness of The Almighty must be considered by us all until we come to trust and believe in the wondrous glory and all the miracles of being a Follower of the Jeculin Brotherhood. We must strive to ever draw nearer to The Almighty, to revere and serve to the very best of our abilities. Earth life may fence us around, yet it is up to us to see we are not caged in – the door to the greater life must ever remain ajar and it will eventually stand wide for us to travel to our destined paths, leading through our dear Flocen to The Almighty. To have knowledge and belief in The Almighty is to have peace in the heart and mind. To love everyone and everything, as we are bidden, is to cast out mean and petty thoughts, leaving the satisfying glow of knowing we do the will of The Flocen who is the voice and hands of The Almighty – the everlasting Power of Love, the greatest power the whole of the universe has ever known, or will ever know! Have faith in the power, and the word, and be true to it for it's not the mountain that moves, only the ocean of your thoughts.

(Nitesi, January 1975)

How can a spirit grow? Tenderly, lovingly, vibrantly, triumphantly!

Feed it with the bread of knowledge and it will expand beyond all expectations, with great and flowing abundance. Awareness of the need to enhance our spirits in the eyes of The Almighty is the *beginning* of seeing the light that is to lead us to salvation, therefore we must do all in our power to become fairer and more resilient to the teachings of our good mentors to learn and grow better by what we have been taught. One person, filled with true belief in The Holy Spirit of our dear Flocen, can achieve far more than a thousand people who do not know or receive The Holy Ghost, no matter what their earnestness or gifts may consist of – if they have not the knowledge of The Holy Ghost, the thousand will do nothing as compared to the *one* in which The Holy Spirit is recognised and loved. Through one true believer a multitude of converts can add to the Holy Power of Love. Through faith the divine life flows into us, preparing us to let it flow out again to others who need our love, as we need the love of The Almighty, and as it flows through us, inwards and outwards, the spirit grows to ever greater dimensions and attains increasing beauty of Aura, thus making us more acceptable in the eyes of The Flocen and that tiny bit nearer to our goal. The Almighty Power of Love.

(Nitesi, April 1976)

WHERE LOVE IS LACKING
(Teresi)

Where love is lacking, life is incomplete. The soul thirsts for love which should not be denied, for the soul is the inner self and is that part of you which is closest to The Almighty, who *is* love. Do not be misled into thinking that love is a purely physical thing, or merely to be given to your chosen beloved ones. All of life, all things that live and breathe are part of love, for The Almighty is in all things and all of life must return this love to The Great One and to all other beings, who are our brothers and sisters. We all being children of The Almighty.

We should all be filled with deep humility to think that we are permitted to know of, and to share in, the great and wondrous works of the universe. There is so much we do not understand, so much we are not even capable of assimilating, yet we are honoured to be trusted and taught by our very dear and patient friends of such things that others have strived for and struggled towards since time immemorial. We must rid ourselves of all selfish desires and prepare ourselves to share our learning with all those who wish to be free of the shackles of misery, which is life for the majority on this Earth. It is not only conscious misery and sadness, but also that of the spirit. Physical life is such a temporary existence in comparison to the life of the spirit and so many people have lived in their spiritual form for thousands of years yet never found fulfillment. Therefore we must endeavour to learn and retain as much knowledge as we are capable of holding and then put all our energies into leading those who are blind and ignorant of the truth into the light and the revelation of the great truths of The Almighty and the wonders of the universe.

We pray to be ever worthy of this great task that has been given to us and that we may always have the love and guidance of The Flocen and all our dear friends. We give our deep love and total devotion to The Almighty, now and for all eternity.

AMEN